Homeland Security

Homeland Security

The Essentials

Jane A. Bullock

George D. Haddow

Damon P. Coppola

AMSTERDAM • BOSTON • HEIDELBERG • LONDON
NEW YORK • OXFORD • PARIS • SAN DIEGO
SAN FRANCISCO • SINGAPORE • SYDNEY • TOKYO
Butterworth-Heinemann is an imprint of Elsevier

Acquiring Editor: Pam Chester
Development Editor: Amber Hodge
Project Manager: Paul Gottehrer
Designer: Eric DeCicco

Butterworth-Heinemann is an imprint of Elsevier
225 Wyman Street, Waltham, MA 02451, USA
The Boulevard, Langford Lane, Kidlington, Oxford, OX5 1GB, UK

Notices
Knowledge and best practice in this field are constantly changing. As new research and experience broaden our understanding, changes in research methods, professional practices, or medical treatment may become necessary.

Practitioners and researchers must always rely on their own experience and knowledge in evaluating and using any information, methods, compounds, or experiments described herein. In using such information or methods they should be mindful of their own safety and the safety of others, including parties for whom they have a professional responsibility.

To the fullest extent of the law, neither the Publisher nor the authors, contributors, or editors, assume any liability for any injury and/or damage to persons or property as a matter of products liability, negligence or otherwise, or from any use or operation of any methods, products, instructions, or ideas contained in the material herein.

Library of Congress Cataloging-in-Publication Data
Application submitted

British Library Cataloguing-in-Publication Data
A catalogue record for this book is available from the British Library.

ISBN: 978-0-12-415803-0

For information on all Butterworth–Heinemann publications
visit our website at http://store.elsevier.com

Printed in China

13 14 15 16 17   10 9 8 7 6 5 4 3 2

Working together to grow
libraries in developing countries

www.elsevier.com | www.bookaid.org | www.sabre.org

ELSEVIER   BOOK AID International   Sabre Foundation

This book is dedicated to Rand Beers who has brought vision, intellect, and leadership to the nation's efforts to understand and implement homeland security programs.

Contents

Acknowledgments

The authors wish to thank the following individuals for their knowledge, analysis, insight, and support, much of which is reflected in the pages of this book: B. Wayne Blanchard, David Gilmore, Ryan Miller, Sarp Yeletaysi, Erdem Ergin, Jack Harrald, Greg Shaw, Joseph Barbera, Ehren Ngo, Bridger McGaw, Don Goff, Barbara Johnson, Terrence Downes, Amber Hodge, Paul Gottehrer, and Pamela Chester.

Introduction

In the decade since operations officially commenced at the U.S. Department of Homeland Security (DHS), the greater profession of homeland security has expanded at an explosive pace. The term homeland security appeared long before the Department's 2002 inauguration, but its connotation at that time was generally limited to include highly specific tasks associated with the physical defense of the nation and of its territories. However, in large part as a result of the sweeping nature of the 2002 Homeland Security Act that created DHS in early 2002, this term and the concepts that accompany it have come to mean so much more. Coinciding with these changes, the pool of individuals and experts who together assure homeland security in its modern context is much more diverse than could ever have been imagined.

The workforce required to support a unified homeland security effort in the modern context is significant, and the profession has expanded in both the public and private domains to meet growing needs. Today, scores of homeland security programs offered at institutions of higher education at the nation's colleges and universities, and by various public and private training institutions, feed the development of this growing workforce. Just a decade ago, such programs were unheard of. And each and every day, those engaged in homeland security monitor the nation's transportation systems, ensure the safety of air and sea ports, maintain the effective collection of tariffs, manage the immigration process and facilitate legal immigration, protect our nation's fisheries, and prepare for and respond to natural and technological disasters, among many other functions.

It has been over a decade since the terrorist attacks of September 11 were carried out, precipitating the dramatic reorganization of government at all levels that resulted in the institutionalization of Homeland Security. The National Commission on Terrorist Attacks upon the United States (informally known as the 9/11 Commission) was formed and issued a report calling for sweeping changes in the U.S. approach for dealing with terrorism. The Department of Homeland Security (DHS) was established, the most comprehensive reorganization of the federal government ever undertaken. Congress continued to pass new laws to address all aspects of national security, including the Patriot Act, which provides the Attorney General of the United States with significant new authorities relative to civil liberties to fight the war on terrorism.

The United States and its allies became embroiled in two significant wars in Iraq and Afghanistan to try to find and dismantle Osama bin Laden's operations and other terrorist organizations. Significant progress has been made as demonstrated by the disruption of the potential threat in New York's Times Square, the failed attempt to detonate explosives on Flight 253 on December 25, 2009, and the publication of the first-ever Quadrennial Homeland Security Review (QHSR) by the DHS in February 2010. Perhaps the most significant action has been the capture and killing of Osama bin Laden in 2011 as well as other key leaders in his organization.

With the U.S. government being increasingly focused on terrorism, natural hazards have continued to impact thousands of our communities, reminding us that the likelihood of a natural disaster far exceeds a terrorist event. The aftermath of Hurricane Katrina brought sweeping legislative changes to the Federal Emergency Management Agency (FEMA), within DHS, and served to remind officials of the exacting toll natural disasters can take on public safety and our social and economic security. The devastating wildfires, floods, weather, and drought problems that impacted the nation in 2011 continued this trend, although the response from FEMA/DHS and other partners was much improved. Striking the right balance, between the various hazards, looking for commonalities among the hazards in mitigation, preparedness response, and recovery, and adopting a more all-hazards approach to homeland security remain a priority to the officials responsible for public safety.

At the same time, concerns continue to be raised on the impacts of illegal and legal immigration on the economic and social stability of our communities, especially along the border areas that consume the activities of the Immigration and Customs Enforcement (ICE). The Coast Guard (CG) is vigilant in maintaining territorial waters and safety and security at our ports that is of the highest priority to ensure homeland commerce can continue.

New emerging and evolving threats require greater attention to cybersecurity, preventing cybercrime, and protecting our critical infrastructure. The complexities and speed with which the cyber environment changes require a diligence and a level of cooperation and coordination between the government and the private sector not evidenced before. As more of our daily lives are dependent on the continual operation of computers and computer systems, for example, transportation, energy, and banking systems, preventing an attack on these systems becomes a critical priority for Homeland Security officials.

This text offers a concise vantage into the diverse function that is homeland security. The authors' goal in writing this book was to provide a source of history, practical information, programs, references, and best practices so that any academic, homeland security official, emergency manager, public safety official, community leader, or individual could understand the foundations of homeland security and be motivated to engage in actions to help make their communities safer and more secure. The homeland security function clearly is an evolving discipline that will continue to change in reaction to the steps we take to reduce the impacts of known hazards and as new threats are identified.

In the end, achieving homeland security will not be accomplished by the Federal government but by each individual, each organization, each business, and each community working together to make a difference.

Homeland Security: The Concept, the Organization

What You Will Learn

- What was the history behind the establishment of homeland security
- How events have altered the concept of homeland security
- What is the homeland security enterprise (HSE)
- How the concept of a homeland security enterprise has changed priorities
- How other agencies and entities besides DHS contribute to the homeland security enterprise

Introduction

In the immediate aftermath of the September 11, 2001 attacks, as search-and-rescue teams were still sifting through the debris and wreckage for survivors in New York, Pennsylvania, and Virginia, the federal government was analyzing what had just happened and what it could quickly do to begin the process of ensuring such attacks could not be repeated. It was recognized that nothing too substantial could take place without longer-term study and congressional review, but the circumstances mandated that real changes begin without delay.

The idea of homeland security was primarily the result of the White House, the federal government, and the U.S. Congress's reactions to September 11 events. However, the movement to establish such broad-sweeping measures was initiated long before those attacks took place. Domestic and international terrorists have been striking Americans, American facilities, and American interests, both within and outside the nation's borders, for decades — though only fleeting interest was garnered in the aftermath of these events. Support for counterterrorism programs and legislation was, therefore, rather weak, and measures that did pass rarely warranted front-page status. Furthermore, the institutional cultures that characterized many of the agencies affected by this emerging threat served as a resilient barrier to the fulfillment of goals. Only the spectacular nature of the September 11 terrorist attacks was sufficient to boost the issue of terrorism to primary standing on all three social agendas: the public, the political, and the media.

Out of the tragic events of September 11, an enormous opportunity for improving the social and economic sustainability of our communities from all threats, but primarily terrorism, was envisioned and identified as homeland security. Public safety officials and emergency managers championed the concept of an all-hazards approach, and despite some unique characteristics, they felt terrorism could be incorporated into that approach as well (Figure 1–1).

However, in the immediate aftermath of 9/11, the single issue of preventing a future terrorist attack was foremost in the minds of federal officials and legislators. On September 20, 2001, just 9 days after the attacks, President George W. Bush announced that an Office of Homeland Security would be established within the White House by executive order. Directing this office would be Pennsylvania Governor Tom Ridge. Ridge was given no real staff to manage, and the funding he would have at his disposal was minimal. The actual order, cataloged as Executive Order 13228, was given on October 8, 2001. In addition to creating the Office of Homeland Security, this order created the Homeland Security Council, "to develop and coordinate the implementation of a comprehensive national strategy to secure the United States from terrorist threats or attacks."

Four days later, on September 24, 2001, President Bush announced that he would be seeking passage of an act entitled "Uniting and Strengthening America by Providing Appropriate Tools Required to Intercept and Obstruct Terrorism," which would become better known as the PATRIOT Act of 2001. This act, which introduced a large number of controversial legislative changes in order to significantly increase the surveillance and investigative powers of law enforcement agencies in the United States (as it states) to "… deter and punish terrorist acts in the United States and around the world," was signed into law by the president on October 26 after very little deliberation in Congress.

FIGURE 1–1 New York City, New York, October 13, 2001 — New York firefighters at the site of the World Trade Center. (Photo by Andrea Booher/FEMA News Photo)

On October 29, 2001, President Bush issued the first of many homeland security presidential directives (HSPDs), which were specifically designed to "record and communicate presidential decisions about the homeland security policies of the United States" (HSPD-1, 2001). Among the HSPD issued post September 11 include:

- **HSPD-1**: Organization and Operation of the Homeland Security Council. Ensures coordination of all homeland security-related activities among executive departments and agencies and promote the effective development and implementation of all homeland security policies.
- **HSPD-2**: Combating Terrorism Through Immigration Policies. Provides for the creation of a task force which will work aggressively to prevent aliens who engage in or support terrorist activity from entering the United States and to detain, prosecute, or deport any such aliens who are within the United States.
- **HSPD-3**: Homeland Security Advisory System. Establishes a comprehensive and effective means to disseminate information regarding the risk of terrorist acts to Federal, State, and local authorities and to the American people.
- **HSPD-4**: National Strategy to Combat Weapons of Mass Destruction. Applies new technologies, increases emphasis on intelligence collection and analysis, strengthens alliance relationships, and establishes new partnerships with former adversaries to counter this threat in all of its dimensions.
- **HSPD-5**: Management of Domestic Incidents. Enhances the ability of the United States to manage domestic incidents by establishing a single, comprehensive national incident management system.
- **HSPD-6**: Integration and Use of Screening Information. Provides for the establishment of the Terrorist Threat Integration Center.
- **HSPD-7**: Critical Infrastructure Identification, Prioritization, and Protection. Establishes a national policy for federal departments and agencies to identify and prioritize United States critical infrastructure and key resources and to protect them from terrorist attacks.
- **Presidential Policy Directive/PPD-8**: National Preparedness. Aimed at strengthening the security and resilience of the United States through systematic preparation for the threats that pose the greatest risk to the security of the nation, including acts of terrorism, cyberattacks, pandemics, and catastrophic natural disasters.
- **HSPD-18**: Medical Countermeasures Against Weapons of Mass Destruction. Establishes policy guidelines to draw upon the considerable potential of the scientific community in the public and private sectors to address medical countermeasure requirements relating to CBRN threats.
- **HSPD-19**: Combating Terrorist Use of Explosives in the United States. Establishes a national policy, and calls for the development of a national strategy and implementation plan, on the prevention and detection of, protection against, and response to terrorist use of explosives in the United States.
- **HSPD-20**: National Continuity Policy. Establishes a comprehensive national policy on the continuity of federal government structures and operations and a single national continuity coordinator responsible for coordinating the development and implementation of federal continuity policies.

These actions were followed closely by organizational changes. The legislation to establish a Department of Homeland Security (DHS) was first introduced in the U.S. House of Representatives by Texas Representative Richard K. Armey on June 24, 2002. Similar legislation was introduced into the Senate soon after. After differences between the two bills were quickly ironed out, the Homeland Security Act of 2002 (P.L. 107–296) was passed by both houses and signed into law by President Bush on November 25, 2002.

FIGURE 1–2 New Orleans, LA, September 8, 2005 — Neighborhoods and roadways throughout the area remain flooded as a result of Hurricane Katrina. (Photo by Jocelyn Augustino/FEMA News Photo)

Creating DHS would provide the United States with a huge law enforcement capability that would deter, prepare, and prevent any future September 11 type events. Agencies such as Federal Emergency Management Agency (FEMA) became part of DHS because it was responsible for the consequences to our communities of natural and technological disasters, and had played a major role in providing federal assistance to recover from the previous terrorist events on U.S. soil: the 1993 World Trade Center bombing and the Murrah Federal Building bombing.

Prior to 9/11, the majority of FEMA's efforts and funding were focused on the mitigation of, preparedness for, response to, and recovery from natural disasters. Much of this changed with the establishment of DHS. Many, if not all, of the grant programs established within the new DHS focused on terrorism. The all-hazards concept was not embraced in the early years of DHS. State and local governments, who were more concerned about their flooding or hurricane threat, had to focus on terrorism.

The decision of the 1980s to focus on nuclear attack planning led to the botched response to Hurricane Andrew, under the first Bush administration. The decision by the leadership of DHS to focus on terrorism, at the expense of other threats, and to diminish the role of FEMA, led directly to the horrible events and aftermath of Hurricane Katrina (Figure 1–2).

Hurricane Katrina, which struck on August 29, 2005, and resulted in the death of over 1,800 people (and the destruction of billions of dollars in housing stock and other infrastructure), exposed significant problems with the United States' emergency management framework. Clearly, the terrorism focus had been maintained at the expense of preparedness and response capacity for other hazards, namely the natural disasters that have proven to be much more likely to occur. FEMA, and likewise DHS, were highly criticized by the public and by Congress in the months following the 2005 hurricane season.

In response, Congress passed the Post-Katrina Emergency Management Reform Act (H.R. 5441, Public Law 109–295), signed into law by the president on October 4, 2006.

This law established several new leadership positions within the Department of Homeland Security, moved additional functions into (several were simply returned) FEMA, created and reallocated functions to other components within DHS, and amended the Homeland Security Act in ways that directly and indirectly affected the organization and functions of various entities within DHS.

In passing this Act, Congress reminded DHS that the natural disaster threats to the United States were every bit as real as the terrorist threats and required changes to the organization and operations of DHS to provide a more balanced approach to the concepts of homeland security in addressing the threats impacting the United States.

The Obama Administration is building on the past efforts of the Bush Administration to understand and implement a more balanced, universal approach to homeland security. This balanced approach is reflected in the first ever Quadrennial Homeland Security Review (QHSR) published by the Obama Administration and DHS in February 2010. In the years since the events of September 11 and the establishment of DHS, knowledge and recognition of the real scope of threats and hazards to the United States has greatly increased.

When we look at how fast ideas, goods, and people move around the world and through the Internet, we recognize that this flow of materials is critical to the economic stability and the advancement of the U.S. interests. However, this globalization of information and commerce creates new security challenges that are borderless and unconventional. As evidenced by the U.S. and Europe an economic recession and the Arab Spring, both of 2011, entire economies and groups organized through social media and the criminal networks and terrorist organizations now have the ability to impact the world with far-reaching effects, including those that are potentially disruptive and destructive to our way of life.

Homeland security is certainly becoming tied to the impacts of globalization. The table below reflects the thinking represented in the QHSR.

Threats, Hazards, and Long-Term Global Challenges and Trends

Threats and Hazards	Global Challenges and Trends
• High-consequence weapons of mass destruction	• Economic and financial instability
• Al-Qaeda and global violent extremism	• Dependence on fossil fuels and the threats of global climate change
• High-consequence and/or wide scale cyberattacks, intrusions, disruptions, and exploitations	• Nations unwilling to abide by international norms
• Pandemics, major accidents, and natural hazards	• Sophisticated and broadly available technology
• Illicit trafficking and related transnational crime	• Other drivers of illicit, dangerous, or uncontrolled movement of people and goods
• Smaller scale terrorism	

Source: Quadrennial Homeland Security Review Report: A Strategic Framework for Secure Homeland, DHS, February 2010, http://www.dhs.gov/xlibrary/assets/qhsr_report.pdf.

■ ■ Critical Thinking ■

Can you identify the reasons why FEMA should not have been incorporated into the new DHS?

A New Concept of Homeland Security

Reflecting the increasingly complex issues surrounding homeland security, the recently completed QHSR has revised the definition of homeland security to incorporate a more global and comprehensive approach. They have now chosen to use a more comprehensive term to categorize homeland security activities and this term is the "homeland security enterprise (HSE).

DHS Secretary Janet Napolitano, in her letter in the QHSR, describes the HSE as, "the Federal, State, local, tribal, territorial, nongovernmental, and private-sector entities, as well as individuals, families, and communities who share a common national interest in the safety and security of America and the American population. DHS is one among many components of this national enterprise. In some areas, like securing our borders or managing our immigration system, the Department possesses unique capabilities and, hence, responsibilities. In other areas, such as critical infrastructure protection or emergency management, the Department's role is largely one of leadership and stewardship on behalf of those who have the capabilities to get the job done. In still other areas, such as counterterrorism, defense, and diplomacy, other Federal departments and agencies have critical roles and responsibilities, including the Departments of Justice, Defense, and State, the Federal Bureau of Investigation, and the National Counterterrorism Center. Homeland security will only be optimized when we fully leverage the distributed and decentralized nature of the entire enterprise in the pursuit of our common goals."

The Executive Summary of the QHSR elaborates on the definition of homeland security as "the intersection of evolving threats and hazards with traditional governmental and civic responsibilities for civil defense, emergency response, law enforcement, customs, border control, and immigration. In combining these responsibilities under one overarching concept, homeland security breaks down longstanding stovepipes of activity that have been and could still be exploited by those seeking to harm America. Homeland security also creates a greater emphasis on the need for joint actions and efforts across previously discrete elements of government and society" (DHS, 2010).

By creating this broader definition of homeland security, DHS is stressing the diversity of organizations and individuals who have responsibility for, and interest in, the safety and security of the United States — from the President, as Commander in Chief, to the Secretary of DHS, Secretaries of other federal departments and agencies (D&A's), to Governors, Mayors, City Council Chairs, business leaders, nongovernmental leaders, educators, first responders, Neighborhood Watch captains, and down to each and every citizen. Under this definition, with the diversity of stakeholders, no single person or entity is wholly responsible for achieving homeland security; it is a shared responsibility.

DHS has defined the following three concepts as the foundation for a comprehensive approach to homeland security:

1. *Security*: Protect the United States and its people, vital interests, and way of life.
2. *Resilience*: Foster individual, community, and system robustness, adaptability, and capacity for rapid recovery.
3. *Customs and exchange*: Expedite and enforce lawful trade, travel, and immigration.

The QHSR says the following about security: "Homeland security relies on our shared efforts to prevent and deter attacks by identifying and interdicting threats, denying hostile actors the ability to operate

FIGURE 1–3 A Customs and Border Patrol (CBP) officer directs a truck with a seaport container to an inspection area at a port. (DHS photo by James R. Tourtellotte. http://www.cbp.gov/xp/cgov/newsroom/multimedia/photo_gallery/afc/field_ops/inspectors_seaports/cs_photo26.xml)

within our borders, and protecting the Nation's critical infrastructure and key resources. Initiatives that strengthen our protections, increase our vigilance, and reduce our vulnerabilities remain important components of our security. This is not to say, however, that security is a static undertaking. We know that the global systems that carry people, goods, and data around the globe also facilitate the movement of *dangerous* people, goods, and data, and that within these systems of transportation and transaction, there are key nodes — for example, points of origin and transfer, or border crossings — that represent opportunities for interdiction. Thus, we must work to confront threats at every point along their supply chain — supply chains that often begin abroad. To ensure our homeland security then, we must engage our international allies, and employ the full breadth of our national capacity — from the Federal Government, to State, local, tribal, and territorial police, other law enforcement entities, the Intelligence Community, and the private sector — and appropriately enlist the abilities of millions of American citizens" (Figure 1–3) (DHS, 2010).

On resilience, the QHSR has the following explanation of resilience: "to foster individual, community, and system robustness, adaptability, and capacity for rapid recovery. Our country and the world are underpinned by interdependent networks along which the essential elements of economic prosperity — people, goods and resources, money, and information — all flow. While these networks reflect progress and increased efficiency, they are also sources of vulnerability. The consequences of events are no longer confined to a single point; a disruption in one place can ripple through the system and have immediate, catastrophic, and multiplying consequences across the country and around the world" (Figure 1–4) (DHS, 2010).

The third concept in the foundation of the HSE as discussed in the QSHR is Customs and Exchange. Under this concept DHS seeks to "expedite and enforce lawful trade, travel, and immigration. The partners and stakeholders of the HSE are responsible for facilitating and expediting the lawful movement of people and goods into and out of the United States. This responsibility intersects with and is deeply linked to the enterprise's security function. We need a smarter, more holistic approach that embeds security and resilience

FIGURE 1–4 Greensburg, KS, May 16, 2007 — The center of town 12 days after it was hit by an F5 tornado with 200 mph winds. Debris removal is moving at a record pace, but reconstruction will likely take years. (Photo by Greg Henshall/FEMA News Photo)

directly into global movement systems. Strengthening our economy and promoting lawful trade, travel, and immigration must include security and resilience, just as security and resilience must include promoting a strong and competitive U.S. economy, welcoming lawful immigrants, and protecting civil liberties and the rule of law. We view security along with customs and exchange as mutually reinforcing and inextricably intertwined through actions such as screening, authenticating, and maintaining awareness of the flow of people, goods, and information around the world and across our borders" (Figure 1–5) (DHS, 2010).

Public safety officials, including police, fire, public health, emergency managers, and border security, will continue to be in the forefront of mitigation, preparedness, response, and recovery from the potential threat of terrorism and natural hazards, as well as other man-made hazards. However, the new concept of a HSE broadens the spectrum of responsibility to include risk managers, computer analysts, public policy officials, health and environmental practitioners, economic development leaders, educators, the media, businesses, and other elected officials responsible for the safety of their communities. Each and every individual is now responsible for helping to achieve the HSE.

Not everyone is enamored with the new homeland security enterprise; several individuals and organizations have questioned whether it is just another example of the DHS trying to rebrand an organization that is not well understood by the public. The main public/DHS interface is either being subjected to TSA security at airports or reading about immigration raids and border patrol problems.

■ ■ Critical Thinking ■

What do you think were the reasons for DHS establishing the HSE?
Based on your current knowledge of homeland security, describe the responsibilities a mayor, a nongovernmental organization leader, or a citizen would have for achieving homeland security.

FIGURE 1–5 A Border Patrol agent uses a computer word translator to assist in determining the needs of this illegal immigrant. (DHS photo by James Tourtellotte. http://www.cbp.gov/xp/cgov/newsroom/multimedia/photo_gallery/afc/bp/32.xml)

The Department of Homeland Security

On November 25, 2002, President Bush signed into law the Homeland Security Act of 2002 (HS Act) (Public Law 107–296), and announced that former Pennsylvania Governor Tom Ridge would become secretary of a new DHS to be created through this legislation. This act, which authorized the greatest federal government reorganization since President Harry Truman joined the various branches of the armed forces under the Department of Defense, was charged with a threefold mission of protecting the United States from further terrorist attacks, reducing the nation's vulnerability to terrorism, and minimizing the damage from potential terrorist attacks and natural disasters.

The sweeping reorganization into the new department, which officially opened its doors on January 24, 2003, joined more than 179,000 federal employees from 22 existing federal agencies under a single, cabinet-level organization. The legislation, which was not restricted to the newly created department, also transformed several other federal agencies that at first glance may have appeared only remotely affiliated with the homeland security mission. To the affected government employees, millions of concerned American citizens, the entire world media, and even the terrorists themselves, it was clear that the U.S. government was entering a new era.

The creation of the DHS was the culmination of an evolutionary legislative process that began largely in response to criticism that increased interagency cooperation between federal intelligence organizations could have prevented the September 11 terrorist attacks. Based on the findings of several pre-September 11 commissions, it appeared that the country needed a centralized federal government agency whose primary reason for existence would be to coordinate the security of the "homeland" (a term that predated the attacks). The White House and Congress were both well aware that any homeland security czar position they conceived would require both an adequate staff and a large budget to succeed. Thus, in early 2002 deliberations began to create a new cabinet-level department that would fuse many of the security-related agencies dispersed throughout the federal government.

For several months during the second half of 2002, Congress jockeyed between differing versions of the homeland security bill in an effort to establish legislation that was passable yet effective. Lawmakers were particularly mired on the issue of the rights of the 179,000 affected employees — an issue that prolonged the legislative process considerably. Furthermore, efforts to incorporate many of the intelligence-gathering and investigative law enforcement agencies, namely, the National Security Agency (NSA), the Federal Bureau of Investigation (FBI), and the Central Intelligence Agency (CIA), into the legislation failed.

Despite these delays and setbacks, after the 2002 midterm elections, the Republican seats that were gained in both the House and Senate gave the president the leverage he needed to pass the bill without further deliberation (House of Representatives, 299–121 on November 13, 2002; Senate, 90–9 on November 19, 2002). While the passage of this act represented a significant milestone, the implementation phase to come presented a tremendous challenge.

■ ■ Critical Thinking ■

Do you think that the CIA should have been moved into DHS? If so, why, or if not, why not?
The Department of Transportation's Office of Lifeline Safety was not moved into DHS. What would the reasons be to keep it in Transportation and not move it to DHS?

The Department of Homeland Security is a massive agency, juggling numerous responsibilities between a staggeringly wide range of program areas, employing approximately 180,000 people, and managing a massive multi-billion-dollar budget and an ambitious list of tasks and goals. The department leverages resources within federal, state, and local governments, coordinating the ongoing transition of multiple agencies and programs into a single, integrated agency focused on protecting the American people and their homeland. In total, more than 87,000 different governmental jurisdictions at the federal, state, and local levels have homeland security responsibilities.

At the federal level, the DHS organizational composition remains in a state of flux. Scattered readjustments have occurred throughout its first years of existence, with multiple offices being passed between the department's components. Though it seemed by the end of DHS Secretary Tom Ridge's years of service that the basic organizational makeup had been established, incoming DHS Secretary Chertoff proposed several fundamental changes to the department's organization, which were implemented under Secretary Chertoff's Reorganization Plan. Again, the department was reorganized following the 2005 hurricane season according to the requirements of the Post-Katrina Emergency Management Reform Act (PKEMRA) of 2006.

The Obama Administration has retained the fundamental organizational structure as mandated by PKEMRA at the agency and subcomponent level, adding one new subcomponent, an Office of Intergovernmental Affairs. At the subcomponent level some minor changes were made. There was hope within the emergency management community that President Obama might move FEMA out of DHS and return it to its former status as an independent Agency. That did not happen nor does it look like it will ever happen unless there is another catastrophic failure as experienced in Hurricane Katrina.

■ ■ Critical Thinking ■

Should President Obama have taken FEMA out of DHS and made it an independent agency? Discuss the pros and cons of your opinion.

Other Federal Departments Responsible for the Homeland Security Enterprise

Appendix A of the QHSR details the roles and responsibilities of the other Federal agencies in the HSE. They are summarized below:

- The Attorney General has lead responsibility for criminal investigations of terrorist acts or terrorist threats by individuals or groups inside the United States, or directed at U.S. citizens or institutions abroad, as well as for related intelligence collection activities within the United States. The Attorney General leads the Department of Justice, which also includes the Federal Bureau of Investigation, Drug Enforcement Administration, and Bureau of Alcohol, Tobacco, Firearms, and Explosives, each of which has key homeland security responsibilities.

- The Secretary of State has the responsibility to coordinate activities with foreign governments and international organizations related to the prevention, preparation, response, and recovery from a domestic incident, and for the protection of U.S. citizens and U.S. interests overseas. The Department of State also adjudicates and screens visa applications abroad.

- The Secretary of Defense leads the Department of Defense (DOD), whose military services, defense agencies, and geographic and functional commands defend the United States from direct attack; deter potential adversaries; foster regional stability; secure and assure access to sea, air, space, and cyberspace; and build the security capacity of key partners. DOD also provides a wide range of support to civil authorities at the direction of the Secretary of Defense or the President when the capabilities of State and local authorities to respond effectively to an event are overwhelmed.

- The Secretary of Health and Human Services leads the coordination of all functions relevant to Public Health Emergency Preparedness and Disaster Medical Response. Additionally, the Department of Health and Human Services (HHS) incorporates steady-state and incident-specific activities as described in the National Health Security Strategy.

- The Secretary of the Treasury works to safeguard the U.S. financial system, combat financial crimes, and cut off financial support to terrorists, WMD proliferators, drug traffickers, and other national security threats.

- The Secretary of Agriculture provides leadership on food, agriculture, natural resources, rural development, and related issues based on sound public policy, the best available science, and efficient management. The U.S. Department of Agriculture (USDA) is the sector-specific agency for the Food and Agriculture Sector, a responsibility shared with the Food and Drug Administration with respect to food safety and defense.

- The Director of National Intelligence serves as the head of the Intelligence Community (IC), acts as the principal advisor to the President and National Security Council for intelligence matters relating to national security, and oversees and directs implementation of the National Intelligence Program. The IC, composed of 16 elements across the U.S. government, functions consistent with law, executive order, regulations, and policy to support the national security-related missions of the U.S. government. It provides a range of analytic products that assess threats to the homeland and inform planning, capability development, and operational activities of HSE partners and stakeholders. In addition to IC elements with specific homeland security missions, the Office of the Director of National Intelligence maintains a number of mission and support centers that provide unique capabilities for homeland security partners, including the National Counterterrorism Center (NCTC), National Counterproliferation Center, and National Counterintelligence Executive. NCTC serves as the primary U.S. government organization for analyzing and integrating all intelligence pertaining to terrorism and counterterrorism, and conducts strategic operational planning for integrated counterterrorism activities.

- The Secretary of Commerce, supportive of national economic security interests and responsive to Public Law and Executive direction, is responsible for promulgating Federal information technology and cybersecurity standards; regulating export of security technologies; representing U.S. industry on international trade policy and commercial data flow matters; security and privacy policies that apply to the Internet's domain name system; protecting intellectual property; conducting cybersecurity research and development; and assuring timely availability of industrial products, materials, and services to meet homeland security requirements.

- The Secretary of Education oversees discretionary grants and technical assistance to help schools plan for and respond to emergencies that disrupt teaching and learning. The Department of Education is a supporting Federal agency in the response and management of emergencies under the *National Response Framework*.

- The Secretary of Energy maintains stewardship of vital national security capabilities, from nuclear weapons to leading edge research and development programs. The Department of Energy (DOE) is the designated federal agency to provide a unifying structure for the integration of federal critical infrastructure and key resources' protection efforts specifically for the Energy Sector. It is also responsible for maintaining continuous and reliable energy supplies for the United States through preventive measures and restoration and recovery actions.

- The Administrator of the Environmental Protection Agency (EPA) is charged with protecting human health and the environment.

- The Secretary of Housing and Urban Development coordinates Federal support to State, tribal, regional, and local governments, nongovernmental organizations (NGOs), and the private sector to enable community recovery from the long-term consequences of extraordinary disasters.

- The Secretary of the Interior develops policies and procedures for all types of hazards and emergencies that impact Federal lands, facilities, infrastructure, and resources; tribal lands; and insular areas. DOI, together with the Department of Agriculture, also operates the National Interagency Fire Center.

- The Secretary of Transportation collaborates with DHS on all matters relating to transportation security and transportation infrastructure protection and in regulating the transportation of hazardous materials by all modes (including pipelines). The Secretary of Transportation is responsible for operating the national airspace system.

- Other federal agencies are also part of the HSE and contribute to the homeland security mission in a variety of ways. This includes agencies with responsibilities for regulating elements of the nation's critical infrastructure to assure public health, safety, and the common defense, developing and implementing pertinent public policy, supporting efforts to protect the homeland (DHS, 2010).

■ ■ Critical Thinking ■

After DHS which federal entity has the most critical role in the HSE and what are the factors that support your choice? In addition, the QHSR defines the roles of State and local governments and the private sector, which are summarized in the following sidebars.

Roles and Responsibilities of State and Local Governments in the Homeland Security Enterprise

- **State and Territorial Governments** coordinate the activities of cities, counties, and intrastate regions. States administer Federal homeland security grants to local and tribal (in certain grant programs) governments, allocating key resources to bolster their prevention and preparedness capabilities. State agencies conduct law enforcement and security activities, protect the Governor and other executive leadership, and administer State programs that address the range of homeland security threats, hazards, and challenges. States government officials lead statewide disaster and mitigation planning. During response, States coordinate resources and capabilities throughout the State and are responsible for requesting and obtaining resources and capabilities from surrounding States. States often mobilize these substantive resources and capabilities to supplement the local efforts before, during, and after incidents.
- **Tribal Leaders** are responsible for the public safety and welfare of their membership. They can serve as both key decision makers and trusted sources of public information during incidents.
- **Tribal Governments**, which have a special status under Federal laws and treaties, ensure the provision of essential services to members within their communities, and are responsible for developing emergency response and mitigation plans. Tribal governments may coordinate resources and capabilities with neighboring jurisdictions, and establish mutual aid agreements with other tribal governments, local jurisdictions, and State governments. Depending on location, land base, and resources, tribal governments provide law enforcement, fire, and emergency services as well as public safety to their members.
- **Local Governments** provide front-line leadership for local law enforcement, fire, public safety, environmental response, public health, and emergency medical services for all manner of hazards and emergencies. Through the Urban Areas Security Initiative (UASI) program, cities (along with counties in many cases) address multijurisdictional planning and operations, equipment support and purchasing, and training and exercises in support of high-threat, high-density urban areas. UASI grants assist local governments in building and sustaining homeland security capabilities. Local governments coordinate resources and capabilities during disasters with neighboring jurisdictions, NGOs, the State, and the private sector.
- **County Governments** provide front-line leadership for local law enforcement, fire, public safety, environmental response, public health, and emergency medical services for all manner of hazards and emergencies. In many cases, county government officials participate in UASIs with other urban jurisdictions to assist local governments in building and sustaining capabilities to prevent, protect against, respond to, and recover from threats or acts of terrorism. County governments coordinate resources and capabilities during disasters with neighboring jurisdictions, NGOs, the State, and the private sector.

Source: Quadrennial Homeland Security Review Report: A Strategic Framework for Secure Homeland, DHS, February 2010, http://www.dhs.gov/xlibrary/assets/qhsr_report.pdf.

ROLE OF PRIVATE SECTOR IN HOMELAND SECURITY ENTERPRISE

- **Critical Infrastructure and Key Resource (CIKR) Owners and Operators** develop protective programs and measures to ensure that systems and assets, whether physical or virtual, are secure from and resilient to cascading, disruptive impacts. Protection includes actions to mitigate the overall risk to CIKR assets, systems, networks, functions, or their interconnecting links, including actions to deter the threat, mitigate vulnerabilities, or minimize the consequences associated with a terrorist attack or other incident. CIKR owners and operators also prepare business continuity plans and ensure their own ability to sustain essential services and functions.
- **Major and Multinational Corporations** operate in all sectors of trade and commerce that foster the American way of life and support the operation, security, and resilience of global movement systems. They take action to support risk management planning and investments in security as a necessary component of prudent business planning and operations. They contribute to developing the ideas, science, and technology that underlie innovation in homeland security. During times of disaster, they provide response resources (donated or compensated)—including specialized teams, essential service providers, equipment, and advanced technologies—through public–private emergency plans/partnerships or mutual aid and assistance agreements, or in response to requests from government and nongovernmental-volunteer initiatives.
- **Small Businesses** contribute to all aspects of homeland security and employ more than half of all private-sector workers. They support response efforts by developing contingency plans and working with local planners to ensure that their plans are consistent with pertinent response procedures. When small businesses can survive and quickly recover from disasters, the nation and economy are more secure and more resilient. They perform research and development, catalyze new thinking, and serve as engines of innovation for development of new solutions to key challenges in homeland security.

Source: Quadrennial Homeland Security Review Report: A Strategic Framework for Secure Homeland, DHS, February 2010, http://www.dhs.gov/xlibrary/assets/qhsr_report.pdf.

Conclusion

The QHSR report establishes a vision for the future of the HSE. It reflects lessons learned from the past that homeland security is not just about terrorism. While building protections, securing our borders, or preventing terrorism, measures are all critical to homeland security, it encompasses so much more. To be successful, the HSE needs to acknowledge and focus on threats other than terrorism, both natural and manmade, that have had devastating impacts on the United States in the past decade. It must recognize and build protective mechanisms for new and evolving threats such as cybercrime. Fundamentally, the HSE is about protecting the American way of life and ensuring our resilience in a challenging world.

As the DHS matures and critical funding continues, we should have better-trained and better-equipped first responders; a stronger, less vulnerable national infrastructure; more rational immigration and border policies; an enhanced delivery system for public health and new technologies; and mechanisms to improve and safeguard our information, communications, and cybernetworks.

In embracing the new concept of a HSE, DHS is one among many components. It is a department with unique expertise such as securing our borders or managing our immigration system. In many other areas, such as emergency management, the Department's role is largely one of leadership among the governmental family to get the job done. In counterterrorism, defense, and diplomacy, other Federal departments and agencies have critical roles and responsibilities, including the Departments of Justice, Defense, and State, the Federal Bureau of Investigation, and the National Counterterrorism Center.

As the QHSR states, "The effectiveness of the evolving concept of homeland security will only be accomplished when we leverage the capabilities of our partners at all levels of government, within the private sector, and among our citizens to achieve the goals of the homeland security enterprise."

Key Terms

Critical Infrastructure: Critical infrastructure includes any system or asset that, if disabled or disrupted in any significant way, would result in catastrophic loss of life or catastrophic economic loss.

Executive Order: A declaration issued by the president or by a governor that has the force of law. Executive orders are usually based on existing statutory authority and require no action by Congress or the state legislature to become effective.

Federal Response Plan: The FRP was developed to establish a standard process and structure for the systematic, coordinated, and effective delivery of federal assistance to address the consequences of any major disaster or emergency declared under the Robert T. Stafford Disaster Relief and Emergency Assistance Act, as amended. This plan was later replaced by the National Response Plan.

Homeland Security Enterprise: A new concept defined as "the Federal, State, local, tribal, territorial, nongovernmental, and private-sector entities, as well as individuals, families, and communities who share a common national interest in the safety and security of America and the American population."

National Incident Management System: This is a system mandated by Homeland Security Presidential Directive (HSPD) 5 that provides a consistent nationwide approach for governments, the private sector, and nongovernmental organizations to work effectively and efficiently together to prepare for, respond to, and recover from domestic incidents, regardless of cause, size, or complexity.

Presidential Directive: A form of executive order issued by the president that establishes an action or change in the structure or function of the government (generally within the Executive Office). Under President Bush, directives have been termed *Homeland Security Presidential Directives* (HSPDs) and *National Security Presidential Directives* (NSPDs). Under President Clinton, they were termed *Presidential Decision Directives* (PDDs) and *Presidential Review Directives* (PRDs).

Quadrennial Homeland Security Review (QHSR): A comprehensive report published by DHS in February 2010 that establishes the future direction of the DHS and the discipline of homeland security.

Statutory Authority: The legally granted authority, bestowed on the named recipient by a legislature, that provides a government agency, board, or commission the power to perform the various functions, expenditures, and actions as described in the law.

Review Questions

1. What is the Quadrennial Homeland Security Review?
2. What legislation required DHS to undertake the QHSR?
3. What changes to the definition of *homeland security* were manifested in the QHSR?
4. How has the PKEMRA influenced the QHSR and DHS?
5. Discuss the role of federal agencies other than DHS in the HSE.
6. Discuss the role of state and local governments in the HSE.
7. Do you think the new concept of a HSE is valid? Explain the pros and cons of your position.

References

Barry, T., Border Lines Blog. http://www.borderlinesblog.blogspot.com/2010/02/Americas-failing-homelandsecurity.html.

Baldwin, T.E., 2002. Historical Chronology of FEMA Consequence Management, Preparedness and Response to Terrorism. Argonne National Laboratory, Argonne, IL.

Clarke, R., 2010. Cyber War: The Next Threat to National Security and What to Do about It. New York, New York.

Communications Sector Coordinating Council. 2007. Communications Sector Specific Infrastructure Protection Plan. Communications Sector Coordinating Council. http://www.dhs.gov/xlibrary/assets/nipp-ssp-communications.pdf.

Department of Homeland Security. 2007. Department Subcomponents and Agencies. www.dhs.gov/xabout/structure.

Department of Homeland Security. 2002. National Strategy for Homeland Security. http://www.dhs.gov/xlibrary/assets/nat_strat_hls.pdf.

Department of Homeland Security. 2003. National Strategy for the Protection of Physical Infrastructure and Key Assets. http://www.dhs.gov/xlibrary/assets/Physical_Strategy.pdf.

Department of Homeland Security. 2006. DHS Releases Cyber Storm Public Exercise Report. http://www.dhs.gov/xnews/releases/pr_1158341221370.shtm.

Department of Homeland Security. 2009a. National Infrastructure Protection Plan. http://www.dhs.gov/files/programs/editorial/gc_1204738275985.shtm.

Department of Homeland Security. 2009b. NIPP: Sector Specific Plans. http://www.dhs.gov/files/programs/gc_1179866197607.shtm.

Department of Homeland Security. 2010. Quadrennial Homeland Security Review Report: A Strategic Framework for a Secure Homeland. http://www.dhs.gov/xlibrary/assets/qhsr_report.pdf.

Department of Homeland Security. 2011. Implementing the Recommendations of the 9/11 Commission. A Progress Report. dhs.gov/xlibrary/assets/progress_report.pdf.

2

Historic Overview of the Terrorist Threat

What You Will Learn

- The evolution of the federal government in responding to emergencies, disasters, and terrorist threats before September 11
- Measures taken to address the terrorism hazard within the United States following the September 11 terrorist attacks
- Significant statutory measures taken before and after September 11
- The actions taken by DHS to address the recommendations in the 9/11 Commission report

Introduction

Harry Truman once said, "The only thing new is the history we don't know." For many Americans, the rush of activities by the government to pass new laws, reorganize government institutions, and allocate vast sums of money in the aftermath of the September 11, 2001, terrorist attacks may have seemed unprecedented. The reality is that similar actions in terms of both type and scope have happened in the past, and these historical experiences can provide insight into the prospect of the ultimate success or failure of the actions that have been taken since the September 11 attacks occurred.

The purpose of this chapter is to provide a historic perspective of the evolution of the programs, policies, and organizations established to address the problem of terrorism, nuclear threats, and other emergencies in the United States. This chapter provides summaries of terrorist events aimed at the U.S. government outside its shores including the Khobar Towers bombing and the attack of the USS Cole. Information is provided for the two terrorist incidents prior to September 11: the 1993 World Trade Center (WTC) bombing and the 1995 Oklahoma City bombing of the Murrah Federal Office Building. This new material will include information on the 9/11 Commission and the July 2011 Department of Homeland Security (DHS) Report on Implementing the Recommendations of the 9/11 Commission.

Before It Was Called Homeland Security: From the 1800s to the Creation of FEMA

The U.S. government has a long history of responding to all types of threats and emergencies before terrorism became an emerging threat in the 1990s. A brief history of the evolution of government's role is outlined below. It is important to note that each major change was event driven, just as the attacks of September 11 drove the adoption of homeland security.

In 1803, a congressional act was passed to provide financial assistance to a New Hampshire town devastated by fire. This is the first example of the federal government becoming involved in a local disaster.

During the 1930s, the Reconstruction Finance Corporation and the Bureau of Public Roads both were granted the authority to make disaster loans available for repair and reconstruction of certain public facilities after disasters. The next notable period of evolution occurred during the 1950s. The Cold War era presented the potential for nuclear war and nuclear fallout as the principal disaster risk. Civil defense programs proliferated across communities during this time. Individuals and communities alike were encouraged to and did build bomb shelters to protect themselves and their families from a nuclear attack by the Soviet Union.

Federal support for these activities was vested in the Federal Civil Defense Administration (FCDA), an organization with few staff and limited financial resources whose main role was to provide technical assistance. A companion office to the FCDA, the Office of Defense Mobilization, was established in the Department of Defense (DOD). The primary functions of this office were to allow for the quick mobilization of materials and the production and stockpiling of critical materials in the event of war. In 1958, these two offices were merged into the Office of Civil and Defense Mobilization.

As the 1960s began, three major natural disasters occurred. In a sparsely populated area of Montana in 1960, the Hebgen Lake earthquake struck, measuring 7.3 on the Richter scale, calling attention to the fact that the nation's earthquake risk extended far beyond California's borders. Later that year Hurricane Donna hit the west coast of Florida and in 1961 Hurricane Carla blew across Texas. The incoming Kennedy administration decided to change the federal approach to disasters. In 1961, it created the Office of Emergency Preparedness inside the White House to deal with these large-scale events. It distinguished these activities from the civil defense responsibilities, which remained in the Office of Civil Defense within DOD.

During the remainder of the 1960s, the United States was struck by a series of major natural disasters. In 1964, in Prince William Sound, Alaska, an earthquake, measuring 9.2 on the Richter scale, killed 123 people and generated a tsunami. Hurricane Betsy struck in 1965 and Hurricane Camille in 1969, together killing and injuring hundreds and causing hundreds of millions of dollars in damage along the Gulf Coast. The response to these events, as with previous disasters, was the passage of ad hoc legislation for funds. During the 1970s, responsibility for dealing with different threats was allotted to more than five separate federal departments and agencies, including the Department of Commerce (weather, warning, and fire protection), the General Services Administration (continuity of government, stockpiling, federal preparedness), the Treasury Department (import investigation), the Nuclear Regulatory Commission (power plants), and the Department of Housing and Urban Development (HUD) (flood insurance and disaster relief).

With the passage of the Disaster Relief Act of 1974, prompted by the previously mentioned hurricanes and the San Fernando earthquake of 1971, the Department of HUD possessed the most significant authority for natural disaster response and recovery through the NFIP, which it administered under the Federal Insurance Administration (FIA) and the Federal Disaster Assistance Administration (FDAA). On the military side, there existed the Defense Civil Preparedness Agency (nuclear attack) and the U.S. Army Corps of Engineers (flood control).

In the 1970s, a partial release of radioactive materials occurred at the Three Mile Island nuclear power plant in Pennsylvania, requiring the evacuation of thousands of residents. This accident brought national media attention to the lack of adequate off-site preparedness around commercial nuclear power plants and the role of the federal government in responding to such an event.

On June 19, 1978, President Carter transmitted to Congress the Reorganization Plan Number 3 (3 CFR 1978, 5 U.S. Code 903). The intent of this plan was to consolidate emergency preparedness, mitigation, and response activities into a single federal emergency management organization. The president stated that the plan would provide for the establishment of the Federal Emergency Management Agency (FEMA).

Reorganization Plan Number 3 transferred the following agencies or functions to FEMA: National Fire Prevention Control Administration (Department of Commerce), Federal Insurance Administration (HUD), Federal Broadcast System (Executive Office of the President), Defense Civil Preparedness Agency (DOD), Federal Disaster Assistance Administration (HUD), and the Federal Preparedness Agency (GSA).

The early and middle 1980s saw a renewed interest and concern for threats from the Soviet Union, causing the federal efforts to once again focus on civil defense and nuclear attack planning. There were no significant natural disasters, and a robust program for commercial nuclear power preparedness was begun as part of the new Nuclear Regulatory Commission (NRC) licensing process so that threat was believed to have dissipated.

As Congress debated and finally passed major reform of federal disaster policy as part of the Stewart McKinney-Robert Stafford Act, FEMA, the agency responsible for responding to any threat, natural or man-made, was having severe problems with leadership and organization, and its ability to support a national threat response remained in doubt. In 1989, two devastating natural disasters, Hurricane Hugo and the Loma Prieta earthquake, called into question the continued existence of FEMA. In 1992, Hurricane Andrew struck Florida and Louisiana and Hurricane Iniki struck Hawaii within months of each other (Figure 2–1). FEMA wasn't ready, and neither were FEMA's partners at the state level. The agency's failure to respond was witnessed by Americans all across the country as major news organizations followed the crisis. It was not just FEMA that failed during Hurricane Andrew; it was the whole federal emergency management process and system. Investigations by the General Accounting Office (GAO) and other governmental and nongovernmental watchdog groups called for major reforms. The threat of a major natural disaster or even multiple

FIGURE 2–1 Hurricane Andrew, Florida, August 24, 1992 — Many houses, businesses, and personal effects suffered extensive damage from one of the most destructive hurricanes ever recorded in America. One million people were evacuated, and 54 died in this hurricane. (Source: FEMA News Photo)

disasters was the U.S. government's concern as the U.S. started the 1990s. Other threats from man-made incidents such as the Valdez oil spill or a nuclear attack seemed remote. There was an increasing awareness of an ever growing terrorist threat throughout the world, but it hadn't really impacted the U.S. mainland or its property. U.S. intelligence agencies were monitoring an increase in terrorist attacks all over. Within the United States, there were many incidents of bombings, but they were perpetrated by homegrown citizens and rarely for ideological reasons. This was to change with the first terrorist attack on U.S. soil on the WTC in 1993.

■ ■ Critical Thinking ■

In light of the events that have transpired, how would you apportion the amount of Federal effort and funding between natural hazards and man-made hazards and terrorism?

World Trade Center Bombing

The bombing of the WTC presented a new threat on U.S. soil, that is, the first large-scale terrorist attack. Prior to this, bombings that occurred at post offices, medical facilities, etc. were considered to be criminal acts by individuals. On February 23, 1993, a massive explosion occurred in the basement parking lot of the WTC in New York City. Six adults and one unborn child were killed and more than 1,000 people sustained injuries. The explosive device, which weighed more than 1,000 pounds, caused extensive damage to seven of the building's floors, six of which were below grade. More than 50,000 people were evacuated, 25,000 of whom were in the twin towers of the Trade Center. The entire evacuation process required approximately 11 hours to complete (Fusco, 1993).

■ ■ ■ ─────────────────────────────

New York Fire Department Responds to World Trade Center Bombing

At the time, the response to the bombing was described as being the largest incident that the City of New York Fire Department (FDNY) had ever managed in its 128-year history. In terms of the number of fire units that responded, the event was described as being "the equivalent of a 16-alarm fire" (Fusco, 1993). The following list provides a summary of relevant data from the bombing event:

- Deaths: 6
- Injuries: 1,042
- Firefighter injuries: 85 (one requiring hospitalization)
- Police officers injured: 35
- EMS workers injured: 1
- Firefighter, police, and EMS deaths: 0
- Number of people evacuated from WTC complex: approximately 50,000
- FDNY engine companies responding: 84
- FDNY truck companies responding: 60
- FDNY special units responding: 26
- FDNY personnel responding: 28 battalion chiefs, 9 deputy chiefs
- Percentage of FDNY on duty staff responding: 45% (Fusco, 1993)

This incident resulted in increased efforts to address the terrorist threat. Through the work of the Joint Terrorism Task Force, four suspects were arrested and convicted of the WTC bombing. In response to these incidents, the Congress passed and President Clinton signed the Violent Crime Control and Law Enforcement Act of 1994. This was the most comprehensive crime legislation in U.S. history.

Murrah Federal Building Bombing

The bombing of the Murrah Federal Building represented the next incident of domestic terrorism. At 9:02 on the morning of April 19, 1995, a bomb exploded from inside a Ryder truck under the Alfred P. Murrah Federal Building in Oklahoma City. The blast caused a partial collapse of all nine floors of the 20-year-old building, and 168 people died (see Figure 2–2).

At this time, Congress was debating the Nunn-Lugar Domenici legislation that was aimed at better preparing this nation and its responsible organizations for a terrorist attack. The Nunn-Lugar-Domenici legislation provided the primary authority and focus for domestic federal preparedness activities for terrorism. Several agencies — including the FEMA, Department of Justice (DOJ), Department of Health and Human Resources (DHHS), DOD, and the National Guard — were involved in the terrorism issue, and all were jockeying for the leadership position. Several attempts at coordination among these various agencies were launched, but in general, each agency pursued its own agenda. The single factor that provided the greatest distinction between these agencies related to the levels of funding they received, with DOD and DOJ controlling the majority of what was allocated. The Oklahoma City bombing set the stage for interagency disagreements over which agency would be in charge of terrorism.

FIGURE 2–2 Oklahoma City, Oklahoma, April 26, 1995 — Search-and-rescue crews work to save those trapped beneath the debris after the Oklahoma City bombing. (Source: FEMA News Photo)

The Nunn-Lugar legislation of 1995 (Defense against Weapons of Mass Destruction Act of 1996) left open the question as to who would be the lead agency in terrorism.

▣ ▣ Critical Thinking ▣

Was there an obvious federal agency to be named as lead? If so, which one and what is the rationale for naming that agency?

Khobar Towers Bombing, Saudi Arabia

On June 25, 1996, a truck bomb was detonated at the U.S. forces command in the Khobar Towers building in Riyadh. The force of the bomb damaged or destroyed six high-rise buildings within the compound. Some security measures that had been previously erected including Jersey barriers and the marble construction of the building minimized damages. The quick actions of an Air Force sentry, noticing the suspicious actions of the terrorists and alerting security, minimized the deaths and injuries. In anonymous communications to the United States prior to the attack, there were indications that some level of attack would occur as an impetus to get the U.S. troops out of the country. In the aftermath of the attack, most people viewed this as an intelligence failure.

The Three Commissions

In 1998, President Clinton and House Speaker Newt Gingrich petitioned Congress to form a 14-member panel called the United States Commission on National Security/21st Century (USCNS/21), also known as the Hart-Rudman Commission, to make strategic recommendations on how the U.S. government could ensure the nation's security in the coming years. The independent panel, created by Congress, was tasked with conducting a comprehensive review of American security with the goal of designing a national security strategy.

The commission's report, titled "Road Map for National Security: Imperative for Change," dated January 31, 2001, recommended the creation of a new independent National Homeland Security Agency (NHSA) with responsibility for planning, coordinating, and integrating various U.S. government activities involved in homeland security. This agency would be built on the FEMA, with the Coast Guard, the Customs Service, and the U.S. Border Patrol (now part of U.S. Customs and Border Protection [CBP] within the DHS) transferred into it. NHSA would assume responsibility for the safety of the American people as well as oversee the protection of critical infrastructure, including information technology. Obviously, the commission's recommendations were not heeded before 2001, but many of its findings would later be integrated into the justification and legislation behind the creation of the DHS.

Two other commissions were established to study the terrorist threat during these years: the Gilmore Commission and the Bremer Commission, as discussed next.

The Gilmore Commission, also known as the Advisory Panel to Assess Domestic Response Capabilities for Terrorism Involving Weapons of Mass Destruction, produced a series of annual reports beginning in 1999. Each of these reports presented a growing base of knowledge concerning the weapons of mass destruction (WMD) risk faced by the United States, and a recommended course of action required to counter that risk.

The Bremer Commission, also known as the National Commission on Terrorism, addressed the issue of the international terrorist threat. The commission was mandated by Congress to evaluate the nation's laws, policies, and practices for preventing terrorism and for punishing those responsible for terrorist events. Its members drafted a report titled "Countering the Changing Threat of International Terrorism." This report, issued in 2000, presented priorities as follows:

- International terrorism poses an increasingly dangerous and difficult threat to America.
- Countering the growing danger of the terrorist threat requires significantly stepping up the U.S. efforts.
- Priority one is to prevent terrorist attacks. U.S. intelligence and law enforcement communities must use the full scope of their authority to collect intelligence regarding terrorist plans and methods.
- A terrorist attack involving a biological agent, deadly chemicals, or nuclear or radiological material, even if it succeeds only partially, could profoundly affect the entire nation. The government must do more to prepare for such an event.
- The president and Congress should reform the system for reviewing and funding departmental counterterrorism programs to ensure that the activities and programs of various agencies are part of a comprehensive plan.

Each of these conclusions and recommendations would take on new meaning in the aftermath of the September 11 attacks, and would guide many of the changes incorporated into the Homeland Security Act of 2002. However, in the absence of a greater recognition of a terrorist threat within the borders of the United States, no major programs were initiated to combat the growing risk.

▓ ▄ Critical Thinking ▪

President Clinton and Congress were concerned enough about terrorism in the late 1990s that they chose to form and fund the three terrorism commissions. Do you feel that the U.S. public was adequately concerned or aware of the threat of terrorism during this time, and leading up to the September 11 terrorist attacks? Do you believe that the U.S. government was adequately concerned during this same time period? Explain your answer.

Presidential Decision Directives 62 and 63

As these commissions were conducting their research, President Clinton was addressing other recognized and immediate needs through the passage of several presidential decision directives (PDDs). In 1996, terrorists carried out a suicide bombing at U.S. military barracks (Khobar Towers) in Saudi Arabia, and in 1998, simultaneous bombings were carried out at the U.S. diplomatic missions in Kenya and Tanzania.

In May 1998, President Clinton issued PDD-62, "Combating Terrorism," which called for the establishment of the Office of the National Coordinator for Security, Infrastructure Protection and Counterterrorism. The directive's primary goal was to create a new and more systematic approach to fighting the terrorist threat. The new national coordinator was tasked with overseeing a broad variety of relevant policies and programs including counterterrorism, critical infrastructure protection, WMD preparedness, and consequence management.

Soon after this directive, President Clinton issued PDD-63, "Protecting America's Critical Infrastructure." This directive tasked all of the departments of the federal government with assessing the vulnerabilities of their cyber and physical infrastructures and with working to reduce their exposure to new and existing threats.

Attorney General's Five-Year Interagency Counterterrorism and Technology Crime Plan

In December 1998, as mandated by Congress, the DOJ, through the FBI, began a coordinated project with other agencies to develop the Attorney General's Five-Year Interagency Counterterrorism and Technology Crime Plan. The FBI emerged as the federal government's principal agency for responding to and investigating terrorism. Congress had intended the plan to serve as a baseline for the coordination of a national strategy and operational capabilities to combat terrorism. The DOJ asserted that the Attorney General's Five-Year Interagency Counterterrorism and Technology Crime Plan, considered together with related PDDs as described earlier, represented a comprehensive national strategy to address the terrorist threat. However, after a thorough review, the GAO, Congress's investigative arm, concluded that additional work remained that would build on the progress that the plan represented. The GAO contended that a comprehensive national security strategy was lacking.

The GAO report "Combating Terrorism: Comments on Counterterrorism Leadership and National Strategy" (GAO-01-55T), released March 27, 2001, stated that the DOJ plan did not have measurable outcomes and suggested, for example, that it should include goals that improve state and local response capabilities. The report argued that without a clearly defined national strategy, the nation would continue to miss opportunities to focus and shape counterterrorism programs to meet the impending threat. It also made the criticism that the DOJ plan lacked a coherent framework to develop and evaluate budget requirements for combating terrorism since there was no single focal point. The report claimed that no single entity was acting as the federal government's top official accountable to both the president and the Congress for the terrorism hazard and that fragmentation existed in both coordination of domestic preparedness programs and efforts to develop a national strategy.

The GAO released another report in early September 2001 titled "Combating Terrorism: Selected Challenges and Related Recommendations" (GAO-01-822), which it finalized in the last days before the terrorist attacks occurred in Washington and New York. The report stated that the federal government was ill equipped and unprepared to counter a major terrorist attack, claiming also that — from sharing intelligence to coordinating a response — the government had failed to put in place an effective critical infrastructure system. It further stated that

> *Federal efforts to develop a national strategy to combat terrorism ... have progressed, but key challenges remain. The initial step toward developing a national strategy is to conduct a national threat and risk assessment ... at the national level (agencies) have not completed assessments of the most likely weapon-of-mass-destruction agents and other terrorist threats. ...*

To prevent terrorist attacks, the GAO recommended:

- A national strategy to combat terrorism and computer-based attacks
- Better protection for the nation's infrastructure
- A single focal point to oversee coordination of federal programs
- Completion of a threat assessment on likely WMD and other weapons that might be used by terrorists
- Revision of the Attorney General's Five-Year Interagency Counterterrorism and Technology Crime Plan to better serve as a national strategy
- Coordination of research and development to combat terrorism

In a later report regarding Homeland Security, "Key Elements to Unify Efforts Are Underway But Uncertainty Remains" (GAO-02-610), the GAO called for more of the same in terms of needing central leadership and an overarching strategy that identifies goals and objectives, priorities, measurable outcomes, and state and local government roles in combating terrorism since the efforts of more than 40 federal entities and numerous state and local governments were still fragmented. It also called for the term *homeland security* to be defined properly since to date it had not.

USS Cole Bombing, Yemen

On October 12, 2000, while refueling in the port of Aden in Yemen, the U.S. Navy destroyer the USS Cole sustained a suicide bomb attack. The terrorist organization Al-Qaeda claimed responsibility for the attack that took the lives of 17 Navy sailors with an additional 39 injured. However, evidence of Al-Qaeda involvement was inconclusive. The 9/11 Commission report does indicate that in December 2000, the Central Intelligence Agency (CIA) had made a preliminary conclusion that Al-Qaeda may have supported the attack. There was thought to be complicity by the government of the Sudan, and a U.S. judge determined that Sudan was liable for the attack. At the time, then President Clinton declared it an "act of terrorism." However, some people have questioned whether an attack against a military installation meets the legal definition of "terrorism" as opposed to an act of war. Both the Clinton and, later, the Bush administrations have been criticized for not responding with military force on this attack before the September 11 attack.

September 11 Attacks on the World Trade Center and the Pentagon

The concept of homeland security was born on September 11, 2001. On that day, terrorists hijacked four planes and crashed them into the twin towers of the WTC in New York City, the Pentagon in Washington, D.C., and a field in Pennsylvania. These actions resulted in the collapse of both twin towers, the collapse of a section of the Pentagon, and the crash of a domestic airliner that resulted in unprecedented deaths and injuries:

- Total deaths for all 9/11 attacks: 2,974 (not counting the 19 terrorists)
- Total injured for all 9/11 attacks: 2,337
- Total deaths in the World Trade Center towers: 2,603
- Total injured at World Trade Center: 2,261
- Total firefighter deaths at World Trade Center: 343
- Total police deaths at World Trade Center: 75
- Total deaths at Pentagon: 125
- Total injured at Pentagon: 76
- Total deaths, American Flight 77, Pentagon: 59
- Total deaths, United Airlines Flight 93, Pennsylvania: 40
- Total deaths, American Airlines Flight 11, WTC North Tower: 88
- Total deaths, United Airlines Flight 175, WTC South Tower: 59 (From: www.september11news .com/911Art.htm

Table 2–1 Top Ten Natural Disasters (Ranked by FEMA Relief Costs)

Event	Year	FEMA Funding
Hurricane Katrina (AL, LA, MS)	2005	$7.2 billion[a]
Northridge Earthquake (CA)	1994	$6.961 billion
Hurricane Georges (AL, FL, LA, MS, PR, VI)	1998	$2.251 billion
Hurricane Ivan (AL, FL, GA, LA, MS, NC, NJ, NY, PA, TN, WVA)	2004	$1.947 billion[b]
Hurricane Andrew (FL, LA)	1992	$1.813 billion
Hurricane Charley (FL, SC)	2004	$1.559 billion[b]
Hurricane Frances (FL, GA, NC, NY, OH, PA, SC)	2004	$1.425 billion[b]
Hurricane Jeanne (DE, FL, PR, VI, VA)	2004	$1.407 billion[b]
Tropical Storm Allison (FL, LA, MS, PA, TX)	2001	$1.387 billion
Hurricane Hugo (NC, SC, PR, VI)	1989	$1.307 billion

[a]Amount obligated from the President's Disaster Relief Fund for FEMA's assistance programs, hazard mitigation grants, federal mission assignments, contractual services, and administrative costs as of March 31, 2006. Figures do not include funding provided by other participating federal agencies, such as the disaster loan programs of the Small Business Administration and the Agriculture Department's Farm Service Agency.
Note: Funding amounts are stated in nominal dollars, unadjusted for inflation.
[b]Amount obligated from the President's Disaster Relief Fund for FEMA's assistance programs, hazard mitigation grants, federal mission assignments, contractual services, and administrative costs as of May 31, 2005. Figures do not include funding provided by other participating federal agencies, such as the disaster loan programs of the Small Business Administration and the Agriculture Department's Farm Service Agency.
Note: Funding amounts are stated in nominal dollars, unadjusted for inflation.
Source: Federal Emergency Management Agency (FEMA), "Top Ten Natural Disasters: Ranked by FEMA Relief Costs," http://www.fema.gov/hazard/topten.shtm.
Last Modified: Wednesday, August 11, 2010, 14:38:40 EDT.

The response to these attacks by fire, police, and emergency medical teams was immediate, and their combined efforts saved hundreds if not thousands of lives, especially at the WTC.

The addition of another stairway in each tower, the widening of existing stairways, and regular evacuation drills — actions implemented in the aftermath of the 1993 WTC bombing — are all credited with facilitating the evacuation of thousands of office workers in the towers before they collapsed. Federal, state, and nongovernmental groups (e.g., Red Cross, Salvation Army) also responded quickly, establishing relief centers and dispensing critical services to victims and first responders.

The second significant aspect of the September 11 attacks is the magnitude and the scope of the economic losses resulting from the attacks. The total economic impact on New York City alone is estimated to be between $82.8 and $94.8 billion. This estimate includes $21.8 billion in lost buildings, infrastructure, and tenant assets; $8.7 billion in the future earnings of those who died; and $52.3 to $64.3 billion gross city product (Curci, 2004). The economic impact of the attacks was felt throughout the United States and the world.

The federal government costs were extraordinary, and spending by FEMA on these events easily exceeded its spending on past natural disasters and disasters that have happened since (see also Table 2–1):

- Direct emergency assistance from FEMA: $297 million
- Aid to individuals and families: $255 million

- Direct housing: 8,957 applications processed; 5,287 applications approved (59%)
- Mortgage and rental assistance: 11,818 applications processed; 6,187 applications approved (52%)
- Individual and family grant program: 43,660 applications processed; 6,139 applications approved (14%)
- Disaster unemployment: 6,657 claims processed; 3,210 claims approved (48%)
- Crisis counseling: $166 million
- Aid to government and nonprofits: $4.49 billion
- Debris removal: $437 million
- Overtime for New York Police Department (NYPD): $295.4 million
- Overtime for the New York Fire Department: $105.6 million (*Source*: Federal Emergency Management Agency, 2003)

The insurance losses resulting from the September 11 events were also extraordinary, especially when considered in light of the relatively small amount of physical property that was directly affected by the events themselves. This comprehensive terrorist attack illustrates the far-reaching indirect, intangible consequences of terrorism, and their potential for damaging a nation's economy.

The Creation of the Department of Homeland Security: 2001–2004

In the immediate aftermath of the September 11 attacks, the federal government was analyzing what had just happened and what it could quickly do to begin the process of ensuring such attacks could not be repeated.

On September 20, 2001, just 9 days after the attacks, President George W. Bush announced that an Office of Homeland Security would be established within the White House by executive order. Directing this office would be Pennsylvania Governor Tom Ridge. Ridge was given no real staff to manage, and the funding he would have at his disposal was minimal. In addition to creating the Office of Homeland Security, this order created the Homeland Security Council, "to develop and coordinate the implementation of a comprehensive national strategy to secure the United States from terrorist threats or attacks."

Four days later, on September 24, 2001, President Bush announced that he would be seeking passage of an act titled "Uniting and Strengthening America by Providing Appropriate Tools Required to Intercept and Obstruct Terrorism," which would become better known as the PATRIOT Act of 2001. This act, which introduced a large number of controversial legislative changes in order to significantly increase the surveillance and investigative powers of law enforcement agencies in the United States was signed into law by the president on October 26 after very little deliberation in Congress.

On October 29, 2001, President Bush issued the first of many homeland security presidential directives (HSPDs), which were specifically designed to "record and communicate presidential decisions about the homeland security policies of the United States" (HSPD-1, 2001). On March 21, 2002, President Bush signed Executive Order 13260 establishing the President's Homeland Security Advisory Council (PHSAC) and Senior Advisory Committees for Homeland Security.

In the flurry of legislation and presidential directives that were enacted immediately after September 11, the PATRIOT Act was clearly the most controversial. This legislation was introduced in the U.S. House of Representatives by Representative F. James Sensenbrenner, Jr. (R-WI) on October 23, 2001, "to deter and punish terrorist acts in the United States and around the world, to enhance law enforcement investigatory tools, and for other purposes" (www.congress.gov 2003).

Under normal circumstances, legislation, especially that which has broad-sweeping reach and which brings into question constitutional rights, requires years and even decades of deliberation before it is finally passed — if that day ever comes. Considering the PATRIOT Act was passed less than a month after the event that inspired it, with almost no significant deliberation, it can be regarded as an anomalous case, and one that, considering its comprehensive nature and its impact on civil liberties, deserves more detailed description.

The principal focus of the PATRIOT Act is to provide law enforcement agencies with the proper legal authority to support their efforts to collect information on suspected terrorists, to detain people suspected of being or aiding terrorists and terrorist organizations, to deter terrorists from entering and operating within the borders of the United States, and to further limit the ability of terrorists to engage in money-laundering activities that support terrorist actions. The major provisions of the PATRIOT Act are as follows:

- Relaxes restrictions on information sharing between U.S. law enforcement and intelligence officers on the subject of suspected terrorists.
- Makes it illegal to knowingly harbor a terrorist.
- Authorizes "roving wiretaps," which allows law enforcement officials to get court orders to wiretap any phone a suspected terrorist would use. The provision was needed, advocates said, with the advent of cellular and disposable phones.
- Allows the federal government to detain non-U.S. citizens suspected of terrorism for up to 7 days without specific charges (original versions of the legislation allowed for the holding of suspects indefinitely).
- Allows law enforcement officials greater subpoena power for e-mail records of terrorist suspects.
- Triples the number of border patrol personnel, customs service inspectors, and INS inspectors at the northern border of the United States and provides $100 million to improve technology and equipment on the U.S. border with Canada.
- Expands measures against money laundering by requiring additional record keeping and reports for certain transactions and requiring identification of account holders.
- Eliminates the statute of limitations for prosecuting the most egregious terrorist acts but maintains the statute of limitation on most crimes at 5–8 years.

The PATRIOT Act immediately sparked concern among citizens and organizations involved in protecting the civil rights and liberties of all Americans, although this concern only became more vocal as the time between the attacks increased due to the emotional sensitivities associated with what had transpired. The critics that have emerged, and which continue to emerge in growing numbers as the act is repeatedly renewed, have questioned the constitutionality of several of the act's provisions and have expressed grave concerns regarding the methods by which some of those new authorities will be used by law enforcement agencies in their pursuit of terrorists.

The U.S. attorney general at the time, John Ashcroft, and the DOJ that operated under his direction countered that these authorities are necessary if the U.S. government is to more effectively track and detain terrorists. Regardless, the act very quickly began generating lawsuits, resistance from community officials, and concern about the way its provisions were being used and abused outside of their intended scope in a way that affected everyday Americans with no association with terrorist activities.

■ ■ Critical Thinking ■

Do you feel that the USA PATRIOT Act counters the basic freedoms bestowed upon Americans by the drafters of the Constitution? Why or why not? Would you be willing to give up some of your freedom for increased security from terrorism?

In the 7 years since the act's passage, numerous communities across the country have passed resolutions opposing parts or all of the act's contents. These resolutions began appearing as early as January 2002, when the city of Ann Arbor, Michigan, voiced its opposition to what they saw as an attack on the basic freedoms and rights that Americans considered sacred. As of December 2007, these resolutions continued to appear, with the latest passed in the city of Wichita Falls, Texas on December 4. The American Civil Liberties Union (ACLU), which monitors these actions, registered 414 local, county, and state resolutions that had been passed as of January 1, 2008, with another 275 efforts currently under debate (to see a complete list of resolutions passed, see http://www.bordc.org/list.phpfisortoAlpha51 or http://www.aclu.org/resolutions). Similar resolutions have been passed in the cities of Dallas, Denver, Detroit, Honolulu, Minneapolis, and Seattle, and at the state level in Vermont, Montana, Maine, Hawaii, and Alaska (Bill of Rights Defense Committee, 2007).

■ ■ ■

In May 2011, Congress voted to extend three provisions of the law that would have otherwise expired. They allow investigators to get "roving wiretap" court orders allowing them to follow terrorism suspects who switch phone numbers or providers; to get orders allowing them to seize "any tangible things" relevant to a security investigation, like a business's customer records; and to get national security wiretap orders to monitor noncitizen suspects who are not believed to be connected to any foreign power.

The Senate passed the extension 72 to 23 late in the afternoon of the day on which the provision would expire and within hours the House approved it 250 to 153. In an unusual move, a White House spokesman said that President Obama, who was in Europe, would "direct the use" of an autopen machine to sign the bill into law without delay.

During the debate, two senators, Ron Wyden and Mark Udall, claimed that the Justice Department had secretly interpreted the act in a twisted way, enabling domestic surveillance activities that many members of Congress do not understand

■ ■ ■

In March 2002, President Bush took another major step and signed Homeland Security Presidential Directive 3 (HSPD-3), which stated that:

The Nation requires a Homeland Security Advisory System to provide a comprehensive and effective means to disseminate information regarding the risk of terrorist acts to Federal, State, and local authorities and to the American people. Such a system would provide warnings in the form of a set of graduated "Threat Conditions" that would increase as the risk of the threat increases. At each Threat Condition, Federal departments and agencies would implement a corresponding set of "Protective Measures" to further reduce vulnerability or increase response capability during a period of heightened alert.

This system is intended to create a common vocabulary, context, and structure for an ongoing national discussion about the nature of the threats that confront the homeland and the appropriate measures that should be taken in response. It seeks to inform and facilitate decisions appropriate to different levels of government and to private citizens at home and at work.

The product outcome of this directive was the widely recognizable color-coded Homeland Security Advisory System (HSAS). The HSAS has been called on repeatedly since its inception to raise and lower the nation's alert levels between elevated (yellow) and high (orange), although the frequency of these movements has decreased over time as standards for such movements have been developed.

On November 25, 2002, President Bush signed into law the Homeland Security Act of 2002 (HS Act) (Public Law 107–296), and announced that former Pennsylvania Governor Tom Ridge would become secretary of a new DHS to be created through this legislation. This act, which authorized the greatest federal government reorganization since President Harry Truman joined the various branches of the armed forces under the DOD, was charged with a threefold mission of protecting the United States from further terrorist attacks, reducing the nation's vulnerability to terrorism, and minimizing the damage from potential terrorist attacks and natural disasters.

The sweeping reorganization into the new department, which officially opened its doors on January 24, 2003, joined more than 179,000 federal employees from 22 existing federal agencies under a single, cabinet-level organization. Since that time, there have been many additions, movements, and changes to both the organizational makeup of the department and its leadership.

■ ■ Critical Thinking ■

Were members of Congress justified in making such a sweeping reform of the federal government as they did in the aftermath of the September 11 attacks? What could have, or should have, been done differently now that the benefit of hindsight exists?

As a result of the September 11 attacks, President Bush established the National Commission on Terrorist Attacks Upon the United States, informally known as the 9/11 Commission. He asked former Congressman Lee Hamilton and former New Jersey Governor Thomas Keane to chair the Commission. Members included a broad range of people including former congressmen and senators and officials from previous administrations. The Commission was charged with looking at the events leading up to the September 11 attacks and the actions that were taken immediately following the attack and making recommendations to the President and the Congress. The major finding of the Commission's report was that there were government failures in policy, capabilities, and management. The main areas they focused on were unsuccessful diplomacy, problems within the intelligence community, problems with the FBI, permeable borders and aviation security, lack of command and control in the response, and underfunding of programs to combat terrorism. The intelligence community, the CIA, and the FBI were highly criticized. Congress also came in for criticism for its failure to financially support counterterrorism programs and the confusion over oversight and jurisdictions within its committee structure.

The final report of the 9/11 Commission was issued on July 22, 2004. The specific recommendations were encompassed in the following categories:

- Attack terrorists and their organizations
- Prevent the continued growth of Islamist terrorism
- Protect against and prepare for terrorist attacks

- Establish a National Counterterrorism Center
- Appoint a National Intelligence Director
- Encourage the sharing of information among government agencies and with state and local officials

A copy of the Final Report is available at http://www.9-11commission.gov/report/911report.pdf.

Homeland Security Focus on Terrorism Results in a Disaster: Hurricane Katrina and Its Aftermath

In the first few years following the creation of the DHS, the nation worked through many of the growing pains associated with such a drastic bureaucratic overhaul. The TSA certainly experienced growing pains as the public was faced with ever more restrictive and evasive security policies. Of the many new and changing policies related to both national security and emergency management, one which sparked significant concern was that the focus of emergency management at all levels of government was being led away from the all-hazards philosophy to that of the single terrorism hazard. Floods, tornadoes, and other events continued to occur, although there were several mild hurricane seasons. However, several members of Congress still proposed legislation to remove the FEMA from DHS, although their efforts were ultimately rebuffed.

In late August 2005, Hurricane Katrina veered into the Gulf Coast states of Louisiana, Mississippi, and Alabama, dealing a blow considered by many emergency planners to be a worst-case scenario. At the last minute, the category 5 storm weakened to a category 3, and its track turned just slightly askew, thus preventing a direct hit on the city of New Orleans, but the damage that followed this glancing blow was still enough to completely overwhelm all mitigation and preparative measures that had been taken to protect the city and its residents. The storm's impact covered a broad geographic area stretching from Alabama, across coastal Mississippi and southeast Louisiana, spanning an estimated 90,000 square miles. As of January 2007, the official death toll attributable to the storm stood at 1,836 with another 705 individuals listed as missing (Figure 2–3).

By any account, Hurricane Katrina was a massive storm, both deadly and destructive. But it was the failed response that followed, which exposed severe cracks that had developed in the nation's emergency management system and its ability to respond to a catastrophic event. Both government and independent after-action reports, and several media accounts, judged the overall response an outright failure. Many of the problems of the immediate response exposed the impacts of a priority focus on terrorism and homeland security that had developed in preceding years, which had likely been a major contributing factor in the decrease in local, state, and national capacities and capabilities.

Congress immediately tackled the apparent emergency management shortfalls, drawing up legislation aimed at patching many of the holes that had been exposed and developing new systems that were hoped would reduce overall risk for the future. For the moment, at least, it seemed as if the nation's emergency management focus was willing to regain its all-hazards approach. The resulting legislation, the Post-Katrina Emergency Reform Act (PKEMRA), was signed into law by the president on October 4, 2006. This law served to reconfigure the leadership hierarchy of the DHS and to return many functions that were stripped from FEMA back into the agency.

This law established several new leadership positions within the DHS, moved additional functions into (several were simply returned) FEMA, created and reallocated functions to other components within DHS, and amended the Homeland Security Act in ways that directly and indirectly affected the organization and functions of various entities within DHS. The changes were required to have gone into effect by

FIGURE 2–3 Biloxi, Mississippi, September 3, 2005 — Damage and destruction to houses. Hurricane Katrina caused extensive damage all along the Mississippi Gulf Coast. (Source: Photo by Mark Wolfe/FEMA News Photo)

March 31, 2007. Transfers that were mandated by the Post-Katrina Emergency Management Reform Act included (with the exception of certain offices as listed in the act):

- United States Fire Administration (USFA)
- Office of Grants and Training (G&T)
- Chemical Stockpile Emergency Preparedness Division (CSEP)
- Radiological Emergency Preparedness Program (REPP)
- Office of National Capital Region Coordination (NCRC)

The law determined that the head of FEMA would take on the new title of administrator. This official would now be supported by two deputy administrators. One is the deputy administrator and chief operating officer, who serves as the principal deputy and maintains overall operational responsibilities at FEMA. The other is the deputy administrator for National Preparedness, a new division created within FEMA.

The National Preparedness Division under FEMA included several existing FEMA programs and several programs that were moved into the former Preparedness Directorate. This division focuses on emergency preparedness policy, contingency planning, exercise coordination and evaluation, emergency management training, and hazard mitigation (with respect to the CSEP and REPP programs). The National Preparedness Division oversees two new divisions: Readiness, Prevention, and Planning (RPP) and the National Integration Center (NIC). RPP is now the central office within FEMA handling preparedness policy and planning functions. The NIC maintains the National Incident Management System (NIMS) and the National Response Plan (NRP), and coordinates activities with the U.S. Fire Administration.

Additional headquarters' positions created at FEMA by the new law included a Disability Coordinator (located in the FEMA Office of Equal Rights), a Small State and Rural Advocate, a Law Enforcement Advisor to the Administrator, and a National Advisory Council.

▪ ▪ Critical Thinking ▪

Several legislators and key emergency management officials proclaimed that, in order to truly reform emergency management in the United States, FEMA would have to be removed from DHS and returned to its cabinet-level status. Do you agree or disagree with their sentiments, and why?

Obama Administration

With the election of President Barak Obama in November 2008, many people expected dramatic change relative to homeland security issues. As a Senator, Mr. Obama voted against the war in Iraq and expressed concerns about civil liberties lost in the aftermath of 9/11. During the campaign, he spoke of wanting to close Guantanamo Bay prison where hundreds of suspected Al-Qaeda conspirators were being kept. There were also some thoughts that the new administration might take FEMA out of DHS and restore it to its independent Agency status. Recognizing that the permeable border remains an issue, President Obama nominated Janet Napolitano, Governor of Arizona, to be Secretary of DHS. She was quickly confirmed by the Senate and was committed to addressing issues facing the Department as well as aggressively tackling the emerging threats such as cybersecurity. Among the high-priority issues were problems with immigration programs, the Transportation Security Administration (TSA) cybersecurity, and critical infrastructure. The TSA was created to address the need for heightened airport security after the hijacking of the planes during 9/11, and has had a mixed record in accomplishing its mission.

On December 25, 2009, a Nigerian national, Umar Farouk Abdulmutallab, on a flight from Amsterdam to Detroit, attempted to explode a plastic device hidden in his underwear. It didn't work and he was immediately arrested when the plane landed. His connections were traced to Yemen and an organized terrorist's organization, possibly Al-Qaeda. This event was a clear blot on the TSA security operations. Initially Secretary Napolitano said the system "worked" but the next day she acknowledged that somewhere the system had failed.

DHS in 2011 published a report on their accomplishments in meeting the recommendations of the 9/11 Commission including in the areas of airline security. Airports now include full body screeners that, hopefully, will prevent any future underwear bombers but these additional security measures are not popular with the general public.

On July 21, 2011, Secretary of DHS Janet Napolitano released a report that highlighted the progress DHS has made in fulfilling the 9/11 Commission recommendations. In releasing the report, the Secretary said, "Now 10 years after the worst terrorist attacks ever on American soil, America is stronger and more resilient than ever before. But threats from terrorism persist. And challenges remain. Over the past decade, we have made great strides to secure our nation against a large attack or disaster, to protect our critical infrastructure and cyber networks, and to engage a broader range of Americans in the shared responsibility for security."

The most significant success for the Obama administration and the intelligence community of homeland security was the capture and subsequent killing of Osama bin Laden on May 2, 2011. The U.S. intelligence community, led by the CIA, began an extensive effort starting in 2002 that culminated in a surveillance program on what was thought to be the Al-Qaeda's leader's compound in 2010. Operation Neptune Spear was authorized by President Obama and executed by the CIA and U.S. Navy Seals. The raid on bin Laden's compound in Pakistan started in Afghanistan. After the successful raid, bin Laden's body was taken back to Afghanistan to be verified and then buried at sea. Following this event, other Al-Qaeda operatives were arrested and the general opinion in the intelligence community was that Al-Qaeda was severely wounded and it would be hard to recover.

Many people have been disappointed by the Obama administration's adoption of Bush-era homeland security practices, including the lack of progress on comprehensive immigration reform, support for continuation of certain segments of the PATRIOT Act, and the failure to resolve issues on the closing of Guantanamo Bay prison. The passage of health care legislation, the problems with unemployment, and a lackluster economy have dominated the administration's agenda, although continuing issues with TSA and airport security, along with significant natural disaster activity, have required some focus on DHS issues.

In May 2011, the Obama administration proposed comprehensive cybersecurity legislation. The highlights in this legislation include consolidating the 47 different state laws that require businesses to report breaches of their cybersystems to consumers and DHS will work with industry to prioritize most important cyberthreats and vulnerabilities; provide clear authority to allow the federal government to provide assistance to state and local governments when there has been a cyberbreach; provide immunity to industry and state and local government when sharing cybersecurity information with DHS; and provide for a new framework to protect individuals' privacy and civil liberties. A more thorough discussion of this legislation is found in Chapter 8.

They also entered into a joint U.S.–U.K. Cooperation on Cyberspace.

Conclusion

The terrorist attacks of September 11 have forever changed America and, in many ways, the world. This event has been termed the most significant disaster since the attack on Pearl Harbor and the first disaster that affected the United States on a national scale. It seemed that every American knew someone or knew of someone who perished in the attacks, and surely every citizen felt the economic impact. Does the killing of Osama bin Laden negate the need for such a focus on terrorism in homeland security? Terrorist organizations that dislike the U.S. government and its policies exist outside of Al-Qaeda. There are new forms of terrorism — in cybersecurity — where major corporations such as Sony and Lockheed-Martin have had their systems compromised. The DOD experienced a major cybersecurity attack, when one of its defense contractors with documentation on a new weapon system was hacked into. Environmental terrorism, depending on your political philosophy, has become more prevalent.

Natural hazards continue to beset a good portion of our nation and impact our economic and social stability. In 2011, record floods impacted the Midwest, whereas in 2010 wildfires destroyed forests and threatened communities.

The threat portfolio under the area of terrorism has only expanded, thereby presenting the nation with a whole new set of hazards about which to worry (e.g., biological, chemical, radiological, and nuclear weapons). The concept of homeland security is impacted by each event that happens — natural or man-made, the level of impact of the event has determines its influence, so the concept of homeland security is still, clearly, a work in progress, reacting to events as opposed to strategically anticipating future events.

Key Terms

Critical Infrastructure: Critical infrastructure includes any system or asset that, if disabled or disrupted in any significant way, would result in catastrophic loss of life or catastrophic economic loss. Some examples of critical infrastructure include the following:
Public water systems
Primary roadways, bridges, and highways
Key data storage and processing facilities, stock exchanges, or major banking centers
Chemical facilities located in proximity to large population centers

Major power generation facilities
Hydroelectric facilities and dams
Nuclear power plants

Cybersecurity: The prevention of damage to, unauthorized use of, or exploitation of, and, if needed, the restoration of electronic information and communications systems and the information contained therein to ensure confidentiality, integrity, and availability. Includes protection and restoration, when needed, of information networks and wire line, wireless, satellite, public safety answering points, and 911 communications systems and control systems (NIPP).

Department of Homeland Security: A federal agency whose primary mission is to help prevent, protect against, and respond to acts of terrorism on U.S. soil.

Emergency Management: The discipline dealing with the identification and analysis of public hazards, the mitigation of and preparedness for public risk, and the coordination of resources in response to and recovery from associated emergency events.

Executive Order: A declaration issued by the president or by a governor that has the force of law. Executive orders are usually based on existing statutory authority and require no action by Congress or the state legislature to become effective.

National Incident Management System: This is a system mandated by HSPD-5 that provides a consistent nationwide approach for governments, the private sector, and nongovernmental organizations to work effectively and efficiently together to prepare for, respond to, and recover from domestic incidents, regardless of cause, size, or complexity.

Statutory Authority: The legally granted authority, bestowed on the named recipient by a legislature, that provides a government agency, board, or commission the power to perform the various functions, expenditures, and actions as described in the law.

References

City of Oklahoma City Document Management, 1996. Final Report: Alfred P. Murrah Federal Building Bombing April 19, 1995. Stillwater: Department of Central Services Central Printing Division.

Curci, Lt. Col. Michael A. 2004. Transnational terrorism's effect on the U.S. economy. United States Army War College Strategy Research Project. Carlisle Barracks, PA: United States Army.

Federal Emergency Management Agency (FEMA), 2003. A Nation Remembers, A Nation Recovers. FEMA, Washington, DC.

Fusco, A.L., 1993. The World Trade Center Bombing: Report and Analysis. U.S. Fire Administration, Emmitsburg, MD.

Library of Congress. July 21, 2003. www.congress.gov.

Schmidle, N. 2011. Getting Bin Laden. The New Yorker, August 8, 2011. http://www.newyorker.com.reporting/2011/08/110808fa_fact_schmidle.

3

Hazards

What You Will Learn

- The various hazards that often result in major emergencies and disasters, including natural hazards, technological hazards, and terrorism (including chemical, biological, radiological, nuclear, and explosive weapons)
- Why it is so difficult to assess and evaluate the likelihood of terrorist attacks, both within the United States and throughout the world

Introduction

Through its various directorates and offices, the Department of Homeland Security is actually responsible for the preparedness for, mitigation of, response to, and recovery from all forms of hazards – not just terrorism. Any destabilizing incident or factor, regardless of origin, threatens national security. Overall, the overwhelming majority of deaths, property damages, and economic losses, occur as a result of damage from natural disasters. Of course, many will argue that the ever-growing threat of a terrorist's use of weapons of mass destruction provides some parity between natural and man-made events as our cities, states, and our country look to the future.

While the nation's natural hazard profile has remained relatively unchanged for decades, factors such as urbanization, increasing societal complexity, and climate change, have gradually increased risk. Today, disasters are happening more frequently, and with greater consequence, thereby demanding greater and greater response capacity and capabilities. In the United States, just like elsewhere in the world, this trend shows no signs of slowing.

The increasing threat or risk posed by terrorism has introduced an expanded set of hazards for many communities. The greatest threat comes from the four principal categories of weapons of mass destruction which include chemical, biological, radiological/nuclear, and explosive (CBRNE). These hazards must now be considered in concert with the myriad traditional natural and technological hazards that have menaced communities for centuries. These hazards present a unique challenge due to the fact that much less is known about them, and they are encountered in an intentional manner.

The Hazards

A *hazard* is defined as a "source of danger that may or may not lead to an emergency or disaster" (National Governors Association, 1982), and it is named after the emergency/disaster that could be so precipitated. Each hazard carries an associated risk, which is represented by the likelihood of the hazard leading to an actual disaster event and the consequences of that event should it occur. The product of realized hazard risk is an emergency event, which is typically characterized as a situation exhibiting negative consequences that require the efforts of one or more of the emergency services (fire, police, emergency medical services [EMS], public health, or others) to manage. When the response requirements of an emergency event exceed the capabilities of those established emergency services in one or more critical areas (e.g., shelter, fire suppression, mass care), the event is classified as a disaster.

Each hazard is distinct with regard to its characteristics. However, there are three umbrella groupings into which all hazards may be sorted that include Natural Hazards, Technological Hazards, and Terrorist Hazards.

Natural Hazards

Natural hazards are those that exist in the natural environment as a result of hydrological, meteorological, seismic, geologic, volcanic, mass movement, or other natural processes, and that pose a threat to human populations and communities. Natural hazards are often intensified in scope and scale by human activities, including development and modification of the landscape and atmosphere. The following hazards are those with the greatest potential to impact humans on a community-wide or greater scale.

Floods

A flood is an overabundance of water that engulfs dry land and property that is normally dry. Floods may be caused by a number of factors, including heavy rainfall, melting snow, an obstruction of a natural waterway, and other generative factors. Floods usually occur from large-scale weather systems generating prolonged rainfall or onshore winds, but they may also result from locally intense thunderstorms, snowmelt, ice jams, and dam failures. Flash floods usually result from intense storms dropping large amounts of rain within a brief period, occur with little or no warning, and can reach full peak in only a few minutes.

Floods are the most frequent and widespread disaster in the United States, primarily as a result of human development in the floodplain. The close relationship that exists between societies and water is the result of commerce, agriculture, and access to drinking water. As development and urbanization rates increase, so does the incidence of flooding in large part as a result of this relationship. FEMA estimates that approximately 10 million households are at risk from flooding in the United States, which sustained an average of $2.7 billion each year during the period from 2001 to 2010.

Earthquakes

An earthquake is a sudden, rapid shaking of the earth's surface that is caused by the breaking and shifting of tectonic (crustal) plates. This shaking can affect both the natural and built environments, with even moderate events leading to the collapse of buildings and bridges; disruptions in gas, electric, and phone service; landslides; avalanches; fires; and tsunamis. Structures constructed on unconsolidated landfill, old waterways, or other unstable soil are generally at greatest risk unless seismic mitigation has been utilized. Seismicity is not seasonal or climate dependent and can therefore occur at any time of the year.

Each year hundreds of earthquakes occur in the United States, though the vast majority are barely perceptible. As earthquake strength increases, its likelihood of occurrence decreases. Major events, which are greater than 6.5 to 7 on the Richter scale, occur only once every decade or so, but such events have been among the most devastating in the experience of the United States. The Northridge earthquake that struck California in 1994, for instance, is the second most expensive natural disaster to ever occur in the United States as ranked by FEMA relief costs, resulting in almost $7 billion in federal funding (and second only to Hurricane Katrina). It is anticipated that a major earthquake along the New Madrid Fault could cause catastrophic damage across eight states, and result in indirect damages throughout the entire country that would significantly impact the nation's economy.

Hurricanes

Hurricanes are cyclonic storms that occur in the Western Hemisphere where the majority of the United States land is located. When these storms affect the Pacific island territories, such as Guam, American Samoa, and the Northern Mariana Islands (among others), they are called *cyclones*. These very strong wind storms begin as tropical waves and grow in intensity and size as they progress to become tropical depressions and tropical storms (as determined by their maximum sustained wind speed). The warm-core depression becomes a tropical storm when the maximum sustained surface wind speeds fall between 39 miles per hour and 73 miles per hour (mph). Tropical cyclonic storms are defined by their low barometric pressure, closed-circulation winds originating over tropical waters, and an absence of wind shear. Cyclonic storm winds rotate counterclockwise in the Northern Hemisphere and clockwise in the Southern Hemisphere.

A *hurricane* is a cyclonic tropical storm with sustained winds measuring 74 mph or more. Hurricane winds extend outward in a spiral pattern as much as 400 miles around a relatively calm center of up to 30 miles diameter known as the *eye*. Hurricanes are fed by warm ocean waters. As these storms make landfall, they often push a wall of ocean water known as a *storm surge* over coastal zones. Once over land, hurricanes cause further destruction by means of torrential rains and high winds. A single hurricane can last for several weeks over open waters and can run a path across the entire length of the eastern seaboard.

Hurricane season runs annually from June 1 through November 30. August and September are peak months during the hurricane season. Hurricanes are commonly described using the Saffir–Simpson scale. To date, the costliest disaster in U.S. history was Hurricane Katrina that occurred in August of 2005 and required over $29 billion in federal funding.

Historically, high winds and flood caused by storm surge have been the principal contributors to the loss of life and injuries and the property and infrastructure damage caused by hurricanes. Inland flooding caused by hurricane rainfall has also resulted in large losses of life and severe property damage, especially in zones of hilly or mountainous topography. Damage to the environment is another important factor related to hurricane-force winds and flooding.

Storm Surges

Storm surges, defined as masses of water that are pushed toward the shore by meteorological forces, are the primary cause of the injuries, deaths, and structural damages associated with hurricanes, cyclones, nor'easters, and other coastal storms. When the advancing surge of water coincides with high tides, the resulting rise in sea level is further exacerbated. Storm surges may reach several dozen feet under the right conditions, as was the case in Hurricane Katrina. Wind-driven turbulence becomes superimposed on the storm tide, thereby causing further damage to structures that are inundated through wave action (each cubic yard of water results in 1,700 lb of pressure on affected structures). The surge height at landfall is ultimately dictated by the expanse and intensity of the storm, the height of the tide at the time of landfall, and the slope of the sea floor approaching land. The longer and shallower the sea floor, the greater the storm surge will be. Because much of the United States' densely populated Atlantic and Gulf Coast coastlines lie less than 10 ft above mean sea level, storm surge risk is extreme.

Tornadoes

A *tornado* is a rapidly rotating vortex or funnel of air extending groundward from a cumulonimbus cloud, exhibiting wind speeds of up to 300 mph. Approximately 1,200 tornadoes are spawned by thunderstorms each year in the United States. Most tornadoes remain aloft, but the few that do touch the ground are devastating to everything in their path. The forces of a tornado's wind are capable of lifting and moving huge objects, destroying or moving whole buildings, and siphoning large volumes from bodies of water and ultimately depositing them elsewhere. Because tornadoes typically follow the path of least resistance, people living in valleys have the greatest exposure to damage.

Collapsing buildings and flying debris are the principal factors behind the deaths and injuries tornadoes cause.

Buildings that are directly in the path of a tornado have little chance of surviving unless they are specifically designed to withstand not only the force of the winds but also the force of the debris "missiles" that are thrown about.

Wildfires

Wildfires (often called "wildland fires") are classified into three categories: surface fires, the most common type, which burn along the floor of a forest, moving slowly and killing or damaging trees; ground fires, which are usually started by lightning and burn on or just below the forest floor; and crown fires, which burn through the forest canopy high above the ground and therefore spread much more rapidly due to wind and direct contact with nearby trees. As residential areas expand into relatively untouched wildlands (called the *wildland–urban interface*), the threat to the human population increases dramatically. Protecting structures located in or near the wildland poses special problems and often stretches firefighting resources beyond capacity. Wildland fires also cause several secondary hazards. For instance, when heavy rains follow a major fire, landslides, mudflows, and floods can strike on or downhill from the newly unanchored soil. These fires can also severely scorch the land, destroying animal habitats and causing barren patches that may persist for decades, increasing the likelihood of long-term erosion.

Several terms are used to classify the source and behavior of wildland fires:

- *Wildland fires*. Fueled almost exclusively by natural vegetation, these fires typically occur in national forests and parks, where federal agencies are responsible for fire management and suppression.
- *Interface or intermix fires*. These fires occur in or near the wildland–urban interface, affecting both natural and built environments and posing a tactical challenge to firefighters concerned with the often conflicting goals of firefighter safety and property protection.
- *Firestorms*. Events of such extreme intensity that effective suppression is virtually impossible, firestorms occur during extreme weather and generally burn until conditions change or the available fuel is exhausted.
- *Prescribed fires and prescribed natural fires*. These are fires that are intentionally set or selected natural fires that are allowed to burn for the purpose of reducing available natural fuel.

Mass Movements

The general category of mass movements includes several different hazards caused by the horizontal or lateral movement of large quantities of physical matter. Mass movements cause damage and loss of life through several different processes, including the pushing, crushing, or burying of objects in their path, the damming of rivers and waterways, the subsequent movement of displaced bodies of water (typically in the form of a tsunami), destruction or obstruction of major transportation routes, and alteration of the natural environment in ways in which humans are negatively impacted. Mass-movement hazards are most prevalent in areas of rugged or varied topography, but they can occur even on level land, as in the case of subsidence. The following are the categories of mass movement hazards:

- *Landslides*. Landslides occur when masses of relatively dry rock, soil, or debris move in an uncontrolled manner down a slope.
- *Mudflows*. Mudflows are water-saturated rivers of rock, earth, and other debris that are drawn downward by the forces of gravity.
- *Lateral spreads*. Lateral spreads occur when large quantities of accumulated earth or other materials spread downward and outward due to gradual hydrologic and gravitational forces.
- *Liquefaction*. When saturated solid material becomes liquid-like in constitution due to seismic or hydrologic activity, it can exacerbate lateral spreading.
- *Rockfalls*. Rockfalls occur when masses of rock or other materials detach from a steep slope or cliff and descend by freefall, rolling, or bouncing.
- *Land subsidence*. Land subsidence is the loss of surface elevation caused by the removal of subsurface support.
- *Expansive soils*. Soils and soft rock that tend to swell or shrink when their moisture content changes are referred to as *expansive soils*.

Tsunamis

A *tsunami* is wave or series of waves that is generated by a mass displacement of sea or lake water. The most common generative factor behind tsunamis is undersea earthquakes that cause ocean floor displacement, but large tsunamis have also been caused by volcanic eruptions and landslides. Tsunami waves travel outward as movements of kinetic energy (rather than traveling water) at very high speeds in all directions from the area of the disturbance, much like the ripples caused by a rock thrown into a pond. As the waves approach shallow coastal waters, wave speed quickly decreases and the water is drawn upward and onto land. Tsunamis can strike at heights of up to and over 100 ft and extend onto land for a mile or more (depending upon topography). The force of the water causes near total destruction of everything in its path.

Volcanic Eruptions

A volcano is a break in the earth's crust through which molten rock from beneath the earth's surface (magma) erupts. Over time, volcanoes will grow upward and outward, forming mountains, islands, or large, flat plateaus called *shields*.

When pressure from gases and molten rock becomes strong enough to cause an explosion, violent eruptions may occur. Gases and rock shoot up through the opening and spill over or fill the air with lava fragments. Volcanoes cause injuries, death, and destruction through a number of processes, including direct burns, suffocation from ash and other materials, trauma from ejected rocks, floods and mudflows from quickly melted snow and ice, burial under burning hot "pyroclastic" burning ash flows, and others. Airborne ash can affect people hundreds of miles away from the eruption and influence global climates for years afterward.

Volcanic ash contaminates water supplies, causes electrical storms, and can cause roofs to collapse under the weight of accumulated material. Eruptions may also trigger tsunamis, flash floods, earthquakes, and rock falls. Sideways-directed volcanic explosions, known as *lateral blasts*, can shoot large pieces of rock at very high speeds for several miles. These explosions can kill by impact, burial, or heat. They have been known to knock down entire forests. Most deaths attributed to the Mount St. Helens volcano were a result of lateral blast and trees that were knocked down.

Severe Winter Storms

Severe winter storms occur when extremely cold atmospheric conditions coincide with high airborne moisture content, resulting in rapid and heavy precipitation of snow and/or ice (either as freezing rain or hail). When combined with high winds, the event is known as a *blizzard*. In the United States, these hazards originate from four distinct sources:

- In the Northwest, cyclonic weather systems originate in the North Pacific Ocean or the Aleutian Islands region.
- In the Midwest and Upper Plains, Canadian and Arctic cold fronts push ice and snow deep into the heart of the nation—in some instances, traveling as far south as Florida.
- In the Northeast, lake-effect snowstorms develop when cold weather fronts pass over the relatively warm surfaces of the Great Lakes.
- The eastern and northeastern states are affected by extratropical cyclonic weather systems in the Atlantic Ocean and the Gulf of Mexico that produce snow, ice storms, and occasional blizzards.

Drought

Drought is defined as a prolonged shortage of available water, primarily due to insufficient rain and other precipitation or because exceptionally high temperatures and low humidity cause a drying of agriculture and a loss of stored water resources. Drought hazards differ from other natural hazards in three ways:

1. A drought's onset and conclusion are difficult to determine because the effects accumulate slowly and may linger even after the apparent termination of an episode.
2. There is no precise or universally accepted determination of what conditions constitute official drought conditions or the degree of drought severity.
3. The drought's effects are less obvious and spread over a larger geographic area.

Extreme Temperatures

Major diversions in average seasonal temperatures can cause injuries, fatalities, and major economic impacts when they are prolonged or coincide with other natural or technological events. Extreme heat, called a *heat wave*, occurs when temperatures of 10 or more degrees above the average high temperature persist across a geographic region for several days or weeks. Humid or muggy conditions, which add to the discomfort of high temperatures, can occur when a "dome" of high atmospheric pressure traps hazy, damp air close to the ground. Excessively dry conditions that coincide with extreme heat can provoke wind and dust storms.

While there is no widely accepted standard for extreme cold temperatures, periods of colder than normal conditions exhibit a range of negative consequences, depending on where they occur and exactly how cold temperatures fall. Any time temperatures fall below freezing, there is the risk of death from hypothermia to humans and livestock, with the degree to which populations are accustomed to those temperatures a primary factor in resilience. Extreme cold can also lead to serious economic damages from frozen water pipes; the freezing of navigable rivers, which halts commerce and can cause ice dams; and the destruction of crops.

Thunderstorms

Thunderstorms are meteorological events that bring heavy rains, strong winds, hail, lightning, and tornadoes. Thunderstorms are generated by atmospheric imbalance and turbulence caused by a combination of several conditions, including unstable, warm air rising rapidly into the atmosphere; sufficient moisture to form clouds and rain; and upward lift of air currents caused by colliding weather fronts (cold and warm), sea breezes, or mountains. A thunderstorm is classified as severe if its winds reach or exceed 58 mph, it produces a tornado, or it drops surface hail at least 0.75 in. in diameter. Thunderstorms may occur singly, in clusters, or in lines. Thus, it is possible for several thunderstorms to affect one location in the course of a few hours. These events are particularly devastating when a single thunderstorm affects one location for an extended period. Such conditions lead to oversaturation of the ground and subsequent flash flooding and slope erosion.

Lightning is a major secondary threat associated with thunderstorms.

Hail

Hail is frozen atmospheric water that falls to the earth. Moisture in clouds becomes frozen into crystals at high temperatures and begins to fall under its own weight. Typically, these crystals melt at lower temperatures, but in the right conditions they pick up more moisture as they fall and are then lifted to cold elevations, which causes refreezing. This cycle may continue until the individual hailstones reach several inches in diameter under the right conditions. Because of the strength of severe thunderstorms and tornadoes, both can cause this cyclic lifting, and therefore they are often accompanied by hail. Hailstorms occur more frequently during late spring and early summer when the jet stream migrates northward across the Great Plains. When they fall, they can damage crops, break windows, destroy cars and other exposed properties, collapse roofs, and cause other destruction totaling nearly $1 billion each year in the United States.

Technological Hazards

Technological hazards, or "man-made" hazards as they are often called, are an inevitable product of technological innovation and human development. These hazards, which can occur after the failure of or damage to the many structures and systems upon which humans rely, tend to be much less understood than their natural counterparts. Additionally, as technology advances with each passing year, the number of associated disasters increases, and their scope expands. The most common technological hazards arise from systems and structures related to transportation, infrastructure, industry, and construction.

Structural Fires

Structural fires can be triggered or exacerbated by both natural processes, including lightning, high winds, earthquakes, volcanoes, and floods, or by human origins, including accidents and arson, for example.

Lightning is the most significant natural contributor to fires affecting the built environment. Buildings with rooftop storage tanks for flammable liquids are particularly susceptible. There were 1,348,500 fires in the United States in 2009, of which 35.6% affected structures. While residential fires only very rarely cause a disaster, they result in 85% of the roughly 3,000 civilian deaths associated with fires each year, and 75% of the 17,000 injuries that occur. They are also a major contributor to the 75,000–85,000 fire-fighter injuries that occur annually (National Fire Protection Association, 2010).

Transportation Accidents

Transportation is a technology on which the entire world depends for travel, commerce, and industry. The vast system of land, sea, and air transportation involves complex and expensive infrastructure, humans or machines to conduct that infrastructure, and laws and policies by which the whole system is guided. A flaw or breakdown in any one of these components can and often does result in a major disaster involving loss of life, injuries, property and environmental damage, and economic consequences. Transportation accidents can cause mass casualty incidents, as well as major disruptions to society and commerce, when they occur in any of the transportation sectors (including air travel, sea travel, rail travel, bus travel, and roadways). The accidents do not need to be the result of the vehicles themselves. For instance, the collapse of the I-35 Mississippi Bridge in Minneapolis (August 4, 2007) resulted in 13 fatalities, 145 injuries, and severe financial implications given that 140,000 daily commuters had to find alternate means of crossing the river. Transportation systems and infrastructure are considered a top terrorist target due to these severe consequences.

Infrastructure Failures

Infrastructure hazards are another type of technological hazard, and are primarily related to critical systems of utilities, services, and other assets (both state-run and private) that serve the public. The consequences of infrastructure hazards may include loss of vital services, injury, death, property damage, or a combination of these. As technological innovation, global communication, and global commerce increase, nations are becoming much more dependent upon their critical infrastructure. One of the most common types of infrastructure failures, the power outage (or "blackout"), is the number one concern of businesses and the cause of as much as $80 billion in economic losses each year (LaCommare and Eto, 2004). The primary types of infrastructure hazards include power failures; telecommunications system failures, computer network failures; critical water or sewer system failures; and major gas distribution line breaks.

Dam Failures

Dams are constructed for many purposes, the most common being flood control and irrigation. When dams retaining large quantities of water fail, there exists the potential for large-scale uncontrolled release of stored water downstream. Dam failures pose the most extreme flood risk due to the sudden and severe impacts that can result. Dams most often fail as a result of maintenance neglect, overtopping (as in the case of a flood), poor design, or structural damage caused by a major event such as an earthquake, collision, or blast. However, dams are also considered a critical terrorist risk due to the fact that dam failure would result in immediate and significant deaths and property destruction, and would provide little hope for warning those in the resulting torrent's path. Dams are both publicly and privately owned and maintained, so their monitoring can pose a challenge to offices of emergency management and homeland security charged with assessing associated hazard risk. The United States as a nation boasts the second greatest number of dams worldwide, exceeded only by China.

Hazardous Materials Incidents

Hazardous materials are chemical substances that if released or misused can pose a threat to people and the environment. Chemicals are prevalent in many industries and products, including agriculture, medicine, research, and consumer product development. These materials may be explosive, flammable, corrosive, poisonous, radioactive, or otherwise toxic or dangerous. Releases typically occur as a result of transportation accidents or accidents at production and storage facilities. Depending on the nature of the chemical, the result of a release or spill can include death, serious injury, long-lasting health effects, and damage to buildings, homes, and other property.

The majority of hazardous materials incidents occur in homes, and the quantities released are almost always too small to cause more than a highly localized hazard. However, it is the transportation or industrial use of these same products that leads to major disaster events when releases occur due to the massive volumes or quantities involved. At present, hazardous materials are manufactured, used, or stored at an estimated 4.5 million facilities in the United States—from major industrial plants to local dry cleaning establishments or gardening supply stores. Since the Oklahoma City and World Trade Center bombings, monitoring of many of these chemicals has increased. However, it was in the wake September 11, with recognition of the terrorist potential at a great many other facility types, that tracking became institutional. This is discussed in greater detail later in this chapter as well as in Chapter 8 (Cybersecurity and Infrastructure Protection).

Nuclear Accidents

Radioactive materials are prevalent in modern society, allowing such things as power generation medical treatments, detection, and imaging, scientific experiments, and more. However, radiation can cause immediate and lasting tissue damage to humans and animals upon exposure. National and international law strictly dictates who may possess these materials, how they can be used, and how and where they must be disposed of. Radiation exposure can be accidental or intentional, and can come in many forms (including gasses, liquids, solids, powders, and more.)

In the United States, the greatest threat of exposure to radioactive materials comes from an accident or sabotage at one of the nation's many nuclear power plants. As the distance to a nuclear power plant decreases, the risk of exposure increases, and the likelihood of surviving in the event of a large-scale release of materials decreases. A catastrophic failure of a nuclear reactor is called a *meltdown*, indicative of the failure of the reactor's containment due to the incredibly high heat caused by a runaway nuclear reaction.

Terrorism Hazards

Terrorism hazards, or "intentional hazards" as they are often called, are means or mechanisms through which terrorists are able to carry out their attacks.

This section presents basic information about various categories of terrorist methods and weapons. Cyberterrorism, one of the foci of cybersecurity, is addressed in Chapter 8, "Cybersecurity and Infrastructure Protection."

Conventional Explosives and Secondary Devices

Conventional explosives have existed for centuries. Traditional (manufactured) and improvised explosive devices (IEDs) are generally the easiest weapons for terrorists to obtain and use. These widely available weapons, when skillfully used, can inflict massive amounts of destruction to property and can cause significant injuries and fatalities to humans. Conventional explosives are most troubling as weapons of mass destruction (WMD) in light of their ability to effectively disperse chemical, biological, or radiological agents.

Conventional explosives and IEDs can be either explosive or incendiary nature. Explosives use the physical destruction caused by the expansion of gases that result from the ignition of "high- or low-filler" explosive materials to inflict damage or harm. Examples of explosive devices include simple pipe bombs, made from common plumbing materials; satchel charges, which are encased in a common looking bag such as a backpack, and left behind for later detonation; letter or package bombs, delivered through the mail; or a car bomb, which can be used to deliver a large amount of explosives. Incendiary devices, also referred to as firebombs, rely on the ignition of fires to cause damage or harm. Examples include Molotov cocktails (gas-filled bottles capped with a burning rag), napalm bombs, and fuel-air explosives (thermobaric weapons).

Explosions and conflagrations can be delivered via a missile, or projectile device, such as a rocket, rocket-propelled grenade (RPG), mortar, or air-dropped bomb. Nontraditional explosive delivery methods are regularly discovered, and include the use of fuel-filled commercial airliners flown into buildings as occurred on September 11, 2001. Because these weapons rely on such low technology and are relatively easy to transport and deliver, they are the most common choice of terrorists. Although suicide bombings, in which bombers manually deliver and detonate the device on or near their person, are becoming more common, most devices are detonated through the use of timed, remote (radio, cell phone), or other methods of transmission (light sensitivity, air pressure, movement, electrical impulse, etc.).

■ ■ Critical Thinking ■

Conventional explosives can be manufactured using ingredients commonly found in hardware stores, pharmacies, and other sources available to the general public. What can planners do to prevent terrorists from using these much-needed materials for sinister purposes short of banning them entirely?

Chemical Agents

Like explosives, chemical weapons have existed for centuries and have been used repeatedly throughout history. Chemical weapons are created for the sole purpose of killing, injuring, or incapacitating people. They can enter the body through inhalation, ingestion, or the skin or eyes. Many different kinds of chemicals have been developed as weapons, falling under six general categories that are distinguished according to their physiological effects on victims:

1. Nerve agents (Sarin, VX)
2. Blister agents (mustard gas, lewisite)
3. Blood agents (hydrogen cyanide)
4. Choking/pulmonary agents (phosgene)
5. Irritants (tear gas, capsicum [pepper] spray)
6. Incapacitating agents (BZ, Agent 15)

Terrorists can deliver chemical weapons by means of several different mechanisms. Aerosol devices spread chemicals in liquid, solid (generally powdered), or gas form by causing tiny particulates of the chemical to be suspended into the air. Explosives can also be used to disperse the chemicals through the air in this manner. Devices that contain chemicals, either for warfare or everyday use (such as a truck or train tanker), can be breached, thereby exposing the chemical to the air. Chemicals can also be mixed with water or placed into food supplies. Chemicals that are easily absorbed through the skin can be placed directly onto a victim to cause harm or death.

Chemical attacks, in general, are recognized immediately, although it may be unclear to victims and responders until further testing has taken place that an attack has occurred, and whether the attack was chemical or biological in nature. Chemical weapons may be persistent (remaining in the affected area for long after the attack) or nonpersistent (evaporating quickly, due to their lighter-than-air qualities, resulting in a loss of ability to harm or kill after approximately 10 or 15 minutes in open areas). In unventilated rooms, however, any chemical can linger for a considerable time.

Biological Agents

Biological or "germ" weapons are live organisms (either bacteria or viruses) or the toxic by-products generated by living organisms that are manipulated in order to cause illness, injury, or death in humans, livestock, or plants. Advances in weapons technology have allowed the much more effective reach and application of bioweapons. Bioweapons may be dispersed overtly or covertly by perpetrators. When covertly applied, bioweapons are extremely difficult to recognize because their negative consequences can take hours, days, or even weeks, to emerge. This is especially true with bacteria and viruses, although toxins (which are, in essence, poisons) generally elicit an immediate reaction. Attack recognition is made through a range of methods, including identification of a credible threat, the discovery of weapons materials (dispersion devices, raw biological material, or weapons laboratories), and correct diagnosis of affected humans, animals, or plants. Detection depends on a collaborative public health monitoring system, trained and aware physicians, patients who elect to seek medical care, and equipment suitable for confirming diagnoses. Bioweapons are unique in this regard, in that detection is likely to be made not by a first responder, but by members of the public health community.

The devastating potential of bioweapons is confounded by the fact that people normally have no idea that they have been exposed. During the incubation period, when they do not exhibit symptoms but are contagious to others, they can spread the disease by touch or through the air. Incubation periods can be as short as several hours but as long as several weeks, allowing for wide geographic spreading due to the efficiency of modern travel. Biological weapons are also effective at disrupting economic and industrial components of society, even when they only target animals or plants. Terrorists could potentially spread a biological agent over a large geographic area, undetected, causing significant destruction of crops. If the agent spread easily, the consequences could be devastating to an entire industry.

The primary defense against the use of biological weapons is recognition, which is achieved through proper training of first responders and public health officials. Early detection, before the disease or illness has spread to critical limits, is key to preventing a major public health emergency.

Biological agents are grouped into three categories:

- *Category A*: Agents that have great potential for causing a public health catastrophe, and that are capable of being disseminated over a large geographic area (e.g. anthrax, smallpox, plague, botulism, and tularemia)
- *Category B*: Agents that have low mortality rates, but which may be disseminated over a large geographic area with relative ease (e.g. salmonella, ricin, Q fever, typhus, and glanders)
- *Category C*: Common pathogens that have the potential for being engineered for terrorism or weapon purposes (e.g. hantavirus and tuberculosis) (source: FEMA, 2002)

▦ ▪ Critical Thinking ▨

Why do chemical and biological agents instill such fear into the minds of Americans? Do you think that most people overestimate or underestimate their actual risk? What can be done to correct misperceptions of risk? What is most likely causing these misperceptions?

Nuclear/Radiological

Nuclear and radiological weapons are those that involve the movement of energy through space and through material. There are three primary mechanisms by which terrorists can use radiation to carry out an attack: detonation of a nuclear bomb, dispersal of radiological material, or an attack on a facility housing nuclear material (power plant, research laboratory, storage site, etc.).

Nuclear weapons are the most devastating of the various attack forms listed earlier. They are also the most difficult to develop or acquire, and thus are considered the lowest threat of the three in terms of terrorist potential (likelihood). A nuclear weapon causes damage to property and harm to life through two separate processes. First, a blast is created by the detonation of the bomb. An incredibly large amount of energy is released in the explosion, which is the result of an uncontrolled chain reaction of atomic splitting. The initial shock wave, which destroys all built structures within a range of up to several miles, is followed by a heat wave reaching tens of millions of degrees close to the point of detonation. High winds accompany the shock and heat waves.

The second process by which nuclear weapons inflict harm is through harmful radiation. This radiation and radiological material is most dangerous close to the area of detonation, where high concentrations can cause rapid death, but particles reaching high into the atmosphere can pose a threat several hundreds of miles away under the right meteorological conditions. Radiation can also persist for years after the explosion occurs.

Radiological dispersion devices (RDDs) are simple explosive devices that spread harmful radioactive material upon detonation, without the involvement of a nuclear explosion. These devices are often called "dirty bombs." Radiological dispersion devices also exist that do not require explosives for dispersal. Although illnesses and fatalities very close to the point of dispersal are likely, these devices are more likely to be used to spread terror. Like many biological and chemical weapons, it may be difficult to initially detect that a radiological attack has occurred. Special detection equipment and the training to use it are a prerequisite.

A third scenario involving nuclear/radiological material entails an attack on a nuclear facility. There are many facilities around the country where nuclear material is stored, including nuclear power plants, hazardous materials storage sites, medical facilities, military installations, and industrial facilities. An attack on any of these facilities could result in a release of radiological material into the atmosphere, which would pose a threat to life and certainly cause fear among those who live nearby.

If a radiological or nuclear attack were to occur, humans and animals would experience both internal and external consequences. External exposure results from any contact with radioactive material outside the body, while internal exposure requires ingestion, inhalation, or injection of radiological materials. Radiation sickness results from high doses of radiation, and can result in death if the dosage is high enough. Other effects of radiation exposure can include redness or burning of the skin and eyes, nausea, damage to the body's immune system, and a high lifetime risk of developing cancer (FEMA, 2002).

Combined Hazards

By combining two or more methods of attack, terrorists can achieve a synergistic effect. And in doing so, they often increase the efficacy of each agent in terms of its potential to destroy, harm, or kill, thereby creating a sum total consequence much more devastating than had each agent been used independently. The dirty bomb, in which radiological material is added to a conventional explosive, is a perfect illustration of this effect. Explosives function by causing physical damage resulting from the expansion of gases, while the radiological material works by inducing a range of adverse health effects. The combination of the two results in an attack that not only causes both physical damage and harmful radiation, but disperses the radiological material over a much larger area, contaminates both the crime scene and the surrounding structures and environment, and instills a sense of fear into the entire affected population (which can extend to include the entire nation as would likely be the case if a dirty bomb was used anywhere in the country).

Explosives can also be used to deliver chemical or biological weapons in a similar manner. This presents a dangerous scenario in that the trauma resulting from the explosion will demand immediate attention from responders, who may enter a contaminated attack scene without first recognizing or taking the time to check if a biological or chemical agent is present. Victims who are rushed to hospitals can cause secondary infections or injuries to EMS and hospital staff. Additionally, contaminated debris can help to spread certain viruses that may not otherwise have so easily entered the body. There have even been cases of hepatitis-B positive suicide bombers passing their infection to victims struck with bits of shrapnel and bone, and the CDC has identified several potential infectious diseases that may be transmitted through bombings including HIV.

When multiple chemicals, biological agents, or a combination of the two are used in an attack, the consequences can confound even those considered experts. The combination of symptoms resulting from multiple injuries or infections will make diagnosis extremely difficult, because these diagnoses often depend on a defined set of effects. The multiple agents will cause physiological effects in humans, animals, or plants that do not fit any established models. The extra time required for identification of the agents used will undoubtedly cause an overall increase in the efficacy of the terrorist attack.

Other Armed Attacks Using Firearms or Other Tactics

In addition to the CBRNE weapons described above, terrorists may employ tactical methods to instill terror and cause death and destruction. In fact, the majority (59%) of terrorist attacks involve armed assault, kidnapping, and "other" attack methods. Table 3–1 illustrates how the 2009 attacks were distributed by both method of attack and resulting deaths. Terrorists generally use the weapons that best meet their budget, expertise, target, and the resources they have accessible. Based on these statistics, it is clear that terrorists favor weapons other than CBRNE weapons, and of the CBRNE weapons that are used, the overwhelming majority are explosive or incendiary in nature. Judging by the number of fatalities caused by these explosive attacks, they are much more effective at causing the fatalities sought by the perpetrators.

■ ■ Critical Thinking ■

What is the difference between a terrorist attack and an act of war? Do you think that the terrorist attacks that occur in Iraq are terrorism? Why or why not? Will it ever be possible to eradicate terrorism entirely? Why or why not?

Table 3–1   Worldwide Fatalities by Terrorism Attack Type, 2009

Method of Terrorist Attack	Number of People Killed[a]	Number of Attacks Using the Method[a]
Bombing	7,056	4,050
Armed attack	6,415	4,842
Suicide	3,177	299
Unknown	1,324	709
Assault	1,135	479
Kidnapping	1,017	1,039
Arson/firebombing	981	650
Other	181	172

[a]Note that there is some double counting due to the fact that multiple methods were used in many attacks. The total number of people killed in terrorist attacks in 2009 according to the National Counterterrorism Center was 14,971, and the number of attacks was 10,999.
Source: National Counterterrorism Center. Report on Terrorist Incidents. Washington, DC, April 30, 2010.

Difficulty of Predicting Terror Attacks in the United States

A risk index published on August 18, 2003, by the World Markets Research Center (WMRC), a business intelligence firm based in London, ranked the United States fourth among the top five countries most likely to be targeted for a terrorist attack within the 12-month period that followed (www.wmrc.com). The index also predicted that "another September 11-style terrorist attack in the United States is highly likely." Colombia, Israel, and Pakistan ranked in the top three positions, respectively. After the United States, the Philippines, Afghanistan, Indonesia, Iraq, India, and Britain, which tied with Sri Lanka, rounded out the top 10. North Korea ranked as the least likely country to experience a terrorist attack within that next year. The index, which assessed the risk of terrorism to some 186 countries and their interests, was based on five criteria: "motivation of terrorists; the presence of terror groups; the scale and frequency of past attacks; efficacy of the groups in carrying out attacks; and how many attacks were thwarted by the country." Explaining the U.S. ranking, the index stated that while the presence of militant Islamic networks within the United States is less extensive than in Western Europe, "U.S.-led military action in Afghanistan and Iraq has exacerbated anti-U.S. sentiment" (Homeland Security Monitor, August 19, 2003).

This rank designation made issues such as detection, containment, control, quarantine, and vaccination — to name just a few — significant factors in developing new response and recovery practices for first responders. Political affairs and events across the globe have factored heavily in efforts to prepare populations and to mitigate the impacts of these new hazards on those populations and on critical infrastructure, communities, economies, and the normality of daily life.

During the months that followed the WMRC risk prediction, the actual incidence of terrorism followed drastically different patterns than expected. Who, for instance, could have foreseen that the Maoist insurgency in Nepal would have heated up so quickly, with such deadly consequences? Or who could have guessed that Islamic separatists in the southern provinces of Thailand would have resorted to such brutal measures as to place that country near the top of the terrorism target list for many years to come? The situation in Iraq, by far the ongoing leader in both number of attacks and associated fatalities, spiraled out of control much faster than anyone could have imagined, thanks to the presence of third-world terrorists who imported their deadly methods and materials. The differences in what was predicted and what transpired highlight the difficulty of analyzing and evaluating intentional hazards such as terrorism that are dynamic and that respond to unforeseeable social, political, economic, and other anthropologically generated factors. Table 3–2 presents the top 15 countries ranked by number of people killed in terrorist attacks in 2005 and 2009, adapted from studies conducted by the National Counterterrorism Center (NCTC) and the Federal Bureau of Investigation (FBI). This table illustrates how great uncertainty factors into any terrorism risk prediction from one year to the next.

A general lack of experience with and knowledge about these new hazards, and the realization that they could be deliberately used to harm or kill U.S. citizens, has resulted in a perception by nearly all Americans that they are potential terrorist targets. (See sidebar "Where Will Terrorists Strike?") And unlike hurricanes or tornadoes, which tend to have geographical boundaries, the general terrorist threat and each of the new hazards must be considered national risks. People in Montana do not worry about hurricanes, and it rarely floods in the desert of Nevada. There have been few if any tornadoes reported in Maine. But residents of all states may consider themselves, however remotely, the next possible victims of terrorism, thereby reinforcing what has become a skewed perception of risk. The open nature of our governance system and our society has resulted in widespread press coverage of WMD risk analyses at the federal level, especially in relation to belief among various government officials that terrorists will not only acquire WMD technologies in the near future, but that the heartland of America (i.e., small towns, shopping malls, restaurants, and other locations away from major, obvious, and hardened targets) is the most likely next target.

Table 3–2   Top 15 Countries Ranked by Number of Terrorism-Related Fatalities in 2005 and 2009

Country	Rank in 2005	Number of Fatalities	Rank in 2009 (Change)	Number of Fatalities
Iraq	1	8,262	1 (0)	3,654
India	2	1,361	6 (−4)	663
Colombia	3	813	9 (−6)	323
Afghanistan	4	684	2 (+2)	2,778
Thailand	5	498	7 (−2)	401
Nepal	6	485	N/A	N/A
Pakistan	7	338	3 (+4)	2,670
Russia	8	238	8 (0)	337
Sudan	9	157	10 (−1)	255
DPR Congo	10	154	5 (+5)	1,346
Philippines	11	144	11 (0)	241
Algeria	12	132	12 (0)	128
Sri Lanka	13	130	13 (0)	124
Chad	14	109	N/A	N/A
Uganda	15	109	N/A	N/A
Somalia	N/A	N/A	4	1,441
Iran	N/A	N/A	14	114
Yemen	N/A	N/A	15	73

Where Will Terrorists Strike? Different Theories …

One of the greatest problems facing the Department of Homeland Security is trying to determine where terrorists will strike next. Major U.S. cities are considered the most likely targets for terrorist attacks, as evidenced by risk-based funding for terrorism that has clearly targeted urban centers with the greatest amount of counterterrorism-related funding. There are, however, opinions that conflict with this majority assessment.

In 2003, Deputy Secretary of Health and Human Services Claude Allen stated that rural America should be considered among the most likely sites for the next terror attack in the United States, especially a bioterrorism attack. Deputy Secretary Allen stated that "[s]ome rural communities are among the most vulnerable to attack, simply because of their proximity to a missile silo or to a chemical stockpile. Other rural communities are vulnerable simply because they mistakenly believe that terrorism is an urban problem and they are safe from attack." While Allen said the federal government has increased funding for bioterrorism preparedness, he also noted that rural areas are vulnerable given their "limited infrastructure for public health as well as fewer health care providers and volunteer systems."

In March 2004, CSO Online, an industry journal for security executives, conducted a survey that asked where in the United States terrorists would likely strike next. The results of the poll indicated that these industry experts felt the next target would be the airline industry (3%), a seaport (7%), a large public event (23%), an urban mass transit system (27%), or a "different and unexpected target" (41%). Considering the efforts that are under way to block an attack on known or expected targets, it would follow in this line of thinking that terrorists would seek to exploit an unknown target that would likely be "soft," or more vulnerable to attack. Citing another major area of vulnerability, a Princeton University research group found that most Internet experts feel that a devastating cyber attack will occur within the next 10 years, possibly affecting business, utilities, banking, communications, and other Internet-dependent components of society.

On June 23, 2005, the U.S. Senate Foreign Relations Committee released a report stating that there was a 50% chance of a major WMD-based attack, between 2005 and 2010, somewhere in the world. The report was based on a poll of 85 national security and nonproliferation experts. The reports found that the risks of biological or chemical attacks were comparable to or slightly higher than the risk of a nuclear attack, but that there is a "significantly higher" risk of a radiological attack.

As of late 2011, it seems that many of those security experts questioned by CSO Online were correct in their assessments. Although no successful attacks have been carried out since the October 2001 anthrax attacks, there have been at least 30 incidents thwarted in various stages of planning and development. The most significant of these include:

- Shoe Bomber Richard Reid (2001) – Unsuccessful attempt to destroy a commercial airline in flight
- Jose Padilla (2002) – Planning to use a dirty bomb
- Lackawanna Six (2002) – Attended jihadist training in Pakistan to learn how to attack Americans
- Lyman Faris (2003) – Planning to destroy the Brooklyn Bridge
- Virginia Jihad Network (2003) – Planning undetermined attacks against Americans
- Nuradin Abdi (2003) – Planning to bomb a shopping mall
- Dhiren Barot (2004) – Planning to attack the New York Stock Exchange
- James Elshafay and Shahawar Matin Siraj – Planning to bomb a New York subway station

- Yassin Aref and Mohammed Hossein (2004) – Planning to assassinate a Pakistani diplomat in New York City
- Levar Haley Washington, Gregory Vernon Patterson, Hammad Riaz Samana, and Kevin James (2005) – Planning to attack National Guard facilities, synagogues, and other targets in the Los Angeles area
- Michael Reynolds (2005) – Planning to blow up a natural gas refinery in Wyoming
- Narseal Batiste, Patrick Abraham, Stanley Grant Phanor, Naudimar Herrera, Burson Augustin, Lyglenson Lemorin, and Rotschild Augustine (2006) – Planning to destroy the Chicago Sears Tower, FBI offices, and other government buildings
- Assem Hammoud (2006) – Planning to attack underground transit links between New York City and New Jersey
- Derrick Shareef (2006) – Planning to set off hand grenades in a Chicago-area shopping mall
- Fort Dix Plot (2007) – Six men planned to attack Fort Dix Army post in New Jersey using assault rifles and grenades
- JFK Airport Plot (2007) – Four men planned to blow up aviation fuel tanks and pipelines at the John F. Kennedy International Airport in New York City
- Christopher Paul (2008) – Planning to use weapons of mass destruction against Americans
- Synagogue Terror Plot (2009) – Four men planned to attack Jewish centers in New York and planes at a nearby military base
- Najibullah Zazi (2009) – Planning to detonate explosives on the New York City subway
- Hosam Maher Husein Smadi (2009) – Planning to plant a bomb in a Dallas skyscraper
- Michael Finton (2009) – Attempting to detonate a car bomb in downtown Springfield, IL
- Tarek Mehanna and Ahmad Abousamra (2009) – Planning to kill U.S. politicians, American troops in Iraq, and civilians in local shopping malls
- Umar Farouk Abdulmutallab (2009) – Attempted to detonate a bomb hidden in his underwear on a U.S.-bound international flight as the plane began to land

■ ■ Critical Thinking ■

Will it ever be possible to accurately predict terrorist attacks, whether in the United States or elsewhere? Why or why not? What tools, skills, and other options may be used to increase the accuracy of predictions? What is so different about the assessment of terrorist risk versus other hazard types?

Conclusion

Terrorism has presented emergency managers in the United States with an expanded range of new hazards — many of which are just now emerging, and many others that have existed elsewhere in the world for centuries but are now legitimate threats to the nation. These hazards have required a significant investment in education of the general public, local officials, the media, and our first responders. This requirement is surpassed in cost by the need to invest in training, protective equipment and gear, specialized technical capabilities, and enhancements of our public health networks. The threat of terrorism in the United States has presented a unique opportunity to integrate many groups responsible for mitigating, preparing, responding to, and recovering from less traditional consequences of disasters, such as the public health service, that will likely assist not only with terrorist hazards but also in just about any devastating disaster event that might occur. It has given us the opportunity to include many of these public health concerns into general disaster planning efforts, and has increased cooperation with the private sector in emergency management systems and efforts (often because privately owned and maintained financial and communications infrastructures are primary terrorist targets). The research and development efforts associated with these new hazards, described in greater detail in Chapter 12, have already begun to result in advances spanning a broad spectrum of human activities from medicine to communications technology, and have led to the development of safer personal protective equipment (PPE), vaccines, and other defenses for the first responders that must manage attack consequences. Most importantly, these new hazards, and the financial resources connected with addressing them, can provide an opportunity to actually embrace and apply an all-hazards approach to achieving a homeland that is more secure from the threat of weapons of mass destruction, technological hazards, and natural hazards alike.

Key Terms

Aerosol Device: A tool, device, or machine that converts liquid or solid matter into a gas or otherwise airborne suspension.

Biological Weapon: A warfare or terrorist device capable of projecting, dispersing, or disseminating a biological warfare agent (bacteria, virus, or toxin).

Blister Agent: Also known as a vesicant, a blister agent is any chemical compound that, upon contact with exposed skin, eyes, or other tissue, causes severe pain and irritation.

Blood Agent: Any chemical compound that is inhaled, ingested, or absorbed, which prevents otherwise normal blood cells from carrying oxygen.

Category A Biological Weapon: Organisms that can be easily disseminated or transmitted from person to person; result in high mortality rates and have the potential for major public health impact; might cause public panic and social disruption; and require special action for public health preparedness.

Category B Biological Weapon: Second-highest-priority agents, including those that are moderately easy to disseminate; result in moderate morbidity rates and low mortality rates; and require specific enhancements of diagnostic capacity and enhanced disease surveillance.

Category C Biological Weapon: Third-highest-priority agents, including emerging pathogens that could be engineered for mass dissemination in the future because of availability; ease of production and dissemination; and potential for high morbidity and mortality rates and major health impact.

CBRNE: Weapons that are chemical, biological, radiological/nuclear, or explosive in nature, often referred to as "weapons of mass destruction" (WMDs).

Chemical Weapon: A warfare or terrorist device capable of projecting, dispersing, or disseminating a chemical warfare agent.

Choking/Pulmonary Agent: A chemical weapon affecting the lungs, designed to impede a victim's ability to breathe (ultimately resulting in their suffocation).

Containment: The prevention of spread of biological, chemical, or radiological materials.

Cyberterrorism: The use or destruction of computing or information technology resources aimed at harming, coercing, or intimidating others in order to achieve a greater political or ideological goal.

Detection: Recognition of the existence of a WMD agent, or the consequences of such an attack. Detection is often achieved through various public health service working together to recognize trends in disease symptoms and geographical coverage.

Drought: A prolonged shortage of available water.

Earthquake: A sudden, rapid shaking of the earth's surface that is caused by the breaking and shifting of tectonic plates.

Explosive Weapon (Conventional Explosives): A device relying on the expansion of gases and/or the propelling of bits of metal, glass, and other materials, to achieve bodily harm, death, and destruction.

Flood: An overabundance of water that engulfs dry land and property that is normally dry.

Hazard: A source of danger that may or may not lead to an emergency or disaster.

Hazardous Materials: Chemical substances that, if released or misused, can pose a threat to people and the environment.

High-Filler Explosive: An explosive that combusts nearly instantaneously, thereby producing a violent, shattering effect. High-filler explosives, which are most often used by the military in shells and bombs, may be detonated by a spark, flame, or by impact, or may require the use of a detonator. Examples include TNT, RDX, and HBX.

Hurricane: A cyclonic atmospheric storm occurring in the Western Hemisphere, characterized by sustained wind speeds exceeding 74 mph.

Incapacitating Agent: A chemical warfare agent that produces a temporary disabling condition (physiological or psychological) that persists. Oftentimes, incapacitating agents result in death to those exposed due to unexpected physical reactions.

Incendiary Weapon: A weapon that disperses a chemical weapon that causes fire. Napalm bombs, used extensively in the Vietnam War to reduce forest coverage, are one example.

Irritant: A noncorrosive chemical that causes a reversible inflammatory effect on living tissue at the site of contact (skin, eyes, or respiratory tract).

Low-Filler Explosives: Also called "low explosives," a low-filler explosive is a mixture of a combustible substance and an oxidant that decomposes rapidly once ignited. Under normal conditions, low explosives undergo combustion rates that vary from a few centimeters per second to approximately 400 m/s. It is possible, however, for low-filler explosives to combust so quickly as to produce an effect similar to detonation (see high-filler explosive) as often occurs when ignited in a confined space. Gunpowder and pyrotechnics (including flares and fireworks) are generally low explosives.

Mass Movement: Hazard characterized by a horizontal or lateral movement of large quantities of physical matter.

Natural Hazard: A hazard that exists in the natural environment as a result of hydrological, meteorological, seismic, geologic, volcanic, mass movement, or other natural processes, and that poses a threat to human populations and communities.

Nerve Agent: A chemical weapon that is absorbed through the skin, eyes, or lungs, that disrupts the body's nervous system.

Nuclear Weapon: A weapon whose destructive force is derived from the energy produced and released during a fission or fusion reaction.

Persistent Chemical: A chemical agent or weapon that maintains its toxic properties for an extended period of time following release into the atmosphere (several hours or days).

Quarantine: The imposed isolation placed upon people, animals, or objects that are confirmed or suspected of being contaminated or infected with a chemical or biological agent, for the purpose of limiting the spread of exposure.

Radiological Dispersion Device: A bomb or other weapon used to spread radiological waste across a wide area for the purpose of causing contamination and bodily harm (often called a "dirty bomb").

Radiological Weapon: See "Radiological dispersion device."

Satchel Charge: A powerful yet portable explosive device traditionally used by infantry forces, but which has become a terrorist weapon of choice in that they blend easily for effective concealment in public places.

Storm Surge: Masses of water that are pushed toward the shore by meteorological forces.

Synergistic Effect: Simultaneous action of separate things that have a greater total effect than the sum of their individual effects.

Tornado: A rapidly rotating vortex or funnel of air extending groundward from a cumulonimbus cloud.

Tsunami: A wave or series of waves generated by a mass displacement of sea or lake water.

Vaccination: The process of administering weakened or dead pathogens to a healthy person or animal, with the intent of conferring immunity against a targeted form of a related disease agent.

Volcano: A break in the earth's crust through which molten rock from beneath the earth's surface erupts.

Wildfire: Large fires which spread throughout the natural environment, whether at the surface, close to the ground, or in the forest crown.

Review Questions

1. Discuss the two major differences between traditional hazards (i.e., hurricanes, floods, tornadoes, earthquakes, hazardous materials incidents) and the new hazards associated with terrorism.

2. What are five major categories of hazards associated with terrorism?

3. Discuss the appropriate responses to the new hazards associated with terrorism. For each hazard, when is it appropriate to shelter in place, evacuate, and/or quarantine?

4. Understanding the new hazards associated with terrorism will be critical to reducing the fear among the public of these hazards. This was done very successfully in the past in understanding and dispelling the fear surrounding traditional hazards. How would you design and implement a public education campaign concerning the new hazards? What information would you present and how?

5. If you were a member of Congress, what role would you foresee for the federal government in researching these new hazards, identifying appropriate response and preparedness measures, and educating the public? What role would you have if you were a governor? What role would you have if you were a mayor or county executive?

References

CDC, 2008. Recommendations for Postexposure Interventions to Prevent Infection with Hepatitis B Virus, Hepatitis C Virus, or Human Immunodeficiency Virus, and Tetanus in Persons Wounded During Bombings and Other Mass-Casualty Events. http://www.cdc.gov/mmwr/preview/ mmwrhtml/rr5706a1.htm.%20.stm.

Coppola, D., 2011. Introduction to International Disaster Management, 2nd Edition. Butterworth Heinemann, Burlington, MA.

Federal Emergency Management Agency (FEMA), 2002. Managing the Emergency Consequences of Terrorist Incidents—Interim Planning Guide for State and Local Governments. FEMA, Washington, DC.

Haltman, M., 2010. More Than 30 Incidents of Domestic Terrorism Attacks Thwarted Since 9/11. The Homeland Security Examiner, May 23, http://www.examiner.com/ homeland-security-in-national/more-than-30-incidents-of-domestic-terrorism-attacks-thwarted-since-9-11.

LaCommare, K., Eto, J., 2004. Understanding the Cost of Power Interruptions to US Electricity Consumers. Ernest Orlando Lawrence Berkeley National Laboratory. http:// certs.lbl.gov/pdf/55718.pdf.

NCTC Report, 2009. www.nctc.gov/witsbanner/docs/2009_ report_on_terrorism.pdf.

Governmental Homeland Security Structures

What You Will Learn

- The individual components that compose the Department of Homeland Security, the function of each component, and other interesting facts and figures about each
- The causes and nature of major structural changes that have occurred within the Department of Homeland Security since it was established in 2002
- The federal agencies, in addition to the Department of Homeland Security, that participate in traditional homeland security activities and the nature of those activities
- The various homeland security-related activities that the nation's state and local organizations participate in, and what types of assistance they provide their constituent members

Introduction

The Department of Homeland Security is a massive agency, juggling numerous responsibilities between a staggeringly wide range of program areas, employing approximately 230,000 people, and managing a massive multibillion-dollar budget and an ambitious list of tasks and goals. The Department leverages resources within federal, state, and local governments, coordinating the ongoing transition of multiple agencies and programs into a single, integrated agency focused on protecting the American people and their homeland.

The function of homeland security, however, is not unique to this one federal department. In fact, there are more than 87,000 different governmental jurisdictions at the federal, state, and local level that have homeland security responsibilities.

This chapter presents the structure and makeup of the Department of Homeland Security as it exists today, explains the organizational positioning of its many components, and details how this organizational structure has changed through time. These components are presented according to three organizational groupings, which include components falling within the Office of the Secretary, preexisting offices (which have maintained their structural integrity within the new Department), and new offices and directorates. This chapter also explains several other areas within the federal government, and at the state and local levels, where homeland security functions exist.

Department of Homeland Security Organizational Chart

At the federal level, the Department of Homeland Security (DHS) organizational composition continues to experience regular transition, and as such remains in a constant state of flux. Several readjustments and reorganizations have occurred during the course of its first decade, with multiple offices and responsibilities being passed between the Departments and many functional components. The most recent reorganization followed the 2005 hurricane season per the Post-Katrina Emergency Management Reform Act (PKEMRA) of 2006. In coming years, as a result of a move to consolidate the department into a new location in the Washington, DC area, and in response to the Quadrennial Homeland Security Review (February 2011), more changes should be expected.

The current organization of the Department is provided in Figure 4–1.

The Office of the Secretary of Homeland Security

The Secretary of Homeland Security is a cabinet-level official, within the executive branch, who leads the department. The current DHS Secretary is former Arizona Governor Janet Napolitano, who assumed over office in January of 2009 and remains in the position as of the publication of this book. The secretary and his or her staff are responsible for managing the overall direction of the department and its activities. In conjunction with other federal, state, local, and private entities, as part of a collaborative effort to strengthen the nation's borders, the Office of the Secretary sets the direction for intelligence analysis and infrastructure protection, improved use of science and technology to counter weapons of mass destruction, and the creation of comprehensive response and recovery initiatives. Within the Office of the Secretary are multiple-program and issue-related offices that contribute to the overall homeland security mission. These offices and their purposes include:

- *The Privacy Office*: This office was created to minimize the impact that the DHS mission has on the privacy of individuals, particularly with respect for their personal information and dignity. Privacy remains a major concern of citizens' advocacy groups due to the types of personally identifiable information that must be gathered in the Department's interaction with American citizens.

- *Office of Civil Rights and Civil Liberties*: This office provides legal and policy advice to DHS leadership on civil rights and civil liberties issues; investigates and resolves complaints; and provides leadership to Equal Employment Opportunity Programs. Even more so than privacy concerns, civil liberties advocates have argued that the actions of the Department infringe upon citizens' civil liberties and constitutional rights.

- *Office of the Inspector General*: This office is responsible for conducting and supervising audits, investigations, and inspections relating to DHS programs and operations, and for recommending ways for DHS to carry out its responsibilities in the most effective, efficient, and economical manner possible.

- *Citizenship and Immigration Ombudsman*: This office provides recommendations for resolving individual and employer problems with the U.S. Citizenship and Immigration Services (USCIS) in order to ensure that both the national security and the integrity of the legal immigration system are maintained. The work of this office is a major concern of employers, especially in the agriculture and construction industries, who rely heavily upon a foreign workforce. This office is also tasked with improving the interface that exists between the Department and foreign applicants seeking permission to immigrate to the United States or to become a U.S. citizen.

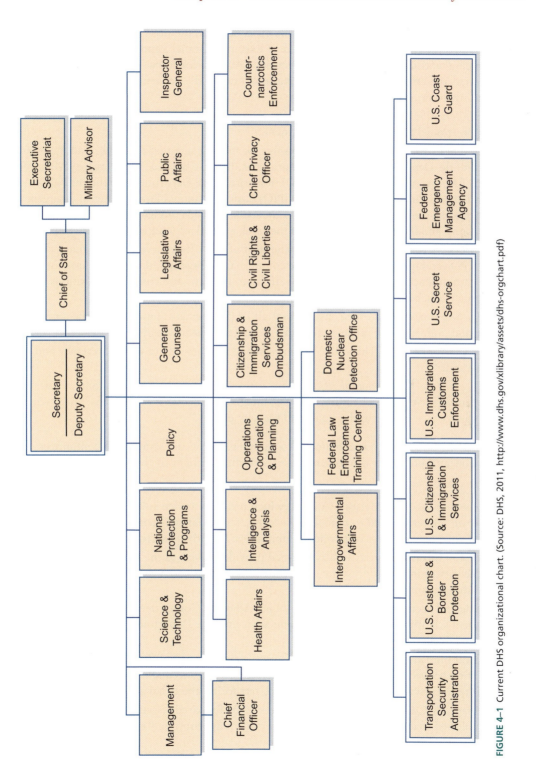

FIGURE 4–1 Current DHS organizational chart. (Source: DHS, 2011, http://www.dhs.gov/xlibrary/assets/dhs-orgchart.pdf)

- *Office of Legislative Affairs*: The staff of this office serve as the primary liaison to members of Congress and their staff, the White House and Executive Branch, and to other federal agencies and governmental entities that have national security roles and concerns. This office is key to ensuring the accurate and effective sharing of information between the department and other key government agencies involved in homeland security.

- *Office of General Counsel*: This office works to integrate the efforts of approximately 1,700 lawyers positioned throughout the Department.

- *Office of Public Affairs*: This office is responsible for making sure that the public and the press are informed of the Department's activities and priorities. Because the Federal Emergency Management Agency (FEMA) is now located within the DHS structure, the Department's Office of Public Affairs also serves as the lead Public Information Office (PIO) during a national-level disaster or emergency event. This office is the primary point of contact for the media, outside (nongovernmental and private-sector) organizations, and the general public, when they seek general information about the Department.

- *Office of Counternarcotics Enforcement*: The staff of this office serve as the primary policy advisers to the DHS Secretary for department-wide counternarcotics issues, develop policies that unify DHS counternarcotics activities, and coordinate efforts to monitor and combat connections between illegal drug trafficking and terrorism.

- *Executive Secretariat*: This office ensures that all DHS officials are included in the correspondence drafting and policymaking process through a managed clearance and control system.

- *Military Advisor's Office*: This office provides sound military advice to the Secretary and other executive staff.

- *The Office of Intergovernmental Affairs*: This office is the primary point of contact with other government agencies at all government levels, integrating the work of the department with that of each of these other entities in their national security efforts.

The Office of the Secretary also maintains a number of advisory panels and committees, which help to form direction and policy on a number of issues deemed critical to the Department's mission. These include:

- The Homeland Security Advisory Council, which provides advice and recommendations to the Secretary on matters related to homeland security. This Council is comprised of leaders from state and local governments, first-responder communities, the private sector, and academia.

- The National Infrastructure Advisory Council provides advice to the Secretary and the President on the security of information systems for the public and private institutions managing or owning critical infrastructure.

- The Homeland Security Science and Technology Advisory Committee serves as a source of independent scientific and technical planning advice for the Department's Under Secretary for Science and Technology.

- The Critical Infrastructure Partnership Advisory Council was established to facilitate effective coordination between federal infrastructure protection programs and infrastructure protection activities of the private sector and of state, local, territorial, and tribal governments.

- The Interagency Coordinating Council on Emergency Preparedness and Individuals with Disabilities was established to ensure that the federal government appropriately supports safety and security for individuals with disabilities in disaster situations.

- The Task Force on New Americans leads the interagency effort to develop programs and communication that helps new immigrants to learn English, to embrace American civic culture, and to otherwise become part of the collective American citizenry.
- The DHS Labor-Management Forum was established in 2010 according to President Obama's Executive Order 13522 (requiring all executive-level agencies with employees represented by labor organizations to establish Labor-Management Forums) to support cooperative and productive labor-management relations.

Preexisting Offices Moved into DHS in 2002

Several agencies that existed elsewhere in the federal government prior to September 11 were transferred with few or no structural changes into the DHS when it was established. The leadership and staff of each of these agencies now report directly to the Office of the Secretary. Most notable of these agencies are the U.S. Coast Guard (USCG) and the U.S. Secret Service. FEMA was originally integrated into one of four original directorates, but after the bungled response to the post-Katrina 2007 reorganization, the agency was reinstated to its standalone status, reporting directly to the DHS Secretary. The Federal Law Enforcement Training Center (FLETC) was similarly incorporated into a DHS entity in 2002, but restored to its independent status under the DHS Secretary as part of the post-Katrina reorganization. These intact agencies are described individually in the following subsections.

The U.S. Coast Guard

The U.S. Coast Guard (USCG) was transferred to DHS as an intact agency on March 1, 2003. The primary function of the Coast Guard within DHS remains consistent with its historic mission, as identified in the following ten mission areas:

- Ports, waterways, and coastal security
- Drug interdiction
- Aids to navigation
- Search and rescue
- Living marine resources
- Defense readiness
- Migrant interdiction
- Marine environment protection
- Ice operations
- Other law enforcement

As lead federal agency for maritime safety and security, the USCG protects several of the nation's vital interests; the personal safety and security of the American population; the natural and economic resources of the United States; and the territorial integrity of the country from both internal and external threats, natural and human-made. As a military, maritime service, the USCG is responsible for a blend of humanitarian, law enforcement, regulatory, diplomatic, and military duties and to provide maritime security, maritime safety, protection of natural resources, maritime mobility, and national defense services (Figure 4–2).

The USCG was recognized after September 11 as being a well-equipped military force with established jurisdiction within U.S. territory. Immediately following September 11, the importance of this

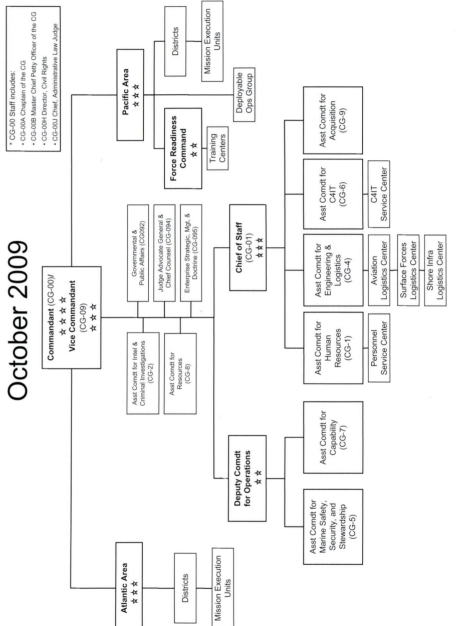

October 2009

* CG-00 Staff includes:
• CG-00A Chaplain of the CG
• CG-00B Master Chief Petty Officer of the CG
• CG-00H Director, Civil Rights
• CG-00J Chief, Administrative Law Judge

Commandant (CG-00)/
Vice Commandant
(CG-09)
★ ★ ★ ★
★ ★ ★ ★

Pacific Area
★ ★ ★

Districts

Mission Execution
Units

Deployable
Ops Group

Force Readiness
Command
★ ★

Training
Centers

Atlantic Area
★ ★ ★

Districts

Mission Execution
Units

Governmental &
Public Affairs (CG092)

Judge Advocate General &
Chief Counsel (CG-094)

Enterprise Strategic, Mgt. &
Doctrine (CG-095)

Asst Comdt for Intel &
Criminal Investigations
(CG-2)

Asst Comdt for
Resources
(CG-8)

Deputy Comdt
for Operations
★ ★

Asst Comdt for Marine Safety,
Security, and
Stewardship
(CG-5)

Asst Comdt for
Capability
(CG-7)

Chief of Staff
(CG-01)
★ ★ ★

Asst Comdt for
Human
Resources
(CG-1)

Personnel
Service Center

Asst Comdt for
Engineering &
Logistics
(CG-4)

Aviation
Logistics Center

Surface Forces
Logistics Center

Shore Infra
Logistics Center

Asst Comdt for
C4IT
(CG-6)

C4IT
Service Center

Asst Comdt for
Acquisition
(CG-9)

FIGURE 4-2 U.S. Coast Guard organizational chart. (Source: DHS, 2011, http://www.uscg.mil/top/about/organization.asp)

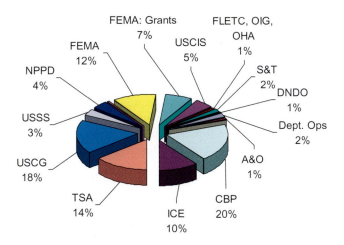

FIGURE 4–3 DHS — Percent of total budget authority by organization. (Source: DHS, 2011, "FY 2012 Budget in Brief," http://www .dhs.gov/xlibrary/assets/budget-bib-fy2012.pdf)

fact was not lost on federal government officials who witnessed how, as naval ships were quickly leaving the nation's ports to protect themselves, the Coast Guard's ships were moving into position inside those same ports.

Since entering DHS, the USCG has received a significant boost in its budget allocation, which has been used primarily to update its fleet of ships and aircraft and to increase staff. As of 2011, the Coast Guard employed 42,576 active duty military members and 8,106 civilian employees. In addition to these, the USCG maintains 8,100 selected reserve and 30,257 auxiliary employees. Between FY 2004 and FY 2012, the USCG saw its budget rise first from $6.994 billion to $10.339 billion. This represents 18% of the total FY2012 DHS budget authorization (see Figure 4–3).

U.S. Secret Service

The U.S. Secret Service (USSS), was transferred to the DHS as an intact agency on March 1, 2003. The Secret Service was able to continue its historic mission of protecting the president and senior executive personnel (and select family members), protecting the country's currency and financial infrastructure and providing security for designated national events. The USSS is also responsible for the protection of presidential candidates, visiting heads of state and their accompanying spouses, and, at the direction of the president, other distinguished foreign visitors to the United States and official representatives of the United States performing special missions abroad.

The USSS also protects residences and buildings associated with these officials and functions.

The Service is organized into two major components, one focused on protection and the other focused on investigation. In 2011, the USSS employed 7,054 people. The Secret Service budget allocation has gained slightly each year, rising from $1.334 billion in FY 2004 to $1.943 billion in FY 2012 (accounting for about 3% of the total FY 2012 DHS budget).

Federal Emergency Management Agency

The Federal Emergency Management Agency (FEMA) is the government agency responsible for leading national efforts to mitigate the risk of and prepare for the response to all types of disasters regardless of origin (Figure 4–4). FEMA is also tasked with managing the federal response and recovery efforts to support affected states and jurisdictions included in presidentially declared disasters.

FEMA maintains a full-time staff of 10,255 employees (as of late 2011), of which over half are supported by the Disaster Relief Fund (i.e., are associated with the response and recovery of specific disaster events). FEMA staff are located at the agency's headquarters in Washington, D.C., at regional and area offices across the country, at the Mount Weather Emergency Operations Center, and at the National Emergency Training Center in Emmitsburg, Maryland.

Through the Disaster Relief Fund, FEMA provides individual and public assistance to help families and communities impacted by disasters to rebuild and recover. FEMA also administers hazard mitigation programs to prevent or to reduce the risk to life and property from floods and other hazards. FEMA has been granted the leadership role, through the National Response Framework (NRF) and the Robert T. Stafford Disaster Relief and Emergency Assistance Act, to manage the DHS response to any sort of natural, technological, or terrorist attack disaster. The agency is also in charge of coordinating the involvement of other federal response teams in the event of a major incident.

FEMA also funds and administers the Citizen Corps Program, which is detailed in Chapter 9 of this book.

In FY 2012, the FEMA budget stands at $10.063 billion. This amount accounts for 18% of the total DHS budget, of which 7% is reallocated outside of FEMA in the form of grants. The FEMA budget can be increased by Congress through emergency appropriations to cover the costs of catastrophic disasters when such a need arises.

▪ ▪ Critical Thinking ▪

Do you believe that FEMA is appropriately placed within the DHS bureaucracy in its current position under the Secretary of Homeland Security, or should it have been placed somewhere else within the federal structure outside of DHS? Explain your answer.

Federal Law Enforcement Training Center

The Federal Law Enforcement Training Center (FLETC) serves as the federal government's principal provider of federal law enforcement personnel training. FLETC provides for the training needs of 85 federal agencies that carry out law enforcement responsibilities. The center also provides training and technical assistance to state and local law enforcement entities, and plans, develops, and presents formal training courses and practical exercise applications related to international law enforcement training. The center offers numerous basic law enforcement training programs of varying lengths, designed specifically for the duties and responsibilities of the personnel to be trained, and conducts numerous advanced and specialized training programs found nowhere else in the country.

FLETC currently operates four training sites throughout the United States. Its headquarters and primary training site is located in Glynco, Georgia. Two other field locations, both of which provide both basic and advanced training, are located in Artesia, New Mexico, and Charleston, South Carolina. The fourth training site, in Cheltenham, Maryland, provides in-service and requalification training for officers and agents in the Washington, D.C., area. In cooperation with the State Department, FLETC also operates International Law Enforcement Academies in Gabarone, Botswana; San Salvador, El Salvador; Bangkok, Thailand;

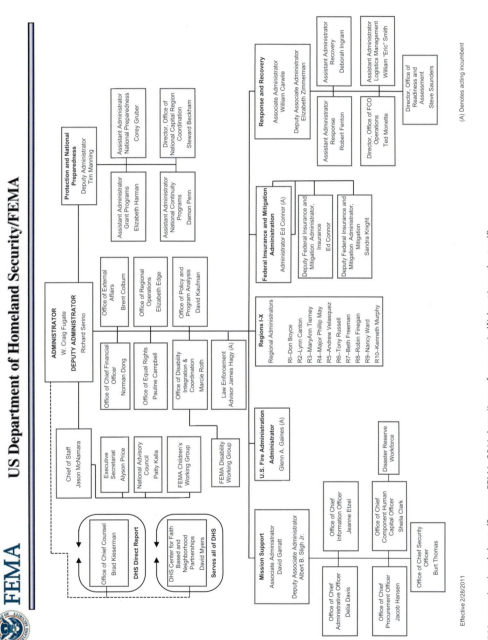

FIGURE 4–4 FEMA organizational chart. (Source: FEMA, 2011, http://www.fema.gov/pdf/about/org_chart.pdf)

and throughout the world through collaboration with U.S. embassies and consulates abroad. FLETC maintained a staff of 1,103 in FY 2012, and saw budget allocations rise from $192 million in FY 2004 to $276 million in FY 2012 (representing less than 1% of the DHS budget).

Transportation Security Administration (TSA)

The Transportation Security Administration (TSA) was created just 2 months after the September 11 terrorist attacks to protect the nation's transportation systems. The efforts of TSA ensure the freedom of movement for both people and commercial goods and services. TSA's focus is on identifying and prioritizing tranportation sector risks, and then managing them to acceptable levels, while working to mitigate the impact of incidents that may occur (Figure 4–5).

TSA began as an agency focused on airline security but has since expanded to address many other transportation modes (e.g., intercity buses, rail travel, and ferry travel). In terms of staff and funding, the primary focus remains on aviation security. TSA's most visible function is the thorough and efficient screening of all airline passengers and baggage, and the screener workforce that carries this out consists primarily of 50,000 passenger and baggage screeners located at more than 450 commercial and privatized airports nationwide. TSA efforts in protecting all forms of transportation are detailed in Chapter 7.

John Pistole is the current administrator of TSA. The TSA maintained an employee base of 58,401 in FY 2011 (primarily federal airport security screeners), and saw its budget rise steadily from $4.578 billion in FY 2004 to $8.115 billion in FY 2012. The TSA budget represents 14% of the total DHS budget.

New Offices and Directorates

Many offices were created within the DHS to manage the wide range of functions that directly and indirectly support national security. Among these are three major multifunctional divisions, termed *directorates*, each of which is led by an undersecretary. Each of the directorates and offices is described in this section

Directorate for National Protection and Programs

The Directorate for National Protection and Programs (NPPD) was created in 2007, and serves to accomplish the Department's risk-reduction mission. NPPD is led by DHS Undersecretary Rand Beers and maintains a full-time staff of 3,167 employees. The NPPD budget has increased from $1.177 billion in FY 2008 to $2.555 billion in FY 2012, representing 4% of the DHS budget request.

NPPD assumed two critical department-wide needs upon its creation, namely:

1. To strengthen national risk management efforts for critical infrastructure
2. To define and synchronize DHS-level doctrine for homeland security protection initiatives that entail aggressive coordination internally within DHS, in planning and integration work across the federal government, and with state, communities, and the private sector

In addition, NPPD provides management support and direction for US-VISIT, an immigration tracking and technology program. NPPD is also the lead office for federal efforts to protect and prevent attacks on critical infrastructure, and as such, it works to improve cybersecurity and communications system resilience. NPPD is the office that interacts with the private sector and with state and local government leaders to ensure the full range of department-wide programs and policies are effectively integrated. This office is also working to standardize DHS risk management efforts.

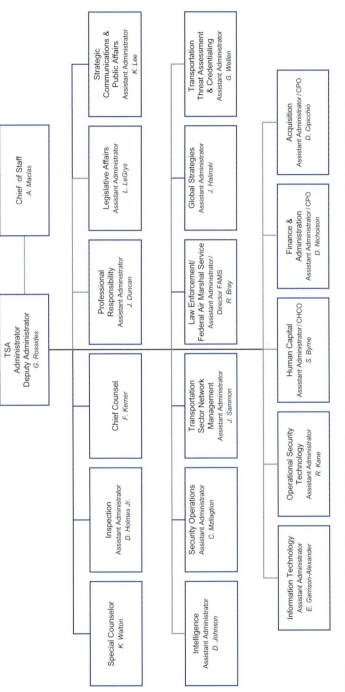

FIGURE 4-5 TSA organizational chart. (Source: TSA, 2011, http://www.tsa.gov/who_we_are/org/editorial_multi_image_with_table_0102.shtm)

- Identifying threats and vulnerabilities to the nation's cyber infrastructure and mitigating against the consequences of a cyber attack
- Protecting and strengthening the nation's national security and emergency communications capabilities' reliability, survivability, and interoperability at the federal, state, local, and tribal levels
- Integrating and disseminating critical infrastructure and key resources' threat, consequence, and vulnerability information and developing risk mitigation strategies that enhance protection and resilience through coordination with critical infrastructure and key resources owners
- Developing and ensuring implementation of the National Infrastructure Protection Plan (NIPP) for the nation's infrastructure through sector-specific plans
- Ensuring a safe and secure environment in which federal agencies can conduct business by reducing threats posed against approximately 9,000 federal facilities nationwide
- Providing biometric and biographic identity management and screening services to other departmental entities as well as to other federal, state, local, and international stakeholders for immigration and border management
- Leading the Department's effort to develop, implement, and share a common framework addressing the overall analysis and management of homeland security risk

There are five components of NPPD which include (and which are detailed in chapters relevant to their foci):

- *The Office of Cybersecurity and Communications (CS&C)*: Programs contained within this office include:
  - The National Communications System
  - The National Cybersecurity Division
  - The Office of Emergency Communications
- *The Office of Infrastructure Protection (OIP)*
- *The Federal Protective Service (FPS)*
- *The Office of Risk Management and Analysis (RMA)*: RMA has two divisions that address critical homeland security needs:
  - *The Risk Governance and Support Division*
  - *The Risk Analytics Division*
- *United States Visitor and Immigrant Status Indicator Technology (US-VISIT)*

Directorate for Science and Technology

The Directorate for Science and Technology (S&T) provides leadership for directing, funding, and conducting research, development, testing and evaluation (RDT&E), and procurement of technologies and systems that can prevent the importation of WMDs and will help the nation protect against and respond to terrorist threats. The S&T Directorate partners and coordinates with federal, state, and local government and private-sector entities in its activities and in ensuring research products and knowledge are disseminated appropriately (Figure 4–6).

S&T is comprised of four groups that address basic research through advanced technology development and transition, spanning six primary divisions that address critical homeland security needs. These lead groups, which are detailed in Chapter 12, include:

- *The Director of Support to the Homeland Security Enterprise and First Responders Group (FRG)*: FRG manages the following offices:
  - Office of Interoperability and Compatibility

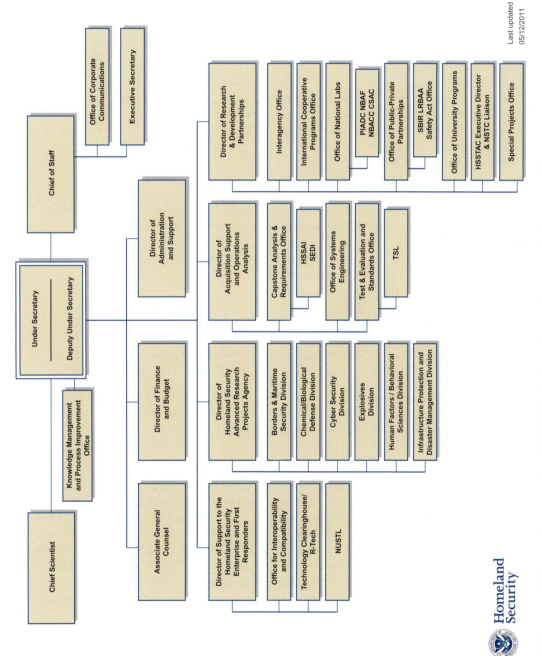

FIGURE 4-6 Science and technology directorate. (Source: DHS, 2011, http://www.dhs.gov/xlibrary/assets/sant-org-chart.pdf)

- Technology Clearinghouse/R-Tech
- National Urban Security Technology Laboratory (NUSTL)
- *The Director of Homeland Security Advanced Research Projects Agency*: HSARPA manages the following technical divisions:
  - *Borders & Maritime Security Division*
  - *Chemical/Biological Defense Division*
  - *Cybersecurity Division*
  - *Explosives Division*
  - *Human Factors/Behavioral Sciences Division*
    - *Infrastructure Protection & Disaster Management Division*
- *The Director of Acquisition Support and Operations Analysis (ASOA)*: ASOA is made up of three primary components including:
  - Office of Systems Engineering (SYS)
  - Capstone Analysis & Requirements Office (CAR)
  - Test & Evaluation and Standards Office (TES)
- *The Director of Research and Development Partnerships (RDP)*: RDP conducts stakeholder outreach and engagement through close partnerships with eight Department science and technology groups which include:
  - The Interagency Office
  - The International Cooperative Programs Office
  - The Office of National Laboratories
- *The Office of Public–Private Partnerships,*
  - The Office of University Programs
  - The Homeland Security Science and Technology Advisory Committee (HSSTAC)
  - The Executive Director & National Science and Technology Council (NSTC) Liaison
  - The Special Projects Office

The S&T Directorate maintained a staff of 505 full-time employees in FY 2012. The S&T budget allocation has fluctuated from $913 million in FY 2004 to $1.368 billion in FY 2006. In FY 2012, the budget stood at $1,176 billion, accounting for 2% of the total DHS budget.

Directorate for Management

The Undersecretary for Management (USM) is responsible for budget, appropriations, expenditure of funds, accounting, and finance; procurement; human resources and personnel; information technology systems; facilities, property, equipment, and other material resources; and identification and tracking of performance measurements relating to the responsibilities of the DHS. The Office of the USM maintained a budget of $249 million in FY 2012 and a staff of 941. The Office of the USM is but one component of the function termed *"Departmental Management and Operations"*. This function, which received a budget of $947 million in FY 2012, provides leadership, direction, and management to the whole Department and is comprised of separate appropriations which include (in addition to the Directorate of Management) the following:

- Office of the Secretary and Executive Management (OSEM): Provides central leadership, management, direction, and oversight of all the Department's components.
- The Undersecretary for Management (USM): Delivers administrative support services and provides leadership and oversight for all Departmental Management and Operations functions that include

IT, budget and financial management, procurement and acquisition, human capital, security, and administrative services.

- Office of the Chief Financial Officer (OCFO): Provides guidance and oversight of the Department's budget, financial management, financial operations for all Departmental management and operations, the DHS Working Capital Fund, grants and assistance awards, and resource management systems to ensure that funds necessary to carry out the Department's mission are obtained, allocated, and expended in accordance with DHS priorities and relevant law and policies.

Office of the Chief Information Officer (OCIO): Responsible for all the information technology projects in the Department, including the provision of IT leadership, products and services; ensuring the effective and appropriate use of IT across DHS; coordination of acquisition strategies to minimize costs and improve consistency of IT infrastructure; and development and maintenance of the DHS Information Security Program.

- The National Special Security Events (NSSE) State and Local Fund: Provides funding to state and local governments hosting major events considered nationally significant by the President or the DHS Secretary.
- The DHS Headquarters Consolidation Project (HQ): Responsible for Department consolidation into a facility that has been purchased on the outskirts of Washington, DC (the former St. Elizabeth's campus).

Office of the Inspector General

The DHS Office of the Inspector General (OIG) is an independent and objective inspection, audit, and investigative body that safeguards public tax dollars by promoting effectiveness, efficiency, and economy in DHS programs and operations, and by preventing and detecting fraud, abuse, mismanagement, and waste in such programs and operations. This office also works to prevent and detect fraud, abuse, mismanagement, and waste in programs and operations. The inspector general reports to both the DHS secretary and to Congress, thereby allotting special authoritative powers. The massive changes relative to the Departments creation and the billions of dollars being spent on the department's mission together make such a function critical. In 2012, OIG maintained a staff of 676 people and a budget of $144 million, representing less than 1% of the total DHS budget.

United States Citizenship and Immigration Services

The U.S. Citizenship and Immigration Services (USCIS) is the component of DHS that facilitates legal immigration for people seeking to enter, reside, or work in the United States. USCIS assumed the immigration functions from the former Immigration and Naturalization Service (INS) of the Department of Justice after September 11th. USCIS was specifically given responsibility for the former INS immigration services (applications for residence, for instance), while other DHS offices assumed the responsibility for enforcing immigration law within the United States and maintaining customs and border protection (Figure 4–7).

USCIS processes more than seven million applications each year. The office maintained a staff of 11,633 in FY 2012, and saw their budget rise from $1.550 billion in FY 2004 to $2.906 billion in FY 2012 (5% of the department's total budget).

United States Customs and Border Protection

U.S. Customs and Border Protection (CBP) is responsible for protecting the nation's borders, at and between official ports of entry. CBP is responsible for ensuring that all persons and cargo entering the United States do so both legally and safely. CBP inspectors are responsible for preventing cross-border smuggling of such contraband as controlled substances, weapons of mass destruction (WMDs), and illegal plants and animals. They also ensure that travelers and immigrants have appropriate documentation

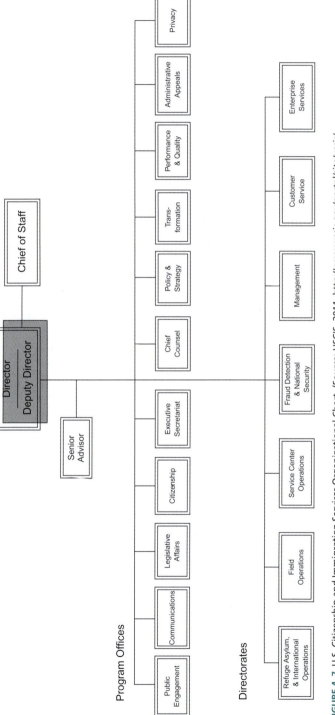

USCIS Organizational Chart

Effective 01/06/10

FIGURE 4-7 U.S. Citizenship and Immigration Services Organizational Chart. (Source: USCIS, 2011, http://www.uscis.gov/portal/site/uscis/menuitem.5af9bb95919f35e66f61 4176543f6d1a/?vgnextchannel=2af29c7755cb9010VgnVCM10000045f3d6a1RCRD&vgnextoid=476fcf021c599110VgnVCM1000004718190aRCRD)

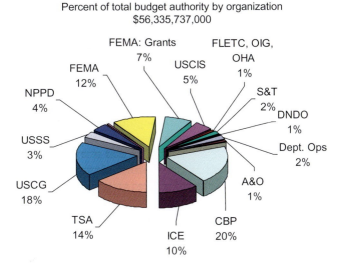

FIGURE 4–8 DHS FY2011 budget — percent of total budget authority by organization. (Source: DHS, 2010, "FY2011 Budget in Brief," http://www.dhs.gov/xlibrary/assets/budget_bib_fy2011.pdf)

necessary to enter the country legally. Other tasks include preventing the illegal export of U.S. currency or other negotiable instruments, the export of stolen goods and strategically sensitive technologies. The Border Patrol, which operates under the direction of CBP, is responsible for controlling all of America's land borders between ports of entry and maritime borders (in partnership with the USCG). The full scope of CBP border security functions are detailed in Chapter 6.

In FY 2012, CBP maintained a staff of 61,354, and saw budgets rise steadily from $5.997 billion in FY 2004 to $11.846 billion in FY 2012 (the single greatest item on the DHS budget, accounting for 21% of the total) (Figure 4–8).

Immigration and Customs Enforcement

As the largest investigative arm of DHS, U.S. Immigration and Customs Enforcement (ICE) enforces federal immigration and customs laws. ICE protects America and upholds public safety by identifying and dismantling criminal organizations that exploit the nation's borders. ICE agents and investigators identify, apprehend, and remove (deport) criminal and other illegal aliens from the United States. The various components of this directorate are as follows:

- The Office of Investigations (OI)
- The Office of International Affairs (OIA)
- The Office of Detention and Removal Operations (DRO)
- The Secure Communities/Comprehensive Identification and Removal of Criminal Aliens (SC/CIRCA) Program Office
- The Office of Intelligence
- The Office of the Principal Legal Advisor (OPLA)

In FY 2012, ICE employed 20,546 employees, and saw allocations rise steadily from $3.616 billion in FY2004 to $5.823 billion in FY 2012 (representing 10% of the department's budget) (Figure 4–9).

Office of Policy

The Office of Policy formulates and coordinates homeland security policy and procedures for the DHS. This office helps the enormous, widespread department to maintain a centralized, coordinated focus. Through their actions, the Office of Policy coordinates the department's prevention, protection, response, and recovery missions. The Office of Policy operates through the actions of seven offices, which include:

- *Office of Policy Development*
- *Office of Strategic Plans*
- *Office of State and Local Law Enforcement*
- *Office of International Affairs*
- *Office of Immigration Statistics*
- *Private-Sector Office*
- *Homeland Security Advisory Council*

The budget of this office falls within the Directorate for Management.

Office of Health Affairs

The Office of Health Affairs (OHA) coordinates all DHS medical activities to ensure appropriate preparation for and response to incidents having "medical significance." OHA serves as the principal medical adviser for the DHS Secretary and FEMA Administrator by providing timely incident-specific management guidance for the medical consequences of disasters. Additionally, OHA leads the department's bio- and chemical defense activities; leads the Department's food, agriculture, and veterinary defense; works with partner agencies to ensure medical readiness for catastrophic incidents; and supports the DHS mission through department-wide standards and best practices for the occupational health and safety of employees. The office is led by the Chief Medical Officer, who maintains the title of Assistant Secretary for Health Affairs and Chief Medical Officer.

The OHA has two main divisions:

- *The Health Threats Resilience Division*: Strengthens national capabilities to prepare and secure the nation against the health impacts of CBRN incidents and other intentional and naturally occurring events
- *The Workforce Health and Medical Support Division*: Ensures coordination of medical first responders by providing operational medical support; enhances occupational health in the Department by developing strategy, policy, requirements and metrics for the medical aspects of an occupational health and safety program; and ensures medical quality assurance

The president's FY 2012 budget request for this new office, which maintains a full-time staff of 118 employees, is $161 million.

Offices of Intelligence and Analysis and Operations Coordination

The Office of Intelligence and Analysis (I&A) is responsible for using the information and intelligence gleaned from the myriad sources throughout the federal government to identify and assess current and

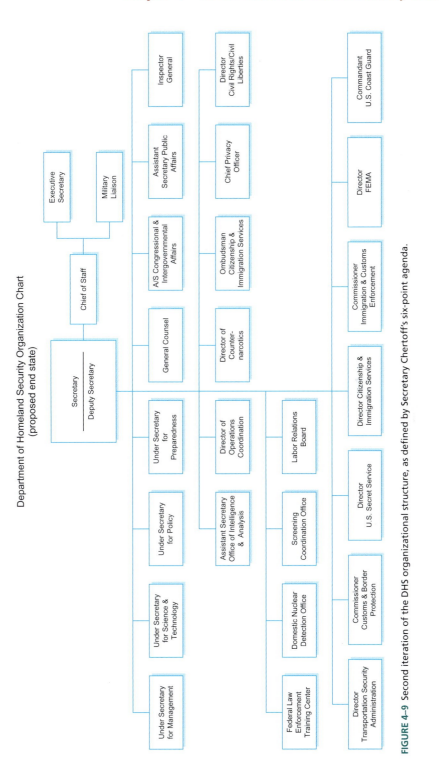

Department of Homeland Security Organization Chart (proposed end state)

FIGURE 4-9 Second iteration of the DHS organizational structure, as defined by Secretary Chertoff's six-point agenda.

future threats to the United States, and for intelligence and information-gathering and -sharing capabilities for and among all components of DHS, state, local, and private sector partners and the IC. The Office of Operations Coordination is responsible for monitoring national security and coordinating activities within DHS and with governors, Homeland Security Advisors, law enforcement partners, and critical infrastructure operators throughout the country. Greater detail about how these offices support national intelligence efforts is described in Chapter 6.

These two offices operate under a joined budget, termed *Analysis and Operations*, for which $355 million was appropriated in 2012. Together, these offices employed 1,017 people in FY 2012.

Domestic Nuclear Detection Office

The Domestic Nuclear Detection Office (DNDO) works to enhance the nuclear detection efforts of federal, state, territorial, tribal, and local governments and the private sector and to ensure a coordinated response to such threats. DNDO was established April 15, 2005, to improve the capability of the U.S. government to detect and report unauthorized attempts to import, possess, store, develop, or transport nuclear or radiological material for use against the nation, and to further enhance this capability over time.

The DNDO employed 142 people in FY 2012. The DNDO budget has remained at approximately $315 to $330 million since FY 2006, and was $332 million in FY 2012.

▦ ▦ Critical Thinking ▦

Do you believe that it is possible to effectively lead a single federal department like the DHS, with over 220,000 employees, or does its existence combine too many unrelated functions under a single organizational mission? Explain your answer.

Agency Reorganization

At various points throughout the first decade of the Department's existence, reorganizations have been necessary. Offices have been added or expanded and reduced or eliminated. There have been two specific situations, however, where the nature of these organizations was of such great scope as to merit special mention. These include Secretary (Michael) Chertoff's DHS Reorganization Plan and the PKEMRA. Both are described below.

Secretary Chertoff's DHS Reorganization Plan

On July 13, 2005, DHS Secretary Michael Chertoff released a six-point agenda that was used to guide the first major DHS reorganizations. His intentions were to streamline inefficient and cumbersome efforts and operations. The review closely examined the department in search of ways in which leadership could better manage risk in terms of threat, vulnerability, and consequence; prioritize policies and operational missions according to this risk-based approach; and establish a series of preventive and protective steps that would increase security at multiple levels. According to the six-point agenda, changes were focused on the following:

- Increasing overall preparedness, particularly for catastrophic events
- Creating better transportation security systems to move people and cargo more securely and efficiently
- Strengthening border security and interior enforcement and reforming immigration processes
- Enhancing information sharing (with partners)

- Improving financial management, human resource development, procurement, and information technology within the department
- Realigning the department's organization to maximize mission performance

Secretary Chertoff initiated several new policy initiatives that were included in the overhaul of the department.

One of the most significant changes that occurred as result of the six-point agenda was an organizational restructuring of the department (Figure 4–9). Chertoff asserted that these changes were made "to increase [the Department's] ability to prepare, prevent, and respond to terrorist attacks and other emergencies." Changes included the following:

- The creation of a Directorate of Policy (which later became the Office for Policy)
- Creation of the Office of Intelligence and Analysis
- Establishment of a Director of Operations Coordination, with a corresponding Operations Coordination office
- Renaming of the Information Analysis and Infrastructure Protection Directorate to the Directorate for Preparedness, which consolidated preparedness assets from across the department.
- Removal of FEMA from the Emergency Preparedness & Response Directorate
- Transfer of the Federal Air Marshal Service from ICE to TSA
- Creation of an Office of Legislative and Intergovernmental Affairs
- Movement of the Office of Security into the Directorate for Management

■ ■ Critical Thinking ■

Do you believe that the problems attributed to FEMA in the response to Hurricane Katrina would have happened regardless of Secretary Chertoff's reorganization plan, or that it was something about this structure that caused the inefficiencies and shortfalls that were observed? Or were the problems entirely unrelated to the DHS structure? Explain your answer.

The Post-Katrina Emergency Management Reform Act

Hurricane Katrina exposed significant problems with the United States' emergency management framework. A terrorism focus had been maintained at the expense of preparedness and response capacity for other hazards, namely, the natural disasters that have proven to be much more likely. FEMA, and likewise DHS, was highly criticized by the public and by Congress in the months following the 2005 hurricane season. In response, Congress passed the Post-Katrina Emergency Management Reform Act (PKEMRA) (H.R. 5441, Public Law 109-295), signed into law by the president on October 4, 2006.

PKEMRA established several new leadership positions within DHS, moved additional functions into FEMA, created and reallocated functions to other components within DHS, and amended the Homeland Security Act in ways that directly and indirectly affected the organization and functions of various entities within DHS.

PKEMRA mandated transfers into FEMA included:

- United States Fire Administration (USFA)
- Office of Grants and Training (G&T)

- Chemical Stockpile Emergency Preparedness Division (CSEP)
- Radiological Emergency Preparedness Program (REPP)
- Office of National Capital Region Coordination (NCRC)

PKEMRA dictated that the head of FEMA would take on the new title of administrator, and would be supported by two deputy administrators. One is the deputy administrator and chief operating officer, who serves as the principal deputy and maintains overall operational responsibilities at FEMA. The other is the deputy administrator for National Preparedness, a new division created within FEMA. The National Preparedness Division under FEMA included several existing FEMA programs and several programs that were moved into the former Preparedness Directorate. This division focuses on emergency preparedness policy, contingency planning, exercise coordination and evaluation, emergency management training, and hazard mitigation. The National Preparedness Division oversees two new divisions: Readiness, Prevention and Planning (RPP), and the National Integration Center (NIC). RPP is now the central office within FEMA handling preparedness policy and planning functions. The NIC maintains the NIMS and the National Response Plan (NRP) and coordinates activities with the U.S. Fire Administration.

The existing Office of Grants and Training (OGT) was moved into the newly expanded FEMA and was renamed the "Office of Grant Programs." The training and systems support divisions of the OGT were transferred into the NIC. The Office of the Citizen Corps was transferred into the FEMA Office of Readiness, Prevention and Planning.

Additional headquarters positions created at FEMA by the new law included a disability coordinator (located in the FEMA Office of Equal Rights), a small state and rural advocate, a law enforcement advisor to the administrator, and a national advisory council.

This act specifically excluded certain elements of the former DHS Preparedness Directorate from transfer into FEMA. The Preparedness Directorate was renamed the National Protection and Programs Directorate (NPPD), and it remained under the direction of a DHS Undersecretary (currently Rand Beers).

And finally, the law created the OHA, described earlier in this chapter.

DHS Budget

Table 4–1 details the FY 2012 DHS budget proposed by department function or component.

Other Agencies Participating in Community-Level Funding

As mentioned in the introduction to this chapter, the DHS may be the most recognized embodiment of federal homeland security action and have the most central role in its implementation, but it is not alone in the federal government by any means in this mission. Several other federal agencies outside of the new department have both maintained existing programs and created entirely new programs, each addressing some aspect of homeland security. Many of these also fund or support homeland security efforts at the state and local levels as well. Several of these programs, as discussed next, are either in the transitional or in the developmental phase but have already begun active participation within the greater homeland security context.

The White House (the Executive Office of the President)

The President of the United States and the White House (the Executive Office of the President) play an important homeland security role as the primary drivers of federal policy and as a result of the role of the President as Commander in Chief. Through the National Security and Homeland Security Councils and the National Security Staff, the President provides overall homeland security policy direction and

Table 4–1   FY 2012 Proposed DHS Budget ($ in thousands)

Budget Item	FY 2010	FY 2011	FY 2012 Proposed	Year Over Year Change	Year Over Year (%)
Departmental Operations	809,531	800,931	947,231	146,300	18
Analysis and Operations (A&O)	333,030	335,030	355,368	20,338	6
Office of the Inspector General (OIG)	113,874	129,874	144,318	14,444	11
U.S. Customs & Border Protection (CBP)	11,540,501	11,544,660	11,845,678	301,018	3
U.S. Immigration & Customs Enforcement (ICE)	5,741,752	5,748,339	5,822,576	74,237	1
Transportation Security Administration (TSA)	7,656,066	7,649,666	8,115,259	465,593	6
U.S. Coast Guard (USCG)	10,789,076	10,151,543	10,338,545	187,002	2
U.S. Secret Service (USSS)	1,710,344	1,722,644	1,943,531	220,887	13
National Protection and Programs Directorate (NPPD)	2,429,455	2,432,756	2,555,449	122,693	5
Office of Health Affairs (OHA)	136,850	139,250	160,949	21,699	16
Federal Emergency Management Agency (FEMA)	6,200,618	6,181,718	6,218,433	36,715	1
FEMA: Grant Programs	4,165,200	4,165,200	3,844,663	(320,537)	−8
U.S. Citizenship & Immigration Services (USCIS)	2,870,997	3,054,829	2,906,866	(147,963)	−5
Federal Law Enforcement Training Center (FLETC)	282,812	282,812	276,413	(6,399)	−2
Science & Technology Directorate (S&T)	1,006,471	1,006,471	1,176,432	169,961	17
Domestic Nuclear Detection Office (DNDO)	383,037	383,037	331,738	(51,299)	−13
Total budget authority:	56,169,614	55,728,760	56,983,449	1,254,689	2.25
Mandatory, fee, and trust funds	(10,179,438)	(9,697,347)	(9,578,910)	118,437	−1.22
Discretionary offsetting fees	(3,533,561)	(3,442,780)	(4,180,357)	(737,577)	21
Net discount budget authority	42,456,615	42,588,633	43,224,182	635,549	–
Less rescission of prior-year carryover — regular appropriations	(151,582)	(40,474)	(41,942)	–	0
Adjusted net discount budget authority	42,305,033	42,548,159	43,182,240	634,081	1

coordination. As a result of Presidential Study Directive 1 (2009), which directed an examination of ways to reform the White House organization for counterterrorism and homeland security, the White House merged the staffs of the National Security Council and the Homeland Security Council into a single new integrated National Security Staff (NSS). The new NSS supports all White House policymaking activities related to international, transnational, and homeland security matters. The NSS was established under the direction of the National Security Advisor. The NSS is maintained as the principal venue for interagency deliberations on national security issues including terrorism, WMDs, and natural disasters, among others. Within the NSS, a number of new directorates and positions were created to deal with new and emerging threats including cybersecurity, WMD terrorism, transborder security, information sharing, and resilience.

U.S. Department of Agriculture

Considering the varied and wide-reaching impacts that both terrorism and other natural disasters (such as plant and animal diseases) could have on the both the U.S. food supply and on the U.S. economy, agriculture has assumed a very important role in the overall homeland security approach of the United States. Shortly after September 11, the U.S. Department of Agriculture (USDA) formed a Homeland Security Council (within USDA) to develop a department-wide plan and coordinate efforts among all USDA agencies and offices. Their efforts have since focused on three key areas of concern:

- Safety and security of the food supply and agricultural production
- Protection of USDA facilities
- USDA staff and emergency preparedness

The USDA contributes to an ongoing DHS effort of protecting the nation's food supply by keeping foreign agricultural pests and diseases from entering the country. In this vein, there has been a drastic increase in the number of veterinarians and food import surveillance officers that have been posted at borders and ports of entry. Although approximately 2,600 members of the USDA border inspection force were transferred to DHS as stipulated in the Homeland Security Act of 2002, USDA has continued to train inspectors and set policy for plants, animals, and commodities entering the United States.

USDA continues to contribute to homeland security efforts in the following ways:

- By protecting the health and safety of farm animals, crops, and natural resources
- By ensuring the safety of the nation's food supply
- By protecting research and laboratory facilities
- By preparing for and responding to emergencies involving agriculture
- By protecting infrastructure upon which agriculture relies, or which crosses agricultural lands
- By securing information technology related to agricultural production or safety

Department of Commerce

The Department of Commerce promotes homeland security through actions conducted in three of its many offices and agencies. These include:

- Bureau of Industry and Security (BIS): The BIS's mission is to advance U.S. national security, foreign policy, and economic interests. BIS's activities include regulating the export of sensitive goods and technologies and enforcing export control and public safety laws; cooperating with and assisting foreign countries on export control; helping U.S. industry to comply with international arms control agreements; and monitoring the U.S. defense industrial base to ensure that it is capable of handling national and homeland security needs.
- National Institute for Standards and Technology (NIS): NIS supports homeland security by developing the infrastructure used to establish safety and security standards, including such things as building security, biometric identification, and various radiation detection systems, among others.
- National Oceanographic and Atmospheric Administration (NOAA): NOAA monitors meteorological conditions, makes forecasts about storm risks, and recommends preparedness measures to FEMA and other federal, state, and local government agencies. The NOAA National Weather Service (NWS), under which the All-Hazards Radio Warning Network is managed, is another vital component to the overall homeland security needs of the nation. The weather radio system may be activated to provide warning in advance of any type of disaster event.

Department of Education

The Department of Education is responsible for, among other things, taking a leadership position in establishing standards and technical assistance for school safety. Schools are not only vulnerable to the effects of natural and technological disasters, but have been identified by many terrorism experts to be a primary target for terrorist activities due to the emotional factor involved with the injury or death of children. Schools have often been the target of terrorist attacks, both within and outside the United States. The office of Safe and Drug-Free Schools manages all Department of Education activities related to safe schools, crisis response, alcohol and drug prevention, and health and well-being of students, and is today responsible for leading the homeland security efforts of the department.

The Department has created a "one-stop shop" for schools to locate information to plan for all types of disasters, whether they are natural, terrorist, or other.

The Environmental Protection Agency

The Environmental Protection Agency (EPA) is charged with protecting human health and the environment. The EPA has played a very important role in emergency management and homeland security for decades, most notably in the water sector. The EPA is concerned primarily with emergencies involving the release, or threatened release, of oil, radioactive materials, or hazardous chemicals that have the potential to affect communities and the surrounding environment. These releases may be accidental, deliberate, or the result of a natural disaster. EPA works with a variety of private and public entities to prevent, prepare for, and respond to spills and other environmental emergencies.

The EPA has a responsibility for preparing for and responding to terrorist threats involving WMDs. Because of its inherent role in protecting human health and the environment from possible harmful effects of certain chemical, biological, and nuclear materials, the EPA is actively involved in counterterrorism planning and response efforts.

Several offices within the agency are involved in these efforts, including:

- The EPA office of Emergency Management (OEM): Works with other federal partners to prevent accidents as well as to maintain the response capabilities of the Agency. This office is tasked with providing information about response efforts, regulations, tools, and research that will help the regulated community, government entities, and concerned citizens prevent, prepare for, and respond to emergencies. OEM also administers the Oil Pollution Act and several other environmental statutes that relate to environmental emergencies and, more importantly, their prevention. OEM provides EPA with a leading role within the federal government in building programs to respond to and prevent chemical, biological, and radiological threats and accidents.
- The office of Superfund Remediation Technology Innovation (OSRTI): Manages the Superfund program, which was created to protect citizens from the dangers posed by abandoned or uncontrolled hazardous waste sites
- The office of Air and Radiation (OAR): Develops national programs, technical policies, and regulations for controlling air pollution and radiation exposure. With regard to homeland security, this office is responsible for emergency response to radiation disasters, helping to design and implement air protection measures, monitoring ambient air, and maintaining a national air monitoring system.

In March 2004, the EPA Homeland Security Collaborative Network (HSCN) was established to facilitate the agency's collective approach to analyzing homeland security issues while formulating policy recommendations and actions cooperatively. There are several program offices that are members of the HSCN which have distinct homeland security tasks.

The Department of Justice

The Department of Justice has lead responsibility for criminal investigations of terrorist acts or terrorist threats by individuals or groups inside the United States or directed at U.S. citizens or institutions abroad, as well as for related intelligence collection activities within the United States. Following a terrorist threat or an actual incident that falls within the criminal jurisdiction of the United States, the Attorney General identifies the perpetrators and makes every effort through the various DOJ agencies to bring those perpetrators to justice. These agencies include the Federal Bureau of Investigation (FBI), the Drug Enforcement Administration (DEA), and Bureau of Alcohol, Tobacco, Firearms, and Explosives (ATF), each of which has key homeland security responsibilities.

The Department of State

The Department of State has the responsibility to coordinate activities with foreign governments and international organizations related to the prevention, preparation, response, and recovery from domestic disasters, and for the protection of U.S. citizens and U.S. interests overseas. The Department of State political officers located at the various embassies and consulates, found throughout all countries of the world maintaining diplomatic relations with the United States, monitor emerging and known threats through establishment of local contacts and monitoring of events. The Department of State also provides direction to the Office of the President on areas where diplomatic pressure may be utilized to control emerging and known threats to domestic security (see sidebar "Diplomatic Pressure"). The Department of State also has an important counterterrorism role through its adjudication of visa applications, which helps to prevent easy access to the nation for possible terrorists (as identified through the various intelligence efforts).

The Department of Defense

The Department of Defense (DOD) ensures the security of the United States by acting both as a military deterrent to nations and groups who might otherwise wish to attack American soil and by pursuing and eliminating threats around the world. DOD military services, defense agencies, and geographic and functional commands also work to ensure regional stability by participating in conflict around the globe, securing and assuring access to sea, air, space, and cyberspace, and building the security capacity of key partners. DOD supports civil authorities in disaster events, at the direction of the Secretary of Defense or the President, when the capabilities of state and local authorities to respond effectively to an event are overwhelmed.

The Department of Health and Human Services

The Department of Health and Human Services (HHS) leads the coordination of all functions relevant to Public Health Emergency Preparedness and Disaster Medical Response. Additionally, HHS incorporates steady-state and incident-specific activities as described in the National Health Security Strategy. HHS is the coordinator and primary agency for NRF Emergency Support Function (ESF) #8 — Public Health and Medical Services, providing the mechanism for coordinated federal assistance to supplement state, local, tribal, and territorial resources in response to a public health and medical disaster, potential or actual incident requiring a coordinated federal response, and/or during a developing potential health and medical emergency.

The Department of the Treasury

The Department of the Treasury (Treasury) works to safeguard the U.S. financial system, combat financial crimes, and cut off financial support to terrorists, WMD proliferators, drug traffickers, and other national security threats. After the 9/11 terrorist attacks, Treasury initiated the Terrorist Finance Tracking Program (TFTP) to identify, track, and pursue terrorists and terror networks (e.g., Al Qaeda). The Treasury Department is uniquely positioned to track terrorist money flows and assist in broader U.S. government efforts to uncover terrorist cells and map terrorist networks here at home and around the world. As the policy development and outreach office for Terrorism and Financing Intelligence (TFI), the Office of Terrorist Financing and Financial Crimes (TFFC) works across all elements of the national security community — including the law enforcement, regulatory, policy, diplomatic, and intelligence communities — and with the private sector and foreign governments to identify and address the threats presented by all forms of illicit finance to the international financial system. TFFC advances this mission by developing initiatives and strategies to deploy a full range of financial authorities to combat money laundering, terrorist financing, WMD proliferation, and other criminal and illicit activities both at home and abroad. These include not only systemic initiatives to enhance the transparency of the international financial system, but also threat-specific strategies and initiatives to apply and implement targeted financial measures to the full range of national security threats.

The Director of National Intelligence

The Director of National Intelligence (DNI) serves as the head of the IC, acts as the principal advisor to the President and National Security Council for intelligence matters relating to national security, and oversees and directs implementation of the National Intelligence Program. The IC, composed of 16 elements across the U.S. Government, functions consistent with law, Executive order, regulations, and policy to support the national security-related missions of the U.S. Government. The homeland security role of DNI is explained in much greater detail in Chapter 5.

Department of Energy

The Department of Energy (DOE) maintains stewardship of vital national security capabilities, from nuclear weapons to research and development programs. DOE is the designated federal agency to provide a unifying structure for the integration of federal critical infrastructure and key resources' protection efforts, specifically for the energy sector. It is also responsible for maintaining continuous and reliable energy supplies for the United States through preventive measures and restoration and recovery actions. DOE is the coordinator and primary agency for ESF #12 (Energy) when disasters are declared by the President.

The Department of Housing and Urban Development

The Department of Housing and Urban Development (HUD) is the coordinator and primary agency for ESF #14 — Long-Term Community Recovery, which provides a mechanism for coordinating federal support to state, tribal, regional, and local governments, nongovernmental organizations (NGOs), and the private sector to enable community recovery from the long-term consequences of extraordinary disasters.

Department of the Interior

The DOI develops policies and procedures for all types of hazards and emergencies that impact federal lands, facilities, infrastructure, and resources; tribal lands; and insular areas. DOI is also a primary agency for ESF #9 (Search and Rescue), providing specialized lifesaving assistance to state, tribal, and local authorities when activated for incidents or potential incidents requiring a coordinated federal response. DOI, together with the Department of Agriculture, also operates the National Interagency Fire Center.

Department of Transportation

The Department of Transportation (DOT) collaborates with DHS on all matters relating to transportation security and transportation infrastructure protection and in regulating the transportation of hazardous materials by all modes (including pipelines). The Secretary of Transportation is responsible for operating the national airspace system. DOT is the coordinating agency for ESF #1 (Transportation) in the event of disasters declared by the president.

The Corporation for National and Community Service

The Corporation for National and Community Service (CNCS) is a government agency that administers several individual volunteer-based but grant-funded programs that contribute to homeland security and emergency management, including AmeriCorps, Senior Corps, and Learn and Serve America.

Citizen Corps Program

Citizen Corps is a FEMA-administered program that provides opportunities for citizens who want to help make their communities more secure. Since its January 2002 establishment, tens of thousands of people from all 50 states and U.S. territories have volunteered to work with one or more of the Citizen Corps programs. These programs, which are detailed in Chapter 9, include:

- Citizen Corps Councils (CCCs): Established at the state and local level to promote, organize, and run the various programs that fall under the Citizen Corps umbrella.
- Community Emergency Response Teams (CERTs): Train average citizens to perform basic search and rescue, first aid, and other critical emergency response skills. CERT teams remain active in the community before a disaster strikes, sponsoring events such as drills, neighborhood cleanup, and disaster-education fairs.
- Volunteers in Police Service (VIPS): Created in the aftermath of September 11, 2001 to address the increased demands on state and local law enforcement by training civilian volunteers to support police officers (thereby permitting them to spend more time on the street).
- The Medical Reserve Corps (MRC): Establishes teams of local volunteer medical and public health professionals who can contribute their skills and experience when called on in times of need.
- The Neighborhood Watch Program: Organizes neighbors who work together to fight crime in their neighborhoods and thereby increase security on a very local level.
- Fire Corps: Similar to the VIPS program, but trains volunteers to backfill their local fire department staff in order to allow them to focus more on the operational and emergency functions of their jobs.

NRF Participant Agencies

Many other federal agencies other than those just listed are involved in homeland security efforts, although most of these actions occur as a result of their contractual obligations set out in NRF. Although these actions will be described in greater detail in Chapter 9, the following is a list of the federal agencies that participate in the response to disasters within the United States:

- Corporation for National and Community Service
- Department of Agriculture
- Department of Commerce
- Department of Defense
- Department of Education
- Department of Energy
- Department of Health and Human Services
- Department of Homeland Security
- Department of Housing and Urban Development
- Department of the Interior
- Department of Justice
- Department of Labor
- Department of State
- Department of Transportation
- Department of the Treasury
- Department of Veterans Affairs
- Central Intelligence Agency
- Environmental Protection Agency
- Federal Bureau of Investigation
- Federal Communications Commission
- General Services Administration
- National Aeronautics and Space Administration
- National Transportation Safety Board
- Nuclear Regulatory Commission
- Office of Personnel Management
- Small Business Administration
- Social Security Administration
- Tennessee Valley Authority
- United States Agency for International Development
- U.S. Postal Service

■ ■ Critical Thinking ■

Why do you think certain homeland security-related functions are still performed by other federal agencies that were not incorporated into DHS? Should they have been? Why or why not?

Activities by State and Local Organizations

State and local governments have expended considerable human and financial resources to secure their jurisdictions from the perceived threat of terrorism. Although considerable amounts of federal funding have gone to helping state and local agencies to better prepare for the terrorist threat, many of these efforts have been performed without any federal compensation. Also, each time a homeland security alert is issued, or when a major event that is identified as being a potential terrorist target is held within a jurisdiction, local leaders must divert sparse financial and human resources from other areas of need to adequately address those threats. These collective strains have prompted the many organizations representative of state and local governments to become actively engaged in the homeland security debate, from the passage of the Homeland Security Act of 2002 until today.

As early as September 2002, the municipal organizations, which include the U.S. Conference of Mayors (USCM), the National League of Cities (NLC), the National Association of Counties (NACo), and the National Governors Association (NGA), and the emergency management organizations, which include the National Emergency Management Association (NEMA) and the International Association of Emergency Managers (IAEM), began fighting for first-responder funding for state and local governments and about the way the money was allocated — whether it would be to the states or directly to the local municipalities. Clearly, these organizations were and continue to be involved in informing the federal government's approach to funding state and local homeland security efforts.

United States Conference of Mayors

The U.S. Conference of Mayors (USCM) is the official nonpartisan organization of the nation's 1,192 U.S. cities with populations of 30,000 or more. It's primary role is to:

- Promote the development of effective national urban/suburban policy
- Strengthen federal–city relationships
- Ensure that federal policy meets urban needs
- Provide mayors with leadership and management tools
- Create a forum in which mayors can share ideas and information

The conference has historically assumed a national leadership role, calling early attention to serious urban problems and pressing successfully for solutions.

In December 2001, 3 months after the 9/11 attacks, the USCM released "A National Action Plan for Safety and Security in America's Cities." The document was prepared as part of the Mayors Emergency Safety and Security Summit held in Washington, DC, on October 23–25, 2001. It contained recommendations in four priority areas that described the initial homeland security concerns of local jurisdictions, namely:

- Transportation security
- Emergency preparedness
- Federal–local law enforcement, and
- Economic security

In this document, the mayors made the following critical point:

It is important to understand that while the fourth area, economic security, is viewed as the ultimate goal of a nation, it cannot be achieved in the absence of the first three. That is, securing our transportation system, maximizing our emergency response capability, and coordinating our law enforcement response to threats and incidents at all levels are viewed as prerequisites to eliminating the anxiety that has accelerated the nation's economic downturn, and to achieving economic security for the nation.

The USCM leadership has repeatedly expressed concern that a significant amount of funding from the federal government has not reached the cities for combating terrorism. The mayors expressed that they have been working on initiatives related to homeland security, largely without any federal assistance. Select initiatives, related to communities, that they mentioned include the following:

1. Conducting exercises to help prepare for emergencies and improve response capabilities
2. Expanding public information and education efforts, and
3. Conducting vulnerability assessments of potential key targets

In 2006, the USCM conducted a survey to determine levels of emergency and disaster readiness at the city level in the United States. The results of this survey were issued in a report titled "Five Years Post 9/11 and One Year Post Hurricane Katrina: The State of America's Readiness," showed that cities still have a long way to go. The USCM has continued to fight for municipal homeland security issues in the years since. In January 2007, the mayors released a 10-point legislative agenda that included a section on homeland security. This plan identified three areas of concern for the cities, many of which remain relevant to this day. These included:

- *Interoperable communications*: The mayors called for a well-funded, standalone, federal emergency communications grant program designed to improve interoperable communications, including flexible direct grants to cities and first responders.
- *Transit security*: The mayors called for a flexible federal transit security initiative to improve security in the areas of communications, surveillance, detection systems, personnel, and training.
- *Funding mechanism*: The mayors contend that improvements must be made in the application process and delivery mechanism for federal homeland security grant resources to make sure that the process is more user-friendly, the funding reaches cities quickly, and the funding is flexible enough to meet local needs.

National League of Cities

The NLC is the oldest and largest national organization representing municipal governments throughout the United States. The NLC serves as a resource to and is an advocate for the more than 19,000 cities, villages, and towns it represents. More than 1,600 municipalities of all sizes pay dues to NLC and actively participate as leaders and voting members in the organization. The NLC provides numerous benefits to its network of members, including:

- Advocates for cities and towns in the Washington, D.C. area
- Promotes cities and towns and the image of local government through an aggressive media and communications program
- Empowers local leaders by providing training programs and services
- Keeps leaders informed of critical issues

- Recognizes and awards municipal achievements and gathers and promotes examples of best practices and lessons learned
- Partners with state leagues to supplement resources and strengthen the voice of local government in the nation's capital and all state capitals

Like the USCM, the NLC has also focused on the first-responder funding issue. The NLC has continued to lobby Congress and the Executive Office to increase or maintain funding support to strengthen "hometown" and homeland security, and develop extensive policy on these issues. The NLC reports the results of surveys on municipal responses to terrorism regarding vulnerable targets and the need for federal guidance and support. A variety of publications that NLC generates offer practical guidance to local officials to assist in their ongoing efforts to develop and refine local and regional homeland security plans.

In July 2007, NLC representatives met with DHS officials to exchange views and perspectives on homeland security in towns and cities. At this meeting, the NLC reiterated that all emergency situations are local events and that local elected officials involved in the day-to-day operations of local government shoulder the burden of ensuring that public safety resources are available to citizens in times of emergency or disaster. At this meeting, NLC highlighted the following seven topics as priorities for local elected officials:

1. Emergency communications
2. Emergency Management Assistance Compacts (EMACs)/Mutual Aid
3. All-hazards planning
4. Federalization of the National Guard
5. Intragovernmental collaboration and communication
6. Full funding of federal mandates
7. Immigration/border security

National Association of Counties

NACo was created in 1935, and remains the only national organization that represents county governments in the United States. NACo maintains a membership of more than 2,000 counties (over 80% of the U.S. population), but represents all of the nation's 3,068 counties to the White House and to Congress. NACo is a full-service organization that provides many services to its members, including legislative, research, technical, and public affairs assistance.

In 2001, NACo created the "Policy Agenda to Secure the People of America's Counties" which stated that counties are often the front line of response in the event of both terrorist attacks and natural disasters. Soon after, NACo established a 43-member NACo Homeland Security Task Force that, on October 23, 2001, prepared a set of 20 recommendations in four general categories concerning homeland security issues relevant to counties:

- Public health
- Local law enforcement and intelligence
- Infrastructure security
- Emergency planning and public safety

Since that time, NACo has continued to release policy recommendations that promote the homeland security needs of counties. Like the other municipal organizations listed earlier, NACo is vitally interested in homeland security funding issues and works to help its member counties to locally address the complex issues. In addition to advocacy, NACo develops toolkits and other publications that counties can use to decipher the flood of information that exists.

National Governors Association

The NGA — the bipartisan organization of the nation's governors — promotes visionary state leadership, shares best practices, and speaks with a unified voice on national policy for states' needs. Its members are the governors of the 50 states and 5 territories.

In August 2002, the NGA released a list of the states' ten homeland security priorities, which clearly illustrated the main concerns of the state leadership in light of the massive changes that were occurring at the federal level and included the following:

- Coordination must involve all levels of government.
- The federal government must disseminate timely intelligence to the states.
- The states must work with local governments to develop interoperable communications and to set aside adequate wireless spectrum to do the job.
- State and local governments need help and technical assistance to identify and protect critical infrastructure.
- Both the states and federal government must focus on enhancing bioterrorism preparedness and strengthening the nation's public health system.
- The federal government should provide adequate federal funding and support to ensure that homeland security needs are met.
- The federal government should work with states to protect sensitive security information.
- An effective system must be developed that secures points of entry at borders, airports, and seaports without placing an undue burden on commerce.
- The National Guard should remain under the control of the governor during times of crises.
- Federal agencies should integrate their command systems into existing state and local incident command systems rather than requiring state and local agencies to adapt to federal command systems. (NGA Center for Best Practices, Issue Brief, August 19, 2002)

Since 2004, the National Governors Association Center for Best Practices (NGA Center) has tracked the states' progress in developing homeland security structures and programs through an annual survey of state homeland security officials.

These surveys have shown that the states' priorities, which remain largely unchanged from year to year, include:

- Developing interoperable communications
- Coordinating state and local efforts
- Protecting critical infrastructure
- Developing state fusion centers
- Strengthening citizen preparedness

National Emergency Management Association

The National Emergency Management Association (NEMA) is a nonpartisan, nonprofit association that works to enhance public safety. State emergency management directors form the core membership, but members also include key state staff, homeland security advisers, federal agencies, nonprofit organizations, private-sector companies, and concerned individuals.

NEMA's mission is to:

- Provide national leadership and expertise in comprehensive emergency management
- Serve as a vital emergency management information and assistance resource
- Advance continuous improvement in emergency management through strategic partnerships, innovative programs, and collaborative policy positions

Following September 11, NEMA created the National Homeland Security Consortium, which includes key state and local organizations, elected officials, the private sector, and others with roles and responsibilities for homeland security prevention, preparedness, response, and recovery activities. Participating organizations began meeting in 2002. The consortium is an outgrowth of those initial discussions regarding the need for enhanced communication and coordination between disciplines and levels of government. The consortium is now recognized by DHS and works in partnership with other federal agencies such as the Centers for Disease Control and Prevention. The mission of the consortium is to provide a forum wherein key ideas on homeland security can be shared among and between various levels of government.

International Association of Emergency Managers

The International Association of Emergency Managers (IAEM) is a nonprofit organization dedicated to promoting the goals of saving lives and protecting property during emergencies and disasters. IAEM brings together emergency managers and disaster response professionals from all levels of government, as well as the military, the private sector, and volunteer organizations in the United States and around the world. The purpose of IAEM is to serve the emergency management community by:

- Encouraging the development of disaster-resistant communities to reduce the effect of disasters on life and property
- Acting as a clearinghouse for information on comprehensive management issues
- Providing a forum for creative and innovative problem-solving on emergency management issues
- Maintaining and expanding standards for emergency management programs and professionals
- Fostering informed decision making on public policy in the emergency management arena

The IAEM often issues policy briefs that relay the position of the nation's and the world's emergency managers about salient issues being debated or considered in Congress.

Homeland Security Activity of State and Tribal Governments

Each governor is responsible for overseeing and ensuring the prevention of hazard risk within that state, including the assessment of threats and vulnerability, the mitigation of hazard risks, the funding and coordination of local offices of emergency management, and the coordination with federal emergency management agencies and entities. The governor is also tasked with leading the state's response to any emergency or disaster, and must therefore take an active role in ensuring that other state officials and agencies are able to address these many hazards and ongoing challenges.

During a disaster event, the governor will likely take on a number of roles, including the state's principal source of information to the public. This might include the issuance of evacuations, details about the scope of the disaster, and the availability of assistance. Governors command the state's National Guard resources and maintain the authority to mobilize them in times of disaster. During disasters, it is the responsibility of the governor to assess the need for a disaster declaration and to make that request to the President and/or mutual aid partners if such a determination for need is made.

The state or territorial government itself is tasked with coordinating the activity of cities, counties, and intrastate regions. States administer federal homeland security grants to local and tribal (in certain grant programs) governments, allocating key resources to bolster their prevention and preparedness capabilities. Several state agencies and offices are tasked with ensuring the enforcement of state and federal law and for carrying out other security activities. State government agencies have expanded their roles with regard to the homeland security function since 9/11 as many key components of critical infrastructure, as well as key resources, exist or are maintained at the state level. Moreover, because many risk reduction and other emergency management/homeland security programs are coordinated and funded at the state level, the state government is tasked with providing the necessary direction and guidance for these efforts. During actual disaster events, states must often mobilize their various response resources, as stipulated in the state emergency plan, and help to coordinate federal and other resources as they are provided.

Like governors, tribal leaders are responsible for the public safety and welfare of their membership. They can serve as both key decision makers and trusted sources of public information during incidents. Tribal governments, which have a special status under federal laws and treaties, ensure the provision of essential services to members within their communities and are responsible for developing emergency response and mitigation plans. Tribal governments may coordinate resources and capabilities with neighboring jurisdictions, and establish mutual aid agreements with other tribal governments, local jurisdictions, and state governments. Depending on location, land base, and resources, tribal governments provide law enforcement, fire, and emergency services as well as public safety to their members.

Local Government Homeland Security Activities

Like their counterpart governors at the state level, mayors and other local elected and appointed officials are responsible for ensuring the public safety and welfare of their residents. Local chief elected officials serve as their jurisdiction's chief communicator and a primary source of information for homeland security-related information, and ensure their governments are able to carry out emergency response activities. They are typically the key decision makers in times of disaster as stipulated in the local emergency operations plan.

The local government manages a number of key government functions, many of which pertain directly to emergency management and homeland security. These include, for example, law enforcement, fire safety and suppression, public safety, environmental response, public health, and emergency medical services. In times of disaster, this role is put to the forefront as the local government maintains operational control of incidents in accordance with the U.S. federal system of government.

Through individual cooperation, as well as supported by other state and federal programs (such as the UASI program), cities and counties address multijurisdictional planning and operations, equipment support and purchasing, and training and exercises in support of high-threat, high-density urban areas. Federal grant money helps local governments to build and sustain their homeland security capabilities. Local governments coordinate resources and capabilities during disasters with neighboring jurisdictions, NGOs, the state, and the private sector.

County leaders serve as chief operating officers of county governments, in a fashion similar to what exists at the local level. The role of the county (or parish in the case of Louisiana) changes from state to state. This role typically includes supporting and enabling the county governments to fulfill their responsibilities to constituents, including public safety and security. County governments provide frontline leadership for local law enforcement, fire, public safety, environmental response, public health, and emergency medical services for all manner of hazards and emergencies. County governments coordinate resources and capabilities during disasters with neighboring jurisdictions, NGOs, the state, and the private sector.

Emergency preparedness, mitigation, response, and recovery all occur at the local community level. It is at the local level that the critical planning, communications, technology, coordination, command, and spending decisions matter the most. The priorities of groups such as the National Conference of Mayors and the National Association of Counties are to represent these very concerns shared by local communities about what is necessary for them to become resilient from the threat of terrorism. The drive toward a reduction in vulnerability from terrorism has spawned a series of new requirements in preparedness and mitigation planning for most local-level officials that, prior to September 11, rarely considered such issues.

The events of September 11 brought to the surface the notion that the security of community infrastructure, which was suddenly recognized as a potential target for terrorist attacks, was vital to the security of the nation as a whole. Community infrastructure has always been vulnerable to natural and other technological disaster events — so much so that FEMA's largest disaster assistance program, Public Assistance, is designed to fund the rebuilding of community infrastructure damaged by a disaster event. However, local government officials and local emergency managers were suddenly finding themselves dedicating a greatly increased amount of funding and personnel to protecting and securing community infrastructure from the increased threat of terrorist attack. They have also had to boost the abilities of the local public health system, which has been recognized by the federal government as the most likely area where an outbreak caused by a bioterrorism agent will be identified.

▪ ▪ Critical Thinking ▪

Terrorism prevention and preparedness have added significant strain to already stretched local budgets. Do you feel that the local governments should determine their risk and act accordingly, or should they be expected to subscribe to a minimum level of preparedness regardless of the effect it has on other local programs that may suffer as a result of budget reallocations?

Role of Private Sector in Homeland Security and Changes in Business Continuity and Contingency Planning

Businesses are profoundly impacted by disasters, whether terrorist, technological, or natural in origin. The terrorist attacks of September 11 affected thousands of private businesses, not just businesses in New York or near the Pentagon, but businesses that were as far away as Hawaii and Seattle. The attacks killed nearly 3,000 people, most of whom were employees of private corporations that had offices in or near the World Trade Center (WTC). In downtown Manhattan, almost 34.5 million square feet of office space was destroyed. Totaling almost $70 billion in insured losses, the WTC attack became one of the costliest disasters in U.S. history. Most of these direct economic losses were incurred by the private sector. In addition to the physical resources and systems lost by businesses in the WTC, changes in public behavior following the attacks had a severe impact on travel, tourism, and other businesses. Because the biggest portion of the impact was absorbed by the private sector, September 11 has been perceived as a sudden wake-up call for disaster preparedness, business continuity planning, and corporate crisis management in the private sector.

The changes in private-sector disaster preparedness after September 11 can be analyzed from two perspectives: (1) the direct involvement of the private sector in disaster preparedness and response in coordination with the DHS and as foreseen by the NRF and NIMS, and (2) the self-reassessment of the private sector in terms of corporate crisis management and business continuity as a competitive requirement as opposed to cost of business.

Expectations of DHS from the Private Sector

The National Strategy for Homeland Security defines the basic approach of DHS and briefly describes the characteristics of the partnership the department is planning to achieve with the private sector. Given the fact that almost 85% of the infrastructure of the United States is owned or managed by the private sector, there is no doubt that the private sector must be included as a major stakeholder in homeland security. Reducing the vulnerabilities and securing the private sector means the same as securing the vast portion of U.S. infrastructure and economic viability.

According to the National Strategy for Homeland Security, a close partnership between the government and private sectors is essential in ensuring that existing vulnerabilities of critical infrastructures to terrorism are identified and eliminated as quickly as possible. The private sector is expected to conduct risk assessments on their holdings and invest in systems to protect key assets. The internalization of these costs is interpreted by the DHS as not only a matter of sound corporate governance and good corporate citizenship but also an essential safeguard of economic assets for shareholders, employees, and the nation.

Since the events of September 11, many businesses have increased their investments in security in light of the new threat environment. Similarly, the private sector looks to the government for assistance when the threat at hand exceeds an enterprise's capability to protect itself beyond a reasonable level of additional investment. In this light, the federal government promises to collaborate with the private sector (and state and local governments) to ensure the protection of nationally critical infrastructures and assets; provide timely warning and ensure the protection of infrastructures and assets that face a specific, imminent threat; and promote an environment in which the private sector can better carry out its specific protection responsibilities. The critical infrastructure information sharing and analysis centers (ISACs) are an example of this collaboration. ISACs are established by the owners and operators of a national critical infrastructure to better protect their networks, systems, and facilities within the coordination of DHS.

Corporate Crisis Management, Business Continuity, and Contingency Planning: The New Cost of Doing Business

September 11 was the most devastating day in modern history for American corporations. The attack in New York City was a direct attack on not only the symbols of corporate America, but also on the businesses themselves. The private sector lost human resources, expertise, buildings, office space, data, records, and revenue. Some of these losses were irreplaceable, such as people. The affected companies also suffered time-dependent and continuous losses such as business interruption, loss of customer trust, and employee loyalty. The property and human losses could not have been prevented because the private sector itself could not have stopped the hijacked planes from crashing into the towers. However, effective corporate crisis management and business continuity planning absolutely could have, and in many places did, minimize the continuous losses.

Despite common perceptions that terrorist strikes against military and government targets are most pervasive, it is the soft-target private-sector facilities that are most often chosen. Remarkably, a reduction in the number of attacks on businesses worldwide occurred after 2001, attributable to several possible factors. One of these is the increased global effort to reduce terrorist acts, led primarily by the United States and its allies. However, this does not account for why the reduction in the total number of attacks to businesses is greater than other types of targets, diplomatic facilities, government buildings, and military or other facilities. It must be assumed that the actions of businesses to protect themselves has helped to make them 'harder' targets for terrorists to attack.

Corporate Security

Terrorists often select targets they consider to be soft — that is, those that are easy to hit. Therefore, it is not only the operational benefits gained by corporate security programs, but also their visibility, that serves as a deterrent for terrorists. For example, if a terrorist organization aims to damage a country's tourism sector, it may attempt to detonate a bomb in a hotel. As terrorists determine which hotel to attack, they will likely consider several alternatives and select that which has the least visible security. Overall, business sector preparedness is much greater today than it was in 2001, which is one obvious explanation for why attacks on business targets have decreased. This reduction can be attributed to businesses "hardening" themselves against their former "soft target" image.

Another effect that the September 11th, 2001, attacks have had is on private-sector perceptions of the value of insurance, and in taking the necessary measures to ensure an event does not heavily impact the businesses' 'bottom line.' A great private-sector perceptions amount of damage to businesses is not physical but rather a factor of business opportunities lost. In the September 11, 2001, attacks this amounted to a significant portion of the damage, one over which we have some degree of control if adequate business impact analysis and business continuity planning activities can be established before the crisis. One needs to remember that despite significant losses in the 2001 attack, due to the 1993 WTC bombing and the potential Y2K threat, private-sector members located inside the WTC complex were among the more prepared stakeholders compared to private organizations in other parts of the nation.

By launching of the Terrorism Risk Insurance Act, in a sense the U.S. government has agreed to act as a re-insurer of insurance companies by guaranteeing to absorb a significant amount of losses after terrorist incidents that qualify to trigger the program. In doing so, the government has enabled an insurance market that would not otherwise be sustainable (nor affordable to most businesses) to exist. By buying into this market, businesses are also contributing to its existence as the risk must be spread across a great many participants in the insurance scheme for it to adequately cover the few businesses that are ultimately impacted. Since the Act was first passed in 2002, it has been amended to expand coverage to acts that occur within the United States (while before it only covered those that occurred outside the country).

Homeland Security Role of Nongovernmental Organizations (NGOs)

The American Red Cross (ARC) is probably one of the most significant NGO players in the homeland security field. ARC is a key player in U.S. emergency management preparedness and response, and is currently a supporting agency to the mass care functions of ESF #6 — Mass Care, Emergency Assistance, Housing, and Human Services under the NRF. As the nation's largest mass care service provider, ARC provides sheltering, feeding, bulk distribution of needed items, basic first aid, welfare information, and casework, among other services, at the local level as needed. In its role as a service provider, ARC works closely with local, tribal, and state governments to provide mass care services to victims of every disaster, large and small, in an affected area.

VOADs, or voluntary organizations active in disasters, are associations of NGOs who have a common goal of assisting in major emergencies and who work together to better coordinate their efforts in times of need. At the national level, the National Voluntary Organizations Active in Disaster (NVOAD) is a consortium of approximately 50 national organizations and 55 state and territory equivalents that typically send representatives to the FEMA's National Response Coordination Center to represent the voluntary organizations and assist in response coordination. Members of NVOAD form a coalition of nonprofit organizations that respond to disasters as part of their overall mission. Each state maintains a VOAD which includes organizations that work statewide, and to a growing degree communities are establishing community VOADs.

Individual NGOs are becoming a vital part of the nation's response and recovery network, providing shelter, emergency food supplies, counseling services, and other services to support official emergency management organizations and agencies. They often provide specialized services that help individuals with special needs, including those with disabilities, and provide resettlement assistance and services to arriving refugees. NGOs also play key roles in engaging communities to integrate lawful immigrants into American society and reduce the marginalization or radicalization of these groups. Through the communities, and in some cases official community organizations, many homeland security needs are met. There are a number of established community-based organizations that act toward this common goal, including Neighborhood Watch, the CERTs, and other civic and professional organizations (such as the Lions Club or Rotary International.) These groups may possess the knowledge and understanding of the threats, local response capabilities, and special needs within their jurisdictions and have the capacity necessary to alert authorities of those threats, capabilities, or needs. Additionally, during an incident these groups may be critical in passing along vital incident communications to individuals and families and to supporting critical response activities in the initial stages of a crisis.

Homeland Security Role of Individuals

Finally, individuals and families take the basic steps to prepare themselves for emergencies, including understanding the threats and hazards that they may face, reducing hazards in and around their homes, preparing an emergency supply kit and household emergency plans (that include care for pets and service animals), monitoring emergency communications carefully, volunteering with established organizations, mobilizing or helping to ensure community preparedness, enrolling in training courses, and practicing what to do in an emergency. These individual and family preparedness activities strengthen community resilience and mitigate the impact of disasters. In addition, individual vigilance and awareness can help communities remain safer and bolster prevention efforts.

Conclusion

Emergency management in the United States was forever changed by the events of September 11, 2001, and many would say for the better. This opinion is in wide dispute, however, for a variety of reasons that are unique to each successive level of government, primarily in terms of a loss of dedication to more traditional, nonterrorism hazards. Regardless, it is undeniable that emergency management, and now homeland security, has been thrust to the forefront of the public and the policy agendas, and is one of many primary concerns of federal, state, and local administrators.

For local governments, terrorism is a new threat that greatly expands their already strained safety and security requirements and adds to a long list of needs and priorities. But the threat of terrorism is one that cannot be ignored, and state and local governments have not done so. At these local levels, the dramatic increase in funding that has provided training and equipment to local first responders has been greeted with mixed emotion. Many recipients feel it has remained singular in focus, addressing mainly the terrorism threat. Historically, and including the 2001 terrorist attacks, natural disasters have taken many more lives and have caused much more financial harm. These natural and technological hazards will continue to pose a threat and will continue to result in disaster. It is undeniable that a more comprehensive approach to building the capacity of the local government to respond would provide more long-term benefits. Whether or not these local government agencies will be better prepared overall remains to be seen.

At the state level, governors and state emergency management directors have resisted the push toward local control and have been accused on many occasions of holding out federal homeland security funding from the local governments for which it was intended. In many circumstances it was determined that these accusations were correct. But state officials feel the same concerns about the terrorist threat as do the locals, and have called for better coordination, new communications technologies, and, as always, more and more funding.

At the federal government level, the changes that have resulted with regard to emergency management have been the most visible — and the most dramatic. The creation in 2002 of the DHS, which absorbed FEMA and most of the former federal government disaster management programs, has resulted in DHS taking the lead in addressing these new issues. This new agency has been tested on several occasions, as is displayed throughout this chapter, and has enjoyed relatively mixed but primarily positive success. Under the leadership of DHS, many federal disaster response, recovery, and mitigation programs have so far fared well, although their priorities have seen a drastic shift to accommodate the new terrorist concern. In general, the United States has taken the typical response to a new problem in that it reorganized and committed huge amounts of funding to reducing the newly recognized problem.

Key Terms

Civil Rights: The rights belonging to an individual by virtue of citizenship.

Cybersecurity: The protection of data and systems in networks that are connected to the Internet.

Directorate (DHS): A major division within the Department of Homeland Security that oversees several offices addressing a similar broad-reaching topic (like Science and Technology, for instance).

Ombudsman: A person or an office that investigates complaints and mediates fair settlements.

Superfund: Another name for the Comprehensive Environmental Response, Compensation, and Liability Act of 1980 (CERCLA), which sought to define liability for individual toxic waste sites and then clean up those sites from a fund built from taxes and fines.

Review Questions

1. What is the principal role of emergency management in homeland security? Identify the other major players and their roles in homeland security.
2. Identify the three directorates of the Department of Homeland Security and discuss their respective missions.
3. Discuss the homeland security role of federal agencies other than DHS.

4. Make the case for retaining an all-hazards approach to emergency management that includes terrorism and its associated hazards as one of many hazards. Discuss the pros and cons of such an approach as it relates to all four phases of emergency management: mitigation, preparedness, response, and recovery.

5. If you had been in charge of establishing the Department of Homeland Security (DHS), would you have included the Federal Emergency Management Agency in DHS or would you have retained it as an independent executive branch agency reporting directly to the president? Discuss the possible ramifications of moving FEMA into DHS in terms of FEMA's mission, programs, and reporting structure. The director of FEMA no longer reports directly to the president; will this be a problem in future natural and terrorist-related disasters? What will the impact of FEMA's inclusion in DHS be on the nation's emergency management system?

References

Department of Homeland Security. 2011. FY 2012 Budget in Brief. http://www.tsa.gov/what_we_do/tsnm/mass_transit/force_multipliers.shtm

5

Intelligence and Counterterrorism

What You Will Learn

- Elements of the intelligence community and restructuring of statutory authority based on recommendations of the 9/11 Commission
- Detailed overview of essential intelligence agencies such as the CIA, NSA, NRO, and NGA
- New coordination body of national intelligence: Office of the Director of National Intelligence
- Information Sharing and Analysis Centers (ISACs)

Introduction

Accurate and actionable intelligence is key to ensuring the security of a nation. A government must be aware of the potential and brewing threats that exist, and must also be able to understand the nature of those threats, the sources of risk associated with them, and the options that exist to control or otherwise neutralize them. The events of September 11th, 2001 were considered by many to be a failure of intelligence — not because the scope of intelligence required to predict the attacks didn't exist, but rather because the mechanisms for information sharing between the agencies responsible for managing such risk were absent or ineffective.

The original basis for creating a Department of Homeland Security was to join together the many disparate government intelligence agencies in order to prevent failures of the scope that occurred in 2001. Despite the great changes that occurred in accordance with the legislation that was ultimately passed, the intelligence function remains dispersed throughout many government agencies. Of course, sharing of information has improved considerably, and maybe even too much so as evidenced by several high-profile intelligence leaks. Intelligence has remained on the forefront of homeland security and as such is integral to its mission. This chapter explores the role of intelligence in homeland security and describes the various governmental agencies that are involved in intelligence and counterterrorism activities.

The Intelligence Community (IC)

The U.S. Intelligence Community (IC) is made up of many agencies and organizations that operate within the executive branch and work both independently and collaboratively to gather the intelligence necessary to conduct national security activities (among other activities). The IC works to collect and convey essential security-related information to the president and members of the policymaking, law enforcement, and military communities as they need to carry out their required functions and duties. The many IC components are spread out across the vast range of civilian and military government departments (Figure 5–1).

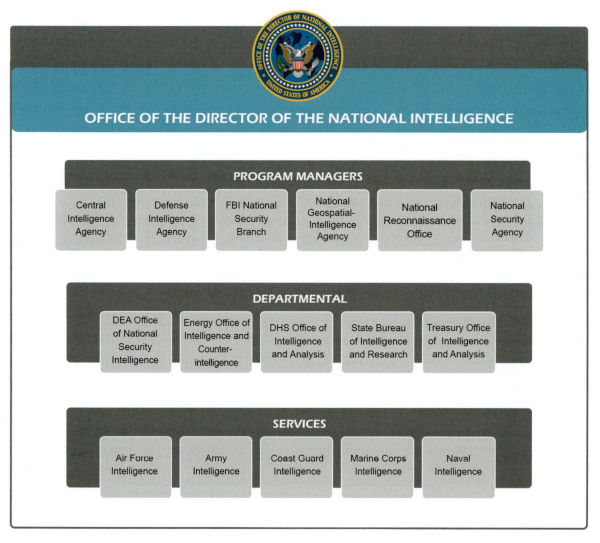

FIGURE 5–1 The U.S. Intelligence Community. (Source: Intelligence.gov, 2011, http://www.intelligence.gov/about-the-intelligence-community/structure/)

While the number of actual agencies has expanded and contracted over time, today 17 agencies perform this function. These agencies include:

- Air Force Intelligence
- Army Intelligence
- Central Intelligence Agency
- Coast Guard Intelligence

- Defense Intelligence Agency
- Department of Energy
- Department of Homeland Security
- Department of State
- Department of the Treasury
- Drug Enforcement Administration
- Federal Bureau of Investigation
- Marine Corps Intelligence
- National Geospatial-Intelligence Agency
- National Reconnaissance Office
- National Security Agency
- Navy Intelligence
- Office of the Director of National Intelligence

These agencies are tasked to varying degrees with the collection and assessment of information regarding national security issues that may include:

- Terrorism
- Weapons (namely nuclear) proliferation, including technologies
- Chemical warfare
- Biological warfare
- Information infrastructure attack
- Narcotics trafficking
- Hostile activities by foreign powers, organizations, persons, and their agents
- Foreign intelligence activities directed against the United States

The IC expanded greatly during the Cold War era, when the perceived national security threat was great, to include 25 different organizations and more than 100,000 people. After the Cold War ended the number of agencies and employees was reduced by consolidation of activities and reduction in budgetary allocations. The military intelligence services saw the steepest cuts (about 20% reductions), but given this capacity grew so large during the Cold War era, a vast intelligence capacity remains despite these cuts.

The IC experienced great change again in the aftermath of the September 11th attacks as a result of the findings of the 9/11 Commission. The findings of this commission, which was formed to study the existing weaknesses in intelligence structure and effectiveness, to form a better understanding of how the IC functions and to identify areas for improvement. The Commission's findings have since profoundly impacted both the IC budgets and the nature of their work and collaboration. Specifically, the Commission found six problems pertaining to the Intelligence Community for which it made recommendations for change, including (9/11 Commission, 2004):

1. *Structural barriers to performing joint intelligence work*
2. *Lack of common standards and practices across the foreign–domestic divide*
3. *Divided management of national intelligence capabilities*

4. *Weak capacity to set priorities and move resources*
5. *Too many job functions held by the Director of Central Intelligence*
6. *Too much complexity and secrecy*

Soon after the 9/11 Commission Report was released, Congress passed the Intelligence Reform and Terrorism Prevention Act (IRTPA) of 2004 (S. 2845) to address these problems. Of particular relevance within this Act is the first of its eight sections that is aptly titled "Reform of the Intelligence Community." Of particular note is that this section called for the creation of two intelligence entities, both described in this chapter.

- Director of National Intelligence
- National Counterterrorism Center

At present, the IC is structured to maximize the effectiveness of intelligence collection and dissemination among its 17 member agencies. Each agency is authorized to operate under its own directive, but all share the common intelligence mission as stated in the IRTPA to collect and convey essential information to the president and other key stakeholders. The current structure of the Intelligence Community is represented in the organizational chart shown in Figure 5–1.

The Intelligence Cycle

The various intelligence agencies convert the information they acquire into clear, comprehensible intelligence and deliver it to end users as required (e.g., the president, policy makers, military commanders). Key to this effort is delivering it in a form they can utilize. The Intelligence Community performs this role according to what is commonly referred to as the "intelligence cycle."

The intelligence cycle begins with the identification of key issues that interest policy makers, and defining the answers they require in order to make educated decisions on action and policy. The individual agencies, under the direction of the Office of the Director of National Intelligence, determine how they will acquire needed information and then act on those plans. Once attained, the intelligence is sorted and analyzed, and any necessary reports and recommendations are prepared and delivered. These reports often reveal other areas of concern, which in turn lead to more questions. In this way, the end of one cycle effectively leads to the start of the next.

The steps of the intelligence cycle include (Figure 5–2):

- *Planning*: Decisions are made regarding what types of information to collect and how to collect it.
- *Collection*: The IC gathers the raw data used to produce finished intelligence products from a range of collection sources (see below).
- *Processing*: Collected information is converted into a usable format, such as by language translation or decryption.
- *Analysis*: Intelligence officers analyze processed information to finished intelligence (typically, though not always, reports).
- *Dissemination*: Intelligence products are provided to those who request them.

IC collection efforts draw from a number of different source types, which include:

- *Open-source intelligence* (OSINT): Publicly available information
- *Human intelligence* (HUMINT): Collected and provided by human sources

FIGURE 5–2 The intelligence cycle. (Source: Intelligence.gov, 2011, "The Intelligence Cycle")

- *Signals intelligence* (SIGINT): Gathered from data transmissions, including:
  - Communications intelligence (COMINT)
  - Electronic intelligence (ELINT)
  - Foreign instrumentation signals intelligence (FISINT)
- *Geospatial intelligence* (GEOINT): Information describing, visually depicting, and accurately locating physical features and human activities on the Earth
- *Measurement and signature intelligence* (MASINT): Produced by quantitative and qualitative analysis of physical attributes of targets and events

Intelligence Oversight

The work of IC agencies and offices is subject to external oversight from the executive and legislative branches, given its sensitive nature. Executive organizations involved in oversight of the Intelligence Community include:

- The President's Foreign Intelligence Advisory Board
- The President's Intelligence Oversight Board
- The Office of Management and Budget

  Within the Congress, principal oversight responsibility rests with the following two entities:

- The Senate Select Committee on Intelligence
- The House Permanent Select Committee on Intelligence

Office of the Director of National Intelligence

The Office of the Director of National Intelligence (DNI) was created according to the recommendations of the National Commission on Terrorist Attacks upon the United States (the 9/11 Commission). Congress set out to establish a presidentially nominated, Senate-confirmed position of DNI, who would serve as the head of the Intelligence Community's distinct intelligence agencies. Congress sought to establish a separate Senate-confirmed director of central intelligence, who would manage the CIA and would be prohibited from serving simultaneously as the DNI. John Negroponte, the former U.S. ambassador to the United Nations and recently the U.S. ambassador to Iraq, was nominated and confirmed into the position of DNI on May 18, 2005.

The DNI was initially tasked with ensuring coordination and cooperation among the IC agencies and authorized to do the following:

- Create national intelligence centers to incorporate capabilities from across the IC
- Control the national intelligence budget
- Transfer IC personnel and funds to respond to emerging threats
- Protect privacy and civil liberties concerns
- Establishing an information-sharing network that facilitates the flow of information between federal, state, and local agencies and the private sector (Congressional Research Service, 2004a; Congressional Research Service, 2004b)

In late 2005, the DNI created the National Clandestine Service within the CIA to boost human intelligence capabilities, and released the National Intelligence Strategy to detail the intelligence framework and established goals, priorities, and measures of effectiveness. A DNI Open Source Center was created to better exploit openly (publicly) available information for intelligence gathering and analysis purposes, and the DNI National Counterproliferation Center (NCPC) was created to unify efforts to prevent the proliferation of weapons of mass destruction (WMDs) (Office of the Director of National Intelligence, 2008a).

Negroponte was succeeded by Admiral Mike McConnell who created the Information Sharing and Steering committee within the DNI to further improve coordination and collaboration among different members of the Intelligence Community. This action led to an agreement between the Department of Defense and the DNI to create the Unified Cross Domain Management Office, tasked with enhancing information sharing between the DOD and the Intelligence Community (Office of the Director of National Intelligence, 2008b).

Today, the DNI serves as the head of the Intelligence Community and is the principal advisor to the president, the National Security Council, and the Homeland Security Council (HSC) for intelligence matters related to national security. The DNI's responsibilities, among others, are to:

- Lead the Intelligence Community
- Oversee the coordination of foreign relationships between IC elements and intelligence services of foreign governments
- Establish requirements and priorities for collection, analysis, production, and dissemination of national intelligence
- Coordinate reform of security clearance and acquisition processes
- Achieve auditable financial statements
- Support legislative, legal, and administrative requirements
- Ensure compliance with statutory and presidentially mandated responsibilities
- Transform the Intelligence Community into a unified, collaborative, and coordinated enterprise

The DNI organization is composed of the DNI staff and Intelligence Community mission and support activities (MSAs). The DNI staff is primarily responsible for Intelligence Community policy and oversight and the preparation of the National Intelligence Program Budget. The MSAs are directly responsible for providing Intelligence Community-wide substantive intelligence, counterintelligence strategy and strategic analysis, research and development, and training and education.

There are four deputy directors of national intelligence, who serve in the following offices:

- *Office of the Deputy Director for Policy, Plans and Requirements* (DDNI/PPR): drives intelligence reform by coordinating IC-wide policy and strategy, plans, and requirements; modernizing security processes; and strengthening relationships with federal, state, local, foreign, and private sector partners
- *Office of the Deputy Director for Collection* (DDNI/C): coordinates collection throughout the IC and ensures that the president's and the DNI's priorities are appropriately reflected in decisions and programming
- *Office of the Deputy Director for Analysis* (DDNI/A): enhances the quality, timeliness, and utility of intelligence analysis
- *Office of the Deputy Director for Future Capabilities* (DDNI/FC): promotes technical innovation, responsive stewardship, and systems acquisition in the IC and acts as the DNI's Science and Technology advisor

The DNI organization includes ten functional mission support activities, which include:

- *National Counterterrorism Center* (NCTC): serves as the primary government organization for integrating and analyzing terrorism intelligence
- *National Counterintelligence Executive* (NCIX): exploits and defeats adversarial intelligence activities directed against U.S. interests, the armed forces, and the IC
- *National Counterproliferation Center* (NCPC): coordinates intelligence strateges and planning aimed at stemming WMD proliferation and delivery systems
- *Special Security Centers* (SSC): assist the DNI in maintaining the secure nature of intelligence information sharing throughout the IC, the U.S. government, U.S. contractors, state, local, and tribal governments, and the foreign partners
- *National Intelligence University* (NIU): promotes a more effective and productive IC through cross-disciplinary education and joint training
- *Intelligence Advanced Research Projects Activity* (IARPA): invests in research aimed at providing an intelligence advantage over adversaries
- *Center for Security Evaluation* (CSE): strengthens overseas security standards and inspections, pursues emerging security technologies, and synchronize IC emergency preparedness activities
- *National Intelligence Council* (NIC): supports the DNI in his or her roles as the head of the Intelligence Community and principal advisor for intelligence matters to the president and the National Security and Homeland Security Councils, and serves as the senior intelligence advisor representing the Intelligence Community's views within the U.S. government
- *National Intelligence Coordination Center* (NIC-C): efficiently coordinate, collaborate, assess, and deploy the nation's total array of intelligence collection capabilities
- *Mission Support Center*: provides support services to all DNI staff and mission support activity components

Central Intelligence Agency

The CIA was created as the Office of Strategic Services (OSS) during World War II in recognition of modern warfare intelligence needs. Functions of the OSS include espionage, covert action (ranging from propaganda to sabotage), counterintelligence, and intelligence analysis.

The OSS was disbanded after the war, but several of its branches were retained and were distributed among other governmental departments. Through the National Security Act of 1947, the CIA was established as an independent agency within the executive office of the president and having five key functions:

1. To advise the National Security Council in matters concerning such intelligence activities of the government departments and agencies as related to national security
2. To make recommendations to the National Security Council for the coordination of such intelligence activities of the departments and agencies of the government as related to national security
3. To correlate and evaluate the intelligence relating to national security, and to provide for the appropriate dissemination of such intelligence within the government using, where appropriate, existing agencies and facilities
4. To perform for the benefit of existing intelligence agencies such additional services of common concern as the National Security Council determines can be more effectively accomplished centrally
5. To perform other such functions and duties related to intelligence affecting the national security as the National Security Council may from time to time direct (US Congress, 1983)

The CIA is composed of distinct directorates. The National Clandestine Service is responsible for the following:

- Clandestine intelligence collection
- Covert action
- Counternarcotics activities
- Counterterrorism activities
- Counterintelligence.

The CIA Directorate of Science and Technology performs the following tasks:

- Developing technical collection systems
- Collecting intelligence from embassy sites (in cooperation with the NSA)
- Recording foreign radio and television broadcasts (through its Foreign Broadcast Information Service)
- Developing and producing technical devices (such as bugging devices, hidden cameras, and weaponry) for agents and officers
- Providing research and development in support of intelligence collection and analysis

The CIA Intelligence and Analysis Directorate is primarily in charge of analyzing the intelligence data and information collected to make sense out of it for the development of more comprehensive intelligence products. Special offices within this directorate which manage distinct intelligence needs include:

- The Crime and Narcotics Center: Focuses on international narcotics trafficking and organized crime for policy makers and the law enforcement community; estimates the impact of the drug trade and of organized crime on U.S. national security, uncovers trafficking trends and routes, and monitors relationships among organized crime groups, traffickers, and terrorists. (Central Intelligence Agency, 2008c)

- Counterintelligence Center/Analysis Group: Identifies, monitors, and analyzes the efforts of foreign intelligence entities against U.S. persons, activities, and interests, focusing on transnational threats posed by foreign intelligence services

- Information Operations Center/Analysis Group: Evaluates foreign threats to U.S. computer systems, particularly those that support infrastructures.

- Office of Asian Pacific, Latin American, and African Analysis (APLAA): Studies the political, economic, leadership, societal, and military developments in Asia, Latin America, and sub-Saharan Africa.

- Office of Collection Strategies and Analysis: Provides comprehensive intelligence collection expertise to the DCI and other key IC staff and policy makers, and crafts new approaches to solving complex collection issues.

- Office of Iraq Analysis: Covers important collection and analysis needs of US Government operations in Iraq.

- Office of Near Eastern and South Asian Analysis (NESA): Provides policy makers with comprehensive analytic support on Middle Eastern and North African countries, as well as on the South Asian nations of India, Pakistan, and Afghanistan.

- Office of Policy Support: Customizes defense intelligence analysis and presents it to a wide variety of policy, law enforcement, military, and foreign liaison recipients.

- Office of Russian and European Analysis: Provides intelligence support on a large set of countries that have long been of crucial importance to the United States as allies or as adversaries and are likely to continue to occupy a key place in U.S. national security policy.

- Office of Corporate Resources: Oversees support to the directorate on a wide variety of issues, including budget, contracts, diversity programs, equal employment opportunity, facilities management, human resources, and resource planning.

- Office of Terrorism Analysis: Informs policy makers and supports the intelligence, law enforcement, homeland security, and military communities by performing the following tasks:
  - Tracking terrorists and the activities of states that sponsor them, and assessing terrorist vulnerabilities by analyzing their ideology and goals, capabilities, associates, and locations
  - Analyzing worldwide terrorist threat information and patterns to provide warnings aimed at preventing terrorist attacks
  - Monitoring worldwide terrorism trends and patterns, including emerging and nontraditional terrorist groups, evolving terrorist threats or operational methods, and possible collusion between terrorist groups
  - Identifying, disrupting, and preventing international financial transactions that support terrorist networks and operations

- Office of Transnational Issues: Produces analytic assessments on critical intelligence-related issues that transcend regional and national boundaries.

- Weapons Intelligence, Nonproliferation, and Arms Control Center: Provides intelligence support aimed at protecting the United States and its interests from all foreign weapons threats by studying the development of the entire spectrum of threats (from WMDs to advanced conventional weapons).

Today, the CIA is the largest producer of national security intelligence for senior U.S. policy makers. The director of the CIA (DCIA) is the national HUMINT manager and serves on behalf of the DNI as the national authority for coordination, deconfliction, and evaluation of clandestine HUMINT operations across the IC.

Defense Intelligence Agency

The Defense Intelligence Agency (DIA) is a major producer and manager of foreign military intelligence for policy makers, to U.S. Armed Forces around the world, and to the U.S. acquisition community and force planners to counter a variety of threats and challenges. The DIA director is a three-star military officer who serves as the principal advisor on intelligence matters to the secretary of defense and the chairman of the Joint Chiefs of Staff, and is the program manager for the General Defense Intelligence Program that funds a variety of military intelligence programs. The director also serves as the program manager for the department's Foreign Counterintelligence Program and is the chairman of the Military Intelligence Board that examines key intelligence issues such as information technology architectures, program and budget issues, and defense intelligence inputs to National Intelligence Estimates.

DIA is headquartered in the Pentagon, but the agency employs more than 15,000 civilian and military personnel around the world. The largest facilities include:

- The Defense Intelligence Analysis Center on Bolling Air Force Base in Washington, D.C.
- The Missile and Space Intelligence Center at Redstone Arsenal in Huntsville, Alabama
- The National Center for Medical Intelligence at Fort Detrick, Maryland

The DIA director is the commander of the U.S. Strategic Command organization. The agency is organized as follows:

- The Directorate for Analysis (DI): Assesses foreign militaries, focusing on include WMDs, missile systems, terrorism, infrastructure systems, and defense-related medical issues.
- The Directorate for Intelligence, Joint Staff (J2): Provides foreign military intelligence to the Joint Chiefs of Staff and senior DOD officials.
- The Directorate for Human Intelligence (DH): Conducts worldwide strategic HUMINT collection operations, overseeing the Defense Attache System that conducts representational duties on behalf of the DOD at embassies overseas and advises U.S. ambassadors on military matters.
- The Directorate for MASINT and Technical Collection (DT): Serves as the defense intelligence center for MASINT collection, analysis and capabilities development.
- The Directorate for Information Management and Chief Information Officer (DS): Serves as DIA's information technology component by managing the DOD, Intelligence Information System (DODIIS) and operates the Joint Worldwide Intelligence Communications System (JWICS).

The Federal Bureau of Investigation (Department of Justice)

The Federal Bureau of Investigation (FBI) is a law enforcement organization that exists at the federal level. However, it is also a threat-based, intelligence-driven national security organization that protects the United States from critical threats while safeguarding civil liberties. As both a component of the

Department of Justice and a full IC member, the FBI serves as a vital link between intelligence and law enforcement communities.

The FBI's top priorities are combating the threat of terrorism, counterintelligence, and cybercrime. As to counterterrorism, the FBI gives particular attention to terrorist efforts to acquire and use WMDs. The FBI also maintains a counterintelligence role, addressing the threat of foreign intelligence services that attempt to infiltrate the U.S. government. A similar threat comes from foreign business interests and students and scientists seeking to steal technology on behalf of foreign governments or commercial interests.

Cyberterrorism and crime are on the forefront of the FBI intelligence efforts as well given the potential for terrorist or foreign state-sponsored elements targeting national information infrastructure. Other areas receiving priority focus are crimes that undermine the health of the economy, including national and transnational gangs, dangerous fugitives, and kidnappers.

Federal law, attorney general authorities, and executive orders give the FBI jurisdiction to investigate all federal crimes not assigned exclusively to another federal agency and to investigate threats to the national security. This gives the FBI the unique ability to address national security and criminal threats that are increasingly intertwined, and to shift between the use of intelligence tools such as surveillance or recruiting sources and law enforcement tools of arrest and prosecution.

The organization of the FBI intelligence operation is as follows:

- The National Security Branch (NSB): Oversees the FBI's national security programs. It includes four divisions plus the Terrorist Screening Center (TSC).
- The Counterterrorism Division (CTD): Focuses on both domestic and international terrorism. It oversees the Joint Terrorism Task Forces (JTTFs).
- The Counterintelligence Division (CD): Prevents and investigates foreign intelligence activities within the US and espionage activities in the US and overseas.
- The Directorate of Intelligence (DI): Is the FBI's intelligence analysis component, with embedded employees at FBI headquarters and in each field office through Field Intelligence Groups (FIGs) and fusion centers.
- The Weapons of Mass Destruction Directorate (WMDD): Prevents individuals and groups from acquiring WMD capabilities and technologies for use against the US, and links all operational and scientific/technology components to accomplish this mission.
- The Terrorist Screening Center (TSC): Created to consolidate the U.S. government's approach to terrorist screening and create a single, comprehensive watch list of known or suspected terrorists.

National Geospatial-Intelligence Agency (NGA)

Imagery has become key to intelligence as technology has advanced. The Intelligence Community has centralized the management of both map-based and imagery-based intelligence under the NGA (formerly NIMA). NGA is tasked with a number of imagery-related functions, including the allocation of targets to imagery collection systems the merging of imagery, maps, charts, and environmental data to produce *geospatial intelligence*, the production and provision of strategic and tactical maps, charts, and databases, and specialized products to support current and advanced weapons and navigation systems (Richelson et al., 2003).

NGA, as NIMA, played a critical role in homeland security following the attacks of September 11. In the response and recovery phases of the disaster in New York City, NIMA partnered with the U.S. Geological Survey (USGS) to survey the World Trade Center site and determine the extent of the destruction. The NGA maintains a headquarters in Bethesda, Maryland, and major facilities in Washington,

D.C., Northern Virginia, and St. Louis, Missouri. NGA activities are organized under the following components:

- *Source Operations and Management Office*: Discovers, acquires, produces, delivers, and manages the data and information used to produce geospatial; manages the end-to-end execution of geospatial intelligence information requirements.
- *Enterprise Operations Directorate*: Responsible for day-to-day systems operations and leveraging technology to ensure and protect the NGA's mission by operating the National System for Geospatial Intelligence (a unified community of geospatial intelligence experts, producers, and users) and providing enterprise, corporate, dissemination, and information services.
- *Analysis and Production Directorate*: Provides geospatial intelligence and services to policy makers, military decision makers and operational "warfighters," and tailored support to civilian federal agencies and international organizations.
- *Acquisition Directorate*: Enables, acquires, and provides systems, supplies, and services that advance NGA's role in geospatial intelligence, including imagery, imagery analysis, and geospatial information.
- *InnoVision Directorate*: Forecasts future environments, defines future needs, establishes plans to align resources, and provides technology and process solutions to help NGA, end users, and partners.

The NGA also provides imagery in support of major disasters.

National Reconnaissance Office

The NRO's primary function has been to oversee the research and development, procurement, deployment, and operation of imaging, signals intelligence, and ocean surveillance satellites. It awards contracts, oversees the research and development efforts of contractors, supervises the launch of the payloads, and, in conjunction with the CIA and the NSA, operates these spacecraft. It has also been involved in the research, development, and procurement of selected aerial reconnaissance systems. From its inception until September 18, 1992, when its existence was formally acknowledged, the NRO operated as a classified organization. A major restructuring of the NRO also began to be implemented in 1992, which turned the NRO into a functional organization instead of a stand-alone organization (Richelson et al., 2003).

In its current setting, the NRO designs, builds, and operates the nation's reconnaissance satellites. NRO products can warn of potential trouble spots around the world, help plan military operations, and monitor the environment. The NRO is a DOD agency and is staffed by DOD and CIA personnel. NRO intelligence gathering and analysis activities are conducted at the request of the secretary of defense and/or the DNI. The director of National Reconnaissance Office (DNRO) is selected by the secretary of defense with the concurrence of the DNI and also serves as the assistant to the secretary of the Air Force. The NRO's workforce of approximately 3,000 includes personnel primarily from the Air Force, the CIA, and the Navy.

The NRO systems provide the foundation for global situational awareness and address many of the nation's most significant intelligence challenges. For instance, the NRO systems are the only collectors able to access critical areas of interest, and data from overhead sensors provide unique information and perspectives not available from other sources.

The NRO systems provide:

- Monitoring the proliferation of WMDs
- Tracking international terrorists, drug traffickers, and criminal organizations

- Developing highly accurate military targeting data and bomb damage assessments
- Supporting international peacekeeping and humanitarian relief operations
- Assessing the impact of natural disasters, such as earthquakes, tsunamis, floods, and fires

Together with other Defense Department satellites, the NRO systems play a crucial role in providing global communications, precision navigation, early warning of missile launches and potential military aggression, signals intelligence, and near real-time imagery to U.S. forces to support the war on terrorism and other continuing operations. The NRO satellites also support civil customers in response to disaster relief and environmental research. Scientists created a global environment database using NRO imagery to help predict climate change, assess crop production, map habitats of endangered species, track oil spills, and study wetlands. Finally, the NRO data form the basis for products that help depict and assess the devastation in areas affected by natural disasters.

National Security Agency

The NSA, which has a longer formal title (the National Security Agency/Central Security Service [NSA/CSS]), is tasked with two primary responsibilities: information assurance and signals intelligence.

The NSA is organized as follows:

- The Information Assurance Directorate (IAD) operates under the authority of the secretary of defense and ensures the availability, integrity, authentication, confidentiality, and nonrepudiation of national security and telecommunications and information systems (national security systems). The IAD is dedicated to providing information assurance solutions that serve to protect U.S. information systems from harm. This mission involves many activities, including the following:
  - Detecting, reporting, and responding to cyberthreats
  - Making encryption codes to securely pass information between systems
  - Embedding information assurance measures directly into the emerging global information grid
  - Building secure audio and video communications equipment
  - Making tamper-proof products
  - Providing trusted microelectronics solutions
  - Testing the security of its partners' and customers' systems
  - Providing operational security assistance
  - Evaluating commercial software and hardware against set standards
- The Signals Intelligence Directorate: Responsible for understanding end-users' intelligence information needs, and for the collection, analysis and production, and dissemination of SIGINT. The NSA's SIGINT mission provides military leaders and policy makers with intelligence to ensure national defense and to advance U.S. global interests, and the information attained is specifically limited to that that focuses on foreign powers, organizations, or persons, and international terrorists.
- The Central Security Service (CSS): Oversees the function of the military cryptologic system, develops policy and guidance on the contributions of military cryptology to the Signals Intelligence/Information Security (SIGINT/INFOSEC) enterprise, and manages the partnership of the NSA and the Service Cryptologic Components. The NSA as a whole is known as "NSA/CSS."
- The NSA/CSS Threat Operations Center: Monitors the operations of the global network to identify network-based threats and protect the nation and allied networks.

- The National Security Operations Center: A nonstop operations center that, on behalf of the NSA/CSS, provides total situational awareness across the NSA/CSS enterprise for both foreign signals intelligence and information assurance, maintains cognizance of national security information needs, and monitors unfolding world events.
- The Research Directorate: Conducts research on signals intelligence and on information assurance for the U.S. government.

DHS Office of Intelligence and Analysis (I&A)

DHS is responsible for leading the unified national effort to secure the nation by preventing and deterring terrorist attacks and responding to threats and hazards. The Intelligence and Analysis (I&A) is a key component of the Intelligence Community. I&A is DHS's headquarters intelligence element and is led by the undersecretary for Intelligence and Analysis, with guidance from the Homeland Security Council and Homeland Security Intelligence Council. As an IC member, I&A is responsible for using information and intelligence from multiple sources to identify and assess current and future threats to the United States. I&A provides actionable intelligence to support national and DHS decision makers while working closely with state, local, tribal, and private sector partners.

I&A focuses on threats related to border security; chemical, biological, radiological, and nuclear (CBRN) issues, to include explosives and infectious diseases; critical infrastructure protection; extremists operating on US soil; and travelers entering the country.

I&A is responsible for using the information and intelligence gleaned from the myriad sources throughout the federal government to identify and assess current and future threats. I&A is also responsible for the Department's intelligence and information gathering and sharing capabilities for and among all components of DHS, state, local, and private sector partners and the IC. I&A serves as the primary federal interface with state and local fusion centers, providing for reciprocal intelligence and information sharing in support of homeland security operations across all levels of government and the private sector. I&A ensures that information is gathered from all relevant DHS field operations and is fused with information from throughout the IC to produce intelligence reports (and other products) for officials who require them inside and outside of DHS.

The Office of Operations Coordination is responsible for monitoring U.S. security on a daily basis and coordinating activities within DHS and with governors, Homeland Security Advisors, law enforcement partners, and critical infrastructure operators in all 50 states and more than 50 major urban areas nationwide. Information is shared daily by the two halves of the office, referred to as the "Intelligence Side" and the "Law Enforcement Side." Each half is identical and functions in tandem with the other but operates under different security clearance standards for information access purposes. The Intelligence Side focuses on pieces of highly classified intelligence and how the information contributes to the current threat picture for any given area. The Law Enforcement Side is dedicated to tracking the different enforcement activities across the country that may have terrorist significance. The two pieces fuse together to create a real-time picture of the nation's threat environment.

Operations Coordination oversees the National Operations Center (NOC), which collects and collates information from more than 35 federal, state, territorial, tribal, local, and private sector agencies. Through the NOC, the office provides real-time situational awareness and monitoring of the nation, coordinates incidents and response activities, and, in conjunction with the I&A, issues advisories and bulletins concerning threats to homeland security, as well as specific protective measures. The NOC — which is always operational — coordinates information sharing to help deter, detect, and prevent terrorist acts and to manage domestic incidents. Information on domestic incident management is shared with Emergency Operations Centers at all levels through the Homeland Security Information Network (HSIN).

Department of State Bureau of Intelligence and Research

The Department of State Bureau of Intelligence and Research (INR) provides expert intelligence analysis to the secretary of state and senior policy makers on decisions regarding the protection of American interests around the world. The INR serves as the State Department focal point for all policy issues and activities involving the IC. The INR assistant secretary reports directly to the secretary of state and serves as his principal adviser on all intelligence matters.

INR foreign affairs analysts utilize all-source intelligence, diplomatic reporting, public opinion polling, and interaction with U.S. and foreign scholars, in conjunction with intelligence gathered by all IC partners, to formulate intelligence products. Their strong regional and functional backgrounds allow them to respond rapidly to changing policy priorities and to provide early warning and analysis of events and trends. The INR analysts — a combination of Foreign Service officers often with extensive in-country experience and Civil Service specialists with in-depth expertise — cover all countries and regional or transnational issues.

The INR provides daily briefings, reports, and memoranda to the secretary of state and other department principals. The INR also briefs members of Congress and their staffs as appropriate. INR products cover the world on foreign relations issues such as political/military developments, terrorism, narcotics, and trade. The INR develops intelligence policy for the Department of State and works to harmonize all agencies' intelligence.

The INR Humanitarian Information Unit (HIU) serves as a nucleus for unclassified information related to complex emergencies and provides a coordinating mechanism for data sharing among the U.S. government, the United Nations, nongovernmental organizations, and foreign governments. HIU also administers the Title VIII Grant Program, an initiative funded by Congress for senior-level academic research in Russian, Eurasian, and East European studies.

Conclusion

Despite the fact that Congress and President Bush were not able to consolidate the various intelligence agencies under a single department "roof," there has been significant improvement in the collection, analysis, and dissemination of intelligence since the 9/11 attacks. These changes appear to have been effective in helping to prevent dozens of attempted terrorist attacks in the years that have followed. Clearly, the means of and policy for sharing information between these disparate agencies are becoming more and more efficient, and should improve further as recommended changes are transformed into policy.

Key Terms

Consequence: The result of a terrorist attack or other hazard that reflects the level, duration, and nature of the loss. For the purposes of the NIPP, consequences are divided into four main categories: public health and safety, economic, psychological, and governance impacts.

Crisis Management: A proactive management effort to avoid crisis, and the creation of strategy that minimizes adverse impacts of crisis to the organization when it could not be prevented. Effective crisis management requires a solid understanding of the organization, its strategy, liabilities, stakeholders, and legal framework combined with advanced communication, leadership, and decision-making skills to lead the organization through the crisis with minimizing potential loss.

Director of Central Intelligence (DCI): Director of the Central Intelligence Agency. In the aftermath of the 9/11 intelligence reform, the DCI is reporting to the Director of National Intelligence for overall intelligence coordination purposes.

Director of National Intelligence (DNI): The statutory authority created on the basis of the recommendations of the 9/11 Commission and tasked by the president to coordinate the holistic intelligence of the United States. Directors of member agencies of the Intelligence Community report to the DNI. The DNI is also responsible for establishing budget priorities for the overall U.S. intelligence effort.

Intelligence: Intelligence is a secret state activity to understand or influence foreign entities (CIA).

Intelligence Community: The collective body of U.S. government agencies that have been tasked with the responsibility of collecting, analyzing, or acting upon intelligence.

Information Sharing and Analysis Center (ISAC): ISACs are sectoral information analysis and sharing centers that bring together representatives and decision makers of a given sector for the purposes of critical infrastructure protection and disaster preparedness.

Unmanned Airborne Vehicles (UAVs): UAVs are airborne vehicles controlled from a ground command center that are used in high-risk intelligence collection efforts and zones as well as in relatively safe target areas where the mission does not require the involvement of a human pilot. UAVs are used in intelligence collection efforts in Iraq as well as for border patrolling activities at the southwest border of the United States.

Review Questions

1. What are the key intelligence agencies in the United States? Briefly comment on their roles in terms of homeland security.
2. Describe how intelligence has evolved in the United States.
3. Is the Office of the National Director of Intelligence a viable alternative for the consolidation of intelligence agencies under one government "roof," as was originally proposed in the early days following the 9/11 attacks?
4. What are the various steps in the intelligence cycle, and what is involved in each?

References

9/11 Commission. 2004. The 9/11 Commission Report. http://govinfo.library.unt.edu/911/report/911Report.pdf.

Central Intelligence Agency. 2007. Offices of CIA. https://www.cia.gov/offices-of-cia/index.html.

Central Intelligence Agency. 2008a. CIA organization chart. https://www.cia.gov/about-cia/leadership/cia-organization-chart.html.

Central Intelligence Agency. 2008b. History of the Intelligence and Analysis Directorate. https://www.cia.gov/offices-of-cia/intelligence-analysis/history.html.

Central Intelligence Agency. 2008c. The CIA Crime and Narcotics Center. https://www.cia.gov/offices-of-cia/intelligence-analysis/organization-1/the-cia-crime-and-narcotics-center.html.

Congressional Research Service. 2004a. RL32506 — The Proposed Authorities of a National Intelligence Director: Issues for Congress and Side-by-Side Comparison of S. 2845, H.R. 10, and Current Law. http://www.fas.org/irp/crs/RL32506.pdf.

Congressional Research Service. 2004b. RS21948 — The National Intelligence Director and Intelligence Analysis. http://www.fas.org/irp/crs/RS21948.pdf.

Office of the Director of National Intelligence. 2008a. Members of the Intelligence Community. http://www.intelligence.gov/about-the-intelligence-community/.

Office of the Director of National Intelligence. 2008b. ODNI Organization. http://www.dni.gov/aboutODNI/organization.htm.

Richelson, J.T., Gefter, J., Waters, M., et al. 2003. U.S. Espionage and Intelligence, 1947–1996. Digital National Security Archive. Mfiche 2552 GRN–MTXT.

6

Border Security, Immigration, and Customs Enforcement

What You Will Learn

- The importance of national borders, and the functions of government that pertain to the movement of people and goods across these borders
- The role of various homeland security organizations in performing immigration and customs enforcement services

Introduction

National borders are strategically important, playing a critical role economic vitality and commerce. Increasing globalization of economic systems and transportation networks has made it possible for every American community to connected to the outside world through a vast system of airports, seaports, pipelines, roadways, and waterways. Borders are gateways for imported and exported goods; therefore, their effectiveness and efficiency are important measures for the trade capacity and capability of the country. Borders also have an important role for the international tourism and travel capability of the country.

At the same time, borders provide access into the country, through both major and clandestine entry points, for illegal immigrants and goods. Therefore, the security and control of borders is of the utmost importance in the drive to mitigate the risk posed by the penetration of unwanted or dangerous people and goods into the country. Human traffickers, smugglers, drug dealers, criminals, terrorists, illegal drugs, conventional weapons, undeclared or counterfeit products, biological agents, and weapons of mass destruction (WMD) are but a small sample of the many possible individuals and items that together mandate strong national borders.

The Department of Homeland Security (DHS) has been tasked with managing the legal movement of goods and people through the nation's borders, and with protecting these same borders from illegal infiltration. This chapter explores the DHS functions of border protection, immigration, and customs enforcement.

Border Security

The United States shares 5,525 miles of border with Canada and 1,989 miles with Mexico. The maritime border includes 95,000 miles of shoreline and a 3.4-million-square-mile exclusive economic zone. Each year, more than 500 million people cross these borders to enter the United States, and approximately 330 million of them are foreign nationals.

Entry points into the country are not limited to its external borders, however. Sea and airports, which are often far from neighboring countries or international bodies of water, serves as potential doorways for illegal and illicit persons and materials. The border security role, therefore, extends far beyond the nation's perimeter.

The United States has had an active border patrol function since the turn of the 20th century, when patrols were conducted by U.S. Immigration Service watchmen on horseback. Since that time, the function has evolved considerably in response to changing pressures related to the control of imported goods and the limiting of access to foreign nationals. Following the 9/11 terrorist attacks, which exposed weaknesses in the nation's border security and immigration systems, it was recognized that these two functions were vital to national security and therefore a natural match for the new DHS. Like most other agencies moved into DHS, the Border Patrol became part of the new agency on March 1, 2003, in the U.S. Customs and Border Protection (CBP).

Immigration

Immigration is defined as the act of entering and settling permanently in another country, and/or becoming a permanent resident or a legal citizen of that country. The nation was founded on the principles of open immigration, and all but a few present-day citizens can trace their roots to immigrants from all countries of the world. Understandably, immigration is closely tied to that of border security, given that a nation's borders exist to ensure that only those transiting legal channels are able to enter the nation. It is through the function of immigration that foreign citizens gain such access.

The granting of residency and citizenship of foreign nationals is guided by the nation's immigration laws. Over the course of the nation's history, these laws have been changed often, reflecting the volatility of national opinions on the value of more open doors in relation to the need for a growing workforce. There has always existed a global demand for U.S. residency and citizenship, given the strength of the U.S. economy, the high standard of living, the availability of jobs, and the prospect of a better life for many who have struggled back home. At the same time, many U.S. businesses have looked elsewhere for manpower as the strength of the U.S. economy made certain low-wage and seasonal jobs hard to fill, given the ability of most U.S. citizens to find alternate ("desirable") employment.

In the first two hundred years of the nation from about 1600 to 1800, it is estimated that less than one million people migrated to the United States. With industrialization, these rates increased rapidly, and approximately 30 million people entered the country from 1820 until 1920. It is during this period that a series of immigration laws were passed and regulatory structures were created. Initially, the Treasury regulated immigration, due to the fact that immigration restrictions were essentially limited to a 50 cents tax levied on each immigrant. The funds collected supported the creation of the Immigration, and a wide range of enforcement mechanisms and facilities followed (including the Ellis Island processing facility in New York). After several changes to governmental immigration structures caused by government reorganizations, the Immigration and Naturalization Service (INS) was created in 1933 within the Department of Labor. Soon after, the INS was transferred to the Department of Justice which reflected the changing the nature of the immigration enforcement function to one of national security.

The emphasis on controlling illegal immigration for reasons of economic and national security and crime control fostered INS's growth in the late 20th century. The INS workforce grew from 8,000 in the

1940s to more than 30,000 in 1998. In 2003, as a direct result of the 9/11 terrorist attacks, the INS was transferred to DHS. Rather than transferring as a distinct unit, the INS divisions were broken into three DHS agencies, namely, the U.S. Citizenship and Immigration Service, U.S. Immigration and Customs Enforcement (ICE), and the U.S. Customs and Border Protection (CBP, 2011a).

Immigration enforcement in the United States is conducted through the following functions, each of which is described in the context of specific DHS components in this chapter:

- Inspections
- Border Patrol
- Investigations
- Detention and Removal

Customs Enforcement

Nations protect their national economic interests through the levying of import taxes, called *duties*, on foreign goods, and by controlling the rate of flow and quantity of specific goods that enter the country. The inspection of goods collection of duties is performed by a customs agency or office, which is a traditional function of government.

The United States' declaration of independence in 1776 was based in large part on the belief that the colonies were denied their right to retain duties collected on imported goods, and one of the first functions of new government was to create a Customs Service under the direct authority of the Secretary of the Treasury. For the 125 years that followed, it was this customs function that generated almost all of the government's revenue, and contributed to the fast growth of the young nation.

The United States remains a major importer of foreign goods, and at present almost 16% of the national budget is supported by income from customs. The U.S. Customs Service ensures that all imports and exports comply with U.S. laws and regulations. The Customs Service collects and protects the revenue, guards against smuggling, and is responsible for the following:

- Assessing and collecting Customs duties, excise taxes, fees, and penalties due on imported merchandise
- Interdicting and seizing contraband, including narcotics and illegal drugs
- Processing persons, baggage, cargo, and mail, and administering certain navigation laws
- Detecting and apprehending persons engaged in fraudulent practices designed to circumvent Customs and related laws
- Protecting American business and labor and intellectual property rights by enforcing U.S. laws intended to prevent illegal trade practices, including provisions related to quotas and the marking of imported merchandise; the Anti-Dumping Act; and, by providing Customs Recordations for copyrights, patents, and trademarks
- Protecting the general welfare and security of the United States by enforcing import and export restrictions and prohibitions, including the export of critical technology used to develop WMD, and money laundering
- Collecting accurate import and export data for compilation of international trade statistics

Border Security, Immigration, and Customs in the Department of Homeland Security

In its initial organization, DHS consolidated the various agencies responsible for the safety, security, and control of the borders under the Directorate of Border and Transportation Security (BTS). These agencies include the ICE agency (previously the INS), the CBP (previously the Customs Service), the USCG, and the U.S. Customs and Immigration Services (USCIS). With the reorganization effort initiated in the latter half of 2005, the Directorate of Border and Transportation Security was replaced with the Directorate of Policy, and its policy functions were transferred to the new directorate. In today's DHS, these agencies have direct reporting responsibility to the secretary of Homeland Security.

Border security, customs enforcement, and immigration are managed throughout the DHS organization, but the most direct responsibilities fall within four specific functional elements, namely:

- U.S. Customs and Border Protection
- U.S. Immigration and Customs Enforcement
- U.S. Coast Guard
- U.S. Citizenship and Immigration Services

U.S. Customs and Border Protection

U.S. Customs and Border Protection (CBP) is the only agency responsible for protecting the sovereign borders of the United States at and between the official Ports of Entry POE. CBP is considered the "front line" in protecting the nation against terrorist attacks. The CBP also ensures national economic security by regulating and facilitating the lawful movement of goods and persons across U.S. borders. CBP is one of DHS's largest and most complex components (Figure 6–1).

The Border Patrol

The mission of the Border Patrol is to prevent terrorists and their weapons (including WMD) from entering the United States, while ensuring that the flow of legal immigration and goods is maintained. The Border Patrol is specifically responsible for patrolling nearly 6,000 miles of Mexican and Canadian international land borders and over 2,000 miles of coastal waters surrounding the Florida Peninsula and the island of Puerto Rico.

A dynamic workforce of over 20,000 agents employed today. Border Patrol agents carry out their mission by maintaining surveillance, following up leads, responding to electronic sensor alarms and aircraft sightings, and interpreting and following tracks. Some of the major activities include maintaining traffic checkpoints along highways leading from border areas and conducting city patrol and transportation checks and antismuggling investigations.

In many places, the U.S. border falls in remote locations, oftentimes in uninhabited deserts, canyons, or mountains. As such, the Border Patrol utilizes specialized equipment and methods to accomplish its mission in these conditions. Electronic sensors are placed at strategic locations along the border to detect people or vehicles entering the country illegally. Video monitors and night vision scopes are also used to detect illegal entries. Border Patrol agents patrol the border in vehicles, boats, and afoot. In some areas,

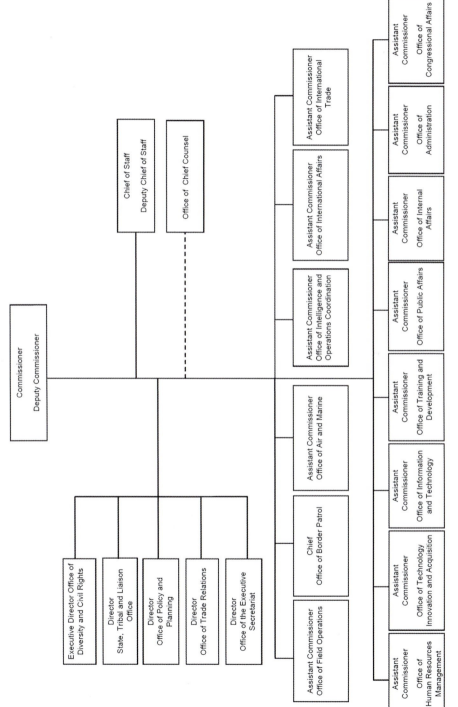

FIGURE 6–1 Customs and Border Protection organizational chart. (Source: CBP, 2011, www.cbp.com)

the Border Patrol even employs horses, all-terrain motorcycles, bicycles, and snowmobiles. Examples of tactics used by the Border Patrol to carry out its mission include the following:

- Linewatch operations: Prevent the illegal entry and smuggling of aliens into the United States, and to intercept those who do enter illegally
- Signcutting operations: Detect and interpret of any disturbances in natural terrain conditions that indicate the presence or passage of people, animals, or vehicles
- Traffic checks: Conducted on major highways leading away from the border (1) to detect and apprehend illegal aliens and narcotics smugglers that have evaded detection at the border
- Transportation checks: Inspections of interior-bound conveyances, which include buses, commercial aircraft, passenger and freight trains, and marine craft
- Marine patrol: Border control activities conducted from the decks of marine craft along the coastal and interior waterways
- Horse and bike patrol: Patrol remote border areas that are inaccessible to standard all-terrain vehicles and in cities where bicycles enjoy greater access

Several CBP programs have helped to better protect the US-Mexico border, including Operation Gatekeeper in San Diego (CA), Operation Hold the Line in El Paso (TX), Operation Rio Grande in McAllen (TX), Operation Safeguard in Tucson (AZ), and the Arizona Border Control Initiative (ABCI).

The heightened presence of Border Patrol agents along the southern border has also helped to curb drug smuggling considerably.

■ ■ Critical Thinking ■

Given the mission of the Border Patrol, do you feel it is appropriately positioned within DHS (as opposed to being an independent agency or under some other federal agency or department)?

CBP Office of Air and Marine

The CBP Office of Air and Marine (OAM) is tasked with protecting people and critical infrastructure through the coordinated use of air and marine forces. This includes the detection, interdiction, and prevention of terrorism ion of and the unlawful movement of people, narcotics, and other contraband toward or across U.S. borders. OAM is the world's largest aviation and maritime law enforcement organization, employing more than 1,200 federal agents and maintaining 270 aircraft and 280 marine vessels operating from 80 locations.

OAM operates a number of Predator B unmanned (drone) aircraft in support of borders security (and occasionally to support disaster relief efforts) (CBP, 2011b; CBP, 2011c).

CBP Office of Technology Innovation and Acquisition (the Secure Border Initiative)

The Secure Border Initiative (SBI) was created in 2005 within CBP to manage the development, deployment, and integration of border security technologies and programs, and integration of border security technologies and programs, and to integrate and coordinate the various border security programs within CBP. Today, the SBI mission is to lead the operational requirements support and documentation as well as the acquisition efforts to develop, deploy, and integrate technology and tactical infrastructure in support of CBP's efforts to gain and maintain effective control of U.S. land border areas. Effective control of the border is achieved by knowing what is going on at the border (situational awareness) and having the ability to respond. CBP utilizes a combination of three tools to achieve effective control: personnel, tactical infrastructure, and technology. These include:

- SBI*net:* A program that seeks to deploy modern technology to focus on the areas between the ports of entry on the southwest border, specifically by integrating new and existing border technology into a networked system that enables CBP personnel to more effectively detect, identify, classify, and respond to border incursions. SBI*net* solutions are focused on the following:
  - Surveillance and detection tools
  - Command, control, and intelligence tools
  - Communications infrastructure
- SBI Tactical Infrastructure: The Facilities Management and Engineering's Office of Border Patrol (OBP) Program Management Office provides the Border Patrol with long-term planning, construction, and maintenance capabilities — including tactical infrastructure (TI) components such as roads, fencing, lights, electrical components, and drainage structures — to help the Border Patrol achieve its primary homeland security mission (see Figures 6–2 and 6–3).
- The Northern Border Project: CBP operations along the northern border are more modest than those on the border with Mexico. However, CPB is deploying integrated technology to meet the needs that exist, including those that address the special vulnerabilities of the northern border maritime (river/lake), cold weather environment.

Secure Freight Initiative

The Secure Freight Initiative (SFI) was created in 2006 to support the deployment of radiation detection and container imaging equipment to be operated in seaports worldwide. SFI seeks to prevent use of nuclear or other radiological materials to attack the global maritime supply chain or to use cargo containers to acquire such resources for a domestic attack. Through the program, containers arriving at participating seaports overseas are scanned with both nonintrusive radiographic imaging and passive radiation detection equipment. Optical scanners identify containers and classify them by destination. Sensor and image data gathered in the U.S. ports are encrypted and transmitted near real-time to the CBP National Targeting Center for final assessment and risk classification. If the scanning data indicate concerns, the specific container will be inspected further. SFI is actively preparing a complementary risk-scoring capability that will fuse certain existing, but not currently collected, data associated with a container's movement to increase the effectiveness of these efforts. The program's long-term vision is to create a globally networked array of detection equipment that will be configured to enable real-time streaming of container images and radiological detection data to other countries engaged in maritime trade (DHS, 2006).

Container Security Initiative

The Container Security Initiative (CSI) was created by the U.S. Customs Service soon after the 9/11 attacks. It was recognized at that time that, like the use of airlines as weapons in 2001, containers could be used by terrorists to easily deliver a WMD device. CSI was created to address the threat to border security and global trade posed by this potential terrorist methodology.

CSI proposes a security regime to ensure all containers that pose a potential risk for terrorism are identified and inspected at foreign ports before they are placed on vessels destined for the United States. CBP has stationed multidisciplinary teams of U.S. officers from both CBP and ICE to work together

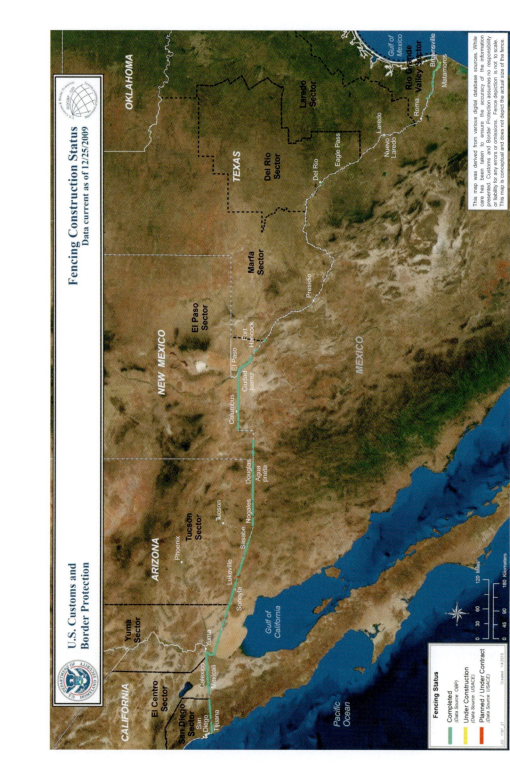

FIGURE 6–2 Southwest border fence. (Source: CBP, 2009)

FIGURE 6–3 Cerrudo services construction workers assemble the southwest border fence in El Paso. (Source: CBP, 2011)

with the host foreign government counterparts. Their mission is to target and prescreen containers and to develop additional investigative leads related to the terrorist threat to cargo destined to the United States.

The three core elements of CSI are:

- Prescreen and evaluate containers before they are shipped
- Identify high-risk containers
- Use technology to prescreen high-risk containers to ensure that screening can be done rapidly without slowing down the movement of trade

Through CSI, CBP officers work with host customs administrations to establish security criteria for identifying high-risk containers. Those administrations use nonintrusive inspection and radiation detection technology to screen high-risk containers before they are shipped to U.S. ports. CSI offers its participant countries the opportunity to send their customs officers to major U.S. ports to target ocean-going containerized cargo to be exported to their countries. Likewise, CBP shares information on a bilateral basis with its CSI partners. Japan and Canada currently station their customs personnel in some U.S. ports as part of the CSI program. CSI is now operational at 58 ports in North America, Europe, Asia, Africa, the Middle East, and Latin and Central America, which represents approximately 86% of all maritime containerized cargo imported into the United States subject to prescreening (CBP, 2008).

Agricultural Inspection

CBP agents work in collaboration with inspection agents from the U.S. Department of Agriculture to prevent the introduction of harmful pests into the United States. CBP agricultural specialists have extensive training and experience in agricultural and biological inspection, and are also able to recognize and prevent the entry of organisms that could be used for biological warfare or terrorism.

CBP employs more than 2,000 agriculture specialists who intercept thousands of shipments of prohibited meat, plant materials, or animal products each day at POE. CBP continues to work in close consultation with USDA, both in training the inspection force and in setting regulations and policies for which plants, animals, and other commodities may legally enter the country.

CBP agriculture specialists use detector dogs to sniff out hidden prohibited agricultural items. CBP agriculture specialists and canine teams work at key U.S. POE, including international airports, land borders, and international mail facilities, inspecting both commercial cargo and passengers/pedestrians.

CBP Immigration Inspection Program

Travelers and other individuals seeking to enter the United States must pass through an immigration inspection station at all U.S. POE, including international airports. CBP officers inspect their documents and determine their admissibility. The inspection process includes all work performed in connection with the entry of aliens and U.S. citizens into the United States, including pre-inspection performed by the immigration inspectors outside the United States. The visa process, wherein permission is granted to travel to a U.S. port for entry examination, is conducted by the U.S. Department of State at overseas missions (embassies and consulates). However, it is the DHS that maintains the final say on whether or not the person is able to enter. The CBP officer is responsible for determining the nationality and identity of each person who presents, and must prevent the entry of ineligible aliens, including criminals, terrorists, and drug traffickers, among others. CBP agents will automatically admit U.S. citizens upon verification of citizenship.

Under the authority granted by the INA, as amended, a CBP officer may question, under oath, any person coming into the United States to determine his or her admissibility. In addition, an inspector has authority to search without warrant the person and effects of any person seeking admission, when there is a reason to believe that grounds of exclusion exist, which would be disclosed by such search. The INA is based on the law of presumption: An applicant for admission is presumed to be an alien until he or she shows evidence of citizenship; an alien is presumed to be an immigrant until he or she proves that he or she fits into one of the nonimmigrant classifications.

The mission of the inspections program is to control and guard the boundaries and borders of the United States against the illegal entry of aliens in a way that (CBP, 2011b):

- Functions as the initial component of a comprehensive, immigration enforcement system;
- Prevents the entry of terrorists, drug traffickers, criminals, and other persons who may subvert the national interest;
- Deters illegal immigration through the detection of fraudulent documents and entry schemes;
- Initiates prosecutions against individuals who attempt or aid and abet illegal entry;
- Cooperates with international, federal, state, and local law enforcement agencies to achieve mutual objectives;
- Contributes to the development and implementation of foreign policy related to the entry of persons;
- Facilitates the entry of persons engaged in commerce, tourism, and/or other lawful pursuits;
- Respects the rights and dignity of individuals;
- Examines individuals and their related documents in a professional manner;

- Assists the transportation industry to meet its requirements;
- Responds to private sector interests, in conformance with immigration law;
- Continues to employ innovative methods to improve the efficiency and cost-effectiveness of the inspections process.

CBP maintains a number of "trusted-traveler" programs that allow preapproved, low-risk travelers to expedite their immigration inspection through the use of dedicated lines and kiosks.

CBP Search Authority

The border search authority exercised by CBP officers border is derived from federal statutes and regulations that date back to the 1930s. For instance, 19 USC Section 1467, effective June 25, 1938, states that, "Whenever a vessel from a foreign port or place or from a port or place in any Territory or possession of the United States arrives at a port or place in the United States or the Virgin Islands, whether directly or via another port or place in the United States or the Virgin Islands, the appropriate customs officer for such port or place of arrival may, under such regulations as the Secretary of the Treasury may prescribe and for the purpose of assuring compliance with any law, regulation, or instruction which the Secretary of the Treasury or the Customs Service is authorized to enforce, cause inspection, examination, and search to be made of the persons, baggage, and merchandise discharged or unladen from such vessel, whether or not any or all such persons, baggage, or merchandise has previously been inspected, examined, or searched by officers of the customs." Another key authority reflecting more current ammendments is 19 C.F.R. 162.6, which states that, "All persons, baggage and merchandise arriving in the Customs territory of the United States from places outside thereof are liable to inspection by a CBP officer."

Unless exempt by diplomatic status, all persons entering the United States, *including U.S. citizens*, are subject to examination and search by CBP officers. CBP officers must determine the nationality of each applicant for admission and, if determined to be an alien, whether or not the applicant meets the requirements of the Immigration and Nationality Act for admission to the United States. CBP Officers use diverse factors to refer individuals for targeted examinations (often referred to as *secondary inspections*) where more detailed questions are asked of individuals seeking entry to better determine their eligibility. Although the constitutionality of these searches has been questioned in many instances, the Supreme Court has upheld the legal authority of CBP's search procedures in all cases brought before them (CBP, 2010).

U.S. Immigration and Customs Enforcement

Immigration and Customs Enforcement (ICE) is the principal investigative arm of DHS and the second largest investigative agency in the federal government. Created in 2003 through a merger of the investigative and interior enforcement elements of the U.S. Customs Service and the INS, ICE now has more than 20,000 employees in offices in all 50 states and 48 foreign countries.

The primary mission of ICE is to promote homeland security and public safety through the criminal and civil enforcement of federal laws governing border control, customs, trade, and immigration. The agency has an annual budget of more than $5.7 billion, primarily devoted to its two principal operating components — Homeland Security Investigations (HSI) and Enforcement and Removal Operations (ERO). Traditionally, the primary mission of the customs enforcement component of ICE was to combat various forms of smuggling. Over time, however, this mission has been expanded to other violations of law involving terrorist financing, money laundering, arms trafficking (including WMD), technology exports, commercial fraud, and child pornography, to name a few.

In total, ICE enforces more than 400 different laws and regulations, including those of 40 other agencies. Within ICE, there are several distinct offices that carry out separate tasks related to the general agency mission. Many of these programs and offices are described below.

ICE Enforcement and Removal Operations

ERO is charged with the enforcement of U.S. immigration laws. It identifies and apprehends removable aliens, detains them if necessary, and deports them. ERO prioritizes the apprehension, arrest, and removal of convicted criminals who pose a threat to national security, fugitives, and recent illegal border crossers.

ERO staff transport removable aliens from point to point, manage aliens in custody or in an "alternative to detention" program, provide access to legal resources and representatives of advocacy groups, and remove individuals from the United States who have been ordered to be deported. ERO manages six Service Processing Centers, oversees seven contract detention facilities, and houses aliens in over 240 facilities under intergovernmental service agreements. ERO's mission is broad and requires a diverse workforce made up of law enforcement officers, medical professionals, administrative specialists, and many others to ensure the success of the mission.

The On-Site Detention Compliance Oversight Program was established within ERO to enhance oversight and care of detainees in the ICE custody as part of the agency's commitment to immigration detention reform. The ERO Detention Monitoring Unit conducts compliance monitoring on a continuous or periodic basis. The unit is composed of Detention Service Managers (DSMs) who are embedded in ICE detention facilities, allowing them to assess potential problems and address these problems with the facility and respective field offices before they occur, or to ensure corrective action in a timely manner.

■ ■ Critical Thinking ■

How is the management of lawful immigration efforts related to the security of the nation? How could people harm the country or its citizens by misusing the lawful immigration mechanisms?

Definitions of Immigration Enforcement Terms

- Administrative Removal: The removal of an alien not admitted for permanent residence or an alien admitted for permanent residence on a conditional basis, under a DHS order based on the determination that the individual has been convicted of an aggravated felony. The alien may be removed without a hearing before an immigration court.
- Deportable Alien: An alien who has been admitted into the United States but who is subject to removal under INA § 237.
- Detention: The seizure and incarceration of an alien in order to hold him/her while awaiting judicial or legal proceedings or return transportation to his/her country of citizenship.
- Expedited Removal: The removal of an alien who is inadmissible because the individual does not possess valid entry documents or attempted to enter the United States by fraud or misrepresentation of material fact. The alien may be removed without a hearing before an immigration court.
- Inadmissible Alien: An alien seeking admission into the United States who is ineligible to be admitted according to the provisions of INA § 212.

- Reinstatement of Final Removal Orders: The removal of an alien based on the reinstatement of a prior removal order, where the alien departed the United States under an order of removal and illegally reentered the United States. The alien may be removed without a hearing before an immigration court.
- Removal: The compulsory and confirmed movement of an inadmissible or deportable alien out of the United States based on an order of removal. An alien who is removed has administrative or criminal consequences placed on subsequent reentry owing to the fact of the removal.
- Return: The confirmed movement of an inadmissible or deportable alien out of the United States not based on an order of removal.

Source: Office of Immigration Statistics, 2011. Immigration Enforcement Actions, 2011, Department of Homeland Security Policy Office, http://www.dhs.gov/xlibrary/assets/statistics/publications/enforcement-ar-2010.pdf.

Secure Communities Program

ICE policy ensures that the removal of criminal aliens, namely, those who pose a threat to public safety, and repeat immigration violators are given priority attention. The Secure Communities program helps the agency to carry out this priority goal. Secure Communities uses an already existing federal information-sharing partnership between ICE and the Federal Bureau of Investigation (FBI) that helps to identify criminal aliens without imposing new or additional requirements on state and local law enforcement. Through Secure Communities, the FBI sends the fingerprints of arrested individuals that are collected by local jurisdictions (who for decades have shared these with the FBI for cross-checking purposes) to ICE to check against its immigration databases. If these checks reveal that an individual is unlawfully present in the United States or otherwise removable due to a criminal conviction, ICE takes enforcement action. Such people are prioritized for removal, thereby minimizing the threat to public safety caused by illegal aliens.

DHS has expanded Secure Communities from 14 jurisdictions in 2008 to more than 1,300 today, including all jurisdictions along the southwest border where risk is highest. DHS is on track to expand this program to all law enforcement jurisdictions nationwide by 2013. Through April 30, 2011, more than 77,000 immigrants convicted of crimes, including more than 28,000 convicted of aggravated felony (level 1) offenses like murder, rape, and the sexual abuse of children, were removed from the United States after identification through the program. These removals significantly contributed to a 71% increase in the overall percentage of convicted criminals removed by ICE, with 81,000 more criminal removals in FY 2010 than in FY 2008. As a result of the increased focus on criminals, this period also included a 23% reduction or 57,000 fewer noncriminal removals.

The Secure Communities Program is important because ICE only receives enough funding to remove a portion of the more than 10 million individuals estimated to be in the United States illegally or who are removable because of criminal convictions. This program ensures that security is improved, given the nature of how deportation is focused.

ICE Homeland Security Investigations

The ICE Homeland Security Investigations (HSI) Directorate is a critical asset in the ICE mission, responsible for investigating a wide range of domestic and international activities arising from the illegal movement of people and goods into, within, and out of the United States. HSI investigates immigration crime; human rights violations and human smuggling; smuggling of narcotics, weapons, and other types of contraband; financial crimes; cybercrime; and export enforcement issues. ICE special agents conduct investigations aimed at protecting critical infrastructure industries that are vulnerable to sabotage, attack, or exploitation.

In addition to ICE criminal investigations, HSI oversees the agency's international affairs operations and intelligence functions. HSI consists of more than 10,000 employees, consisting of 6,700 special agents, who are assigned to more than 200 cities throughout the United States and 46 countries around the world.

HSI is made up of six key divisions, which include:

- Domestic Operations
- Intelligence
- International Affairs
- Investigative Programs
- Mission Support
- National Intellectual Property Rights (IPR) Coordination Center

ICE Project Shield America

Project Shield America is an ICE program aimed at preventing WMD trafficking by illegal exporters, targeted foreign countries, terrorist groups, and international criminal organizations. This program also works to stop organized criminal and state-sponsored efforts from obtaining and illegally exporting licensable commodities, technologies, conventional munitions and firearms; exporting stolen property; and engaging in financial transactions that support these activities or violate U.S. sanctions and embargoes.

The U.S. government protects both the economic and national security interests of the country in this regard. Foreign adversaries regularly attempt to acquire and steal technologies developed in the United States by both legal and illegal means. Those who succeed in acquiring such technologies often do so without having to expend the great amounts of resources required by the innovative U.S. company or governmental or nongovernmental agency. Moreover, such technologies can be used against the country to jeopardize national security and/or the U.S. economy.

Examples of strategic technology sought by certain proscribed countries include:

- Modern manufacturing technology for the production of microelectronics, computers, digital electronic components, and signal processing systems.
- Technology necessary for the development of aircraft, missile, and other tactical weapon delivery systems.
- All types of advanced signal and weapons detection, tracking, and monitoring systems.
- Technology and equipment used in the construction of nuclear weapons and materials.
- Biological, chemical warfare agents and precursors, and associated manufacturing equipment.

Project Shield America was designed and implemented to work in concert with the three-pronged effort of its Export Enforcement Program, namely:

- *Inspection/Interdiction* — Specially trained U.S. CBP inspectors stationed at high-threat ports selectively inspect suspect export shipments.

- *Investigations* — ICE agents deployed throughout the country initiate and pursue high-quality cases that result in the arrest, prosecution, and conviction of offenders of the Export Administration Act, Arms Export Control Act, Trading with the Enemy Act, International Emergency Economics Powers Act, and other related statutes. ICE investigations aim to detect and disrupt illegal exports before they can cause damage to the national security interests of the United States.
- *International Cooperation* — ICE international attaché offices enlist the support of their host governments to initiate new investigative leads and to develop information in support of ongoing domestic investigations.

The Joint Terrorism Task Force

The ICE National Security Investigation Division's (NSID) National Security Unit (NSU) represents ICE participation on the Joint Terrorism Task Force (JTTF). The JTTF investigates, detects, interdicts, prosecutes, and removes terrorists and dismantles terrorist organizations. ICE is involved in almost every foreign terrorism investigation related to cross-border crime. ICE is the largest federal contributor to the JTTF through active participation in each of the 104 local JTTFs nationwide. The agency also plays a critical leadership role on the national JTTF.

Border Enforcement Security Task Force

In response to the dramatic increase in cross-border crime and violence in recent years (due in part to feuds between Mexican drug cartels and criminal smuggling organizations), ICE partnered with federal, state, local, and foreign law enforcement counterparts to create the Border Enforcement Security Task Force (BEST). BEST is a series of multiagency teams developed to identify, disrupt, and dismantle criminal organizations posing significant threats to border security. Several international law enforcement agencies serve as key members of the team.

On the southwest border, the participation of the Mexican Secretaria de Seguridad Publica, or SSP, is vital. On the northern border, Canadian law enforcement agencies like the Canada Border Services Agency, the Royal Canadian Mounted Police, the Ontario Provincial Police, the Niagara Regional Police Service, the Toronto Metropolitan Police, the Windsor Police Service, and the Amherstburg Police Service are active members. The Argentinean customs agency is part of the Miami BEST and the Colombian National Police is part of both the Miami and New York–New Jersey BESTs. Currently, there are 21 BESTs with locations around the United States and in Mexico. Since BEST's inception, investigators have collectively initiated more than 6,400 cases.

Counterterrorism and Criminal Exploitation Unit

The Counterterrorism and Criminal Exploitation Unit (CTCEU) prevents terrorists and other criminals from exploiting U.S. immigration. CTCEU staff also review the immigration status of known and suspected terrorists, combat criminal exploitation of the Student and Exchange Visitor Program (SEVP), and leverage HSI's expertise to identify national security threats.

CTCEU is composed of three sections:

- National Security Threat Task Force (NSTTF)
- SEVIS Exploitation Section (SES)
- Terrorist Tracking Pursuit Group (TTPG)

NSTTF identifies, disrupts, and prosecutes people listed in the Terrorist Identities Datamart Environment (TIDE), a database of individuals who have fraudulently obtained U.S. immigration benefits. The task force identifies individuals for TIDE and coordinates their litigation and removal proceedings on behalf of ICE. Identified violators are subject to the full judicial prosecutorial process.

SEVIS SES analyzes and refers educational/school fraud criminal investigation leads to the respective ICE field office. It implements and manages the Agent/SEVIS School Outreach Program that educates others about SEVP exploitation. The program also improves communication between designated school officials and HSI field agents and provides subject matter expertise to partnering agencies when exploitation is suspected.

TTPG leverages ICE expertise across partnering agencies dedicated to promoting national security. This group leads the Targeted Enforcement Program (TEP), an initiative with U.S. CBP that tracks how long individuals identified as security risks stay in the United States. The program works jointly with the FBI's Foreign Terrorist Threat Task Force (FTTTF) that also proactively identifies known or suspected terrorists. TTPG also initiates high-priority nonimmigrant overstay investigations as dictated by the Compliance Enforcement Advisory Panel (CEAP).

Counterproliferation Investigations

ICE is the only federal law enforcement agency with full statutory authority to investigate and enforce criminal violations of all U.S. export laws related to military items, controlled "dual-use" commodities, and sanctioned or embargoed countries. The magnitude and scope of such threats increase significantly each year. ICE agents in the field who conduct counterproliferation investigations (CPI) focus on the trafficking and illegal export of the following commodities and services:

- WMD materials
- Chemical, biological, radiological, nuclear (CBRN) materials
- Military equipment and technology
- Controlled dual-use commodities and technology
- Firearms and ammunition
- Financial and business transactions with sanctioned and embargoed countries and terrorist organizations

The U.S. Coast Guard

The U.S. Coast Guard (USCG) is one of the five armed forces of the United States and the only military organization within the DHS. The Coast Guard protects the maritime economy and the environment, defends the nation's maritime borders, and rescues those in peril. The Coast Guard is simultaneously and at all times an armed force and federal law enforcement agency (Figure 6–4). National defense responsibilities remain one of the Coast Guard's most important functions. In times of peace, the agency operates as part of the DHS, serving as the nation's front-line agency for enforcing the nation's laws at sea, protecting the marine environment and the nation's vast coastline and ports, and saving life. In times of war, or at the direction of the President, the Coast Guard serves under the Navy Department.

For over two centuries, the Coast Guard has guarded U.S. maritime interests domestically, in the ports, at sea, and around the globe. The Coast Guard has nearly 42,000 men and women on active duty today. By law, the Coast Guard has 11 missions (three of which are starred, representing an association

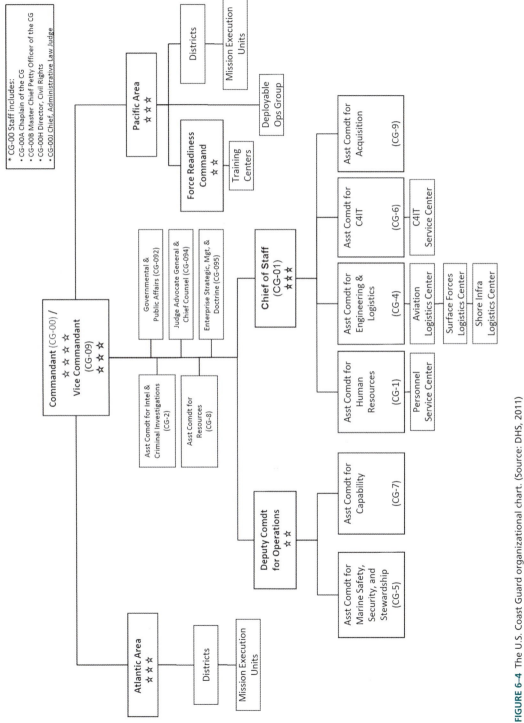

FIGURE 6-4 The U.S. Coast Guard organizational chart. (Source: DHS, 2011)

with border security, customs, or immigration, and which are described in greater detail below). The full list of 11 missions includes:

- Ports, waterways, and coastal security*
- Drug interdiction*
- Aids to navigation
- Search and rescue
- Living marine resources
- Marine safety
- Defense readiness
- Migrant interdiction
- Marine environmental protection
- Ice operations
- Other law enforcement*

Drug Interdiction

The Coast Guard is the lead federal agency for maritime drug interdiction and shares lead responsibility for air interdiction with the U.S. Customs Service. As such, it is a key player in combating the flow of illegal drugs to the country. The Coast Guard's drug interdiction mission is to reduce the supply of drugs from the source by denying smugglers the use of air and maritime routes in the Transit Zone, a six-million square-mile area that includes the Caribbean, the Gulf of Mexico, and Eastern Pacific. In meeting the challenge of patrolling this vast area, the Coast Guard coordinates closely with other federal agencies and countries within the region to disrupt and deter the flow of illegal drugs. The Coast Guard drug interdiction accounts for nearly 52% of all U.S. government seizures of cocaine each year.

The Coast Guard has been conducting drug interdiction missions since the late 19th century, when Chinese drug smugglers began illegally importing opium on ships. In the prohibition days, the Coast Guard saw a rather large increase in resources and funding to fight alcohol smuggling, which included the chasing of now-legendary rum-runners. Today, maritime drug smuggling is a very significant problem, and smugglers are using new technologies to evade capture (including submersible ships that are very difficult to detect). Since its first drug seizures in the early 1970s, the Coast Guard has seized well over 1 million pounds of cocaine and marijuana.

Other Border-Area Law Enforcement Roles

Countries need to protect their commercial fishing interests as a matter of economic, environmental, and food supply security. Commercial fishery zones extending from the nation's borders are protected by federal and international laws, and the USCG is tasked with enforcing these laws. Coast Guard vessels prevent illegal foreign fishing vessels from entering and exploiting the U.S. "Exclusive Economic Zone" (EEZ) encroachment as part of the Coast Guard mission. In addition, the Coast Guard is tasked with the duty of enforcing international agreements aimed at controlling illegal, unreported, and unregulated (IUU) fishing activity on the high seas. In 2008, the Coast Guard detected 81 incursions by foreign fishing vessels into the U.S. EEZ. The Coast Guard also participated in the 2008 multinational high seas drift net (HSDN) enforcement campaign, Operation North Pacific Watch. Through this campaign, the Coast Guard interdicted two Chinese HSDN vessels, facilitating their seizure by Chinese officials.

U.S. Citizenship and Immigration Services

U.S. Citizenship and Immigration Services (USCIS) is the DHS component that oversees lawful immigration to the United States. USCIS is tasked with ensuring the security of the nation by providing accurate and useful information to intending immigrants, granting immigration and citizenship benefits, promoting an awareness and understanding of citizenship, and ensuring the integrity of the U.S. immigration system (Figure 6–5).

USCIS currently employs 18,000 people, many of whom are contractors, at approximately 250 locations throughout the world. USCIS employees facilitate the immigration process, which can be cumbersome, time-consuming, and at times technically challenging (due to the requirements under U.S. immigration law). Because intelligence has shown terrorists to be interested in exploiting the U.S. immigration system to gain entry to the United States, USCIS faces an ongoing challenge to maintain system integrity and innovation. At the same time, to serve the millions of people who are adhering to all immigration policies and laws, USCIS must ensure the immigration system is effective, flexible, and customer-oriented.

Services provided by USCIS include:

- Citizenship (including citizenship through naturalization): Intending immigrants who wish to become U.S. citizens submit applications to USCIS. USCIS determines each applicant's eligibility, processes his or her applications, and, if approved, schedules the applicant for a ceremony to take the Oath of Allegiance. USCIS also determines eligibility and provides documentation of U.S. citizenship for people who acquired or derived U.S. citizenship through their parents.
- Family member immigration: USCIS manages the process that allows current permanent residents and U.S. citizens to bring close relatives to live and work in the United States.
- Employment for foreign nationals: USCIS manages the process that allows individuals from other countries to work in the United States.
- Verifying an individual's legal right to work in the United States (e-verify): USCIS maintains the e-verify system, which allows employers to electronically verify an employee's employment eligibility.
- Humanitarian programs: USCIS administers programs that provide protection to individuals inside and outside the United States who are displaced by war, famine, and civil and political unrest, and those who are forced to flee their countries to escape the risk of death and torture.
- Adoptions: USCIS manages the first step in the process for U.S. citizens to adopt children from other countries. Approximately 20,000 adoptions take place each year.
- Civic integration: USCIS promotes instruction and training on citizenship rights and responsibilities and provides immigrants with the information and tools necessary to successfully integrate into American civic culture.

Office of Citizenship

The Office of Citizenship engages and supports the citizenship process by helping new immigrants to succeed in their adoptive country. This includes promotion of the English language and education on the

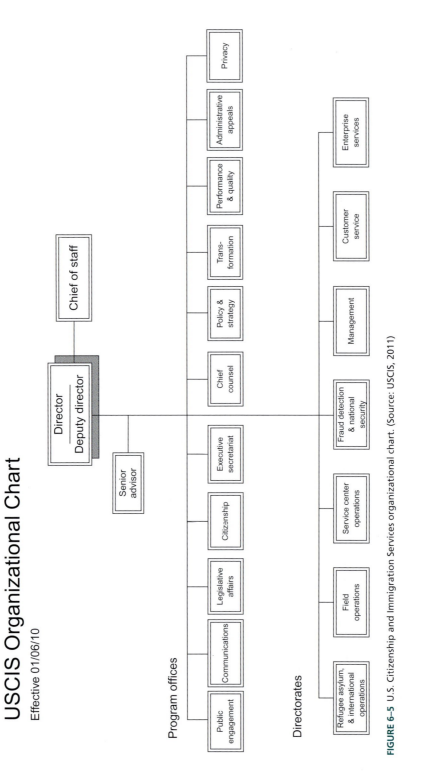

FIGURE 6–5 U.S. Citizenship and Immigration Services organizational chart. (Source: USCIS, 2011)

rights and responsibilities of citizenship, for instance. The Office of Citizenship is tasked with the following activities:

- Developing and enhancing educational products and resources that welcome immigrants, promote English language learning and education on the rights and responsibilities of citizenship, and prepare immigrants for naturalization and active civic participation
- Leading initiatives to promote citizenship awareness and demystify the naturalization process for aspiring citizens
- Supporting national and community-based organizations that prepare immigrants for citizenship by providing grants, educational materials, and technical assistance
- Building collaborative partnerships with state and local governments and nongovernmental organizations to expand integration and citizenship resources in communities
- Conducting training workshops and enhancing professional development and classroom resources for educators and organizations preparing immigrants for citizenship
- Promoting integration policy dialogue among different sectors of society and coordinating with stakeholders at all levels to foster integration and community cohesion

The Office of Citizenship is divided into three divisions:

- Testing, Education, and Training
- Policy and Programs
- Grants

Fraud Detection and National Security Directorate

The Fraud Detection and National Security (FDNS) Directorate was created within USCIS in 2004 to strengthen ongoing efforts to ensure that immigration benefits are not granted to individuals who pose a threat to national security or public safety, or who seek to defraud the U.S. immigration system. In 2010, FDNS became a directorate, which elevated the profile of this work within USCIS. FDNS officers are located in every USCIS center, district, field, and asylum office. FDNS officers are also located in other government agencies. FDNS staff enhance USCIS's ability to detect and remove known and suspected fraud from the application process without hampering the process by which legitimate applications are processed. FDNS officers also perform checks of USCIS databases and public information, as well as other administrative inquiries, to verify information provided on, and in support of, applications and petitions. Administrative inquiries may include:

- Fraud assessments (determine the types and volumes of fraud in certain immigration benefits programs)
- Compliance reviews (reviews of certain types of applications or petitions to ensure the integrity of the immigration benefits system)
- Targeted site visits (inquiries conducted in cases where fraud is suspected)

FDNS uses the fraud detection and national security data system (FDNS-DS) to identify fraud and track potential patterns. In July 2009, FDNS implemented the Administrative Site Visit and Verification Program (ASVVP) to conduct unannounced site inspections to verify information contained in certain visa petitions.

Refugee, Asylum, and International Operations Directorate

The Refugee, Asylum, and International Operations (RAIO) Directorate operates both within and outside the United States to provide protection, humanitarian, and other immigration benefits to legitimate foreign citizen applicants, while at the same time ensuring that these benefits are not exploited by terrorists or criminals. Refugees and asylum seekers are people who are typically characterized as:

- Fleeing oppression, persecution, and torture because of their race, religion, nationality, membership in a particular social group, or political opinion
- Confronting an urgent humanitarian situation and needing authorization to enter the United States on a temporary basis

RAIO also provides immigration services to certain groups of foreign citizens who should not or cannot apply for citizenship or immigration permission within the United States itself. These include (for example):

- Active duty members of the U.S. Armed Forces serving overseas who seek to become naturalized citizens
- Lawful permanent residents who are overseas and have lost documentation that would enable them to lawfully return to the United States
- Individuals who live overseas and seek to be reunified with relatives in the United States

RAIO is made up of three divisions, which include:

- The Refugee Affairs Division: it is responsible for providing the humanitarian benefit of refugee resettlement to applicants in need of protection throughout the world while diligently protecting the U.S. homeland through careful national security screening
- The Asylum Division: It manages the U.S. affirmative asylum process, which permits individuals already in the United States. or at a port of entry, who are not in immigration proceedings, to request asylum if they are unable or unwilling to return to their country of origin due to past persecution or a well-founded fear of future persecution
- The International Operations Division: It extends immigration benefits to eligible individuals located overseas.

Office of US-VISIT

The Office of US-VISIT (US-VISIT) is one of five divisions that make up the DHS National Protection and Programs Directorate (NPPD). US-VISIT contributes to border security efforts by providing biometric identification services to federal, state, and local government decision makers to help them accurately identify the people they encounter and determine whether those people pose a risk to the United States.

US-VISIT was created to enhance entry and exit security procedures. It enables consular, border security, and immigration officers to effectively verify the identity of incoming visitors and confirm compliance with visa and immigration policies. The program's goals are to enhance the security of U.S. citizens and visitors who travel in and out of the country, to expedite legitimate travel and trade, and to ensure the integrity of the immigration system while safeguarding the privacy of visitors.

Implementation of the program began in 2004 at 115 airports. Over the years that followed, the biometrics machines were installed at U.S. embassies and consulates throughout the world. Applicants use the machine to digitally scan their fingerprints, and the generated images are saved in a database where other relevant information about the applicants is located. The fingerprints are later used to verify the identity of a visitor when he or she enters or leaves the country.

On arrival in the United States, as part of the enhanced procedures, most visitors traveling on visas will have two fingerprints scanned by an inkless device and a digital photograph taken. All of the data and information are then used to assist the border inspector in determining whether or not to admit the traveler. These enhanced procedures add only seconds to the visitor's overall processing time.

All data obtained from the visitor are securely stored as part of the visitor's travel record. This information is made available only to authorized officials and selected law enforcement agencies on a need-to-know basis in their efforts to help protect against those who intend to harm American citizens or visitors.

The most notable change for international visitors is the new exit procedure. Most visitors who require a visa will eventually need to verify their departure. This checkout process will be completed by use of automated self-service workstations in the international departure areas of airports and seaports. By scanning travel documents and capturing fingerprints on the same inkless device, the system validates the visitor's identity, verifies his or her departure, and confirms his or her compliance with U.S. immigration policy (DHS, 2004, 2011b).

Conclusion

The nation's security and economic stability are contingent upon effective maintenance of secure borders, effective enforcement of immigration laws, and enforceable customs policies and procedures. These three tasks are monumental in their scope, requiring the dedication of hundreds of thousands of government employees, cutting edge technologies, intergovernmental cooperation, and billions upon billions of dollars in budget allocations. By consolidating these functions under the DHS umbrella, the various agencies involved in their conduct have increased the effectiveness of each, and as a result the nation is likely safer and more secure. While legal immigrants and legitimate commerce do form both the foundation and ongoing prosperity of our nation, the truth remains that criminals and terrorists will continue to seek out new and better ways to evade our systems of protection.

Key Terms

Asylum: The protection granted by a nation to a person who has left their native country as a refugee (and would therefore face imminent danger were they to return to that country).

Border: A line that defines geographic and political boundaries or legal jurisdictions.

Containerization: The transportation of cargo in standardized containers that can be seamlessly transferred between ocean-going (ships), rail (trains), and highway (trucks) vehicles without having to unload contents.

Customs: The government function tasked with collecting duties levied on imported goods.

Deportation: The act of forcibly expelling a foreign national from one country to their own country or to a third country willing to accept them.

Drone Aircraft: A powered, pilotless, unmanned aircraft that is typically flown remotely by an operator on the ground.

Duties: Taxes imposed upon goods imported into one country from another, typically imposed for the purposes of protecting domestic business interests, equalizing the charges imposed by other countries on exported goods, and/or generating government revenue.

Excise Tax: Tax imposed on the use or consumption of certain products.

Immigration: The act of a foreign citizen coming to another country for the purposes of residing there permanently, either by legal or by illegal means.

Linewatch Operations: Operations that are conducted near international boundaries and coastlines in areas of Border Patrol jurisdiction to prevent the illegal entry and smuggling of aliens into the United States, and to intercept those who do enter illegally before they can escape from border areas.

Marine Patrol: Border patrol activities conducted along the coastal waterways of the United States and Puerto Rico and interior waterways common to the United States and Canada. Marine patrol activities are typically conducted from the decks of marine craft.

Naturalization: The process under national law by which a foreign-born person is granted citizenship.

Refugee: A person who has been forced to leave their country due to war, persecution, or other reasons for which they fear for their life and safety.

Signcutting Operations: The detection and interpretation of any disturbances in natural terrain conditions that indicate the presence or passage of people, animals, or vehicles.

Visa: An endorsement on a passport that indicates the holder is allowed to enter, exit, and/or stay for a predetermined amount of time in a country. There are numerous classes of visas that each bestow different privileges.

Review Questions

1. How do the nation's borders serve to maintain economic and physical security?
2. What DHS offices are involved in each of the following, and what specific actions do they perform?
   a. Immigration
   b. Border security
   c. Customs enforcement
3. How does DHS balance the protection of the nation's borders with the freedom of movement of legitimate travelers and goods across the borders?

References

CBP, 2008. CSI In Brief. CBP Website. http://www.cbp.gov/xp/cgov/trade/cargo_security/csi/csi_in_brief.xml.

CBP, 2009. Fencing construction status. (December 25). http://www.cbp.gov/linkhandler/cgov/newsroom/highlights/fence_map.ctt/fence_map.pdf.

CBP, 2010. CBP Authority to Search. CBP Website. http://www.cbp.gov/xp/cgov/travel/admissibility/authority_to_search.xml

CBP, 2011a. Immigration inspection program. CBP Website. http://www.cbp.gov/xp/cgov/border_security/port_activities/overview.xml.

CBP, 2011b. Office of air and marine. Fact sheet. http://www.cbp.gov/linkhandler/cgov/newsroom/fact_sheets/marine/air_marine.ctt/air_marine.pdf.

CBP, 2011c. Unmanned aircraft system MQ-9 predator B. CBP fact sheet. http://www.cbp.gov/linkhandler/cgov/newsroom/fact_sheets/marine/uas.ctt/uas.pdf.

Department of Homeland Security, 2004. Fact sheet: Arizona border control initiative. http://www.dhs.gov/xnews/releases/press_release_0520.shtm.

DHS, 2004. US-VISIT program. http://www.dhs.gov/xtrvlsec/programs/content_multi_image0006.htm.

DHS, 2006. Secure freight initiative: vision and operations overview. (December 7). http://www.dhs.gov/xnews/releases/pr_1165943729650.shtm

DHS, 2011a. Securing America's borders: CBP fiscal year 2010 in review fact sheet. (March 15).

DHS, 2011b. Office of US-Visit. http://www.dhs.gov/files/programs/usv.shtm.

7

Transportation Safety and Security

What You Will Learn

- The nature of U.S. transportation systems and infrastructure
- The roles and responsibilities of the Transportation Security Administration

Introduction

Transportation is a general term that refers to the movement of things or people from one location to another. However, in today's modern world, where transportation systems are intertwined into a global network that moves millions of people and products throughout the world on a daily basis, such simple definitions do not give justice to the complexity that exists in this sector. Furthermore, the safety and security needs to address such a complex system are equally complex and interconnected.

Historically, the United States has relied on the private sector for both the transportation network and the promise of domestic transportation safety and security. The events of September 11, 2001, however, illustrated the vulnerabilities of the nation's transportation systems and spurred a massive change in the existing approaches. Transportation security and the identification and reduction of vulnerabilities within the vast transportation networks have since experienced significant challenges and changes. Because of the complexity of these systems as a whole and of the subsystems, that exist, such efforts have proved challenging.

In the United States, the Department of Homeland Security Transportation Security Administration (TSA) is the primary government body that addresses the security of transportation systems and infrastructure, while the Coast Guard and the Department of Transportation address it to a lesser degree. This chapter discusses the various components of the nation's transportation network and describes the agencies and programs that exist to ensure their protection.

The Transportation Network

The general term "transportation" refers to a very wide range of systems, structures, vehicles, and actions. The transportation of people and things (namely goods) takes many forms and affects every American's life in some way or another. There are a number of distinct components that make up the nation's transportation network, and these include the following.

Freight Rail

The nationwide freight railroad network facilitates the transport of both raw materials and marketable goods. This network is a vital component of the U.S. economy, connecting many of the nation's distribution hubs and shipping ports. At present, there are approximately 140,000 miles of active railroad track that are utilized by 565 common carrier freight railroads. These railroads serve nearly every industrial, wholesale, retail, and resource-based sector of the U.S. economy, and are responsible for transporting a majority of the goods and commodities Americans depend on.

The freight rail system is a diverse network of large and small independent companies. In the absence of one single coast-to-coast freight rail operator, these carriers have developed various interchange, joint services, and voluntary access agreements that allow for the transfer of rail cars between carriers, as well as the operation of one carrier's train on the tracks of another. This type of system increases operational efficiency for the railroads and helps to further lower transportation costs, but increases the complexity of the security operation needed to support it.

Highways, Roadways, and Motor Carrier Networks

All Americans depend on the U.S. highway and roadway systems directly through the facilitation of personal transport, and indirectly through the transport of goods and services upon which they depend. This massive infrastructure network includes:

- 46,934 miles of interstate highway
- 116,813 miles of other National Highway System roads
- 3,884,777 miles of other roads
- 599,766 bridges over 20 feet of span
- 366 U.S. highway tunnels over 100 meters in length

The number of registered vehicles in the United States exceeded 254 million, inclusive 26.2 million privately owned trucks, 9.0 million commercially owned trucks (with 6 or more tires and/or combination vehicles), 834,000 buses, 136 million passenger cars, 7.1 million motorcycles, and 101 million other 2-axle vehicles.

The motor carrier industry, which does not include intracity or mass transit buses, consists of three primary components, namely:

- *The U.S. Motor Coach Industry*: 3,137 bus companies operate 29,325 motor coach buses. These provide 118,000 jobs and transport 750 million passengers annually.
- *The Pupil Transportation (School Bus) Industry*: The nation's 475,000 school buses represent the largest fleet of public vehicles in the United States. They serve 19,000 U.S. school districts, and transport 25 million students each day (10 billion student trips per year).
- *The Motor Carrier Freight Industry*: In the United States, there are approximately 703,000 motor carrier companies. These companies employ 4.7 million commercial vehicle drivers, who operate 9.0 million commercial trucks, and 5.1 million commercial trailers. 61,000 of the trucking companies transport 2 billion tons of hazardous materials (HAZMATs) each year.

Ports and Intermodal Freight Transport

Ninety-nine percent of US imports and exports are conducted by ship through the nation's system of seaports. The U.S. seaport infrastructure is owned and operated by multiple stakeholders at the federal, state, and local levels, and in both the private and public domains. Thirty-two states have active public ports, and there are 327 official ports of entry (in addition to 15 preclearance offices in Canada and the Caribbean).

Mass Transit

U.S. law defines *mass transit* to be "transportation by a conveyance that provides regular and continuing general or special transportation to the public, but does not include school bus, charter, or sightseeing transportation" (U.S. Code Title 49, Subtitle III, Chapter 53, §5302). Mass transit modes include:

- Intercity buses
- Trolleybuses
- Subway and commuter rail
- Demand response services
- Heavy and light rail
- Automated guideway transit
- Cable cars
- Monorails
- Ferries

Each year, almost 10 billion passenger rides are conducted on mass transit systems nationwide on over 144,000 vehicles (of which about 56% are buses). The nation's passenger rail system, Amtrak, also operates a nationwide rail transportation network of 22,000 miles of track and serves 21 million passengers per year at more than 500 stations. Interconnectivity of these systems has been fostered such that several different mass transit systems share terminals and other facilities. Ownership of mass transit systems is unique, with many smaller systems independently owned and operated and most medium-to-large size agencies owned and operated by governmental or quasi-governmental organizations.

Ferries continue to serve as a vital component of the U.S. transportation system, with the number of passenger rides provided by almost a quarter-million vehicles approaching 85 million each year. Due to the nature of many waterways, ferries often travel between states, and in certain locations near Mexico and Canada, across international borders. Ferry-related accidents tend to be spectacular in nature given the unique aspect of drowning, and in many historical events dozens and even hundreds to thousands of people have died. As such, ferries have been and continue to be seen as a high-priority target for terrorists.

Pipeline Security

As a conveyor of goods from place to place, the oil and gas pipeline network that spans the nation is considered a component of the transportation infrastructure (Figure 7–1). The national pipeline system is somewhat unique with regard to its status as a transportation system, and as such has unique infrastructure security characteristics and requirements. Pipelines have been a regular target of terrorism throughout the world, and intelligence has found evidence that terrorists consider the U.S. pipeline system a high-value target. Additionally, accidents or other disruptions to the pipeline infrastructure can cause significant impacts to property and to humans, and the economic impacts may be far-reaching.

Virtually all the critical pipeline infrastructure is owned or operated by private entities. There are:

- 161,189 miles of hazardous liquid pipelines operated by over 200 operators
- 309,503 miles of natural gas transmission pipelines operated by over 700 operators
- 1.9 million miles of natural gas distribution pipelines operated by over 1,300 operators

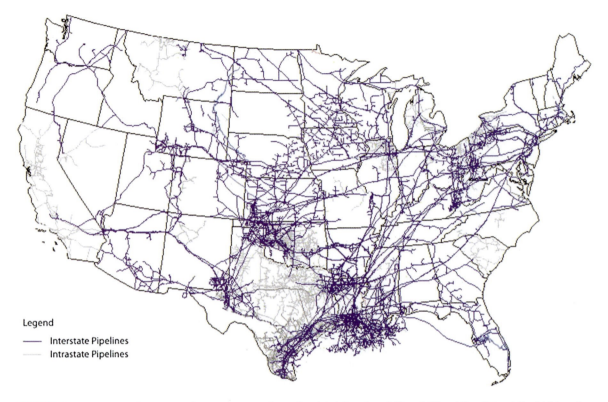

FIGURE 7–1 U.S. pipeline infrastructure. (Source: Energy Information Administration, Office of Oil and Gas, Natural Gas Division, Gas Transportation Information System)

Air Freight

For the 12 months that ended September 2010, almost 10 million tons of freight was transported within the United States and between the United States and other countries using commercial aircraft. The air freight industry provides the speed and efficiency vital for products needed immediately or for which spoilage risk exists. Air freight presents a unique security challenge due to its sheer quantity and the fact that it is transported on both dedicated freight-carrying airplanes and on passenger planes in the cargo hold. When transported on passenger aircraft, passengers are exposed to the risk of these goods, which may be used to conduct terrorist attacks.

Commercial and General Aviation

Commercial aviation has been operating in the United States since 1914. Today, more than 28,000 flights take off or land in the United States each day, representing about half of traffic worldwide. The 599 US airports certified to serve commercial flights transport hundreds of millions of passengers each year, with some of the largest serving tens of millions of passengers each (Reed, 2006).

General Aviation (GA) is a vital component of the aviation sector and the national economy that accounts for some 77% of all flights in the United States. It encompasses a wide range of activities, from pilot training to flying for business and personal reasons, delivery of emergency medical services, and sightseeing. Operations range from short-distance flights in single-engine light aircraft to long-distance international flights in corporate-owned wide-bodies, and from emergency aeromedical helicopter operations to airships seen at open-air sporting events. The sole characteristic that GA operations have in common is that flights are not routinely scheduled; they are on demand.

The Transportation Security Administration

The Aviation and Transportation Security Act (Public Law 107-71), signed by President Bush on November 19, 2001, created the Transportation Security Administration (TSA) within the Department of Transportation. In 2003 this office was absorbed into the newly-formed DHS where it stands as an independent office under the DHS Secretary.

The Aviation and Transportation Security Act fundamentally changed how transportation security is performed and managed in the United States. For instance, aviation security became a direct federal responsibility for the first time, and all transportation security activities under the umbrella of one agency. Aviation security has remained the leading TSA priority in terms of both staff and budget (Figure 7–2).

	FY 2010 Rev. Enacted		FY 2011 Cont. Resolution[1]		FY 2012 Pres. Budget		FY 2012 +/− FY 2011	
	FTE	$000	FTE	$000	FTE	$000	FTE	$000
Aviation Security	49,282	$5,214,040	52,269	$5,214,040	55,284	$5,401,165	3,015	$187,125
Surface Transportation Security	593	110,516	787	110,516	775	134,748	(12)	24,232
Transportation Threat Assessment and Credentialing	246	215,619	252	209,219	481	220,274	229	11,055
Transportation Security Support	1,501	1,001,780	1,517	1,001,780	1,855	1,113,697	338	111,917
Federal Air Marshals	-	860,111	-	860,111	-	991,375	-	131,264
Gross Discretionary	**51,622**	**$7,402,066**	**54,825**	**$7,395,666**	**58,395**	**$7,861,259**	**3,570**	**$465,593**
Mandatory, Fees, & Trust Fund	6	254,000	6	254,000	6	254,000	-	-
Emergency/ Supplemental	-	-	-	-	-	-	-	-
American Reinvestment and Recovery Act (ARRA)	-	-	-	-	-	-	-	-
Total	**51,628**	**$7,656,066**	**54,831**	**$7,649,666**	**58,401**	**$8,115,259**	**3,570**	**$465,593**
Less Prior Year Rescissions	-	(4,000)	-	-	-	-	-	-

[1] The FY 2011 Continuing Resolution funding level corresponds to the FY 2010 Enacted level.

FIGURE 7–2 The TSA budget. (Source: Department of Homeland Security. 2012. Budget in Frief. FY2012. DHS Website. www.dhs.gov/xlibrary/assets/budget-bib-fy2012.pdf.)

TSA's security focus is on identifying risks, prioritizing them, managing these risks to acceptable levels, and mitigating the impact of potential incidents that may arise as result of these risks. Sharing of information among agencies and stakeholders — including intelligence information — has become a cornerstone of its risk management model. TSA has adapted to the complex and unique requirements of both passenger and cargo security, in recognition of the many differences that exist between transportation modes, and to instill confidence in the security of the transportation system. Today, approximately 50,000 Transportation Security Officers (TSOs) provide screening and other security services at approximately 450 US airports. TSOs are trained and certified in constantly evolving rules, methods, and technologies to detect the presence of threats against people and the infrastructure required to maintain safe travel for nearly 2 million passengers each day. Additionally, U.S. air carriers annually transport approximately 12.5 million tons of cargo, 2.8 million tons of which is now secured on passenger planes. The remaining 9.7 million tons of freight, which is shipped in cargo planes, also remains a unique threat to the nation given the destructive physical and psychological impact of a large plane crash.

The full scope of TSA's security mandate is staggering and encompasses a jurisdiction rivaling any other federal agency. This includes more than 9 billion passenger trips per year on the nation's mass transit systems, over 161,000 miles of interstate and national highways and their integrated bridges and tunnels, and nearly 800,000 shipments of hazardous materials. While the United States may not have had another successful attack on its transportation infrastructure in the decade that followed the 9/11 events, these systems remain on the forefront of the security domain in light of the global terrorism experience.

TSA Components

The TSA ensures transportation security through four mechanisms, each of which is described below. These include:

- Transportation Security Grants
- Law enforcement program
- Security programs
- Security screening

Transportation Security Grants

Since 2006, DHS has awarded over $1.6 billion in special grants that target the nation's transportation systems. TSA maintains the department's Transportation Security Grants, which are provided to mass transit and passenger rail systems, intercity bus companies, freight railroad carriers, ferries, and the trucking industry to help protect the public and nation's critical transportation infrastructure against acts of terrorism and other large-scale events. The grants are designed to support "high-impact" security projects that serve to reduce the risk faced by the various transportation systems.

The grant programs include:

- The Freight Rail Security Grant Program (FRSGP): Created to increase security levels within the freight rail industry by funding vulnerability assessments and security plans, providing funding for security training and exercises for frontline personnel, purchasing and installing global positioning systems (GPS) tracking on railroad cars, and hardening of bridges that are used for freight rail transportation.

- The Intercity Bus Security Grant Program (IBSGP): Created to support the work of operators of fixed-route intercity and charter bus services servicing high-risk urban areas. This grant is designed to strengthen the infrastructure upon which these operators depend, and to protect the traveling public against risks associated with potential terrorist attacks.
- The Transit Security Grant Program (TSGP): Provides funds to owners and operators of transit systems, including intracity bus, commuter bus, certain ferry systems, and all forms of passenger rail. These grants are intended to protect critical surface transportation infrastructure and the traveling public from acts of terrorism.

TSA Law Enforcement Functions

TSA is best known for passenger and baggage screening at airport security checkpoints. However, the agency also maintains a number of law enforcement functions across a fairly wide jurisdiction of transportation infrastructure components. TSA law enforcement also includes the training of transportation employees in the knowledge and skills required to maintain the safety and security of the transportation network.

The Federal Air Marshal Service

The Federal Air Marshal Service is a TSA-managed law enforcement agency charged with securing the civil aviation system from both criminal and terrorist acts. Federal Air Marshals are specially trained federal security officers who travel inconspicuously on commercial flights for the purpose of quickly thwarting an attempted criminal or terrorist attack (or to neutralize a potentially dangerous situation involving unruly passengers).

The Federal Air Marshal Service predates TSA by almost 40 years, when hijacking of US commercial flights became an ongoing problem. To address a growing threat, the Federal Air Marshal Service was created within the U.S. Customs Service as the "Customs Air Security Officers Program," or the "Sky Marshal Program" as it was also called. After September of 2001, the program grew from less than 50 armed marshals flying solely on international US carrier flights to the thousands Marshals that serve as the primary law enforcement entity within TSA today.

The Federal Air Marshals have an ever-expanding role in homeland security and work closely with other law enforcement agencies to accomplish their mission. Currently, air marshals staff several positions at different organizations such as the National Counterterrorism Center, the National Targeting Center, and the FBI's Joint Terrorism Task Forces. In addition, they are also distributed among other law enforcement and homeland security liaison assignments during times of heightened alert or special national events.

Due to the nature of their assignment, Federal Air Marshals operate in almost complete independence, without any chance of calling in additional support if needed. The close quarters of the airplane cabin, where any mistake could easily cost an innocent passenger's health or life, demand a standard of firearms accuracy that exceeds that seen in almost all other law enforcement services. They must remain undercover given the importance of surprise and to prevent intending terrorists from knowing whether or not a Federal Air Marshal is on a particular flight.

National Explosives Detection Canine Team

The TSA National Explosives Detection Canine Team Program is tasked with preparing dogs and their handlers to quickly locate and identify dangerous materials that may present a threat to transportation systems. The threat of a cargo- or luggage-based explosive has mandated the need for increased security measures on both cargo and passenger airplanes, but these measures have come at the cost of shipping speed and efficiency. However, trained explosives detection dogs are able to quickly rule out the presence of dangerous materials in unattended packages, structures, or vehicles, allowing the free and efficient flow of commerce.

The TSA Explosives Detection Canine Handler Course is held at Lackland Air Force Base in San Antonio, Texas. Law enforcement officers from throughout the United States travel to this location for training, and are paired with a dog from the TSA "Puppy Program" at that time. Dogs learn how to locate and identify a wide variety of dangerous materials inclusive of search techniques for aircraft, baggage, vehicles, and transportation structures.

Crew Member Self-Defense Training Program

The Federal Air Marshal Service manages a program to reduce terrorism risk in airplanes called Crew Member Self-Defense Training (CMSDT). This no-cost training is available to all U.S. carrier crew members and takes just one day to complete. Topics include hand-to-hand combat, self-defense techniques, and other skills including unruly passenger or potential terrorist detention. CMSDT is delivered in two parts, including self-paced instruction followed by hands-on training.

Armed Security Officer Program

The Armed Security Officer Program is a specialized program created under TSA in partnership with the Department of Defense that focuses on Ronald Reagan Washington National Airport (DCA) in Arlington, Virginia. Because of this airport's proximity to the nation's capital and many key U.S. landmarks, there are a number of special security considerations — the greatest of which is the difficulty associated with thwarting another 9/11-like attack. The DCA Access Standard Security Program (DASSP), as it is also called, allows a total of 48 general aviation flights per day to leave from or fly to designated gateway airports with an Armed Security Officer (ASO) onboard.

Federal Flight Deck Officers Program

The Federal Flight Deck Officers Program further strengthens commercial flights from crime or terrorism by increasing the likelihood that certain cockpit-based flight crew members are able to withstand an attack. Under this program, eligible flight crew members are authorized to use firearms to defend against an act of criminal violence or air piracy attempting to gain control of an aircraft. A flight crew member may be a pilot, flight engineer, or navigator assigned to the flight. This program has since been expanded to include cargo pilots and certain other flight crew members. Each participating crew member is trained by the Federal Air Marshal Service on the use of firearms, use of force, legal issues, defensive tactics, the psychology of survival, and program standard operating procedures.

Law Enforcement Officers Flying Armed Program

Per Code of Federal Regulation (CFR) 1544.219 (Carriage of Accessible Weapons), certain law enforcement officers are able to declare their firearms to the airline and bring them onto the flight to augment security. Attendees in the program are given a structured lesson plan that includes protocols in the handling of prohibited items, prisoner transport, and dealing with an act of criminal violence aboard an aircraft.

TSA Security Programs

TSA is also charged with ensuring the secure operation of various transportation networks. The following are examples of these programs:

Air Cargo Security

Air cargo has remained a major security concern since it was discovered that terrorists considered, and even attempted without success, destroying cargo planes over populated areas (Associated Press, 2010). To assess such issues, the TSA Air Cargo Security Program operates two distinct functions, namely:

- The Transportation Sector Network Management (TSNM) Air Cargo Division
- Office of Security Operations (OSO)

The TSA Air Cargo Division is responsible for coordinating the different actions required to bring about a secure air cargo industry, which includes agencies and partners both within and outside of DHS. This division considers a number of threats and systems, both domestically and internationally, and develops corresponding air cargo regulations, technological solutions, and policies. The challenge is in maintaining constant vigilance while ensuring that commerce is able to continue unimpeded.

This division helped Congress to formulate legal authorities that relate to air cargo, thereby increasing to almost 100% the amount of cargo currently screened.

TSA employs 620 Cargo Transportation Security Inspectors (TSIs) through the office of security operations, who are exclusively dedicated to the oversight of air cargo. TSA also maintains 460 canine teams, of which 120 are specifically assigned to the screening of air cargo at the nation's highest cargo volume airports. This presence has significantly increased the amount of cargo screening TSA is able to conduct.

Flight School Security Awareness Training Program

Federal law requires flight schools to ensure that their employees who have direct contact with students (including flight instructors, ground instructors, chief instructors, and administrative personnel) receive both initial and recurrent security awareness training. Flight schools may choose either to use TSA's security awareness training program or to develop their own program. If a flight school chooses to develop its own program, the program must adhere to standards in the rule.

I-STEP Program

The TSA Intermodal Security Training and Exercise Program (I-STEP) provides exercise, training, and security planning tools and services to the transportation community. The program serves the port and intermodal, aviation, mass transit, freight rail, highway and motor carrier, and pipeline industries. The program coordinates public and private sector partners for exercise, training, information sharing, and to address transportation security issues focused on protecting travelers, commerce, and infrastructure. TSA is also introducing an online transportation security portal called the Exercise Information System (EXIS) that guides users through a step-by-step exercise planning process, provides exercise planning and evaluation tools, and helps to ensure that lessons learned are shared.

TSA Security Screening

Over 600 million people fly each year and carry with them a number of bags and other items that number in the billions. TSA inspectors check each passenger and each item they will carry onto a commercial

FIGURE 7–3 New Orleans, Louisiana, August 30, 2008 — TSA officials check evacuees and baggage with security scanners at the airport during Hurricane Gustav. (Photo by Jacinta Quesada/FEMA News Photo)

aircraft. Screeners work at over 700 security checkpoints and nearly 7,000 baggage screening areas throughout the United States (Figure 7–3).

Passenger Screening

TSA received a legal mandate in 2001, soon after the 9/11 terrorist attacks, to screen air travelers. This role was formerly conducted by private security guards employed by each airport. In what is one of the largest civilian government recruitment campaigns in history, TSA built a screener workforce numbering in the tens of thousands in just a few months. Today, TSA manages 43,000 Transportation Security Officers stationed at commercial airports nationwide, who in conjunction with over 1,000 credentialed security inspectors, screen over 2 million passengers each day. TSA Transportation Security Officers also lead and support security operations in other transportation systems, including mass transit and maritime vessels, although these roles cannot be compared in scope to the role of TSA in the airline industry.

TSA continually works to enhance the effectiveness of screening efforts, including the application of new technologies (e.g., 'backscatter devices') and new methods (e.g., directly engaging passengers to profile suspicious behavior). In some instances, the public and civil liberties groups have protested these actions.

Baggage Screening

TSA maintains a suite of sophisticated technology and equipment that has been developed in recent years to ensure that luggage and other cargo passengers take onto planes are free from terrorist and other potential hazards (such as flammable liquids, aerosols, and radio equipment that may interfere with the flight). TSA Transportation Security Officers electronically screen millions of bags for explosives and other dangerous items each day at over 7,000 baggage screening locations and at over 450 airports nationwide.

Covert Testing

Covert testing is a process by which trained security officials test the effectiveness of screening systems by attempting to successfully board airplanes (or to check baggage on airplanes) while carrying (or packing) banned substances and devices. This can and does typically involve the use of actual explosives and/or weapons. The purpose of covert testing is to ensure that there are no omissions or unknown loopholes in security systems, and to ensure that employees are maintaining high-security standards at all times. Testers try to think like a terrorist or a criminal, and devise new ways in which to fool current screening systems. Whenever they are successful in moving banned substances and devices past security checkpoints, new processes and procedures are developed to prevent such breaches in the future. The details of covert testing are typically kept secret given the need to maintain an element of surprise for screeners.

Trucking Security

Security within the nation's commercial trucking industry is an important component of homeland security given that a significant portion of the nation's hazardous materials (HAZMATs) are transported by these trucks on public highways and roads. Incidents where hazardous materials are spilled or released as a result of commercial truck accidents are fairly common. Moreover, the threat always exists that a terrorist will use a truck carrying some dangerous chemical or other material to cause significant human, property, and environmental damages. Releases involving the volumes or weights of materials contained in these vehicles can have catastrophic effects.

A serious HAZMAT incident is defined by DOT's Research and Special Programs Administration (RSPA) as:

- An incident that involves a fatality or major injury caused by the release of a hazardous material
- The evacuation of 25 or more persons as a result of release of a hazardous material or exposure to fire
- A release or exposure to fire that results in the closure of a major transportation artery
- The alteration of an aircraft flight plan or operation
- The release of radioactive materials from Type B packaging
- The release of over 11.9 gallons or 88.2 pounds of a severe marine pollutant
- The release of a bulk quantity (over 119 gallons or 882 pounds) of a hazardous material

The Office of Hazardous Materials Safety of DOT/RSPA is responsible for coordinating a national safety program for the transportation of hazardous materials by air, rail, highway, and water in the United States. The Code of Federal Regulations (CFR) 49 Part 107 documents the steps being taken to enhance hazardous material transportation security. Subchapter C, Part 107, specifically discusses regulations for HAZMAT transportation on U.S. highways. The subparts of the document include information about regulations for loading and unloading of HAZMAT transportation vehicles, segregation and separation of HAZMAT vehicles and shipments in transit, accidents, and regulations applying to hazardous material on motor vehicles carrying passengers for hire. To supplement safety efforts, Screening Coordination Office performs background checks of drivers of trucks transporting hazardous materials.

TSA supported trucking security through grants administered under the Trucking Security Program (TSP) from 2005 until 2009. However, in 2010, this program was eliminated.

Ports and Shipping Security

DHS considers the securing of goods imported and exported via maritime transport to be a critical task. Given the significance of containerization and maritime commerce on the U.S. economy, it is clear that a successful terrorist attack on a major U.S. port could result in not only significant loss of life and tremendous physical damage, but also serious disruption to the economy of the United States and its trade partners. The SAFE Port Act of October 2006 tasked DHS with the responsibility of assuring maritime transport security and protecting the nation's ports. This is accomplished through risk mitigation, vulnerability analysis, and the establishment of preventive measures in those facilities. The SAFE Port Act also tasked DHS with the creation of a resumption plan to minimize the disruption to economic activity in the case of a major terrorist attack on these seaports.

The USCG is the lead federal agency for maritime homeland security efforts, and is integral to DHS's port and shipping security efforts. The USCG even has its own maritime homeland security strategy wherein duties, responsibilities, and strategic missions are clearly defined. The USCG states its homeland security mission to be the protection of the U.S. maritime domain and the U.S. marine transportation system, the denial of their use and exploitation by terrorists as a means for attacks on U.S. territory, population, and critical infrastructure, and the preparation for and, in the event of attack, conduct of emergency response operations. In accomplishing its homeland security mission, the strategic goals of the Coast Guard are as follows:

- Increasing maritime domain awareness
- Conducting enhanced maritime security operations
- Closing port security gaps
- Building critical security capabilities
- Leveraging partnerships to mitigate security risks
- Ensuring readiness for homeland defense operations

The maritime and port security role of TSA has been to provide grants to support port security and related issues. In 2011, over $235 million was available to 52 port areas considered of highest risk. From 2002 until 2011, DHS awarded more than $2 billion in grants to many port owners, operators, and service providers as part of the Port Security Grant Program. While the focus of these grants changes from year to year, the 2011 priorities indicate the maturity of this effort. The 2011 priorities include:

- Enhancing Maritime Domain Awareness (MDA)
- Enhancing Improvised Explosive Device (IED) and CBRNE prevention, protection, response, and recovery capabilities
- Port resilience and recovery capabilities
- Training and exercises
- Efforts supporting implementation of the Transportation Worker Identification Credential (TWIC)

Assuring the security of seaports is a unique challenge due to the importance of commerce that passes through them and the relatively complex supply chain operations involved. This complexity is the result of both a multistep process required of each cargo item navigating its way to a recipient and the nature of the various stakeholders involved that include private companies and foreign governments. A careful examination of the cargo transit process reveals that nine of 16 typical security steps involved occur outside the jurisdiction of U.S authorities. However, security assurance through the detection and mitigation of actual threats to containers in transit require all 16 steps be performed. To account for this challenge, DHS maintains a cooperative security-focused relationship with foreign governments and their corresponding port authorities, under which each government allows the other to inspect facilities and carry out specific counterterrorism and other inspection measures, as the materials weave their way through the shipment process. For instance, in many key foreign ports, DHS officials perform daily audits and inspections of containers bound for the United States, and work with their foreign counterparts to ensure that chemicals, biological agents, nuclear materials, and explosives that may be hidden in containers are detected and interdicted before they pose a threat to life and commerce. While partner government agencies are invited to conduct the same level of inspection at U.S. ports for materials bound for their own ports, only a handful actually accept.

In light of these challenges, the risk intervention and port security efforts of DHS may be grouped into three distinct phases, namely:

- Overseas vulnerability reduction efforts
- In-transit vulnerability reduction
- Vulnerability reduction in U.S. waters and on U.S. shores

Bus Transportation Security

Bus transportation safety is an often-neglected link in the nation's transportation infrastructure and represents a substantial homeland security vulnerability. The July 7, 2007, terrorist bombing of a London double-decker bus in a coordinated attack on the bus and rail networks of that city, which killed 13 people and injured many more, highlighted the vulnerability of the bus system. Securing the bus transport system is an extremely challenging task as public ground transportation is much more dynamic and state-changing than other transport types. With multiple stops and frequently changing passengers over short periods of time, securing the bus system becomes a very resource intensive and, in some instances, impractical process. However, there are ways to reduce the vulnerabilities even if the security risks of bus transport cannot be eliminated to the degree as exists in other transportation sectors.

To support the intercity bus transportation sector, DHS established the Intercity Bus Security Grant Program under its Infrastructure Protection Program. This program provides funding to intercity bus companies for the improvement of their transport security measures.

Railway Transportation Security

The railroad system is another highly utilized and valuable component of the U.S. transportation infrastructure that requires protective measures to address the growing threat of terrorist attacks and other hazard-related vulnerabilities. DHS made its most noticeable references to the protection of the railway system in the National Strategy for the Physical Protection of Critical Infrastructure and Key Assets and in the announcement of Operation Liberty Shield. This national strategy document refers to potential vulnerabilities of the rail system and expands upon possible terrorist attack scenarios. In light of this, four priorities for improvement in the railroad security are identified, including:

1. The need to develop improved decision-making criteria regarding the shipment of hazardous materials
2. The need to develop technologies and procedures to screen intermodal containers and passenger baggage

3. The need to improve security of intermodal transportation
4. The need to clearly delineate roles and responsibilities regarding surge requirements

The national physical protection strategy clearly identifies the transportation of HAZMAT within the railroad infrastructure as the greatest vulnerability of the system with regards to terrorism risk. The threat associated with HAZMAT transport vulnerability is followed in order, by nuclear and radiological material, food and livestock, and intermodal containers. In 2003, DHS announced the creation of Operation Liberty Shield, which addressed railway security through the following steps:

1. Improvement of rail bridge security
2. An increase in railroad infrastructure security
3. Enhancements of AMTRAK's security measures (to match what was being performed by private rail transport companies)
4. An increase in railroad hazardous material safety measures, including the monitoring of HAZMAT shipments

The 2004 Rail Security Act further enhanced security by increasing rail security funding from $65 million to over $1.1 billion. This act also required that DHS to conduct a vulnerability assessment of the nation's rail systems, including a review of freight and passenger rail transportation, which involved the identification and evaluation of critical assets and infrastructures; threats to those assets and infrastructures; vulnerabilities that are specific to rail transportation of hazardous materials; and security weaknesses. Based on the assessment, DHS developed prioritized recommendations for improving the security of rail infrastructure and facilities, terminals, tunnels, bridges, and other at-risk areas; deploying weapons detection and surveillance equipment; training employees; and conducting public outreach campaigns. The results of the DHS freight and passenger rail transportation vulnerability assessment are also used to distribute future funding for the Rail Security Grant Program.

The Association of American Railroads coordinated and conducted a comprehensive risk analysis of their own, which covered the entire railway industry. This analysis resulted in over 50 permanent changes were made to procedures and operations, including restricted access to facilities, increased tracking of certain shipments, enhanced employee security training, and cybersecurity improvements. In addition to those measures, it was decided that one rail police officer should sit on the FBI's National Joint Terrorism Task Force, and two rail analysts should sit in the DHS intelligence offices to help evaluate data at the top-secret level. The association created a DOD-certified, full-time operations center, working at the secret level to monitor and evaluate intelligence on potential threats and communicate with railroads through the Railway Alert Network (RAN). A Surface Transportation Information Sharing and Analysis Center (ST-ISAC) — operating at the top secret level — was also created to collect, analyze, and disseminate information on physical and cybersecurity threats (Association of American Railroads, 2004).

As rail security grew in stature following the 9/11 attacks, TSA provided the top 10 mass transit and passenger rail agencies with TSA-certified explosives detection canine teams to aid in the identification of explosives materials within the mass transit/rail transportation system. The pilot inspection program was named the Transit and Rail Inspection Pilot (TRIP), which is a first-time rail security technology study conducted by DHS in cooperation with several other entities. TRIP was conducted in three phases. TRIP Phase I occurred at the New Carrollton, Maryland, rail station and evaluated the use of technologies for screening rail passengers and their baggage prior to boarding a train. TRIP Phase II occurred at Union Station in Washington, D.C., and tested the use of screening equipment for checked baggage and cargo prior to their loading onto an Amtrak passenger train, as well as screening of unclaimed baggage and temporarily stored items inside Union Station. TRIP Phase III occurred onboard a Shoreline East commuter rail car. The goal of Phase III was to evaluate the use of existing technologies installed on a rail car to screen passengers and their baggage for explosives, while the rail car is in transit. By 2007, DHS increased its deployment and coverage of explosives detection and canine teams to 13 mass transit systems and a total of 53 canine teams. In addition to the TRIP program, TSA hired and deployed 100 surface transportation (rail) inspectors to enhance the level of national transportation security by leveraging private and public partnerships through a consistent national program of compliance reviews, audits, and enforcement actions pertaining to required standards and directives.

The DHS FY 2011 Freight Rail Security Program was appropriated with total funds of $10 million. The funding priorities for the program were as follows:

1. *GPS tracking*: Owners and offerors of railroad cars containing inhalation/toxic inhalation hazardous (TIH) materials
2. *Infrastructure hardening on rail bridges*
3. *Vulnerability assessments and security plans*
4. *Security training and exercises for railroad frontline employees*

Intermodal Security

Since its creation in 2005, TSA has been steadily expanding the presence of its Visible Intermodal Prevention and Response (VIPR) program. VIPR teams are comprised of officers from several different agencies and backgrounds operating in conjunction, including Federal Air Marshals, explosive-detection canine teams, Aviation Security Inspectors, and Transportation Security Officers, among others. These teams conduct random, announced, high-visibility surges into a transit agency, in addition to enhancing agency resources during special events. What is notable about the VIPR operations is that they often target surface modes of transportation that might not otherwise see such high levels of passenger screening. For instance, VIPR deployments have included the Massachusetts Bay Transportation Authority (MBTA) system in Boston, Amtrak facilities in Boston, upstate New York, Philadelphia and Washington DC, and the Niagara Frontier Transportation Authority.

In 2010, the number of VIPR operations on surface transportation modes alone numbered 3,895 (CNN, 2012; TSA, n/d).

Conclusion

Transportation safety and security are key concepts in the scope of homeland security given the high valuation of these systems to terrorists, the importance of the systems to freedom of movement and the U.S. economy, and because of the high vulnerability these systems have with regard to natural hazards (out of their sheer scope and size). The complexity of each of these systems and their related infrastructure, and the interconnectedness of each of these systems upon which we depend each day, increases our overall vulnerability and increases the difficulty of mitigating the risks we face. In dealing with those distinct vulnerabilities, homeland security agencies at all government levels, and security agencies within the transit authorities and in the private sector, must coordinate on a level that surpasses most other areas of security. The proportional budget appropriation dedicated to transportation security is indicative of these challenges and the growing risk we face as infrastructure ages, as populations move and expand, and as climate change brings about more frequent and devastating events.

Key Terms

Hazardous Material (HAZMAT): Materials, substances, or chemicals that are deemed to have adverse effects on human health and the environment. Typical examples of HAZMAT include but are not limited to biological, chemical, and radiological agents and materials. HAZMAT incidents may be intentional (terrorism) or unintentional (man-made/technological). Oil spills, poisonous gas releases, nuclear waste incidents, and dirty bombs are examples of HAZMAT-related incidents.

Smart Box: Designed to be "tamper evident," the Smart Box couples an internationally approved mechanical seal affixed to an alternate location on the container door with an electronic container security device designed to deter and detect tampering of the container door.

Transportation Workers Identity Card (TWIC): TWICs are tamper-resistant biometric credentials that will be issued to workers who require unescorted access to secure areas of ports, vessels, outer-continental-shelf facilities, and all credentialed merchant mariners.

Review Questions

What are the different transportation modes in the United States? How does the U.S. government protect each? Discuss what types of criteria should be used for prioritizing budgets for protecting different transportation modes.

References

Association of American Railroads. 2004. Freight raill security briefing. http://www.aar.org/Rail_Safety/Security.pdf.

Associated Press. 2010. US knew for years that cargo planes were terror targets. (November 9). http://www.foxnews.com/us/2010/11/09/knew-cargo-planes-vulnerable-years/.

Congressional Research Service. 2004a. Border security and unmanned aerial vehicles. http://www.fas.org/irp/crs/RS21698.pdf/.

Congressional Research Service. 2006. Border security: barriers along the U.S. international border. http://fas.org/sgp/crs/homesec/RL33659.pdf.

Reed, D. 2006. US airports, by the numbers. USA Today (September 27). http://www.usatoday.com/travel/flights/2006-09-26-airport-numbers_x.htm.

Transportation Security Administration. n/d. Building Security Force Multipliers. TSA FY 2004 budget briefing. (June 2005). http://www.tsa.gov/what_we_do/tsnm/mass_transit/force_multipliers.shtm.

8

Cybersecurity and Critical Infrastructure Protection

What You Will Learn

- The meaning of the terms *cybersecurity* and *critical infrastructure*
- The roles of various federal government agencies in maintaining cybersecurity and protecting critical infrastructure
- Local and state government cybersecurity responsibilities
- Private sector cybersecurity and critical infrastructure protection responsibilities
- What programs exist to help entities respond to cybersecurity and critical infrastructure issues
- Recent ideas surrounding the possibility of cyber war

Introduction

Cybersecurity is defined by *Webster's Dictionary* as "measures taken to protect a computer or computer system (as on the Internet) against unauthorized access or attack." *Cyberterrorism* is the newest of all terrorist attack methods, and involves the use or destruction of computing or information technology resources aimed at harming, coercing, or intimidating others in order to achieve a greater political or ideological goal (thus differentiating cyberterrorism from cybercrime, which seeks only personal gain or notoriety).

Cyberterrorism is a major threat, one which continues to increase in severity with each passing year as our nation's and the world's reliance on information technology, computers, and the Internet grows. This reliance has come to exist in virtually all sectors of society, beginning with our economic engines, spanning through almost every component of our critical and other infrastructure systems (including communication systems, power generation facilities, water treatment plants, dams, transportation, and many other areas), and even including the nation's military command and control mechanisms and facilities. The current systems are inherently insecure as demonstrated by the hacking into the systems of the Pentagon and of the defense contractor Lockheed Martin. Adding to the threat are individuals and nations who are adversaries of the U.S. and thus seek to exploit our dependence on cyberspace. While much action has already been taken to protect these systems, whether foreign or domestic, our growing reliance on technology greatly increases the potential consequences were these systems to be compromised, disrupted, or destroyed. Criminals and terrorists are constantly developing new and innovative ways to compromise these ever-more complex systems on which we rely.

Critical infrastructure refers to those assets, systems, and networks that are essential to preserving national security, public safety, economic health, and the social security of our citizens and our communities. Cybersecurity — or protection of the information technology sector — is part of the critical infrastructure matrix. Homeland Security Presidential Directive (HSPD) 7: Critical Infrastructure Identification, Prioritization, and Protection established U.S. policy for enhancing protection of critical infrastructure.

The intent of this chapter is to discuss current policies, programs, and actions that have been undertaken in the areas of cybersecurity and critical infrastructure. Because of the technical nature of these subjects, some materials in this chapter are derived directly from publications of the DHS.

Cybersecurity

Cybersecurity and cyberterrorism have been concerns of the private sector and government agencies, including the military and the FBI, since the 1980s. Following the September 11 terrorist attacks, cybersecurity as a terrorist risk was pushed closer into the limelight and was referred to directly in the National Strategy for Homeland Security as a national concern, and again as a central component of the subsequent National Strategy to Secure Cyberspace. The Comprehensive National Cybersecurity Initiative (CNCI) is an essential part of this strategy as is Presidential Directive 54. Additionally, it was addressed through the executive office by means of the issuance of Homeland Security Presidential Directive (HSPD) 7: Critical Infrastructure Identification, Prioritization, and Protection.

Cybersecurity has a prominent role in the National Security Strategy published by the White House in May 2010, and the Obama Administration has moved aggressively to identify emerging issues and to work with the international community to address cybersecurity.

Excerpts from the White House Cyber Policy Review

Cyberspace touches practically everything and everyone. It provides a platform for innovation and prosperity and the means to improve general welfare around the globe. But with the broad reach of a loose and lightly regulated digital infrastructure, great risks threaten nations, private enterprises, and individual rights. The government has a responsibility to address these strategic vulnerabilities to ensure that the United States and its citizens, together with the larger community of nations, can realize the full potential of the information technology revolution.

The architecture of the nation's digital infrastructure, based largely upon the Internet, is not secure or resilient. Without major advances in the security of these systems or significant change in how they are constructed or operated, it is doubtful that the United States can protect itself from the growing threat of cybercrime and state-sponsored intrusions and operations. Our digital infrastructure has already suffered intrusions that have allowed criminals to steal hundreds of millions of dollars, and nation-states and other entities to steal intellectual property and sensitive military information. Other intrusions threaten to damage portions of our critical infrastructure. These and other risks have the potential to undermine the Nation's confidence in the information systems that underlie our economic and national security interests.

The Federal government is not organized to address this growing problem effectively now or in the future. Responsibilities for cybersecurity are distributed across a wide array of federal departments and agencies, many with overlapping authorities, and none with sufficient decision authority to direct actions that deal with often conflicting issues in a consistent way. Information and communications networks are largely owned and operated by the private sector, both nationally and internationally. Thus, addressing network security issues requires a public-private partnership as well as international cooperation and norms. The United States needs a comprehensive framework to ensure coordinated response and recovery by the government, the private sector, and our allies to a significant incident or threat.

Highlights of the White House Cyber Policy review include:

The Nation is at a crossroads. The globally interconnected digital information and communications infrastructure known as "cyberspace" underpins almost every facet of modern society and provides critical support for the U.S. economy, civil infrastructure, public safety, and national security. This technology has transformed the global economy and connected people in ways never imagined. Yet, cybersecurity risks pose some of the most serious economic and national security challenges of the 21st Century.

The status quo is no longer acceptable. The United States must signal to the world that it is serious about addressing this challenge with strong leadership and vision. This approach requires clarifying the cybersecurity-related roles and responsibilities of federal departments and agencies while providing the policy, legal structures, and necessary coordination to empower them to perform their missions.

The national dialogue on cybersecurity must begin today. The government, working with industry, should explain this challenge and discuss what the Nation can do to solve problems in a way that the American people can appreciate the need for action.

The United States cannot succeed in securing cyberspace if it works in isolation. The Federal government should enhance its partnership with the private sector. The public and private sectors' interests are intertwined with a shared responsibility for ensuring a secure, reliable infrastructure. There are many ways in which the Federal government can work with the private sector, and these alternatives should be explored. The public-private partnership for cybersecurity must evolve to define clearly the nature of the relationship, including the roles and responsibilities of each of the partners.[1,2,3] The Federal government should examine existing public–private partnerships to optimize their capacity to identify priorities and enable efficient execution of concrete actions.[4,5,6] The Nation also needs a strategy for cybersecurity designed to shape the international environment and bring like-minded nations together on a host of issues, such as technical standards and acceptable legal norms regarding territorial jurisdiction, sovereign responsibility, and use of force.

---

[1] Written testimony of Scott Charney (Microsoft) to the House Committee on Homeland Security, Subcommittee on Emerging Threats, Cybersecurity, and Science and Technology, March 10, 2009, at 4.

[2] Cross-Sector Cyber Security Working Group (CSCSWG) Response to 60-day Cyber Review Questions, March 16, 2009, at 2.

[3] Information Technology & Communications Sector Coordinating Councils, March 20, 2009, at 2.

[4] Center for Strategic and International Studies (CSIS) Commission on Cybersecurity for the 44th Presidency, *Securing Cyberspace for the 44th Presidency*, December 2008, at 43.

[5] TechAmerica, Response to 60-Day Cyber Security Review, at 6.

[6] Business Software Alliance, *National Security & Homeland Security Councils Review of National Cyber Security Policy*, March 19, 2009, at Q3.

The Federal government cannot entirely delegate or abrogate its role in securing the Nation from a cyber incident or accident. The Federal government has the responsibility to protect and defend the country, and all levels of government have the responsibility to ensure the safety and wellbeing of citizens. The private sector, however, designs, builds, owns, and operates most of the digital infrastructures that support government and private users alike. The United States needs a comprehensive framework to ensure a coordinated response by the Federal, State, local, and tribal governments, the private sector, and international allies to significant incidents.

Working with the private sector, performance and security objectives must be defined for the next-generation infrastructure. The United States should harness the full benefits of technology to address national economic needs and national security requirements.

The White House must lead the way forward. The Nation's approach to cybersecurity over the past 15 years has failed to keep pace with the threat. We need to demonstrate abroad and at home that the United States takes cybersecurity-related issues, policies, and activities seriously. This requires White House leadership that draws upon the strength, advice, and ideas of the entire Nation.

Table 8–1 Near-Term Action Plan

1. Appoint a cybersecurity policy official responsible for coordinating the Nation's cybersecurity policies and activities; establish a strong NSC directorate, under the direction of the cybersecurity policy official dual-hatted to the NSC and the NEC, to coordinate interagency development of cybersecurity-related strategy and policy.
2. Prepare for the President's approval an updated national strategy to secure the information and communications infrastructure. This strategy should include continued evaluation of CNCI activities and, where appropriate, build on its successes.
3. Designate cybersecurity as one of the President's key management priorities and establish performance metrics.
4. Designate a privacy and civil liberties official to the NSC cybersecurity directorate.
5. Convene appropriate interagency mechanisms to conduct interagency-cleared legal analyses of priority cybersecurity-related issues identified during the policy-development process and formulate coherent unified policy guidance that clarifies roles, responsibilities, and the application of agency authorities for cybersecurity-related activities across the Federal government.
6. Initiate a national public awareness and education campaign to promote cybersecurity.
7. Develop U.S. Government positions for an international cybersecurity policy framework and strengthen our international partnerships to create initiatives that address the full range of activities, policies, and opportunities associated with cybersecurity.
8. Prepare a cybersecurity incident response plan; initiate a dialog to enhance public-private partnerships with an eye toward streamlining, aligning, and providing resources to optimize their contribution and engagement
9. In collaboration with other EOP entities, develop a framework for research and development strategies that focus on game-changing technologies that have the potential to enhance the security, reliability, resilience, and trustworthiness of digital infrastructure; provide the research community access to event data to facilitate developing tools, testing theories, and identifying workable solutions.
10. Build a cybersecurity-based identity management vision and strategy that addresses privacy and civil liberties interests, leveraging privacy-enhancing technologies for the Nation.

Source: www.whitehouse.gov/issues/cybersecurity.

Components of Cybersecuity

Cyberinfrastructure includes electronic information and communication systems, and the information contained in these systems. Computer systems, control systems such as Supervisory Control and Data Acquisition (SCADA) systems, and networks such as the Internet are all part of the cyberinfrastructure.

Information and communications systems are composed of hardware and software that process, store, and communicate data of all types. Processing includes the creation, access, modification, and destruction of information. Storage includes paper, magnetic, electronic, and all other media types. Communications include sharing and distribution of information.

Information technology (IT) critical functions are sets of processes that produce, provide, and maintain products and services. IT critical functions encompass the full set of processes (e.g., R&D, manufacturing, distribution, upgrades, and maintenance) involved in transforming supply inputs into IT products and services.

DHS Cybersecurity Efforts

Through Presidential directives, DHS was tasked with leading and managing the nation's cyberterrorism threat through its risk management division, the Directorate for National Protection and Programs. In the Quadrennial Homeland Security Review published by DHS in February 2010, the fourth stated mission of the Department was Safeguarding and Securing Cyberspace. In this document, they state, "Our vision is a cyberspace that supports a secure and resilient infrastructure, that enables innovation and prosperity, and that protects privacy and other civil liberties by design. It is one in which we can use cyberspace with confidence to advance our economic interests and maintain national security under all conditions. We will achieve this vision by focusing on two goals: (1) helping to create a safe, secure, and resilient cyber environment; and (2) promoting cybersecurity knowledge and innovation. We must enhance public awareness and ensure that the public both recognizes cybersecurity challenges and is empowered to address them. We must create a dynamic cyber workforce across government with sufficient capacity and expertise to manage current and emerging risks. We must invest in the innovative technologies, techniques, and procedures necessary to sustain a safe, secure, and resilient cyber environment. Government must work creatively and collaboratively with the private sector to identify solutions that take into account both public and private interests, and the private sector and academia must be fully empowered to see and solve ever larger parts of the problem set. Finally, because cybersecurity is an exceedingly dynamic field, we must make specific efforts to ensure that the nation is prepared for the cyber threats and challenges of tomorrow, not only of today. To do this, we must promote cybersecurity knowledge and innovation. Innovation in technology, practice, and policy must further protect — not erode — privacy and civil liberties."

National Cyber Incident Response Plan

The President's Cybersecurity Policy Review called for "a comprehensive framework to facilitate coordinated responses by Government, the private sector, and allies to a significant cyber incident." DHS coordinated the interagency, state and local governments, and private sector working group that developed the National Cyber Incident Response Plan.

The plan enables DHS to coordinate the response of multiple federal agencies, state and local governments, international partners, and private industry to incidents at all levels. It is designed to be flexible and adaptable to allow synchronization of response activities across jurisdictional lines. The NCIRP was tested during the Cyber Storm III national exercise, which simulated a large-scale attack on the nation's critical information infrastructure. Seven Cabinet agencies, eleven states, twelve international partners, and sixty private-sector companies participated in the Cyber Storm III exercise.

National Cybersecurity and Communications Integration Center (NCCIC)

The NCCIC is a 24-hour, DHS-led coordinated watch and warning center that will serve as the nation's principal hub for organizing cyberresponse efforts and maintaining the national cyber and communications common operational picture.

The NCCIC combines two of DHS's operational organizations: the U.S. Computer Emergency Readiness Team (US-CERT) and the National Coordinating Center for Telecommunications (NCC), the operational arm of the National Communications System. It integrates the efforts of DHS's National Cybersecurity Center (NCSC), which coordinates operations among the six largest federal cybercenters, the DHS Office of Intelligence and Analysis, and private-sector partners. Additional representatives from federal agencies, the private sector, and state and local governments are also collocated at the NCCIC.

U.S. Computer Emergency Readiness Team

US-CERT is the operational arm of NCSD that provides response support and defense against cyberattacks for the Federal Civilian Executive Branch (.gov) networks. US-CERT also collaborates and shares information with state and local governments, industry, and international partners to address cyberthreats and develop effective security responses. US-CERT is a partnership between DHS and the public and private sectors. The team was established in 2003 to protect the nation's Internet infrastructure. The team is charged with protecting the nation's Internet infrastructure by coordinating defense against and response to cyberattacks. It is responsible for analyzing and reducing cyberthreats and vulnerabilities, disseminating cyberthreat warning information, and coordinating incident response activities. US-CERT interacts with federal agencies, industry, the research community, state and local governments, and others to disseminate reasoned and actionable cybersecurity information to the public. The National Cyber Response Coordination Group (NCRCG), made up of 13 federal agency representatives, acts as the principal federal agency mechanism for cyberincident response. In the event of a nationally significant cyber-related incident, the NCRCG will help to coordinate the federal response, with representatives from US-CERT, law enforcement, and the intelligence community. One of the tools created and used by US-CERT to create public awareness and to disseminate information about known cyberthreats is the Cyber Security Preparedness and the National Cyber Alert System where both technical and nontechnical computer users can stay prepared for these threats by receiving current information by signing up to receive automatic notifications from the system. Another initiative of the National Cybersecurity Division is the "Cyber Cop Portal" which is an Internet portal where more than 5,300 cybercrime investigators worldwide can share information and collaborate.

What Is DHS Doing about Phishing?

US-CERT is collecting phishing email messages and web site locations so that we can help people avoid becoming victims of phishing scams.

You can report phishing to us by sending email to phishing-report@us-cert.gov.

What is Phishing?

Phishing is an attempt by an individual or group to solicit personal information from unsuspecting users by employing social engineering techniques. Phishing emails are crafted to appear as if they have been sent from a legitimate organization or known individual. These emails often attempt to entice users to click on a link that will take the user to a fraudulent web site that appears legitimate. The user then may be asked to provide personal information such as account usernames and passwords that can further expose them to future compromises. Additionally, these fraudulent web sites may contain malicious code.

Source: http://www.uscert.gov/cas/alldocs.html.

Four products in the National Cyber Alert System offer a variety of information for users with varied technical expertise. Those with more technical interest can read the Technical Cyber Security Alerts or the Cyber Security Bulletins. Users looking for more general-interest pieces can read the Cyber Security Alerts and Cyber Security Tips. All past issues of the following products are available:

- Technical Cyber Security Alerts provide timely information about current security issues, vulnerabilities, and exploits.
- Cyber Security Bulletins provide weekly summaries of new vulnerabilities. Patch information is provided when available.
- Cyber Security Alerts provide timely information about current security issues, vulnerabilities, and exploits. They outline the steps and actions that non-technical home and corporate computer users can take to protect themselves from attack.
- Cyber Security Tips provide advice about common security issues for the general public.

The EINSTEIN Program

The EINSTEIN system is designed to provide the U.S. Government with an early warning system for intrusions to Federal Executive Branch civilian networks, near real-time identification of malicious activity, and automated disruption of that malicious activity.

EINSTEIN 1: The first iteration of the EINSTEIN system was developed in 2003. It automates the collection and analysis of computer network security information from participating agency and government networks to help analysts identify and combat malicious cyberactivity that may threaten government network systems, data protection, and communications infrastructure.

EINSTEIN 2: The second phase of EINSTEIN was developed in 2008. It incorporated intrusion detection capabilities into the original EINSTEIN system. DHS is currently deploying EINSTEIN 2 at federal Executive Branch civilian agencies and Networx Managed Trusted Internet Protocol Services (MTIPS) providers, private Internet service providers that serve federal agencies to assist them with protecting their computers, networks, and information.

EINSTEIN 2 has now been deployed at 15 of 19 departments and agencies. In addition, the four MTIPS providers currently service to seven federal agencies.

In 2010, EINSTEIN 2 sensors registered 5.4 million hits, an average of over 450,000 hits per month. A hit is an alert triggered by a predetermined intrusion detection signature that corresponds to a known threat.

EINSTEIN 3: DHS is developing the third phase of the EINSTEIN system — an intrusion prevention capability which will provide DHS with the ability to automatically detect and disrupt malicious activity before harm is done to critical networks and systems.

National Strategy for Trusted Identities in Cyberspace

In July 2010, the White House published a draft National Strategy for Trusted Identities in Cyberspace — which seeks to secure the identities of individuals, organizations, services, and devices during online transactions, as well as the infrastructure supporting the transaction — fulfilling one of the near-term action items of the President's *Cyberspace Policy Review*. The Strategy supports the protection of privacy and civil liberties by enabling only the minimum necessary amount of personal information to be transferred in any particular transaction.

In March 2010, Secretary Napolitano launched the National Cybersecurity Awareness Challenge, which called on members of the public and private sector companies to develop creative and innovative ways to enhance awareness of the importance of cybersecurity and safeguard America's computer systems and networks from attacks.

In July 2010, seven of the more than 80 proposals were selected and recognized at a White House ceremony. The winning proposals helped inform the National Cybersecurity Awareness Campaign, *Stop. Think. Connect.*

Private Cyber Infrastructure Protection

Private industry owns and operates the vast majority of the nation's critical infrastructure and cybernetworks. Consequently, the private sector plays an important role in cybersecurity. DHS is engaged in several pilot programs to promote public–private-sector collaboration. In 2010, DHS launched two critical initiatives with the private sector. Along with DoD and the Financial Services Information Sharing and Analysis Center, DHS launched a pilot program designed to help protect key critical networks and infrastructure within the financial services sector by sharing actionable, sensitive information. In June 2010, DHS implemented the Cybersecurity Partners Local Access Plan, which allows security-cleared owners and operators of CIKR, as well as state technology officials and law enforcement officials, to access secret-level cybersecurity information and video teleconference calls via local fusion centers.

■ ■ Critical Thinking ■

Based on what you have read, do you think that DHS is the appropriate federal entity to lead the government's cybersecurity programs? If so, why; if not, what other Agency would be more appropriate and what is your reasoning?

Based on your knowledge, what do you think are the biggest cybersecurity threats to the United States and why?

Department of Defense

In July 2011, the DOD announced their first comprehensive strategy on cybersecurity entitled Department of Defense's Strategy for Operating in Cyberspace. The strategy covers both cybersecurity and cyberwar. The blueprint was produced by the U.S. Cyber Command, a new military unit with the mission to protect military networks from attack. Much of the recent DOD activity can be traced to an incident in which 24,000 files documenting a new weapons system being developed for DOD were stolen from the federal contractor doing the work. DOD officials believed it was the work of a foreign intelligence organization.

The strategy has five components: (1) cyberspace as an operational domain, (2) new defenses and operating concepts for DOD networks, (3) partnerships with DHS and the private sector to support critical infrastructure, (4) international cooperation, and (5) research and development.

There is some controversy over the decision to identify cyberspace as a military domain, the same as land or sea. In March 2011, the White House prepared draft guidance to assist agencies in the careful application of the use of the word, indicating its preference for the use of the term *cyberspace* (Makashima).

DOD has already developed systems that are used to deter an adversary from using computer hacking or other computer means to attack the United States. They have developed viruses that can be used to corrupt critical networks outside of the United States.

Other Federal Agencies

Each federal agency is responsible for protecting their own networks and vary in the level of their cybersecurity efforts. For example, the Department of Commerce is responsible for establishing standards and issuing guidelines through the National Institute of Standards and Technology, and has issued some preliminary guidelines. The Department of State handles international efforts in coordination with DOD. The National Science Foundation supports research and development in concert with the National Telecommunications and Information Administration.

The Department of Education has been particularly active in this area. In partnership with DHS, they have established the National Initiative for Cybersecurity Education (NICE) from the CNCI. In May 2010, the NICE extended the scope of cybereducation beyond the federal workplace to include the public and students in kindergarten through post-graduate school. The goal of NICE is to establish an operational, sustainable, and continually improving cybersecurity education program for the nation to promote the use of sound cyberpractices that will enhance the nation's security. NICE has since grown to include over 20 federal departments and agencies, to ensure coordination, cooperation, focus, public engagement, technology transfer, and sustainability.

The Environmental Protection Agency (EPA) has developed several cybersecurity road maps including for the water sector, green building, and the emerging technology of smart grids.

■ ■ Critical Thinking ■

Based on what you have read, does the proliferation of government committees and initiatives in cybersecurity make sense and do you think there are other actions that they should consider taking? What are your thoughts on DOD making cyberspace a new area, or domain, requiring military vigilance?

Response to the 9/11 Commission Recommendations

On July 21, 2011, DHS Secretary Napolitano announced the release of a report highlighting DHS progress in fulfilling the 9/11 Commission Recommendations. Several of these recommendations applied to cybersecurity and critical infrastructure. What follows are pertinent excerpts of the DHS progress report, entitled Department of Homeland Security: Progress in Implementing 9/11 Commission Recommendations.

Recommendation: Assess Critical Infrastructure and Readiness

Over the past ten years, DHS has made significant strides in enhancing the security of the nation's critical physical infrastructure as well as its cyber infrastructure and networks. Key tools include the National Cybersecurity Protection System (NCPS) — of which the EINSTEIN cyber intrusion detection system is a key component — and the NCCIC, a DHS-led coordinated watch and warning center that serves as the nation's principal hub for organizing cyber response efforts. In addition, DHS and DOD signed a landmark memorandum of agreement to align and enhance America's capabilities to protect against threats to critical civilian and military computer systems and networks. Further, DHS led the effort to develop the National Infrastructure Protection Plan (NIPP).

In Safeguarding Cyber Infrastructure and Networks

In October 2010, Secretary Napolitano and Secretary of Defense Robert Gates signed a Memorandum of Agreement to align and enhance America's capabilities to protect against threats to critical civilian and military computer systems and networks. The Agreement embeds DOD cyber analysts within DHS and sends DHS privacy, civil liberties, and legal personnel to DOD's National Security Agency to strengthen the nation's cybersecurity posture and ensure the protection of fundamental rights.

In November 2010, the Multi-State Information Sharing and Analysis Center, funded in part by DHS, opened the Cyber Security Operations Center, a 24-hour watch and warning facility, to enhance situational awareness at the state and local level and allow the federal government to quickly and efficiently provide critical cyber risk, vulnerability, and mitigation data to state and local governments.

Protecting Critical Infrastructure and Its Connections to Cyberspace

DHS developed the first-ever National Cyber Incident Response Plan in September 2010 to coordinate the response of multiple federal agencies, state and local governments, and hundreds of private firms, to incidents at all levels. DHS tested this plan during the Cyber Storm III national exercise. In October 2009, DHS opened the new NCCIC — a 24-hour, DHS-led coordinated watch and warning center.

Protecting the dot-gov World

In close partnership with other federal agencies and the private sector, DHS utilizes NCPS, of which the EINSTEIN intrusion detection system is a key component, to protect the dot-gov domains. Once fully deployed, EINSTEIN 2 and EINSTEIN 3 will provide cyber protection capabilities to more than 110 federal civilian executive branch departments and agencies.

Intelligence and Cybersecurity

By embedding intelligence analysts at US-CERT, the ICS-CERT, and the NCCIC, I&A is able to analyze intrusion detection information gathered from DHS sensors like EINSTEIN as well as investigative information from DHS components to provide a national intelligence perspective to cyber incidents.

Recent Initiatives

In an address in 2009, President Obama announced that cybersecurity was one of the top priorities of his administration. To support this, he later released the *Cyberspace Policy Review* which built upon the CNCI. He appointed a cybersecurity advisor at the White House and created a cybersecurity directorate within the National Security Council (NSS), charging them to update the national strategy initially promulgated under Presidential Directive 54. The administration proposed comprehensive cybersecurity legislation in May 2011. Among the highlights in this legislation include consolidating the 47 different state laws that require businesses to report breaches of their cybersystems to consumers — DHS will work with industry to prioritize the most important cyberthreats and vulnerabilities — provide clear authority to allow the federal government to provide assistance to state and local governments when there has been a cyberbreach, provides immunity to the industry, state and local governments when sharing cybersecurity information with DHS, and provides for a new framework to protect individuals' privacy and civil liberties.

Critical Infrastructure Protection

The DHS defines *critical infrastructure* as " the assets, systems and networks, whether physical or virtual, so vital to the United States that their incapacitation or destruction would have a debilitating effect on security, national economic security, public health or safety, or any combination thereof."

Before the creation of DHS, the Clinton Administration was concerned about issues of the U.S. critical infrastructure. This concern became heightened after bombings of U.S. embassies and facilities. In 1998, President Clinton issued Presidential Decision Directive/NSC-63, May 22, 1998.

The comprehensive nature of the Clinton Directive formed the backbone of federal government actions to preserve and protect the nation's critical infrastructure. Many of the ideas and programs established by PDD-63 were carried over into the Bush Administration, although it took the events of September 11 to add a new criticality to the U.S. efforts in critical infrastructure protection. The full text is available online at http://www.fas.org/irp/offdocs/pdd-63.

After September 11, two major documents provided significant authority for the federal government to develop critical infrastructure protections, the Homeland Security Act of 2002 and the Homeland Security Presidential Directive 7 (HSPD-7).

The Homeland Security Act of 2002 provides primary authorization for DHS, assigning DHS the responsibility for developing a comprehensive plan to secure critical infrastructure. It also required that DHS recommend measures to protect the key resources and critical infrastructure of the United States.

HSPD 7 establishes a framework for DHS and partners to identify, prioritize, and protect the critical infrastructure in their communities from terrorist attacks. The directive identified 17 critical infrastructure sectors and, for each sector, designates a federal sector-specific agency (SSA) to lead protection and resilience-building programs and activities. The directive requires DHS to identify gaps in existing sectors and establish new sectors to fill the gaps. For example, in March 2008, DHS established the Critical Manufacturing Sector as the 18th sector.

In 2009, DHS published a revised NIPP, which was originally published by DHS in 2006. The NIPP provides the structure for coordination and integration of the wide range of efforts to enhance protection and resiliency of the nation's CIKR into a single national program. The goal of the NIPP is to "build a safer, more secure and resilient America by preventing, deterring, neutralizing, or mitigating the effects of deliberate efforts by terrorists to destroy, incapacitate or exploit elements of our nation's CIKR and to strengthen national preparedness, timely response, and rapid recovery of CIKR in the event of an attack, natural disaster or other emergency."

In the context of the NIPP, this includes actions to deter the threat, mitigate vulnerabilities, or minimize the consequences associated with a terrorist attack or other man-made or natural disaster. Protection can include a wide range of activities such as improving security protocols, hardening facilities, building resiliency and redundancy, incorporating hazard resistance into facility design, initiating active or passive countermeasures, installing security systems, leveraging "self-healing" technologies, promoting workforce surety programs, implementing cybersecurity measures, training, and exercises, and business continuity planning, among others. Protection includes actions to mitigate the overall risk to CIKR assets, systems, networks, functions, or their interconnecting links resulting from exposure, injury, destruction, incapacitation, or exploitation.

The basic framework of the NIPP focuses on managing risk, organizing and partnerships, information sharing and program sustainability. To support managing risks, the plan defines a process that includes steps to identify, assess, and prioritize risks; implement protective measures; and measure the effectiveness of those measures.

The NIPP has an extensive network for coordination among the levels of government and the private sector and among the sectors. Elements of this network include a national-level coordination council, sector partnership councils, regional coordination councils, and international protocols, all of which emphasize the information-sharing aspects of the CIKR. The NIPP supports the development of sector-specific plans (SSPs), which detail the application of the NIPP framework to the unique characteristics of their sector. The NIPP promotes a series of activities to support program sustainability, including building national awareness through education, training, and exercises, supporting research and development, building and protecting databases and systems such as the National CIKR Protection Data System, and organizational exercises.

There are very fundamental reasons for the federal government to make a substantial and coordinated effort to protect this nation's infrastructure. Attacks on critical infrastructure could significantly disrupt the functioning of both government and industry and provide cascading effects beyond the original target, for example, disruption of the Alaska pipeline.

The current critical infrastructure sectors number 18 and each has a single designated SSA or some have multiple agencies working in partnership. The sectors are listed below with the designated SSA(s):

- *Agriculture and Food*: Department of Agriculture (DOA) and Health and Human Services (HHS)
- *Banking and Finance*: Department of the Treasury (Treasury)
- *Chemical*: DHS
- *Commercial Facilities*: DHS
- *Communications*: DHS

- *Critical Manufacturing*: DHS
- *Dams*: DHS
- *Defense Industrial Base*: DOD
- *Emergency Services*: DHS
- *Energy*: Department of Energy (DOE)
- *Government Facilities*: DHS
- *Health Care and Public Health*: HHS
- *Information Technology*: DHS
- *National Monuments and Icons*: Department of the Interior (DOI)
- *Nuclear Reactors, Materials, and Waste*: DHS
- *Postal and Shipping*: DHS
- *Transportation Systems*: DHS
- *Water*: Environmental Protection Agency (EPA)

▓ ▓ Critical Thinking ▓

Under the Clinton PDD-63, sector responsibility was spread among the federal agencies but now the DHS has assumed lead responsibilities for many of the CIKR sectors. Do you have an opinion on which approach is better?
Under the DHS approach, do you think any of these could be better done by another agency? For example, assigning Nuclear Reactors, Materials, and Waste to the Nuclear Regulatory Commission.

State and Local Governments

The NIPP established a partnership framework that allows federal, state, local, tribal, and territorial governments to work with each other and private sector partners.

Under the NIPP, state, local, tribal, and territorial governments are responsible for implementing the homeland security mission, protecting public safety and welfare, and ensuring the provision of essential services to communities and industries within their jurisdictions. They play a very important and direct role in enabling CIKR protection and resilience, including CIKR under their control, as well as that owned and operated by other NIPP partners within their jurisdictions. The efforts of these public entities are critical to the effective implementation of the NIPP, SSPs, and various jurisdictionally focused protection and resiliency plans. They are equally critical in terms of enabling time-sensitive, post-event CIKR response and recovery activities.

State (and territorial, where applicable) governments are responsible for establishing partnerships, facilitating coordinated information sharing, and enabling planning and preparedness for CIKR protection within their jurisdictions. They serve as crucial coordination hubs, bringing together prevention, protection, response, and recovery authorities; capabilities; and resources among local jurisdictions, across sectors, and between regional entities. States and territories also act as conduits for requests for federal assistance when the threat or incident situation exceeds the capabilities of public and private sector partners at lower jurisdictional levels. States receive CIKR information from the federal government to support national and state CIKR protection and resiliency programs.

Among the responsibilities for protection of the CIKR that exist at the state and territorial levels include:

- Acting as a focal point for and promoting the coordination of protective and emergency response activities, preparedness programs, and resource support among local jurisdictions, regional organizations, and private sector partners;
- Developing a consistent approach to CIKR identification, risk determination, mitigation planning, and prioritized security investment, and exercising preparedness among all relevant stakeholders within their jurisdictions;
- Identifying, implementing, and monitoring a risk management plan and taking corrective actions, as appropriate;
- Participating in significant national, regional, and local awareness programs to encourage appropriate management and security of cybersystems;
- Facilitating the exchange of security information, including threat assessments and other analyses, attack indications and warnings, and advisories, within and across jurisdictions and sectors therein;
- Participating in the NIPP sector partnership model, including: sector-specific GCCs; the State, Local, Tribal, and Territorial Government Coordinating Council (SLTTGCC); SCCs; and other CIKR governance and planning efforts relevant to the given jurisdiction;
- Ensuring that funding priorities are addressed and that resources are allocated efficiently and effectively to achieve the CIKR protection mission in accordance with relevant plans and strategies;
- Sharing information on CIKR deemed to be critical from national, state, regional, local, tribal, and/or territorial perspectives to enable prioritized protection and restoration of critical public services, facilities, utilities, and functions within the jurisdiction;
- Addressing unique geographical issues, including trans-border concerns, dependencies, and interdependencies among the sectors within the jurisdiction;
- Identifying and implementing plans and processes for increasing protective measures that align to all-hazards warnings; specific threats, as appropriate; and each level of the HSAS;
- Providing response and protection, as appropriate, where there are gaps and where local entities lack the resources needed to address those gaps.

▪ ▪ Critical Thinking ▪

Consider the community you live in and identify the CIKR that exist within that community. Choose one CIKR asset and describe its potential vulnerabilities.

Private Sector

The private sector is especially critical since significant portions of this nation's critical infrastructure is owned or managed by the private sector. The issue of a private company sharing information with the federal government has not been completely resolved. Since the events of September 11, many businesses have increased their threshold investments and undertaken enhancements in security in an effort to meet the demands of the new threat environment. For most enterprises, the level of investment in security reflects implicit risk-versus-consequence trade-offs, which are based on (1) what is known about the risk environment, (2) what is economically justifiable and sustainable in a competitive marketplace or in an environment of limited government resources, (3) potential consequences of disasters, and (4) priorities for the protection of human capital, processes, physical infrastructure, organizational reputation, stakeholder confidence, and vital records that require immediate attention. Given the dynamic nature of the terrorist threat and the severity of the consequences associated with many potential attack scenarios, the private sector naturally looks to the government for better information to help make its crucial security investment decisions. The private sector is continuing to look for better data, analysis, and assessment from DHS to use in the corporate decision-making process.

Similarly, the private sector looks to the government for assistance when the threat at hand exceeds an enterprise's capability to protect itself beyond a reasonable level of additional investment. In this light, the federal government promises to collaborate with the private sector (and state and local governments) to ensure the protection of nationally critical infrastructures and assets; to provide timely warning and ensure the protection of infrastructures and assets that face a specific, imminent threat; and to promote an environment in which the private sector can better carry out its specific protection responsibilities.

Private owners have an economic interest in protecting their investments and ensuring a continuity of operations of their facilities and systems from a variety of threats both internal and external. Private owners and operators are usually best able to assess what risks they face and how to set some priorities among the risks for prevention purposes. For many private sector enterprises, the level of investment in security reflects risk-versus-consequence trade-offs that are based on two factors: (1) what is known about the risk environment, and (2) what is economically justifiable and sustainable in a competitive marketplace or within resource constraints. Within this context, among the many actions the NIPP suggests that the private sector can take, the following are suggested to better protect their CIKR assets:

- Performing comprehensive risk assessments on their specific sector, enterprise, or facility risk landscape;
- Implementing protective actions and programs to reduce identified vulnerabilities appropriate to the level of risk presented;
- Participating in the NIPP sector partnership model (including SCCs and information-sharing mechanisms);
- Developing an awareness of critical dependencies and interdependencies at the sector, enterprise, and facility levels;
- Assisting and supporting federal, state, local, and tribal government CIKR data collection and protection efforts;
- Developing and coordinating CIKR protective and emergency response actions, plans, and programs with appropriate federal, state, and local government authorities;
- Adhering to recognized industry best business practices and standards, including those with a cybersecurity nexus;
- Establishing resilient, robust, and/or redundant operational systems or capabilities associated with critical functions;
- Sharing security-related best practices and entering into operational mutual-aid agreements with other industry partners; and
- Working to identify and reduce barriers to public–private partnerships.

International

The federal government and private sector corporations have a significant number of facilities located outside the United States that may be considered CIKR. The NIPP addresses international CIKR protection, including interdependencies and vulnerabilities based on threats (and associated consequences) that originate outside the country or pass through it. The federal government and the private sector work with foreign governments and international/multinational organizations to enhance the confidentiality, integrity, and availability of cyberinfrastructure and products. High priority is placed on the protection of assets, systems, and networks that operate across or near the borders with Canada and Mexico, or rely on other international aspects to enable critical functionality. These also include any assets that require coordination with and planning and/or sharing resources among neighboring governments at all levels, as well as private sector CIKR owners and operators.

The NIPP recognizes several areas where special considerations exist: first, when CIKR is extensively integrated into an international or global market (e.g., financial services, agriculture, energy, transportation, telecommunications, or information technology) or when a sector relies on inputs that are not within the control of U.S. entities; and second, when government facilities and functions are directly affected by foreign-owned and -operated commercial facilities.

The federal government, working in close coordination and cooperation with the private sector, launched the Critical Foreign Dependencies Initiative in 2007 to identify assets and systems located outside the United States, which, if disrupted or destroyed, would critically affect public health and safety, the economy, or national security. The initiative produced a strategic compendium which guides the engagement with foreign countries in the CIKR protection mission.

Conclusion

It is clear that cybersecurity continues to be the next frontier of homeland security. A frontier where new questions and challenges arise each day and where computers and computer systems run many aspects of our daily lives including most of our transportation systems, our power supplies, banking and ATM machines, etc., and even what is available on the shelves of our grocery stores. The newest elements of the federal government's research agenda are looking for trustworthy spaces, which means creating different security levels on the Internet and identifying economic incentives to promote adoption of cybersecurity defense systems by individuals and businesses.

Privacy and the issues of civil liberties remain a major issue when discussing cyberspace. The legislation proposed by the Obama Administration in 2011 includes a framework that ensures the protection of individuals' privacy and liberties while dealing with the challenges presented by cybersecurity.

Richard Clarke, the prescient and brilliant former National Security Advisor to Presidents Clinton and Bush, along with Robert Knake, a fellow at the International Council on Foreign Relations, have recently published a book entitled *Cyber War*, which sets out an agenda for what the United States should be doing to protect its national security from a cyberattack. His book provides some chilling examples of previous, real-life cyberattacks on DOD systems and U.S. infrastructure systems. Among other thing they call for the creation of a Defensive Triad. The Triad would "stop malware on the Internet, hardens the controls of the electric grid, and increase the security of the Defense Department's networks and the integrity of its weapons." They also suggest the possibility of establishing a Cyber Defense Administration within DHS to allow DHS to better operate as part of the Triad. Both ideas warrant careful consideration as we move homeland security into the next frontier.

Key Terms

ACAMS: A web-enabled information services portal that helps state and local governments build CIKR programs.

CFATS: The Chemical Facilities Anti-Terrorism Standards (CFATS) were established by DHS to provide guidance on hardening the facilities that produce, utilize, or store chemical substances, both public and private, throughout the United States.

Consequence: The result of a terrorist attack or other hazard that reflects the level, duration, and nature of the loss resulting from the incident. For the purposes of the NIPP, consequences are divided into four main categories: public health and safety, economic, psychological, and governance impacts. (*Source*: NIPP)

Crisis Management: A proactive management effort to avoid crisis, and the creation of strategy that minimizes adverse impacts of crisis on the organization when it could not be prevented. Effective crisis management requires a solid understanding of the organization, its strategy, liabilities, stakeholders, and legal framework combined with advanced communication, leadership, and decision-making skills to lead the organization through the crisis while minimizing potential loss.

Critical Infrastructure: Assets, systems, and networks, whether physical or virtual, so vital to the United States that the incapacity or destruction of such assets, systems, or networks would have a debilitating impact on security, national economic security, public health or safety, or any combination of those matters. (*Source*: NIPP)

Critical Infrastructure (and Key Resources) Government Coordinating Council (GCC): The GCC brings together diverse federal, state, local, and tribal interests to identify and develop collaborative strategies that advance critical infrastructure protection. GCCs serve as a counterpart to sector coordinating councils for each CIKR sector. They provide interagency coordination around CIKR strategies and activities, policy and communication across government, and between government and the sector to support the nation's homeland security mission. Government coordinating councils for each sector are comprised of representatives from DHS, the SSA, and the appropriate supporting federal departments and agencies. (*Source*: DHS)

Cybersecurity: The prevention of damage to, unauthorized use of, or exploitation of, and, if needed, the restoration of electronic information and communications systems and the information contained therein to ensure confidentiality, integrity, and availability. Includes protection and restoration, when needed, of information networks and wire line, wireless, satellite, public safety answering points, and 911 communications systems and control systems. (*Source*: NIPP)

Environmental Protection Agency (EPA): The U.S. Environmental Protection Agency is an agency of the federal government of the United States responsible for protecting the natural environment (i.e., air, water, and land) and therefore the health of citizens.

Federal Energy Regulatory Commission (FERC): The FERC regulates and oversees energy industries in the economic, environmental, and safety interests of the American public.

Information and communications systems are composed of hardware and software that process, store, and communicate data of all types.

Information Technology (IT) critical functions are sets of processes that produce, provide, and maintain products and services. IT critical functions encompass the full set of processes (e.g., R&D, manufacturing, distribution, upgrades, and maintenance) involved in transforming supply inputs into IT products and services.

Information Sharing and Analysis Center (ISAC): ISACs are sectorial information analysis and sharing centers that bring together representatives and decision makers of a given sector for the purposes of critical infrastructure protection and disaster preparedness.

National Infrastructure Protection Plan (NIPP): U.S. government plan that lays the framework for critical infrastructure and key asset protection activities. The plan is complemented with sector-specific annexes that detail sector-specific planning, response, and coordination bodies for effective disaster preparedness and incident response.

National Response Coordination Center (NRCC): The NRCC is FEMA's primary operations center during disaster response. The center is also vital for resource coordination between different emergency support functions.

National Response Team (NRT): The U.S. National Response Team is an organization of 16 federal departments and agencies responsible for coordinating emergency preparedness and response to oil and hazardous substance pollution incidents. The Environment Protection Agency (EPA) and the U.S. Coast Guard (USCG) serve as chair and vice chair, respectively.

Sector-Specific Agency (SSA): The federal agency designated to lead identification, assessment, protection, and resilience-building programs and activities for each CI sector.

Sector Coordinating Council: These councils are private sector counterparts to the GCCs. They are self-organized, self-run, and self-governed organizations that are representative of a spectrum of key stakeholders within a sector. SCCs serve as the government's principal point of entry into each sector for developing and coordinating a wide range of CIKR protection activities and issues. (*Source*: NIPP)

U.S. Computer Emergency Readiness Team (US-CERT): Established in 2003 to protect the nation's Internet infrastructure, US-CERT coordinates defense against and responses to cyberattacks across the nation.

Vulnerability: The vector of physical, social, geographical, and political factors that influence or define the combined susceptibility to a disaster of a given person, place, or other physical entity.

References

Blumenthal, H., 2003. Government Symposium on Information Sharing and Homeland Security, Department of Human Services Private Sector Information Sharing: ISAC Program, Pennsylvania.

Clarke, R., 2010. Cyber War: The Next Threat to National Security and What to Do about it. Ecco, New York.

Communications Sector Coordinating Council, 2007. Communications sector specific infrastructure protection plan. http://www.dhs.gov/xlibrary/assets/nipp-ssp-communications.pdf.

Communications Sector Coordinating Council, 2008. What is the CSCC? http://www.commscc.org/.

Congressional Research Service, 2007a. Terrorism and security issues facing the water infrastructure sector. http://www.fas.org/sgp/crs/terror/RL32189.pdf.

Congressional Research Service, 2007b. Terrorism and security issues facing the water infrastructure sector. http://www.fas.org/sgp/crs/terror/RL32189.pdf.

Congressional Research Service, 2008. FY 2009 appropriations for state and local homeland security. http://www.fas.org/sgp/crs/homesec/RS22805.pdf.

Coppola, D., 2003. Annotated Organizational Chart for the Department of Homeland Security. Bullock & Haddow, LLC, Washington, DC.

Department of Homeland Security, 2002. National strategy for homeland security. http://www.dhs.gov/xlibrary/assets/nat_strat_hls.pdf.

Department of Homeland Security, 2003. National strategy for the protection of physical infrastructure and key assets. http://www.dhs.gov/xlibrary/assets/Physical_Strategy.pdf.

Department of Homeland Security, 2004. The national plan for research and development in support of critical infrastructure protection. http://www.dhs.gov/xlibrary/assets/ST_2004_NCIP_RD_PlanFINALApr05.pdf.

Department of Homeland Security, 2005. FY 2006 critical infrastructure protection program. http://www.ojp.usdoj.gov/odp/newsreleases/FY06_IPP_PressKit.pdf.

Department of Homeland Security, 2006a. DHS releases cyber storm public exercise report. http://www.dhs.gov/xnews/releases/pr_1158341221370.shtm.

Department of Homeland Security, 2006b. FY 2007 critical infrastructure protection program. http://www.dhs.gov/xlibrary/assets/grants-2007-infrastructure-protection.pdf.

Department of Homeland Security, 2007a. FY 2008 critical infrastructure protection program. http://www.fema.gov/government/grant/ipp/index.shtm#tsp.

Department of Homeland Security, 2007b. Overview: FY 2007 infrastructure protection program awards. http://www.dhs.gov/xlibrary/assets/grants-2007-infrastructure-protection.pdf.

Department of Homeland Security, 2009a. National infrastructure protection plan. http://www.dhs.gov/files/programs/editorial/gc_1204738275985.shtm.

Department of Homeland Security, 2009b. NIPP: sector specific plans. http://www.dhs.gov/files/programs/gc_1179866197607.shtm.

Department of Homeland Security, 2010. Quadrennial homeland security review report: a strategic framework for a secure homeland. http://www.dhs.gov/xlibrary/assets/qhsr_report.pdf.

Department of Homeland Security, 2011. Implementing the recommendations of the 9/11 commission, a progess report. http://www.dhs.gov/xlibrary/assets/progress_report.pdf.

Government Accountability Office, 2006. GAO-07-39 critical infrastructure protection: progress coordinating government and private sector efforts varies by sectors' characteristics. http://www.gao.gov/new.items/d0739.pdf.

Greenberg, W.J., 2003. September 11, 2001: a CEO's story. Harvard Business Review, vol.10.1225/R0210D, pp. 7–8.

Harrald, C., Coppola, D.P., and Yeletaysi, S., 2003. Assessing the Financial Impacts of the World Trade Center Attacks on Publicly Held Corporations. TIEMS Conference Proceedings. Provence, France.

Ignatius, D., 2011. Department of internet defense. The Washington Post. http://www.washingtonpost.com/opinions/department-of-internet-defense/2011/08/12.

Lerbinger, O., 1997. The Crisis Manager. Lawrence Erlbaum Associates, New York.

Nagesh, G., 2011. Cyber attacks on U.S. grow. Hillicon Valley Blog, http://thehill.com/blogs/hillcon-valley/technology/173595.

National Commission on Terrorist Attacks Upon the United States, 2004, Final report of the National Commission on Terrorists Attacks upon the United States.

Pershing, B., 2011. On cybersecurity, a turf battle. *The Washington Post*.

Pincus, W., 2010. Government devotes more money to cybersecurity. *The Washington Post*. http://www.washingtonpost.com/wp-dyn/content/article/2010/06/22.

The White House, 2003. National strategy to secure cyberspace. http://www.whitehouse.gov/pcipb/cyberspace_strategy.pdf.

The White House, 2011. Fact sheet: cybersecurity legislative proposal. http://www.whitehouse.gov/the-press-office/2011/05/12/fact-sheet.pdf.

Symantec, 2010. The Symantec Internet Security Threat Report. http://www.symantec.com/business/theme%20jsp?themeid=threatreport.

u SD Times, Expert backs new security certification for coders. http://www.sdtimes.com/EXPERT_BACKS_NEW_SECURITY_CERTIFICATION_FOR_CODERS/About_SECURITY_and_SOFTWAREDEVELOPMENT_and_ISC2/32912.

Times Online, 2007. China's cyber army is preparing to march on America, says Pentagon. http://www.technology.timesonline.co.uk/tol/news/tech_and_web/the_web/article2409865.ece.

All-Hazards Emergency Response and Recovery

What You Will Learn

- How large-scale emergencies are declared at each level of government, and what kinds of declarations are made
- Legislative actions taken since the September 11 terrorist attacks that affect the nation's response capabilities
- The many federal homeland security grant programs that are available to states and local communities
- The response roles assumed by each level of government, from local to national (including those of the Department of Homeland Security as well as other federal agencies and offices), and by private and nonprofit organizations
- What homeland security volunteer programs exist, what each does, and how they are distributed across the country
- How the National Incident Management System and the National Response Framework guide all-hazards emergency response to major incidents in the United States

Introduction

When a natural disaster such as a flood, earthquake, or hurricane occurs, or when a technological incident or terrorist attack happens, local police, fire, and emergency medical personnel are generally the first to respond. Their mission is to rescue and attend to victims, suppress any secondary fires that may have resulted, secure and police the disaster area, and begin the process of restoring order. They are supported in this effort by local emergency management personnel and community government officials.

The 9/11 attacks were truly a watershed event in emergency management history. In their shadow, agencies at the national, state, and local government levels were prompted to initiate evaluations that sought to improve existing response procedures and protocols in light of the vast new knowledge and experience that had been attained. The spectacular nature of the attacks, and the apparent threat of subsequent events of equal or greater magnitude, mandated the generation of after-action reports that spurred many changes and improvements in the procedures and protocols that first responders have since applied to their emergency management efforts. Considering the devious and dangerous potential posed by future terrorism events, many of these evaluations focused their attention on what appeared to be a relatively new concept for most of the agencies involved: how best to protect first responders from harm in future attacks.

The federal government responded to this shift in response procedures by updating the Federal Response Plan (FRP). A new prescriptive and functional document, the National Response Plan (NRP), was the product of these efforts. The NRP was released in January 2005, and was billed as an all-discipline, all-hazards plan. The NRP was designed to establish a single, comprehensive framework for the management of domestic incidents, which would likely involve many participants from all government levels. The plan directly addressed the prevention of terrorist attacks, as well as the reduction in vulnerability to all natural and man-made hazards. Finally, it attempted to offer guidance on minimizing the damage and assisting in the recovery from any type of incident that occurred.

To carry out the coordinated response approach prescribed in the NRP, the federal government created the National Incident Management System (NIMS). On March 1, 2004, former Department of Homeland Security (DHS) Director Tom Ridge announced the release of NIMS and stated that it was created in order to "provide a consistent nationwide approach for federal, state, and local governments to work effectively and efficiently together to prepare for, respond to, and recover from domestic incidents, regardless of cause, size, or complexity."

Hurricane Katrina (2005) exposed several problems that existed within the new NRP, the most significant reported to be its sheer length. In response, the federal government developed a much more concise National Response Framework (NRF), based heavily upon the systems and organization contained within the original NRP. A final NRF was released on January 22, 2008. It remains to be seen what improvements this progression, from FRP, to NRP, to NRF, will have with regard to streamlining the multiagency response that is required during major national-level disasters, including those involving terrorist intent.

Overall, the changing nature of the terrorist threat (e.g., greater population exposure, possible use of weapons of mass destruction [WMDs]) has been the motivator for developing a new approach to response operations. This new approach has sought to initiate a profound transformation on the response community at the state and local levels through implementation of the following four goals:

- To unify crisis and consequence management (CM) as a single, integrated function, rather than two separate functions, and integrate all existing federal emergency response plans into a single document (the NRF)
- To provide interoperability and compatibility among federal, state, and local capabilities (through NIMS)
- To enhance response and preparedness capabilities of first responders and state and local governments against all kinds of hazards and threats by providing extensive funding for equipment, training, planning, and exercises
- To integrate the private sector and the business communities at a greater extent into response activities and responsibilities in order to increase resources in hand

It is the purpose of this chapter to describe the functional and operational performance of the U.S. response system, to identify and describe the changes brought about by the creation of the DHS and the actions of DHS and Congress, and to discuss their consequences. The chapter highlights in this regard include legislative and budgetary issues, local and state response capacities, volunteer group response mechanisms, an overview of the Incident Command System (ICS) and the NIMS, NRP, and NRF, and the recovery function including various programs available to assist in recovery.

■ ■ Critical Thinking ■

Should the federal emergency management role be crafted by the Department of Homeland Security, by the state and local emergency management organizations that ultimately benefit from the federal assistance provided, or by collaboration among all levels? What benefits and shortcomings would result from each of these three different planning scenarios?

Response Processes

Whenever the national emergency number 911 is called, in any event ranging from a simple traffic accident, to a tornado sighting, or for someone showing signs of a viral disease, the first responders that answer the call are always local officials. But when the size of the incident grows so large that response requirements exceed these local capabilities, and the costs of inflicted damage surpass what the local government can manage, the mayor or county executive must turn to the governor and state government resources for assistance in responding to the event and in helping the community to recover. Each state then calls upon an established system whereby the governor crafts a response that combines various personnel (including the state emergency management agency and the state National Guard), equipment, and funding. And should the disaster exceed the state's abilities to manage, then it is likely that a national disaster has occurred and federal emergency management efforts are required.

The new NRF, like that of its predecessors, dictates the rules by which states initiate an appeal for assistance, and by which that assistance is granted should the president choose to declare a disaster. The new disaster reporting process is similar to that which was stipulated under the original FRP, although fundamental changes have certainly occurred. The following gives a brief overview of the declaration process that exists under the NRF, which is described in much greater detail later in this chapter.

Should the governor decide, based on information and damage surveys generated by community and state officials, or predictions of impending disaster or terrorist threat, that the size of the actual or anticipated disaster event has exceeded or will exceed the state's capacity to respond, the governor will make a formal request to the president for a presidential major disaster declaration or an emergency declaration. This request is prepared by state officials in cooperation with regional staff from the Federal Emergency Management Agency (FEMA).

At the federal level, the governor's request is analyzed first by FEMA's regional administrator, who evaluates the damage and requirements for federal assistance and makes a recommendation to the FEMA administrator. The FEMA administrator, acting through the Secretary of Homeland Security, may then recommend a course of action to the president.

The president considers the FEMA administrator's recommendation, and decides whether or not to declare the disaster a presidential major disaster declaration or an emergency declaration. What constitutes each of these is described in the sidebar "Types of Presidential Declarations."

■ ■ ■ ────────────────────────────────────

Types of Presidential Declarations

Presidential Major Disaster Declaration

A Presidential Major Disaster Declaration (Major Declaration) is defined by FEMA to be "any natural catastrophe (including any hurricane, tornado, storm, high water, wind-driven water, tidal wave, tsunami, earthquake, volcanic eruption, landslide, mudslide, snowstorm, or drought), or, regardless of cause, any fire, flood, or explosion, in any part of the United States, which in the determination of the

President causes damage of sufficient severity and magnitude to warrant major disaster assistance under the [Stafford] Act to supplement the efforts and available resources of States, local governments, and disaster relief organizations in alleviating the damage, loss, hardship, or suffering caused thereby."

A Presidential major disaster declaration puts into motion long-term Federal recovery programs, some of which are matched by State programs, and designed to help disaster victims, businesses, and public entities.

Emergency Declaration

An Emergency Declaration is defined by FEMA to be "any occasion or instance for which, in the determination of the President, Federal assistance is needed to supplement State and local efforts and capabilities to save lives and to protect property and public health and safety, or to lessen or avert the threat of a catastrophe in any part of the United States."

An emergency declaration is more limited in scope and without the long-term Federal recovery programs of a major disaster declaration. Generally, Federal assistance and funding are provided to meet a specific emergency need or to help prevent a major disaster from occurring.

Sources: Federal Emergency Management Agency (FEMA), "Number of Declarations per Calendar Year Since 1998," Washington, DC: FEMA, 2008; FEMA, "National Response Framework (DRAFT)," Washington, DC: FEMA, 2007.

Once a presidential declaration has been made, the FEMA administrator, acting on behalf of the Secretary of Homeland Security and/or senior staff designated by the FEMA administrator determines the need to activate components of the NRF to conduct further assessment of the situation, initiate interagency coordination, share information with affected jurisdictions, and/or initiate the deployment of resources. At this time, federal departments and agencies are notified by the DHS National Operations Center (NOC), and may be called on to staff the National Response Coordination Center (NRCC) or the National Infrastructure Coordinating Center (NICC).

If an incident has already occurred, the NRF priority shifts to immediate and short-term response activities. The purpose of these activities is to preserve lives, protect property, and prevent further harm to the environment. The social, economic, and political structures of the affected community or communities are protected as well. Response actions could include the participation of law enforcement officers, fire officials, emergency medical services (mass care, public health, and medical services), officials involved in infrastructure restoration, environmental protection officials, and more.

Either during (if appropriate) or immediately following the response phase, the long-term recovery is initiated (Figure 9–1).

■ ■ Critical Thinking ■

When the Federal Response Plan (FRP) was replaced by the National Response Plan (NRP), the president gained the power to initiate a federal response in support of the states, under specific circumstances as outlined in the plan, regardless of a request from a governor. This power was transferred into the new National Response Framework (NRF). Do you feel that this takes too much authority away from the states or that this is a necessary tool?

FIGURE 9–1 Tuscaloosa, AL, May 25, 2011 — FEMA Community Relations (CR) Specialists Aron Thompson (far left), and Tony Bronk (center) are providing FEMA disaster recovery information at a disaster benefit concert. FEMA CR outreach efforts attempt to get FEMA registration and other helpful recovery information to survivors of the deadly April tornado. (Source: Photo by George Armstrong/FEMA)

Legislative Actions

The establishment of the state of homeland security as it exists today involved several bills and laws, essentially determined by homeland and national security presidential directives delivered during the years following the 9/11 attacks. The most significant include the following:

- The USA PATRIOT Act of 2001
- The Aviation and Transportation Security Act of 2001
- The SA 4470 Amendment
- The Public Health Security and Bioterrorism Preparedness and Response Act of 2002
- The Enhanced Border Security and Visa Entry Reform Act of 2002
- The Maritime Transportation Security Act of 2002
- The Homeland Security Act of 2002

These laws, among many other goals, attempted to clearly define the mission and organization of emergency management and terrorism preparedness in the United States. The single greatest change that resulted from these laws in the spectrum of emergency management — and also in terms of the changes that have occurred within the federal government itself — was the creation of the DHS. The new department, which integrated 22 existing federal agencies under the direction of a single cabinet-level official for the purpose of streamlining emergency management and counterterrorism activities, was vigorously debated, but finally came into existence in March 2003.

The Homeland Security Act of 2002 describes the responsibilities of FEMA, within DHS, as follows:

- Helping to ensure the preparedness of emergency response providers for terrorist attacks, major disasters, and other emergencies
- Establishing standards, conducting exercises and training, evaluating performance, and providing funds in relation to the Nuclear Incident Response Team (defined in Section 504 of the bill)
- Providing the federal government's response to terrorist attacks and major disasters
- Aiding the recovery from terrorist attacks and major disasters
- Working with other federal and nonfederal agencies to build a comprehensive national incident management system
- Consolidating existing federal government emergency response plans into a single, coordinated national response plan
- Developing comprehensive programs for developing interoperable communications technology and ensuring that emergency response providers acquire such technology

The responsibility of providing the federal government's response to terrorist attacks and major disasters — item 3 above — is explained in detail in the act, and includes the following:

- Coordinating the overall response to terrorist attacks
- Directing the Domestic Emergency Support Team (DEST), the Strategic National Stockpile (SNS), the National Disaster Medical System (NDMS), and the Nuclear Incident Response Team (each described later in this chapter)
- Overseeing the Metropolitan Medical Response System (MMRS) and coordinating other federal response resources

It is important to note that the new responsibilities of FEMA are not intended to detract from other important functions transferred to DHS, such as those of the U.S. Fire Administration (USFA). In almost all areas, DHS has fully preserved the authority to carry out the original functions of FEMA, including support for community initiatives that promote homeland security.

The following agencies were transferred to DHS, and were integrated into FEMA as a result, through the provisions of the Homeland Security Act of 2002:

- The Integrated Hazard Information System of the National Oceanic and Atmospheric Administration (NOAA), which was renamed "FIRESAT"
- The National Domestic Preparedness Office (NDPO) of the Federal Bureau of Investigation (FBI)
- The Domestic Emergency Support Teams (DEST) of the Department of Justice (DOJ)
- The Office of Emergency Preparedness (OEP), the National Disaster Medical System (NDMS), and the Metropolitan Medical Response System (MMRS) of the Department of Health and Human Services (HHS) (the NDMS was transferred back into HHS in 2007)
- The Strategic National Stockpile (SNS) of HHS

On an operational level, minor disasters occur daily in communities around the United States. Local fire, police, and emergency medical personnel respond to these events in a routine, systematic, and well-planned course of action (Figure 9–2). Firefighters, police officers, and emergency medical technicians respond to the scene and take immediate actions. Their job is to secure the scene and maintain order, rescue and treat

FIGURE 9–2 New York City, NY, October 5, 2001 — Rescue workers continue their efforts at the World Trade Center. (Source: Photo by Andrea Booher/FEMA News Photo)

those who are injured, contain and suppress fire or hazardous conditions, and retrieve the dead. Some notable facts about first responders who assert their role as the real front line in the nation's defense from disasters of all categories follow:

- There are more than 1 million firefighters in the United States, of whom approximately 750,000 are volunteers.
- Local police departments have an estimated 556,000 full-time employees, including about 436,000 sworn enforcement personnel.
- Sheriffs' offices reported about 291,000 full-time employees, including about 186,000 sworn personnel.
- There are more than 155,000 nationally registered emergency medical technicians (EMTs) (Department of Homeland Security, www.dhs.gov).

▪ ▪ Critical Thinking ▪

The nation's system of emergency management relies predominantly upon the efforts of unpaid volunteer first responders. Is this type of system sustainable? Why or why not? What could be done to improve it, and at what cost?

The actions of local first responders are driven by procedures and protocols developed by the responding agencies themselves (e.g., fire, police, and emergency medical). Most communities in the United States have developed community-wide emergency plans, mandated by the Disaster Mitigation Act of 2000 (DMA, 2000), which incorporate these procedures and protocols. In the aftermath of the September 11 terrorist events, many communities have reworked or are reviewing and reworking their community emergency plans to include new and improved methodologies for responding to all forms of terrorist attacks including bioterrorism and other WMDs.

The federal government has continued to support local-level first responders heavily through funding, as described earlier in the discussion of budgets. This funding support has been provided to address four primary areas of focus, including:

- *Planning*: Support of state and local governments in developing comprehensive plans to prepare for and respond to a terrorist attack
- *Equipment*: Assistance for state and local first-responder agencies for the purchase of a wide range of equipment needed to respond effectively to a terrorist attack, including personal protective equipment, chemical and biological detection systems, and interoperable communications gear
- *Training*: Resources to train firefighters, police officers, and emergency medical technicians to respond and operate in response to terrorist attacks, most notably for those that result in a chemically or biologically hazardous environment
- *Exercises*: Support for a coordinated, regular program of exercises that improve response capabilities, practice mutual aid, and assess operational improvements and deficiencies

First-Responder Roles and Responsibilities

The roles and responsibilities of first responders are usually detailed in the community emergency operations plan (EOP). Citing the responsibilities of first responders after a terrorist incident provides a useful example of the scope of the changes that these officials are experiencing, as displayed in the following list detailing several of the main objectives for the first responders to a terrorist incident:

- Protect the lives and safety of the citizens and other first responders
- Isolate, contain, and/or limit the spread of any cyber, nuclear, biological, chemical, incendiary, or explosive devices
- Identify the type of agent and/or devices used
- Identify and establish control zones for the suspected agent used
- Ensure emergency responders properly follow protocol and have appropriate protective gear
- Identify the most appropriate decontamination and/or treatment for victims
- Establish victim services
- Notify emergency personnel, including medical facilities, of dangers and anticipated casualties and proper measures to be followed
- Notify appropriate state and federal agencies
- Provide accurate and timely public information
- Preserve as much evidence as possible to aid in the investigation process
- Protect critical infrastructure
- Oversee fatality management
- Develop and enhance medical EMS
- Protect property and environment (Bullock & Haddow, LLC, 2003)

Local Emergency Managers

It is primarily the responsibility of the designated local emergency manager to develop and maintain community-level emergency plans. Often, this individual shares a dual responsibility in local government, such as fire or police chief, and serves only part-time as the community's emergency manager. The emergency management profession, and the professional skill and knowledge of the local emergency manager, has progressively matured since the 1980s.

The roles and responsibilities of the county emergency manager are defined by the County EOP. The job descriptions of these individuals exhibit the same levels of variance as those in the local first-responder community, primarily on account of the broadening incident threat spectrum that likewise poses a threat at the county level. Although no specific guidelines are given for the new roles of either local or county emergency managers, the essential differences between legacy and more modern EOPs are based on the following requirements:

- Changes in established procedures for handling terrorist incidents
- Changes in necessary response equipment
- Changes in the structure of responding agencies and protocols of operations and interagency cooperation
- Changes in neighboring local, state, and federal emergency operation plans

▪ ▪ Critical Thinking ▪

If you could design any grant program to increase the nation's preparedness to cope with all forms of hazards, what types of items or actions would that grant program support? How would you craft the program regarding eligibility? At what levels would your program need to be funded in order for it to make an actual difference in performance levels nationwide?

State Response

States make up the second tier of emergency response in the United States. State emergency management provides mitigation and preparedness support throughout the year, but comes into play only when called upon by an overwhelmed community, county, or region. Each of the 50 states and 6 territories that make up the United States maintains a state government Office of Emergency Management. However, where the emergency management office resides within the government structure varies from state to state. In California, the California Emergency Management Agency reports to the Governor's office. In Tennessee, the Tennessee Emergency Management Agency (TEMA) reports to the adjutant general. In Florida, the emergency management function is located in the Office of Community Affairs. Today, National Guard adjutant generals manage state emergency management offices in less than one-quarter of the states and territories, a number that has fallen from more than 50% only 5 years ago. Civilian employees lead all other state emergency management offices, a growing trend that recognizes the comprehensive intergovernmental organizational role that is central to the office of emergency management.

Not surprisingly, response capabilities and capacities are strongest in those states and territories that experience the highest levels of annual disaster activity. All states and territories, however, being in possession of critical assets and resources, find themselves suddenly striving to reinforce their capabilities against the possibility of a terrorist incident. North Carolina is a state that regularly manages the risk of and response to hurricanes and floods. How the North Carolina Department of Emergency Management describes its response process presents a good example of some of the individual aspects of a mature state response function.

The changes that continue to occur regarding the roles and responsibilities of the state emergency managers are based on the same principles as those occurring at the local level (i.e., changes in procedures to handle terrorist incidents, response equipment, responding agencies and protocols of cooperation, and in local/state/federal operation plans). The sidebar "State, Territorial, or Tribal Emergency Management Responsibilities …" summarizes the responsibilities of the various political entities for the public safety and welfare of the residents of each, as stated in the NRF.

■ ■ Critical Thinking ■

Should the states take a more active role in emergency management at the local level? Do you feel there is anything that the states could do to improve local capacities without infringing on their jurisdictional rights?

Volunteer Group Response

Volunteer groups are often on the front line of disaster response. National groups such as the American Red Cross and the Salvation Army maintain rosters of local chapters of volunteers who are trained in emergency response. These organizations work collaboratively with local, state, and federal authorities to address the immediate needs of disaster victims. They provide shelter, food, and clothing to disaster victims who have had to evacuate or lost their homes to disasters large and small. Each year, the range of response and recovery functions assumed by volunteer groups in lieu of traditional government response agency efforts only grows.

In addition to the Red Cross and the Salvation Army, there are numerous volunteer groups across the country that provide aid and comfort to disaster victims. The National Volunteer Organizations Against Disasters (NVOAD) is composed of an association of 50 national member organizations, 56 state and territorial VOADs, and a quickly growing number of county, community, regional, and other local VOADs that are involved in disaster response and recovery operations around the country and abroad. Formed in 1970, NVOAD helps member groups at a disaster location to coordinate and communicate in order to provide the most efficient and effective response. A list of the NVOAD member organizations follows:

- ACTS World Relief (Foundation of Hope)
- Adventist Community Services
- All Hands Volunteers, Inc.
- Alliance of Information and Referral Systems (AIRS)
- American Baptist Men
- American Radio Relay League, Inc.
- American Red Cross
- Billy Graham Rapid Response Team
- Brethren Disaster Ministries
- Buddhist Tzu Chi Foundation
- Catholic Charities USA Learn More

- Christian Reformed World Relief Committee
- Churches of Scientology Disaster Response
- Church World Service
- City Team Ministries
- Convoy of Hope
- Cooperative Baptist Fellowship
- Episcopal Relief and Development
- Feeding America
- Feed the Children
- Habitat for Humanity International
- Hands on Network generated by Points of Light Foundation
- Hope Coalition America (Operation Hope)
- HOPE Worldwide, Ltd.
- Humane Society of the United States
- International Critical Incident Stress Foundation
- International Relief and Development
- The Jewish Federations of North America
- Latter-Day Saints Charities
- Lutheran Disaster Response
- Mennonite Disaster Service
- Mercy Medical Airlift
- National Association of Jewish Chaplains
- National Baptist Convention USA
- National Organization for Victim Assistance
- Nazarene Disaster Response
- NECHAMA — Jewish Response to Disaster
- Noah's Wish
- Operation Blessing
- Presbyterian Church in America — Mission North America
- Presbyterian Disaster Assistance
- Samaritan's Purse
- Save the Children
- Society of St. Vincent DePaul
- Southern Baptist Convention/North American Mission Board
- The Salvation Army
- United Church of Christ
- United Methodist Committee on Relief
- United Way Worldwide
- World Vision (NVOAD, 2011, http://www.nvoad.org/member/national-members)

DHS Volunteer Programs

Citizen Corps is the arm of U.S. Freedom Corps that provides opportunities for citizens who want to help make their communities safer and more secure. In the first 5 years of its existence, following a call by President George W. Bush for 2 years of volunteer service from every American citizen, almost 24,000 people from all 50 states and U.S. territories volunteered to work with one or more of the Citizen Corps programs. Since then, the numbers have increased. The programs contained within Citizen Corps include:

- Citizen Corps Councils
- Community Emergency Response Teams (CERT)
- Volunteers in Police Service (VIPS)
- Medical Reserve Corps
- Neighborhood Watch
- Fire Corps

Citizen Corps Councils

Citizen Corps Councils (CCCs) are established at the state and local levels to promote, organize, and run the various programs that fall under the Citizen Corps umbrella. Funding for these councils is provided by the federal government through grant awards. As of August 2011, there were CCCs in 56 states and U.S. territories, and 1,101 local communities, all of which serve 61% of the total population of the United States.

Community Emergency Response Teams

The Community Emergency Response Team (CERT) program began in Los Angeles, California, in 1983. City administrators there recognized that in most emergency situations, average citizens — neighbors, co-workers, and bystanders, for example — were often on the scene during the critical moments before professional help arrived. These officials acted on the belief that, by training average citizens to perform basic search and rescue, first aid, and other critical emergency response skills, they would increase the overall resilience of the community. Additionally, should a large-scale disaster like an earthquake occur, where first-response units would be stretched very thin, these trained citizens would be able to augment official services and provide an important service to the community.

Beginning in 1993, FEMA began to offer CERT training on a national level, providing funding to cover start-up and tuition costs for programs. As of August 2011, CERT programs had been established in more than 1,807 communities in all 50 states, the District of Columbia, and several U.S. territories. CERT teams remain active in the community before a disaster strikes, sponsoring events such as drills, neighborhood cleanup, and disaster-education fairs. Trainers offer periodic refresher sessions to CERT members to reinforce the basic training and to keep participants involved and practiced in their skills. CERT members also offer other nonemergency assistance to the community with the goal of improving the overall safety of the community.

Volunteers in Police Service Program

Since September 11, 2001, the demands on state and local law enforcement have increased dramatically. Limited resources at the community level have resulted from these increased demands, and regular police work has ultimately suffered. To address these shortfalls, the Volunteers in Police Service (VIPS) program was created. The basis of the program is that civilian volunteers are able to support police officers by doing much of the behind-the-scenes work that does not require formal law enforcement training, thereby allowing officers to spend more of their already strained schedules on the street. Although the concept is not new, federal support for such programs is.

The VIPS draws on the time and recognized talents of civilian volunteers. Volunteer roles may include performing clerical tasks, serving as an extra set of eyes and ears, assisting with search and rescue activities, and writing citations for accessible parking violations, just to name a few. As of August 2011, there were 2,180 official VIPS programs registered throughout the United States.

Medical Reserve Corps Program

The Medical Reserve Corps (MRC) was founded after the 2002 State of the Union Address, to establish teams of local volunteer medical and public health professionals who can contribute their skills and experience when called on in times of need. The program relies on volunteers who are practicing and retired physicians, nurses, dentists, veterinarians, epidemiologists, and other health professionals, as well as other citizens untrained in public health but who can contribute to the community's normal and disaster public health needs in other ways (which may include interpreters, chaplains, legal advisers, etc.).

Local community leaders develop their own MRC units and recruit local volunteers who address the specific community needs. For example, MRC volunteers may deliver necessary public health services during a crisis, assist emergency response teams with patients, and provide care directly to those with less serious injuries and other health-related issues. MRC volunteers may also serve a vital role by assisting their communities with ongoing public health needs (e.g., immunizations, screenings, health and nutrition education, and volunteering in community health centers and local hospitals). The MRC unit decides, in concert with local officials (including the local CCC), on when the community MRC is activated during a local emergency. As of August 2011, there were 952 MRC programs established throughout the United States.

Neighborhood Watch Program

The Neighborhood Watch program has been in existence for more than 30 years in cities and counties throughout the United States. The program is based on the concept that neighbors who join together to fight crime will be able to increase security in their surrounding areas and, as a result, provide an overall better quality of life for residents. Understandably, after September 11, 2001, when terrorism became a major focus of the U.S. government, the recognized importance of programs like Neighborhood Watch took on much greater significance.

The Neighborhood Watch program is not maintained by the National Sheriff's Association, which founded the program initially. At the local level, the CCCs help neighborhood groups who have banded together to start a program to carry out their mission. Many printed materials and other guidance are available for free to help them carry out their goals.

Neighborhood Watch programs have successfully decreased crime in many of the neighborhoods where they have been implemented. In total, as of January 2008, there were 14,791 programs spread out throughout the United States and the U.S. territories. In addition to serving a crime prevention role, Neighborhood Watch has also been used as the basis for bringing neighborhood residents together to focus on disaster preparedness and terrorism awareness; to focus on evacuation drills and exercises; and even to organize group training, such as the CERT training.

Fire Corps

The Fire Corps was created in 2004 under the umbrella of U.S. Freedom Corps and Citizen Corps. The purpose of the program, like the VIPS program with the police, was to enhance the ability of fire departments to utilize citizen advocates and provide individuals with opportunities to support their local fire departments with both time and talent.

Fire Corps was created as a partnership between the International Association of Fire Chiefs' Volunteer Combination Officers Section (VCOS), the International Association of Fire Fighters (IAFF), and the National Volunteer Fire Council (NVFC). By participating in the program, concerned and interested citizens can assist in their local fire department's activities through tasks such as administrative assistance, public education, fund-raising, data entry, accounting, public relations, and equipment and facility maintenance, to name just a few.

DHS Response Agencies

With the passage of the Homeland Security Act of 2002, several government agencies and offices that managed components of the nation's response framework were consolidated into the DHS. Originally, these various components were brought into DHS and merged together to form an EP&R Directorate, composed most prominently by the functions of the original FEMA. During the course of the DHS's thus-far-brief history, several of these components have moved within the structure of DHS — many falling under the direction of the newly reformed FEMA while others have since been removed from the Department entirely or are facing permanent closure. These agencies and offices, each of which is described in detail below, include:

> Federal Emergency Management Agency (FEMA)
> Integrated Hazard Information System of the National Oceanic and Atmospheric Administration
> National Domestic Preparedness Office of the Federal Bureau of Investigation
> Domestic Emergency Support Teams of the Department of Justice
> Office of Emergency Preparedness
> National Disaster Medical System
> Metropolitan Medical Response System
> Strategic National Stockpile

Federal Emergency Management Agency

The Federal Emergency Management Agency — a former independent agency that became part of the new DHS in March 2003 — is tasked with responding to, planning for, recovering from, and mitigating against disasters. The FEMA Response Division provides the core operational and logistical disaster response capability of the federal government, which is called upon to save and sustain lives, minimize suffering, and protect property in a timely and effective manner in communities that become overwhelmed by natural disasters, acts of terrorism, or other emergencies. FEMA response program activities encompass the coordination of all federal emergency management response operations, response planning, and logistics programs and integration of federal, state, tribal, and local disaster programs. This coordination is designed to facilitate the delivery of immediate emergency assistance to individuals and communities impacted and overwhelmed by emergency and disaster events (see Figure 9–3).

FIGURE 9–3 Joplin, MO, August 3, 2011 — Damage sustained at St. John's Regional Medical Center after the May 22 EF-5 tornado that struck the city. FEMA is working to provide assistance to those affected by the tornado. (Source: Photo by Elissa Jun/FEMA)

FEMA's disaster response responsibilities within DHS, which are very similar to those maintained by the agency prior to its incorporation into DHS, include (among others):

- Coordinating with local and state first responders to manage disasters requiring federal assistance and to recover from their effects (as stipulated in the NRF)
- Administering the Disaster Relief Fund
- Maintaining administration of the National Flood Insurance Program
- Administering the training and other responsibilities of the U.S. Fire Administration
- Offering mitigation grant programs, including the Hazards Mitigation Grant Program, the Pre-Disaster Mitigation Program, and the Flood Mitigation Assistance Program
- Administering the Citizen Corps Program

Integrated Hazard Information System

The Integrated Hazard Information System (IHIS) was transferred from the NOAA into the DHS EP&R Directorate. At the time of transfer, its name was changed to "FIRESAT." IHIS, originally named the Hazards Support System (HSS), was a classified information system developed by the Department of Defense (DOD) in 1997 to compile data obtained from various satellites and sensors, such as those used to detect ballistic missiles and others that continuously monitor weather conditions in the United States. In late 2000, after DOD tested the system, HSS was turned over to the U.S. Geological Survey (USGS) in the Department of the Interior and renamed IHIS, where it would be used to detect wildfires and volcanic eruptions around the world. However, Congress directed USGS to cease expenditures on IHIS, apparently because of concerns about unauthorized reprogramming of those funds. Since then, no funding has been authorized for IHIS. The agreement by Congress and the administration to move IHIS to DHS included "the transfer of workstations, software, documentation, and its communications component." However, the president did not request funding for FIRESAT for FY 2004 (Bea et al., 2003).

National Domestic Preparedness Office

The National Domestic Preparedness Office (NDPO), within the DOJ, coordinated all federal efforts, including those of the DOD, FEMA, the HHS, the Department of Energy (DOE), and the Environmental Protection Agency (EPA), to assist state and local first responders with planning, training, equipment, and exercises necessary to respond to a conventional or nonconventional WMD incident.

NDPO's various functions were transferred into the new DHS and placed under the direction of the FEMA-dominated EP&R Directorate. Among the functions of the NDPO transferred were:

- Serve as a single program and policy office for WMD to ensure that federal efforts are in harmony and represent the most effective and cost-efficient support to the state and local first-responder community
- Coordinate the establishment of training curriculum and standards for first-responder training to ensure consistency based on training objectives and to tailor training opportunities to meet the needs of the responder community
- Facilitate the efforts of the federal government to provide the responder community with detection, protection, analysis, and decontamination equipment necessary to prepare for, and respond to, an incident involving WMD
- Provide state and local governments with the resources and expertise necessary to design, conduct, and evaluate exercise scenarios involving WMD
- Communicate information to the state and local emergency response community

Domestic Emergency Support Team

The Domestic Emergency Support Team (DEST) is designed to be an interagency team of experts, operating on a stand-by basis, which can be quickly mobilized. This team, even within DHS (and directed by FEMA per the Stafford Act), is led by the FBI to provide an on-scene commander (OSC) (special agent in charge) with advice and guidance in situations involving WMDs, or other significant domestic threats. The DEST guidance can range from information management and communications support to instructions on how to best respond to the detonation of a chemical, biological, or nuclear weapon, or a radiological dispersal device (RDD). As specialized predesignated teams, DEST has no permanent staff at DHS, the FBI, or any other federal agency.

Office of Emergency Preparedness

The Office of Emergency Preparedness (OEP) was responsible for oversight, coordination, and management of EP&R and recovery activities in the HHS prior to its transfer to DHS. There were two principal programs of OEP that now exist within DHS under separate functional units. They are the NDMS and the MMRS and are described in further detail later.

Before its move into DHS, OEP served as the lead for Emergency Support Function (ESF) #8 within the FRP — Health and Medical. Under the NRF, HHS has maintained this responsibility under the new

ESF #8, Public Health and Medical Services. The tasks performed by the NDMS and MMRS, which were fulfilled within ESF #8, are still performed as before but under different direction.

National Disaster Medical System

The National Disaster Medical System (NDMS), which originally resided within the Office of Emergency Preparedness of HHS, was transferred to the DHS EP&R Directorate per the Homeland Security Act of 2002, but now falls back under the direction of HHS as stipulated in the post-Katrina Emergency Management Reform Act of 2006 (including its $33.8 million budget). NDMS is a federally coordinated system that is responsible for supporting federal agencies in the management and coordination of the federal medical response to major emergencies and federally declared disasters. In doing so, it establishes a single, integrated national medical response capability for assisting state and local authorities in dealing with the medical and health effects of major disasters. NDMS also cares for casualties of U.S. military operations overseas who have been airlifted back to the United States.

NDMS consists of more than 8,000 volunteer health professionals and support personnel organized into disaster assistance teams that can be activated and deployed anywhere in the country to assist state and local emergency medical services. Several operational units within NDMS assist in this function:

- *Disaster Medical Assistance Team (DMAT)*: A DMAT is a group of professional and paraprofessional medical personnel, supported by logistical and administrative staff, designed to provide medical care during a disaster or other event.
- *Disaster Mortuary Operational Response Team (DMORT)*: DMORTs, like DMATs, are composed of private citizens, each with a particular field of expertise, who are activated in the event of a disaster. During an emergency response, DMORTs work under the guidance of local authorities by providing technical assistance and personnel to recover, identify, and process deceased victims. Teams are composed of funeral directors, medical examiners, coroners, pathologists, forensic anthropologists, medical records technicians and transcribers, fingerprint specialists, forensic odontologists, dental assistants, X-ray technicians, mental health specialists, computer professionals, administrative support staff, and security and investigative personnel. Their duties include setting up temporary morgue facilities, victim identification, forensic dental pathology, forensic anthropology, and processing, preparation, and disposition of remains.
- *Veterinary Medical Assistance Team (VMAT)*: VMATs are composed of private citizens who are activated in the event of a disaster. During an emergency response, VMATs work under the guidance of local authorities by providing technical assistance and veterinary services. Teams are composed of clinical veterinarians, veterinary pathologists, animal health technicians (veterinary technicians), microbiologist/virologists, epidemiologists, toxicologists, and various scientific and support personnel. Their tasks include assessing the medical needs of animals, medical treatment and stabilization of animals, animal disease surveillance, zoonotic disease surveillance and public health assessments, technical assistance to ensure food and water quality, hazard mitigation, animal decontamination, and biological and chemical terrorism surveillance.
- *Federal Coordinating Centers (FCCs)*: FCCs recruit hospitals and maintain local nonfederal hospital participation in the NDMS, coordinate exercise development and emergency plans with participating hospitals and other local authorities in order to develop patient reception, transportation, and communication plans, and during system activation, coordinate the reception and distribution of patients being evacuated to the area.

- *National Pharmacy Response Team (NPRT)*: NPRTs are located in each of the 10 DHS regions. NPRTs are activated in times of disaster to assist in chemo-prophylaxis (preventive medicine) or the vaccination of hundreds of thousands, or even millions of Americans. They may be activated in any scenario that is expected to require the assistance of hundreds of pharmacists, pharmacy technicians, and students of pharmacy.
- *National Nurse Response Team (NNRT)*: NNRTs are specialty DMATs designed for use in scenarios expected to require the activation of hundreds of nurses to assist in chemoprophylaxis, a mass vaccination program, or a scenario that overwhelms the nation's supply of nurses in responding to a WMD event. The NNRTs are directed by the NDMS in conjunction with a regional team leader in each of the 10 standard federal regions. Each NNRT is composed of approximately 200 civilian nurses. National Nurse Response Team members are required to maintain appropriate certifications and licensure within their discipline, stay current in treatment recommendations for diseases compatible with WMDs, complete web-based training courses in disaster response, humanitarian relief, bioterrorism, and other relevant training, participate in regular training exercises, and be available to deploy when needed.

Metropolitan Medical Response System

The Metropolitan Medical Response System (MMRS) provides funding to cities that upgrade and improve their own planning and preparedness to respond to mass casualty events. The concept for the program began in 1995 in the Washington, D.C., metropolitan area with the creation of the Metropolitan Medical Strike Team (MMST). This first team, which pooled resources from several adjoining jurisdictions, was created primarily for the response to chemical incidents, but was able to provide on-site emergency health and medical services following WMD terrorist incidents.

The MMST concept was expanded to several cities under the guidance and funding of the federal government through the authority of the Defense against Weapons of Mass Destruction Act of 1996 (Nunn-Lugar-Domenici legislation). The program's name was changed to the Metropolitan Medical Response System to highlight its national system-oriented approach. The program has grown from the 25 teams created in 1995 to almost 124 municipalities.

Strategic National Stockpile

The Strategic National Stockpile (SNS) began in 1999, when Congress charged HHS and Centers for Disease Control and Prevention (CDC) with the establishment of the capability to provide a resupply of large quantities of essential medical material to states and communities during an emergency within 12 hours of the federal decision to deploy to that region. The system that was developed was called the National Pharmaceutical Stockpile (NPS).

As stipulated in the Homeland Security Act of 2002, on March 1, 2003, the NPS was transferred from HHS to DHS, and was given the new title, Strategic National Stockpile. The program was established so that it could be managed jointly by DHS and HHS and be able to work with governmental and nongovernmental partners to continually seek ways to upgrade the nation's public health capacity to respond to national emergencies. With the signing of the BioShield legislation, however, the SNS program was returned to HHS for oversight and guidance.

During a national emergency, state, local, and private stocks of medical material will be depleted quickly. The SNS is designed to help all state and local first responders bolster their response to a national emergency, through the provision of specially designed 12-hour Push Packages, private vendors, or a combination of both, depending on the situation. Like most federal response programs, the SNS is not a first-response tool, but one that supplements the initial local response efforts.

The SNS is a national repository of antibiotics, chemical antidotes, antitoxins, life-support medications, IV administration supplies, airway maintenance supplies, and medical/surgical items. The SNS is designed to supplement and resupply state and local public health agencies in the event of a national emergency anywhere and at any time within the United States or its territories. The system is also set up to allow for the acquisition of additional pharmaceuticals and/or medical supplies not maintained directly by the SNS through the use of private vendors (which can ship supplies to arrive within 24–36 hours of the request). In some areas, the vendors, which are preregistered under the program, can actually provide the first wave of supplies that arrive.

Urban Search and Rescue

The concept of formally maintained Urban Search and Rescue (US&R or USAR) teams was introduced in the early 1980s. The Fairfax County (Virginia) Fire and Rescue and the Metro-Dade County (Florida) Fire Department each created specialized search and rescue teams trained for rescue operations in collapsed buildings. US&R involves the location, rescue (extrication), and initial medical stabilization of victims trapped in confined spaces. Structural collapse is most often the cause of victims being trapped, but victims may also be trapped in transportation accidents, mines, and collapsed trenches. The initial teams created to carry out these tasks were so successful in this specialty that they were often sent abroad on missions, representing the U.S. government relief efforts, through support of the Department of State and the Office of Foreign Disaster Assistance (OFDA) of the U.S. Agency for International Development (USAID). These teams have deployed to Mexico City, the Philippines, and Armenia, providing vital search and rescue support in earthquake-induced disasters in each of these areas (see Figure 9–4).

FIGURE 9–4 Sabine Pass, TX, September 14, 2008 — Members of the FEMA Urban Search and Rescue team, Indiana Task Force 1 go into neighborhoods impacted by Hurricane Ike to search for people needing help getting out of the area. (Source: Photo by Jocelyn Augustino/FEMA)

Beginning in 1991, US&R became a component of federal response operations under the FRP, when the US&R concept was incorporated as an individual ESF. From that starting point, the size of the US&R system grew considerably, with FEMA sponsoring the creation of 25 national US&R task forces. There are now a total of 28 national task forces, staffed and equipped to conduct around-the-clock search and rescue operations following any disaster that requires their specialized talents and equipment. In 2003, when FEMA was transferred into DHS, the US&R system transferred with FEMA, intact. FEMA, under DHS, maintains its primary agency designation under ESF #9, Search and Rescue.

Maritime Search and Rescue

The USCG maintains several distinct missions within DHS, but one of those, search and rescue, has resulted in strong cooperation with FEMA and the EP&R Directorate. Specifically, USCG maintains the authority and responsibility for the various tasks related to maritime search and rescue.

Maritime search and rescue (SAR) is one of the Coast Guard's oldest missions. Minimizing the loss of life, injury, property damage, or loss by rendering aid to persons in distress and property in the maritime environment has always been a Coast Guard priority. Coast Guard SAR response involves multiple-mission stations, cutters, aircraft, and boats linked by communications networks. The Coast Guard is the SAR coordinator for U.S. aeronautical and maritime search and rescue regions that are near America's oceans, including Alaska and Hawaii. To meet this responsibility, the Coast Guard maintains SAR facilities on the East, West, and Gulf coasts; in Alaska, Hawaii, Guam, and Puerto Rico; and on the Great Lakes and inland U.S. waterways.

Other Response Agencies

Each of the agencies listed in the preceding section operates under the management of DHS, and in several cases, under FEMA, regardless of whether or not a disaster declaration has occurred. However, there are several other agencies within the federal government that bring emergency response capabilities to the federal response system, in many cases operating in their respective organizations without any clear day-to-day contact with DHS outside of a declared disaster. As stipulated in the NRF, these agencies can all be called upon to provide their services in times of need, under the coordination efforts of FEMA, in response to major disasters that require federal support (namely, presidentially declared disasters and emergencies). These departments and agencies are discussed individually.

Federal Bureau of Investigation

The Federal Bureau of Investigation (FBI), part of the Department of Justice, is the lead federal agency (LFA) for crisis management and investigation of all terrorism-related matters, including incidents involving a WMD. Within the FBI's role as LFA, the FBI federal on-scene commander (OSC) coordinates the overall federal response until the attorney general transfers the LFA role to FEMA (Figure 9–5).

Department of Defense

In the event of a terrorist attack or an act of nature on American soil resulting in the release of chemical, biological, radiological, or nuclear material or high-yield explosive (CBRNE) devices, the local law enforcement, fire, and emergency medical personnel who are first to respond may become quickly overwhelmed by the magnitude of the attack. The Department of Defense (DOD) has many unique war-fighting support

FIGURE 9–5 New York City, NY, September 18, 2001 — FBI members look toward the wreckage at the World Trade Center. (Source: Photo by Andrea Booher/FEMA News Photo)

capabilities, both technical and operational, that could be used in support of state and local authorities, if requested by DHS, as the LFA, to support and manage the consequences of such a domestic event.

When requested, the DOD will provide its unique and extensive resources in accordance with the following principles. First, DOD will ensure an unequivocal chain of responsibility, authority, and account-ability for its actions to ensure the American people that the military will follow the basic constructs of lawful action when an emergency occurs. Second, in the event of a catastrophic CBRNE event, DOD will always play a supporting role to the LFA in accordance with all applicable law and plans. Third, DOD support will emphasize its natural role, skills, and structures to mass mobilize and provide logistical support. Fourth, DOD will purchase equipment and provide support in areas that are largely related to its war-fighting mission. Fifth, reserve component forces are DOD's forward-deployed forces for domestic CM.

Department of Energy

Through its Office of Emergency Response, the Department of Energy (DOE) manages radiological emer-gency response assets that support both crisis and CM response in the event of an incident involving a WMD. DOE is prepared to respond immediately to any type of radiological accident or incident with its radiological emergency response assets.

Through its Office of Nonproliferation and National Security, DOE coordinates activities in nonproliferation, international nuclear safety, and communicated threat assessment.

Department of Health and Human Services

The Department of Health and Human Services (HHS), as the LFA for ESF #8 (health and medical ser-vices), provides coordinated federal assistance to supplement state and local resources in response to pub-lic health and medical care needs following a major disaster or emergency. Additionally, HHS provides support during developing or potential medical situations and has the responsibility for federal support of food, drug, and sanitation issues. Resources are furnished when state and local resources are overwhelmed and public health and/or medical assistance is requested from the federal government.

HHS, in its primary agency role for ESF #8, coordinates the provision of federal health and medical assistance to fulfill the requirements identified by the affected state/local authorities having jurisdiction. Included in ESF #8 are overall public health response; triage, treatment, and transportation of victims of the disaster; and evacuation of patients out of the disaster area, as needed, into a network of military services, veterans affairs, and pre-enrolled nonfederal hospitals located in the major metropolitan areas of the United States.

Other than the agencies integrated under FEMA, the CDC may also be used in response activities. CDC is the federal agency responsible for protecting the public health of the country through prevention and control of diseases and response to public health emergencies. CDC works with national and international agencies to eradicate or control communicable diseases and other preventable conditions. The CDC's Bioterrorism Preparedness and Response Program oversees the agency's effort to prepare state and local governments to respond to acts of bioterrorism. In addition, CDC has designated emergency response personnel throughout the agency who are responsible for responding to biological, chemical, and radiological terrorism. CDC has epidemiologists trained to investigate and control outbreaks or illnesses, as well as laboratories capable of quantifying an individual's exposure to biological or chemical agents.

Environmental Protection Agency

The Environmental Protection Agency (EPA) is chartered to respond to WMD releases under the National Oil and Hazardous Substances Pollution Contingency Plan (NCP) regardless of the cause of the release. EPA is authorized by the Comprehensive Environmental Response, Compensation, and Liability Act (CERCLA); the Oil Pollution Act; and the Emergency Planning and Community Right-to-Know Act to support federal, state, and local responders in counterterrorism.

EPA will provide support to the FBI during crisis management in response to a terrorist incident. In its crisis management role, the EPA on-scene commander (OSC) may provide the FBI special agent in charge (SAC) with technical advice and recommendations, scientific and technical assessments, and assistance (as needed) to state and local responders. The EPA's OSC will support DHS during consequence management for the incident. EPA carries out its response according to the FRP's ESF #10, Hazardous Materials. The OSC may request an environmental response team that is funded by the EPA if the terrorist incident exceeds available local and regional resources. The EPA chairs the National Response Team (NRT).

Department of Agriculture

It is the policy of the U.S. Department of Agriculture (USDA) to "be prepared to respond swiftly in the event of national security, natural disaster, technological, and other emergencies at the national, regional, state, and county levels to provide support and comfort to the people of the United States." USDA has been charged with ensuring the safety of the nation's food supply. Since September 11, the concern that bioterrorism will impact agriculture in rural America, namely, crops in the field, hoofed animals, and food-safety issues in the food chain between the slaughterhouse and/or processing facilities and the consumer, has only grown.

Nuclear Regulatory Commission

The Nuclear Regulatory Commission (NRC) is the LFA (in accordance with the FRERP) for facilities or materials regulated by NRC or by an NRC agreement. NRC's counterterrorism-specific role, at these facilities or material sites, is to exercise the federal lead for radiological safety while supporting other federal, state, and local agencies in crisis and CM.

▦ ▦ Critical Thinking ▦

How does the involvement of the Department of Defense in the nation's emergency management system differ from all other federal agencies? Why is this difference significant? Do you feel that anything should be done to change the way the military supports domestic emergency management?

National Incident Management System (NIMS)

A difficult issue in any response operation is determining who is in charge of the overall response effort at the incident. This concept of control, or leadership, is most commonly referred to in the emergency management community as *incident command*. With the significant shift in legislation brought about by the creation of DHS, and the new emphasis on terrorism, the issue of incident command was in danger of becoming even more difficult and, likewise, confusing and even conflicting. To address the concerns that many officials at the local, state, and federal levels expressed in light of the changes that were occurring in the emergency management world, President George W. Bush called on the Secretary of Homeland Security, by means of Homeland Security Presidential Directive (HSPD)-5, to develop a nationally based ICS. The purpose of this system, it was assumed, was to provide a consistent nationwide approach for federal, state, tribal, and local governments to work together to prepare for, prevent, respond to, and recover from domestic incidents — regardless of their cause, size, or complexity.

On March 1, 2004, NIMS was released. The NIMS represents a core set of doctrine, principles, terminology, and organizational processes to enable the management of disasters at all government levels. One very important aspect of this new framework is that it recognized the value of an existing system, the ICS, and stressed the importance of effective incident command as a way of better managing disaster events. The well-known National Commission on Terrorist Attacks Upon the United States (the 9/11 Commission) identified ICS as an answer to many of the coordination problems that arose during the response to the September 11 attacks, and recommended a national adoption of ICS to enhance command, control, and communications capabilities during disaster response (Figure 9–6).

There are multiple functions in the ICS, including common use of terminology, integrated communications, a unified command (UC) structure, resource management, and action planning. A planned set of directives includes assigning one coordinator to manage the infrastructure of the response, and assigning personnel, deploying equipment, obtaining resources, and working with the numerous agencies that respond to the disaster scene. In most instances, the local fire chief or fire commissioner is designated the incident commander.

The ICS was designed to remain effective at each of the following three levels of incident escalation:

1. Single jurisdiction and/or single agency
2. Single jurisdiction with multiagency support
3. Multijurisdictional and/or multiagency support

There are five major management systems within the ICS. They include command, operations, planning, logistics, and finance. Each is described here:

- *Command*: The command section includes developing, directing, and maintaining communication and collaboration with the multiple agencies on site, as well as working with local officials, the public, and the media to provide up-to-date information regarding the disaster.

FIGURE 9–6 New York City, NY, September 21, 2001 — Rescue operations continue far into the night at the World Trade Center. (Source: Photo by Andrea Booher/FEMA News Photo)

- *Operations*: The operations section handles the tactical operations, coordinates the command objectives, develops tactical operations, and organizes and directs all resources to the disaster site.
- *Planning*: The planning section provides the necessary information to the command center to develop the action plan to accomplish the objectives. This section also collects and evaluates information as it is made available.
- *Logistics*: The logistics section provides personnel, equipment, and support for the command center. This section handles the coordination of all services that are involved in the response from locating rescue equipment to coordinating the response for volunteer organizations such as the Salvation Army and the Red Cross.
- *Finance*: The finance section is responsible for the accounting for funds used during the response and recovery aspect of the disaster. This section monitors costs related to the incident and provides accounting procurement time recording cost analyses.

Under the ICS, there is almost always a single incident commander. However, even under this single command figure, the ICS allows for something called a *unified command* (UC). UC is often used when there is more than one agency with incident jurisdiction or when incidents cross multiple political jurisdictions. Within this UC framework, agencies are able to work together through the designated members of the UC, often with a senior official from each agency or discipline participating in the UC, to establish a common set of objectives and strategies and a single plan of action. Due to the nature of disasters, multiple government agencies often need to work together to monitor the response and manage a large number of personnel responding to the scene. ICS allows for the integration of the agencies to operate under a single response management.

NIMS establishes standardized incident management processes, protocols, and procedures that all responders, whether they are federal, state, tribal, or local, can use to coordinate and conduct their cooperative response actions. Using these standardized procedures, it is presumed that all responders will be able to share a common understanding and will be able to work together with very little mismatch. The following are the key components of the new incident management system:

- *Incident Command System (ICS)*: NIMS establishes ICS as a standard incident management organization with five functional areas — command, operations, planning, logistics, and finance/administration — for management of all major incidents. To ensure further coordination, and during incidents involving multiple jurisdictions or agencies, the principle of UC has been universally incorporated into NIMS. This UC not only coordinates the efforts of many jurisdictions, but also provides for and ensures joint decisions on objectives, strategies, plans, priorities, and public communications.

- *Communications and Information Management*: Standardized communications during an incident are essential, and NIMS prescribes interoperable communications systems for both incident and information management. NIMS recognizes that responders and managers across all agencies and jurisdictions must have common access to the full operational picture, thereby allowing for efficient and effective incident response.

- *Preparedness*: Preparedness incorporates a range of measures, actions, and processes accomplished before an incident happens. NIMS preparedness measures include planning, training, exercises, qualification and certification, equipment acquisition and certification, and publication management. NIMS stresses that each of these measures helps to ensure that preincident actions are standardized and consistent with mutually agreed-on doctrine. NIMS further places emphasis on mitigation activities to enhance preparedness. Mitigation includes public education and outreach; structural modifications to reduce the loss of life or destruction of property; code enforcement in support of zoning rules, land management, and building codes; and flood insurance and property buy-out for frequently flooded areas.

- *Joint Information System (JIS)*: The Joint Information System provides the public with timely and accurate incident information and unified public messages. This system employs JICs and brings incident communicators together during an incident to develop, coordinate, and deliver a unified message. This is performed under the assumption that it will ensure that federal, state, and local levels of government are releasing the same information during an incident.

- *NIMS Integration Center (NIC)*: To ensure that NIMS remains an accurate and effective management tool, a NIMS NIC will be established by the DHS Secretary to assess proposed changes to NIMS, capture and evaluate lessons learned, and employ best practices. The NIC will provide strategic direction and oversight, supporting both routine maintenance and continuous refinement of the system and its components over the long term. It will also develop and facilitate national standards for NIMS education and training, first-responder communications and equipment, typing of resources, qualification and credentialing of incident management and responder personnel, and standardization of equipment maintenance and resources. Finally, the NIC will continue to use the collaborative process of federal, state, tribal, local, multidisciplinary, and private authorities to assess prospective changes to NIMS.

Federal Response

It has traditionally been the case that a federal response may be initiated in two ways: a governor can request a presidential disaster declaration or the president can declare a presidential emergency upon damage to federal entities (as was the case for the *Discovery* tragedy). Today, however, there is a third mechanism. The president, through FEMA, can predeploy resources (personnel and equipment) to a location where a disaster declaration is imminent due to an impending disaster. These authorities first appeared in the NRP, and remain unchanged under the NRF. It is important to note that, although a formal declaration does not have to be signed by the president for the federal government to begin response, the governor of the affected state must make a formal request for assistance to occur and must specify in the request the specific needs of the disaster area. Under the new NRF, the president may unilaterally declare a major disaster or emergency if extraordinary circumstances exist. For summaries of procedures on disaster declaration by the president and assistance without the president's declaration, see the sidebars "Presidential Major Disaster Declaration Process Guidelines" and "Federal Assistance without a Presidential Declaration," respectively.

Presidential Major Disaster Declaration Process Guidelines

- The Stafford Act (§401) requires that: "All requests for a declaration by the President that a major disaster exists shall be made by the Governor of the affected State." A State also includes the District of Columbia, Puerto Rico, the Virgin Islands, Guam, American Samoa, and the Commonwealth of the Northern Mariana Islands. The Marshall Islands and the Federated States of Micronesia are also eligible to request a declaration and receive assistance.
- Contact is made between the Governor of the affected State (including the District of Columbia), or territory, and the FEMA Regional Administrator. This contact may take place prior to or immediately following the disaster.
- State and Federal officials conduct a preliminary damage assessment (PDA) to estimate the extent of the disaster and its impact on individuals and public facilities. This information is included in the Governor's request to show that the disaster is of such severity and magnitude that effective response is beyond the capabilities of the State and the local governments and that Federal assistance is necessary. Normally, the PDA is completed prior to the submission of the Governor's request. However, when an obviously severe or catastrophic event occurs, the Governor's request may be submitted prior to the PDA. Nonetheless, the Governor must still make the request.
- Based on the PDA findings, the Governor submits a request to the president through the FEMA Regional Administrator for either a major disaster or an emergency declaration and identifies the affected counties. As part of the request, the Governor must take appropriate action under State law and direct execution of the State's emergency plan. The Governor has to provide in the request information on the nature and amount of State and local resources that have been or will be committed to alleviating the results of the disaster, provide an estimate of the amount and severity of damage and the impact on the private and public sector, and provide an estimate of the type and amount of assistance needed under the Stafford Act.
- The completed request, addressed to the President, is submitted through the FEMA Regional Administrator, who evaluates the damage and requirements for Federal assistance and makes a recommendation to the FEMA Administrator.
- The FEMA Administrator, acting through the Secretary of Homeland Security, may then recommend a course of action to the President.

- Based on the Governor's request, the president may declare that a major disaster or emergency exists, thereby activating the NRP and setting in motion the full array of available Federal programs to assist in the response and recovery effort. The Governor, appropriate Members of Congress, and Federal departments and agencies are immediately notified of a Presidential declaration.

Source: Federal Emergency Management Agency, "National Response Framework," 2008, http://www.fema .gov/emergency/nrf/.

Federal Assistance Without a Presidential Declaration

In many cases, assistance may be obtained from the Federal government without a Presidential declaration. For example, FEMA places liaisons in State EOCs and moves commodities near incident sites that may require Federal assistance prior to a Presidential declaration. Additionally, some types of assistance, such as Fire Management Assistance Grants — which provide support to States experiencing severe wildfires — are performed by Federal departments or agencies under their own authorities and do not require Presidential approval. Finally, Federal departments and agencies may provide immediate lifesaving assistance to States under their own statutory authorities without a formal Presidential declaration.

Source: Federal Emergency Management Agency, "National Response Framework," 2008, www.fema.gov.

Under the NRF, the president maintains the ultimate discretion in making a disaster declaration. There are no set criteria by which he or she is bound and no government regulations to guide which events are declared disasters and which are not. FEMA has developed a number of factors it considers in making its recommendation to the president, including individual property losses per capita, level of damage to existing community infrastructure, level of insurance coverage, repetitive events, and other subjective factors. But in the end, the decision to make the declaration is the president's alone. One major change in the verbiage of the plan, as changed in the NRP, concerns the prevention of terrorist attacks. In situations where the Homeland Security Operations Center determines that a terrorist threat exists for which federal intervention is required to prevent an incident from occurring, DHS provides support as necessary under the direction of the attorney general, through the FBI.

National Response Framework (NRF)

The National Response Framework (NRF) was developed to be a single document by which emergency management efforts at all levels of government could be structured. The NRF has been described by FEMA as being "a guide to how the Nation conducts all-hazards response." It is meant to be scalable, flexible, and adaptable in coordinating the key roles and responsibilities of response participants throughout the country, at all levels of government. It describes specific authorities and practices for managing incidents that range from serious local events to large-scale national-level terrorist attacks or catastrophic natural disasters. The NRF was built directly upon the structure of the NIMS, itself developed to provide a consistent template for managing incidents.

The NRF is built upon the template established under the NIMS, which was called for by HSPD-5 in the aftermath of the September 11 terrorist attacks. NIMS enables all levels of government, the private sector, and nongovernmental organizations (NGOs) to work together during an emergency or disaster event. The NRF and NIMS, working together, seek to ensure that all stakeholders are operating under a common set of emergency management principles.

The NRF can be either partially or fully implemented in the lead-up or response to an emergency or disaster threat, thereby allowing for what is considered a "scaled" response that tasks only those agencies and resources that are actually needed.

Organization of NRF

The NRF is composed of:

- *A core document*: Describes the principles that guide national response roles and responsibilities, response actions, response organizations, and planning requirements that together work to achieve an effective national response to any incident that occurs
- *Emergency Support Function (ESF) Annexes*: Group federal resources and capabilities into functional areas that are most frequently needed in a national response (e.g., transportation, firefighting, mass care)
- *Support Annexes*: Describe essential supporting aspects that are common to all incidents (e.g., financial management, volunteer and donations management, private-sector coordination)
- *Incident Annexes*: Address the unique aspects of how we respond to seven broad incident categories (e.g., biological, nuclear/radiological, cyber, mass evacuation)
- *Partner Guides*: Provide ready references describing key roles and actions for local, tribal, state, federal, and private-sector response partners

The NRF describes the roles and responsibilities not only of public-sector agencies, but also of the private sector, NGOs, and individuals and households. Communities, tribes, states, the federal government, NGOs, and the private sector are each informed of their respective roles and responsibilities, and how their actions complement each other. Each governmental level is tasked with developing capabilities needed to respond to incidents, including the development of plans, conducting assessments and exercises, providing and directing resources and capabilities, and gathering lessons learned.

Types of Federal Disaster Assistance Available under the NRF

The National Response Framework (NRF) makes available the following types of assistance.

Preincident Services

- Interagency information and intelligence sharing is conducted to enable counterterrorism activities.
- Resources and staff can be prepositioned to ensure effective response in anticipation of a disaster.

Immediate Relief Delivery — Response Actions

- Assets are mobilized and resources are deployed to support the incident.
- Teams with specialized capabilities such as the NDMS, the HHS Secretary's Emergency Response Team, the Epidemic Intelligence Service, HHS behavioral health response teams, the U.S. Public Health Service Commissioned Corps, and Urban Search and Rescue teams are deployed.
- A Joint Field Office (JFO) and other field facilities are established to provide incident management, public health, and other community support.
- Assistance is provided to support immediate law enforcement, fire, ambulance, and emergency medical service actions; emergency flood fighting; evacuations; transportation system detours; emergency public information; actions taken to minimize additional damage; urban search and rescue; the establishment of facilities for mass care; the provision of public health and medical services, food, ice, water, and other emergency essentials; debris clearance; the emergency restoration of critical infrastructure; control, containment, and removal of environmental contamination; and protection of responder health and safety.
- During the response to a terrorist event, law enforcement actions to collect and preserve evidence and to apprehend perpetrators are conducted.

Assistance to Speed Recovery and Reduce Damage from Future Occurrences

- Loans and grants to repair or replace damaged housing and personal property are provided.
- Grants to repair or replace roads and public buildings, incorporating to the extent practical hazard-reduction structural and nonstructural measures, are provided.
- Technical assistance to identify and implement mitigation opportunities to reduce future losses is provided.
- Other assistance, including crisis counseling, tax relief, legal services, and job placement may also be provided.

Roles and Responsibilities Defined by the NRF

The NRF Core Document provides an overview of the roles and responsibilities of key emergency management stakeholders at the local, tribal, state, and federal levels who are involved in the implementation of the NRF, including the private sector and NGOs.

Local Level

Disaster response almost always begins locally, and remains local in terms of actual incident command and control responsibility. This responsibility rests both with the individual members of the community themselves and with the public officials elected by them in the county and city governments. The responsibilities of the following individuals are specifically mentioned in the NRF.

Chief Elected or Appointed Official

A mayor, city manager, or county manager, as a jurisdiction's chief executive officer, is responsible for ensuring the public safety and welfare of the people of that jurisdiction. Specifically, this official provides strategic guidance and resources during preparedness, response, and recovery efforts.

Emergency Manager

The local emergency manager has the day-to-day authority and responsibility for overseeing emergency management programs and activities. They must work with chief elected and appointed officials to ensure that there are effective emergency plans in place and activities being conducted. Their role includes:

- Coordinating all components of the local emergency management program, to include assessing the availability and readiness of local resources most likely required during an incident and identifying and correcting any shortfalls
- Coordinating the planning process and working cooperatively with other local agencies and private-sector organizations
- Developing mutual aid and assistance agreements
- Coordinating damage assessments during an incident
- Advising and informing local officials about emergency management activities during an incident
- Developing and executing public awareness and education programs
- Conducting exercises to test plans and systems and obtain lessons learned
- Involving the private sector and NGOs in planning, training, and exercises

Department and Agency Heads

The local emergency manager is assisted by, and coordinates the efforts of, employees in departments and agencies that perform emergency management functions. The emergency management responsibilities of department and agency heads include:

- Collaborating with the emergency manager during the development of local emergency plans and providing key response resources
- Participating in the planning process to ensure that specific capabilities (e.g., firefighting, law enforcement, emergency medical services, public works, environmental and natural resources agencies) are integrated into a workable plan to safeguard the community
- Developing, planning, and training to internal policies and procedures to meet response and recovery needs safely
- Participating in interagency training and exercises to develop and maintain the necessary capabilities

Individuals and Households

Although not formally a part of emergency management operations, individuals and households are considered as playing an important role in the overall emergency management strategy under the NRF. Specifically, the NRF states that community members can contribute by:

- Reducing hazards in and around their homes
- Preparing an emergency supply kit and household emergency plan

- Monitoring emergency communications carefully
- Volunteering with an established organization
- Enrolling in emergency response training courses

Private Sector and NGOs

In almost every large-scale emergency incident, and some small-scale ones, the government must work together with private-sector and NGO groups as partners in emergency management. The roles of private-sector organizations include:

- Providing for the welfare and protection of their employees in the workplace
- Private-sector components of the nation's critical infrastructure, including water, power, communications, transportation, medical care, security, and numerous other services, must work together with emergency managers to ensure effective response and recovery
- Planning for the protection of information and the continuity of business operations
- Planning for, responding to, and recovering from incidents that impact their own infrastructure and facilities
- Collaborating with emergency management personnel before an incident occurs to ascertain what assistance may be necessary and how they can help
- Developing and exercising emergency plans before an incident occurs
- Establishing mutual aid and assistance agreements, where appropriate, to provide specific response capabilities
- Providing assistance (including volunteers) to support local emergency management and public awareness during response and throughout the recovery process

Participation of the private sector varies based on the nature of the organization and the nature of the incident. The five distinct roles that private-sector organizations play are summarized in Table 9–1.

The NRF states that NGOs play "enormously important roles before, during, and after an incident." NGOs provide sheltering, emergency food supplies, counseling services, and other vital support services to support response and promote the recovery of disaster victims. These groups often provide specialized services that help individuals with special needs, including those with disabilities. NGOs bolster and support government efforts at all levels — for response operations and planning. NGOs impacted by a disaster may also need government assistance. NGOs collaborate with responders, governments at all levels, and other agencies and organizations. Examples of NGO and voluntary organization contributions include:

- Training and managing volunteer resources
- Identifying shelter locations and needed supplies
- Providing critical emergency services to those in need, such as cleaning supplies, clothing, food and shelter, or assistance with postemergency cleanup
- Identifying those whose needs have not been met and helping coordinate the provision of assistance

State, Territorial, and Tribal Governments

The primary emergency management role of state, territorial, and tribal governments is to supplement and facilitate local efforts before, during, and after an emergency incident occurs. These government agencies provide direct and routine assistance to their local jurisdictions through emergency management program

Table 9–1 Private-Sector Response Role under NRF

Category	Role in This Category
Impacted organization or infrastructure	Private-sector organizations may be impacted by direct or indirect consequences of the incident. These include privately owned critical infrastructure, key resources, and other private-sector entities that are significant to local, regional, and national economic recovery from the incident. Examples of privately owned infrastructure include transportation, telecommunications, private utilities, financial institutions, and hospitals. Critical infrastructure and key resources (CIKR) are grouped into 17 sectors that together provide essential functions and services supporting various aspects of the American government, economy, and society.
Regulated and/or responsible party	Owners/operators of certain regulated facilities or hazardous operations may be legally responsible for preparing for and preventing incidents from occurring and responding to an incident once it occurs. For example, federal regulations require owners/operators of nuclear power plants to maintain emergency plans and facilities and to perform assessments, prompt notifications, and training for a response to an incident.
Response resource	Private-sector entities provide response resources (donated or compensated) during an incident — including specialized teams, essential service providers, equipment, and advanced technologies — through local public–private emergency plans or mutual aid and assistance agreements, or in response to requests from government and nongovernmental-volunteer initiatives.
Partner with state/local emergency organizations	Private-sector entities may serve as partners in local and state emergency preparedness and response organizations and activities.
Components of nation's economy	As the key element of the national economy, private-sector resilience and continuity of operations planning, as well as recovery and restoration from an actual incident, represent essential homeland security activities.

development and by routinely coordinating these efforts with federal officials. They must be prepared to maintain or accelerate the provision of commodities and services to local governments when local capabilities fall short of demands. The roles and responsibilities of the following individuals are described in greater detail in the NRF.

Governor

The public safety and welfare of a state's citizens are fundamental responsibilities of the governor. The governor:

- Is responsible for coordinating state resources and providing the strategic guidance needed to prevent, mitigate, prepare for, respond to, and recover from incidents of all types
- May be able to make, amend, or suspend, in accordance with state law, certain orders or regulations associated with response
- Communicates to the public and helps people, businesses, and organizations cope with the consequences of any type of incident
- Commands the state military forces (National Guard personnel not in federal service and state militias)
- Coordinates assistance from other states through interstate mutual aid and assistance compacts, such as the EMAC

- Requests federal assistance including, if appropriate, a Stafford Act presidential declaration of an emergency or major disaster, when it becomes clear that state capabilities will be insufficient or have been exceeded
- Coordinates with impacted tribal governments within the state and initiates requests for a Stafford Act presidential declaration of an emergency or major disaster on behalf of an impacted tribe when appropriate

State Homeland Security Advisor

The State Homeland Security Advisor serves as a counsel to the governor on homeland security issues and may serve as a liaison between the governor's office, the state homeland security structure, DHS, and other organizations both inside and outside of the state. The adviser often chairs a committee composed of representatives of relevant state agencies, including public safety, the National Guard, emergency management, public health, and others charged with developing prevention, protection, response, and recovery strategies.

Director, State Emergency Management Agency

All states have laws mandating establishment of a state emergency management agency and the emergency plans coordinated by that agency. The state Director of Emergency Management ensures that the state is prepared to deal with large-scale emergencies and is responsible for coordinating the state response in any incident.

Other State Departments and Agencies

State department and agency heads and their staffs develop, plan, and train to internal policies and procedures to meet response and recovery needs safely. They also participate in interagency training and exercises to develop and maintain the necessary capabilities. They are vital to the state's overall emergency management and homeland security programs, as they bring expertise spanning the NRF's ESFs and serve as core members of the state emergency operations center (EOC).

Indian Tribes

The U.S. government has a trust relationship with Indian tribes and recognizes their right to self-government. As such, tribal governments are responsible for coordinating resources to address actual or potential incidents. When local resources are not adequate, tribal leaders seek assistance from states or the federal government. For certain types of federal assistance, tribal governments work with the state, but as sovereign entities they can elect to deal directly with the federal government for other types of assistance. To obtain federal assistance via the Stafford Act, a state governor must request a presidential declaration on behalf of a tribe. The tribal leader is responsible for the public safety and welfare of the people of that tribe. As authorized by tribal government, the tribal leader:

- Is responsible for coordinating tribal resources needed to prevent, protect against, respond to, and recover from incidents of all types. This also includes preparedness and mitigation activities
- May have powers to amend or suspend certain tribal laws or ordinances associated with response
- Communicates with the tribal community, and helps people, businesses, and organizations cope with the consequences of any type of incident
- Negotiates mutual aid and assistance agreements with other tribes or jurisdictions

- Can request federal assistance under the Stafford Act through the governor of the state when it becomes clear that the tribe's capabilities will be insufficient or have been exceeded
- Can elect to deal directly with the federal government. Although a state governor must request a presidential declaration on behalf of a tribe under the Stafford Act, federal departments or agencies can work directly with the tribe within existing authorities and resources

Federal Government

When an incident occurs that exceeds or is anticipated to exceed local or state resources — or when an incident is managed by federal departments or agencies acting under their own authorities — the federal government uses the NRF to involve all necessary department and agency capabilities, organize the federal response, and ensure coordination with response partners. Under the NRF, the federal government's response structures are adaptable specifically to the nature and scope of a given incident.

NRF Emergency Support Functions

Through the NRF, FEMA coordinates response support from across the federal government and certain NGOs by calling up, as needed, one or more of the 15 ESFs. The ESFs are coordinated by FEMA through its NRCC. ESFs are used to coordinate specific functional capabilities and resources provided by federal departments and agencies and with certain private-sector and NGOs when applicable. ESF functions are coordinated by a single agency but may rely on several agencies to provide resources specific to each functional area. The mission of the ESFs is to provide the greatest possible access to capabilities of the federal government regardless of which agency has those capabilities.

For each ESF there is an ESF coordinator, a primary agency, and several support agencies (based upon authorities, resources, and capabilities). The categories of resources provided under the ESFs are consistent with those identified in the NIMS. ESFs may be selectively activated for both presidentially declared and nondeclared incidents as circumstances require, although not all incidents requiring federal support result in the activation of ESFs. FEMA has the ability to deploy assets and emergency management capabilities through the ESFs into an area in anticipation of an approaching storm or event that is expected to cause severe negative consequences.

A list of the 15 ESFs and a description of the scope of each are found in Table 9–2.

Once ESFs are activated, they may have a headquarters, regional, and field presence. At FEMA headquarters, the ESFs support decision making and coordination of field operations within the NRCC. The ESFs deliver regional-level technical support and other services in the RRCs, and in the JFO and incident command posts. At all levels, FEMA issues mission assignments to obtain resources and capabilities from across the ESFs in support of the affected states. At the headquarter, regional, and field levels, ESFs provide staff to support the incident command sections for operations, planning, logistics, and finance/administration, as requested, which enables the ESFs to work collaboratively. Similar structures organize response at the field, regional, and headquarters levels.

The emergency support functions of the NRF are, in order:

- ESF #1, Transportation (Coordinator: Department of Transportation)

ESF #1 supports DHS by assisting federal, state, tribal, and local governmental entities, voluntary organizations, NGOs, and the private sector in the management of transportation systems and infrastructure during domestic threats or in response to incidents. ESF #1 also participates in prevention, preparedness, response, recovery, and mitigation activities.

Table 9–2 NRF Emergency Support Functions and Primary Responsibilities

---

ESF #1 — Transportation

ESF Coordinator: Department of Transportation

Aviation/airspace management and control

Transportation safety

Restoration and recovery of transportation infrastructure

Movement restrictions

Damage and impact assessment

ESF #2 — Communications

ESF Coordinator: DHS (National Communications System)

Coordination with telecommunications and information technology industries

Restoration and repair of telecommunications infrastructure

Protection, restoration, and sustainment of national cyber and information technology resources

Oversight of communications within the federal incident management and response structures

ESF #3 — Public Works and Engineering

ESF Coordinator: Department of Defense (U.S. Army Corps of Engineers)

Infrastructure protection and emergency repair

Infrastructure restoration

Engineering services and construction management

Emergency contracting support for lifesaving and life-sustaining services

ESF #4 — Firefighting

ESF Coordinator: Department of Agriculture (U.S. Forest Service)

Coordination of federal firefighting activities

Support to wildland, rural, and urban firefighting operations

ESF #5 — Emergency Management

ESF Coordinator: DHS (FEMA)

Coordination of incident management and response efforts

Issuance of mission assignments

Resource and human capital

Incident action planning

Financial management

ESF #6 — Mass Care, Emergency Assistance, Housing, and Human Services

ESF Coordinator: DHS (FEMA)

Mass care

Emergency assistance

Disaster housing

Human services

ESF #7 — Logistics Management and Resource Support

ESF Coordinator: General Services Administration and DHS (FEMA)

Comprehensive, national incident logistics planning, management, and sustainment capability

Resource support (facility space, office equipment and supplies, contracting services, etc.)

(Continued)

Table 9–2 (Continued)

ESF #8 — Public Health and Medical Services

ESF Coordinator: Department of Health and Human Services

Public health

Medical

Mental health services

Mass fatality management

ESF #9 — Search and Rescue

ESF Coordinator: DHS (FEMA)

Lifesaving assistance

Search and rescue operations

ESF #10 — Oil and Hazardous Materials Response

ESF Coordinator: Environmental Protection Agency

Oil and hazardous materials (chemical, biological, radiological, etc.) response

Environmental short- and long-term cleanup

ESF #11 — Agriculture and Natural Resources

ESF Coordinator: Department of Agriculture

Nutrition assistance

Animal and plant disease and pest response

Food safety and security

Natural and cultural resources and historic properties protection

Safety and well-being of household pets

ESF #12 — Energy

ESF Coordinator: Department of Energy

Energy infrastructure assessment, repair, and restoration

Energy industry utilities coordination

Energy forecast

ESF #13 — Public Safety and Security

ESF Coordinator: Department of Justice

Facility and resource security

Security planning and technical resource assistance

Public safety and security support

Support to access, traffic, and crowd control

ESF #14 — Long-Term Community Recovery

ESF Coordinator: DHS (FEMA)

Social and economic community impact assessment

Long-term community recovery assistance to states, tribes, local governments, and the private sector

Analysis and review of mitigation program implementation

ESF #15 — External Affairs

ESF Coordinator: DHS

Emergency public information and protective action guidance

Media and community relations

Congressional and international affairs

Tribal and insular affairs

- ESF #2, Communications (Coordinators: DHS/National Protection and Programs/Cybersecurity and Communication/National Communications System)

ESF #2 supports the restoration of the communications infrastructure, facilitates the recovery of systems and applications from cyberattacks, and coordinates federal communications support to response efforts during incidents requiring a coordinated federal response. ESF #2 implements the provisions of the Office of Science and Technology Policy (OSTP) National Plan for Telecommunications Support (NPTS) in Non-Wartime Emergencies. ESF #2 also provides communications support to federal, state, tribal, and local governments and first responders when their systems have been impacted, and provides communications and information technology (IT) support to the JFO and JFO field teams. The National Communications System (NCS) and the National Cybersecurity Division (NCSD) work closely to coordinate the ESF #2 response to cyber incidents.

- ESF #3, Public Works and Engineering (Coordinator: U.S. Army Corps of Engineers)

ESF #3 assists DHS by coordinating and organizing the capabilities and resources of the federal government to facilitate the delivery of services, technical assistance, engineering expertise, construction management, and other support to prepare for, respond to, and/or recover from a disaster or an incident requiring a coordinated federal response. Activities within the scope of this function include conducting preincident and postincident assessments of public works and infrastructure; executing emergency contract support for lifesaving and life-sustaining services; providing technical assistance to include engineering expertise, construction management, and contracting and real estate services; providing emergency repair of damaged public infrastructure and critical facilities; and implementing and managing the DHS/FEMA Public Assistance Program and other recovery programs.

- ESF #4, Firefighting (Coordinator: U.S. Forest Service)

ESF #4 provides federal support for the detection and suppression of wildland, rural, and urban fires resulting from, or occurring coincidentally with, an incident requiring a coordinated federal response for assistance.

- ESF #5, Emergency Management (Coordinator: FEMA)

ESF #5 supports overall activities of the federal government for domestic incident management. ESF #5 serves as the coordination ESF for all federal departments and agencies across the spectrum of domestic incident management from hazard mitigation and preparedness to response and recovery. ESF #5 identifies resources for alert, activation, and subsequent deployment for quick and effective response. During the postincident response phase, ESF #5 is responsible for the support and planning functions. ESF #5 activities include those functions that are critical to support and facilitate multiagency planning and coordination for operations involving incidents requiring federal coordination. This includes alert and notification; staffing and deployment of DHS and FEMA response teams, as well as response teams from other federal departments and agencies; incident action planning; coordination of operations; logistics management; direction and control; information collection, analysis, and management; facilitation of requests for federal assistance; resource acquisition and management; federal worker safety and health; facilities management; financial management; and other support as required.

- ESF #6, Mass Care, Emergency Assistance, Housing, and Human Services (Coordinator: FEMA)

ESF #6 coordinates the delivery of federal mass care, emergency assistance, housing, and human services when local, tribal, and state response and recovery needs exceed their capabilities. When

FIGURE 9–7 Minot, ND, June 24, 2011 — Red Cross shelter in an auditorium that housed flood evacuees. Burleigh and Ward counties were designated a federal disaster area, opening the way for federal disaster assistance from FEMA. (Source: Photo by Andrea Booher/FEMA)

directed by the president, ESF #6 services and programs are implemented to assist individuals and households impacted by potential or actual disaster incidents (see Figure 9–7). ESF #6 is organized into four primary functions:

Mass care: Includes sheltering, feeding operations, emergency first aid, bulk distribution of emergency items, and collecting and providing information on victims to family members.

Emergency assistance: Assistance required by individuals, families, and their communities to ensure that immediate needs beyond the scope of the traditional "mass care" services provided at the local level are addressed. These services include support to evacuations (including registration and tracking of evacuees); reunification of families; provision of aid and services to special needs populations; evacuation, sheltering, and other emergency services for household pets and service animals; support to specialized shelters; support to medical shelters; nonconventional shelter management; coordination of donated goods and services; and coordination of voluntary agency assistance.

Housing: Includes housing options such as rental assistance, repair, loan assistance, replacement, factory-built housing, semipermanent and permanent construction, referrals, identification and provision of accessible housing, and access to other sources of housing assistance. This assistance is guided by the National Disaster Housing Strategy.

Human services: Includes the implementation of disaster assistance programs to help disaster victims recover their nonhousing losses, including programs to replace destroyed personal property, and obtain disaster loans, food stamps, crisis counseling, disaster unemployment, disaster legal services, support and services for special needs populations, and other federal and state benefits.

- ESF #7, Logistics Management and Resource Support (Coordinators: General Services Administration, FEMA)

  Assists DHS by:

  (FEMA) Providing a national disaster logistics planning, management, and sustainment capability that harnesses the resources of federal logistics partners, key public and private stakeholders, and NGOs to meet the needs of disaster victims and responders

  (GSA) Supporting federal agencies and state, tribal, and local governments that need resource support prior to, during, and/or after incidents requiring a coordinated federal response

- ESF #8, Public Health and Medical Services (Coordinator: HHS)

Provides the mechanism for coordinated federal assistance to supplement state, tribal, and local resources in response to a public health and medical disaster, potential or actual incidents requiring a coordinated federal response, and/or during a developing potential health and medical emergency. Public Health and Medical Services includes responding to medical needs associated with mental health, behavioral health, and substance abuse considerations of incident victims and response workers. Services also cover the medical needs of members of the "at risk" or "special needs" population. Public Health and Medical Services includes behavioral health needs consisting of both mental health and substance abuse considerations for incident victims and response workers and, as appropriate, medical needs groups defined in the core document as individuals in need of additional medical response assistance, and veterinary and/or animal health issues.

- ESF #9, Search and Rescue (SAR) (Coordinator: FEMA)

Rapidly deploys components of the federal SAR response system to provide specialized lifesaving assistance to state, tribal, and local authorities when activated for incidents or potential incidents requiring a coordinated federal response. The federal SAR response system is composed of the primary agencies that provide specialized SAR operations during incidents or potential incidents requiring a coordinated federal response. This includes:

Structural Collapse (Urban) Search and Rescue (US&R)
Waterborne Search and Rescue
Inland/Wilderness Search and Rescue
Aeronautical Search and Rescue

- ESF #10, Oil and Hazardous Materials Response (Coordinator: EPA)

Provides federal support in response to an actual or potential discharge and/or uncontrolled release of oil or hazardous materials when activated. Response to oil and hazardous materials incidents is generally carried out in accordance with the National Oil and Hazardous Substances Pollution Contingency Plan (NCP). Appropriate general actions under this ESF can include, but are not limited to, actions to prevent, minimize, or mitigate a release; efforts to detect and assess the extent of contamination (including sampling and analysis and environmental monitoring); actions to stabilize the release and prevent the spread of contamination; analysis of options for environmental cleanup and waste disposition; implementation of environmental cleanup; and storage, treatment, and disposal of oil and hazardous materials.

- ESF #11, Agriculture and Natural Resources (Coordinator: Department of Agriculture)

Supports state, tribal, and local authorities and other federal agency efforts to provide nutrition assistance; control and eradicate, as appropriate, any outbreak of a highly contagious or economically devastating animal or zoonotic disease, or any outbreak of an economically devastating plant pest or disease; ensure the safety and security of the commercial food supply; protect natural and cultural resources and historic properties (NCH); and provide for the safety and well-being of household pets during an emergency response or evacuation situation.

- ESF #12, Energy (Coordinator: DOE)

Facilitates the restoration of damaged energy systems and components when activated for incidents requiring a coordinated federal response. ESF #12 is an integral part of the larger DOE responsibility of maintaining continuous and reliable energy supplies for the United States through preventive measures and restoration and recovery actions. ESF #12 collects, evaluates, and shares information on energy system damage and estimations on the impact of energy system outages within affected areas. Additionally, this function provides information concerning the energy restoration process such as projected schedules, percent completion of restoration, and geographic information on the restoration. It facilitates the restoration of energy systems through legal authorities and waivers. It also provides technical expertise to the utilities, conducts field assessments, and assists government and private-sector stakeholders to overcome challenges in restoring the energy system.

- ESF #13, Public Safety and Security (Coordinator: Department of Justice)

Provides a mechanism for coordinating and providing federal-to-federal support; federal support to state, tribal, and local authorities; and/or support to other ESFs, consisting of law enforcement, public safety, and security capabilities and resources during potential or actual incidents requiring a coordinated federal response.

- ESF #14, Long-Term Community Recovery (Coordinator: FEMA)

Provides a mechanism for coordinating federal support to state, tribal, regional, and local governments, NGOs, and the private sector to enable community recovery from the long-term consequences of extraordinary disasters. ESF #14 accomplishes this by identifying and facilitating availability and use of sources of recovery funding, and providing technical assistance for community recovery and recovery planning support. The function support will vary depending on the magnitude and type of incident.

- ESF #15, External Affairs (Coordinator: DHS)

Ensures that sufficient assets are deployed to provide accurate, coordinated, timely, and accessible information to the various groups affected by the disaster. ESF #15 provides the resource support and mechanisms to implement the NRF Incident Communications Emergency Policy and Procedures (ICEPP) described in the Public Affairs Support Annex. ESF #15 coordinates federal actions to provide the required external affairs support to federal, state, tribal, and local incident management elements to coordinate communications to their audiences. The JIC ensures the coordinated release of information under ESF #15. The planning and products component of External Affairs develops all external and internal communications strategies and products for the ESF #15 organization. And finally, ESF #15 provides the resources and structure for the implementation of the ICEPP.

NRF Support Annexes

The NRF Support Annexes describe how federal departments and agencies; state, tribal, and local entities; the private sector; volunteer organizations; and NGOs coordinate and execute the functional processes and administrative requirements necessary for the management of emergency and disaster incidents. The actions described in these annexes are applicable to nearly every type of incident that may occur, whether natural, technological, or intentional in origin. The annexes, which may be fully or partially implemented, may each support several ESFs, as needed.

The support annexes of the NRF are summarized next.

- Critical Infrastructure and Key Resources (Coordinator: DHS)

Describes policies, roles and responsibilities, and the concept of operations for assessing, prioritizing, protecting, and restoring critical infrastructure and key resources (CIKR) during actual or potential domestic incidents. Specifically, this annex does the following:

> Describes roles and responsibilities for CIKR preparedness, protection, response, recovery, restoration, and continuity of operations
> Establishes a concept of operations for incident-related CIKR preparedness, protection, response, recovery, and restoration
> Outlines incident-related actions to expedite information sharing and analysis of actual or potential impacts to CIKR and facilitate requests for assistance and information from public- and private-sector partners

- Financial Management (Coordinator: FEMA and others)

Provides basic financial management guidance for all NRF departments and agencies providing assistance for incidents requiring a coordinated federal response. The financial management function is a component of ESF #5 (Emergency Management). The processes and procedures described ensure that funds are provided expeditiously and that financial operations are conducted in accordance with established federal laws, policies, regulations, and standards.

- International Coordination (Coordinator: Department of State)

Provides guidance on carrying out responsibilities for international coordination in support of the federal government's response to a domestic incident with an international component. The NRF role of the Department of State is to fully support federal, state, tribal, and local authorities in effective incident management and preparedness planning.

- Private-Sector Coordination (Coordinator: DHS)

Describes the policies, responsibilities, and concept of operations for incident management activities involving the private sector during emergencies and disasters. The annex describes the activities necessary to ensure effective coordination and integration with the private sector, both for-profit and not-for-profit, including the nation's critical infrastructure, key resources, other business and industry components, and NGOs engaged in response and recovery. This annex applies incidents that involve the private sector in any of the following ways:

> Impacted organization or infrastructure
> Response resource
> Regulated and/or responsible party
> Member of the state emergency management organization

- Public Affairs (Coordinator: DHS)

Describes the policies and procedures used to mobilize federal assets to prepare and deliver risk and emergency communications messages to the public. The annex is applicable to all federal departments and agencies responding under the NRF.

- Tribal Relations (Coordinator: DHS)

Describes the policies, responsibilities, and concept of operations for coordination and interaction of federal incident management activities with those of tribal governments and communities during incidents requiring a coordinated federal response. Because tribal governments are fully integrated into the NRF, this annex addresses only those factors in the relationship between federal departments and agencies and the federally recognized tribes.

- Volunteer and Donations Management (Coordinator: FEMA)

Describes the coordination processes used to support the state in ensuring the most efficient and effective use of unaffiliated volunteers, unaffiliated organizations, and unsolicited donated goods to support all ESFs, including offers of unaffiliated volunteer services and unsolicited donations to the federal government.

- Worker Safety and Health (Coordinator: Department of Labor/Occupational Safety and Health Administration)

Provides federal support to response and recovery organizations in assuring response and recovery worker safety and health during emergency incidents. This annex describes the technical assistance resources, capabilities, and other support to ensure that response and recovery worker safety and health risks are anticipated, recognized, evaluated, communicated, and consistently controlled.

NRF Incident Annexes

The incident annexes address contingency or hazard situations requiring specialized application of the NRF. These annexes, which were not reengineered when the NRF was released and are therefore a carryover from the legacy NRP, describe the following components for each of the specialized incident types:

Policies: Each annex explains unique authorities pertinent to that incident, the special actions or declarations that may result, and any special policies that may apply.
Situation: Each annex describes the incident situation as well as the planning assumptions, and outlines the approach that will be used if key assumptions do not hold (e.g., how authorities will operate if they lose communication with senior decision makers).
Concept of operations: Each annex describes the concept of operations appropriate to the incident, integration of operations with NRF elements, unique aspects of the organizational approach, notification and activation processes, and specialized incident-related actions. Each annex also details the coordination structures and positions of authority that are unique to the type of incident, the specialized response teams or unique resources needed, and other special considerations.
Responsibilities: Each incident annex identifies the coordinating and cooperating agencies involved in an incident-specific response; in some cases this responsibility is held jointly by two or more departments.

As is true with the support annexes described above, there are coordinating and cooperating agencies that have been identified for each incident annex. The responsibilities of these agencies in the incident annexes are identical to those detailed in the support annexes. Each of the incident annexes is described below.

- Biological Incident Annex (Coordinator: HHS)

Outlines the actions, roles, and responsibilities associated with response to a disease outbreak of known or unknown origin requiring federal assistance, including threat assessment notification procedures, laboratory testing, joint investigative/response procedures, and activities related to recovery. The broad objectives of the federal government's response to a biological terrorism event, pandemic influenza, emerging infectious disease, or novel pathogen outbreak are to:

Detect the event through disease surveillance and environmental monitoring

Identify and protect the population(s) at risk

Determine the source of the outbreak

Quickly frame the public health and law enforcement implications

Control and contain any possible epidemic (including providing guidance to state and local public health authorities)

Augment and surge public health and medical services

Track and defeat any potential resurgence or additional outbreaks

Assess the extent of residual biological contamination and decontaminate as necessary

- Catastrophic Incident Annex (Coordinator: DHS)

Establishes the context and overarching strategy for implementing and coordinating an accelerated, proactive national response to a catastrophic incident (a more detailed NRF Catastrophic Incident Supplement (NRF-CIS), designated "For Official Use Only," has not been released for public view). A catastrophic incident is any natural or man-made incident resulting in extraordinary levels of mass casualties, damage, or disruption severely affecting the population, infrastructure, environment, economy, national morale, and/or government functions. Recognizing that federal and/or national resources are required to augment overwhelmed state, local, and tribal response efforts, the NRF-CIA establishes protocols to pre-identify and rapidly deploy key essential resources (e.g., medical teams, US&R teams, transportable shelters, and medical and equipment caches) that are expected to be urgently needed/required to save lives and contain incidents. Accordingly, upon designation by the Secretary of Homeland Security of a catastrophic incident, federal resources — organized into incident-specific "packages" — deploy in accordance with the NRF-CIS and in coordination with the affected state and incident command structure. An important factor associated with NRF-CIA-designated disasters is that federal assets unilaterally deployed in accordance with the NRF-CIS do not require a state cost-share. Departments and agencies assigned primary responsibility for one or more functional response areas under the NRF-CIS appendixes include:

Mass care: American Red Cross

Search and rescue: Department of Homeland Security

Decontamination: Department of Homeland Security, Environmental Protection Agency, and Department of Health and Human Services

Public health and medical support: Department of Health and Human Services

Medical equipment and supplies: Department of Health and Human Services

Patient movement: Department of Health and Human Services and Department of Defense

Mass fatality: Department of Health and Human Services

Housing: Department of Homeland Security

Public and incident communications: Department of Homeland Security

Transportation: Department of Transportation

Private-sector support: Department of Homeland Security

Logistics: Department of Homeland Security

- Cyber Incident Annex (Coordinators: DHS, DOD, and DOJ)

Discusses policies, organization, actions, and responsibilities for a coordinated approach to prepare for, respond to, and recover from cyber-related emergency incidents impacting critical national processes and the national economy. A cyber-related emergency may take many forms: an organized cyberattack, an uncontrolled exploit such as a virus or a worm, a natural disaster with significant cyberconsequences, or other incidents capable of causing extensive damage to critical infrastructure or key assets. Federal government responsibilities include:

Providing indications and warning of potential threats, incidents, and attacks
Information sharing both inside and outside the government, including best practices, investigative information, coordination of incident response, and incident mitigation
Analyzing cyber vulnerabilities, exploits, and attack methodologies
Providing technical assistance
Conducting investigations, forensics analysis, and prosecution
Attributing the source of cyberattacks
Defending against the attack
Leading national-level recovery efforts

- Food and Agriculture Incident Annex (Coordinators: Department of Agriculture and HHS)

Describes how the various involved agencies will respond to emergency incidents involving the nation's agriculture and food systems. A food and agriculture incident may threaten public health, animal nutrition, food production, aquaculture, livestock production, wildlife, soils, rangelands, and agricultural water supplies. Responding to the unique attributes of this type of incident requires separate planning considerations that are tailored to specific health and agriculture concerns and effects of the disease (e.g., deliberate contamination versus natural outbreaks, plant and animal versus processed food, etc.). The objectives of a coordinated federal response to an incident impacting food and agriculture are to:

Detect the event through the reporting of illness, disease/pest surveillance, routine testing, consumer complaints, and/or environmental monitoring
Establish the primary coordinating agency
Determine the source of the incident or outbreak
Control and contain the distribution of the affected source
Identify and protect the population at risk
Assess the public health, food, agriculture, and law enforcement implications
Assess the extent of residual biological, chemical, or radiological contamination and decontaminate and dispose as necessary
Support effective and coordinated communication between federal, state, and local responders to a potential or actual incident that requires a coordinated federal response impacting food and agriculture
Minimize public health and economic impacts of a food- and agriculture-related incident
Specify roles and responsibilities of coordinating federal agencies and departments
Provide transition from response to rapid recovery following a food- and agriculture-related incident

- Nuclear/Radiological Incident Annex (Coordinators: DHS, DOD, DOE, EPA, National Aeronautics and Space Administration, and Nuclear Regulatory Commission)

Facilitates an organized and coordinated response by federal agencies to terrorist incidents involving nuclear or radioactive materials, and accidents or incidents involving such material. These nuclear/

radiological incidents, which include sabotage and terrorist incidents, involve the release or potential release of radioactive material that poses an actual or perceived hazard to public health, safety, national security, and/or the environment (including the terrorist use of RDDs), or "dirty bombs," or improvised nuclear devices (INDs), reactor plant accidents (commercial or weapons production facilities), lost radioactive material sources, transportation accidents involving nuclear/radioactive material, and foreign accidents involving nuclear or radioactive material. This annex:

> Provides planning guidance and outlines operational concepts for the federal response to any nuclear/radiological incident, including a terrorist incident that has actual, potential, or perceived radiological consequences within the United States or its territories, possessions, or territorial waters and that requires a response by the federal government
>
> Describes federal policies and planning considerations on which this annex and federal agency-specific nuclear/radiological response plans are based
>
> Specifies the roles and responsibilities of federal agencies for preventing, preparing for, responding to, and recovering from nuclear/radiological incidents
>
> Includes guidelines for notification, coordination, and leadership of federal activities, and coordination of public information, congressional relations, and international activities
>
> Provides protocols for coordinating federal government capabilities to respond to radiological incidents. These capabilities include, but are not limited to:
>
> > The Interagency Modeling and Atmospheric Assessment Center (IMAAC), which is responsible for production, coordination, and dissemination of consequence predictions for an airborne hazardous material release
> >
> > The Federal Radiological Monitoring and Assessment Center (FRMAC), established at or near the scene of an incident to coordinate radiological assessment and monitoring
> >
> > The Advisory Team for Environment, Food, and Health (known as "the Advisory Team"), which provides expert recommendations on protective action guidance

- Oil and Hazardous Materials Incident Annex (Coordinators: EPA and USCG)

Describes the roles, responsibilities, and coordinating mechanisms for managing major oil and hazardous materials pollution incidents. This annex addresses those oil and hazardous materials incidents that are managed through concurrent implementation of the NRF and the National Oil and Hazardous Substances Pollution Contingency Plan (NCP), but are not ESF #10 (Oil and Hazardous Materials Response) activations. The NCP provides the organizational structure and procedures for federal response to releases of oil and hazardous materials, and addresses incident prevention, planning, response, and recovery. The hazardous materials addressed under the NCP include certain substances considered weapons of mass destruction (i.e., chemical agents, biological agents, and radiological/nuclear material). The NCP establishes structures at the national, regional, and local levels that are used to respond to thousands of incidents annually. When an NRF incident does occur, these NCP structures remain in place to provide hazard-specific expertise and support. This annex describes how the NCP structures work with NRF coordinating structures during major emergency or disaster incidents.

- Terrorism Incident Law Enforcement and Investigation Annex (Coordinator: FBI)

Facilitates a federal law enforcement and investigative response to all threats or acts of terrorism within the United States, regardless of whether they are deemed credible and/or whether they are major or minor in scope. This annex provides planning guidance and outlines operational concepts for the federal law enforcement and investigative response to a threatened or actual terrorist incident, and acknowledges and outlines the unique nature of each threat or incident, the capabilities and responsibilities of the local jurisdictions, and the law enforcement and investigative activities necessary to prevent or mitigate a specific threat or incident. The law enforcement and investigative response to a terrorist threat or incident within the United States is a highly coordinated, multiagency state, local, tribal, and federal responsibility. The attorney general holds the lead responsibility for criminal investigations of terrorist acts or terrorist threats by individuals or groups inside the United States, or directed at U.S. citizens or institutions abroad, under HSPD-5. Acting through the FBI, the attorney general, in cooperation with other federal departments and agencies engaged in activities to protect national security, also coordinates the activities of the other members of the law enforcement community to detect, prevent, preempt, and disrupt terrorist attacks. Although not formally designated under this annex, other federal departments and agencies may have authorities, resources, capabilities, or expertise required to support terrorism-related law enforcement and investigation operations. Agencies may be requested to participate in federal planning and response operations, and may be requested to designate liaison officers and provide other support as required.

■ ■ Critical Thinking ■

The NRF is a comprehensive document, but it cannot possibly cover every possible need that may arise in every emergency incident. In light of the wide array of emergencies and disasters that could occur in your community, are there any specific community-level needs that might fall outside the spectrum of the NRF that are not explicitly detailed (e.g., the needs of children in emergencies)?

Recovery

The recovery function is not easy to classify; it often begins in the initial hours and days following a disaster event and can continue for months and in some cases years, depending on the severity of the event. Unlike the response function, where all efforts have a singular focus, the recovery function or process is characterized by a complex set of issues and decisions that must be made by individuals and communities. These issues include the following:

- Rebuilding homes
- Replacing property
- Resuming employment
- Restoring businesses
- Permanently repairing and rebuilding infrastructure

Since the establishment of DHS, the recovery function has remained relatively unchanged, although minor changes affecting the nomenclature and classification of the available assistance, as well as some relief programs and grants, have occurred. Because the recovery function has such long-lasting impacts and usually high costs, the participants in the process are numerous. They include all levels of government, the business community, political leadership, community activists, and individuals. The major players and programs will be listed here and changes, if any, will be described.

Disaster Recovery Operations in the National Response Framework

The NRF addresses the need for structured principles and procedures by which individuals, communities, and the nation recover from the consequences of emergencies and disasters. Recovery operations may require significant contributions from all sectors of society, each of which is addressed. There are two phases of recovery identified in the NRF, including:

Short-term recovery: This is the period when recovery actions that begin immediately upon occurrence of the disaster, which overlap with response actions, are taken. This phase includes actions such as providing essential public health and safety services, restoring interrupted utility and other essential services, reestablishing transportation routes, and providing food and shelter for those displaced by the incident. Although called "short term," some short-term recovery activities may last for weeks. Short-term recovery actions are addressed in several functional areas of the NRF.

Long-term recovery: This is the period that involves the restoration of lives and livelihoods beyond the emergency phase of the disaster, once lifelines and critical societal components have been restored or replaced. This phase falls squarely within the direction of ESF #14, "Long-Term Community Recovery," and often continues for several months or years after the disaster has ended.

Recovery can include the development, coordination, and execution of service- and site-restoration plans; reconstitution of government operations and services; programs to provide housing and promote restoration; long-term care and treatment of affected persons; and additional measures for social, political, environmental, and economic restoration. Under the NRF, recovery operations and programs:

- Identify needs and resources
- Provide accessible housing and promote restoration
- Address care and treatment of affected persons
- Provide recovering victims with appropriate recovery information
- Facilitate community restoration
- Incorporate mitigation measures and techniques, as feasible

Recovery Coordination

As in the response phase, the JFO serves as the central coordination point among local, tribal, state, and federal governments, as well as private-sector and nongovernmental entities that are providing recovery assistance. The NRF outlines several recovery actions that may take place under this structure, including:

Coordinating assistance programs to help individuals, households, and businesses meet basic needs and return to self-sufficiency. Such programs include housing assistance, other needs assistance (ONA), crisis counseling services, disaster legal services, and unemployment or reemployment programs. Other activities include coordinating with local and tribal governments the need for and locations of disaster recovery centers (DRCs).

Establishing DRCs. Federal, state, tribal, local, voluntary, and NGOs determine the need for and location of DRCs. DRC staff provide recovery and mitigation program information, advice, counseling, and related technical assistance.

Coordinating with private-sector and NGOs involved in donations management and other recovery activities. Donations and volunteer management in the past have been chaotic and disorganized, often leading to what is called "the second disaster." The NRF addresses these issues by tasking various federal agencies and offices with the management of these two functions.

Coordinating public assistance grant programs authorized by the Stafford Act. These programs aid local, tribal, and state governments and eligible private nonprofit organizations with the cost of emergency protective services, debris removal, and the repair or replacement of disaster-damaged public facilities and associated environmental restoration.

Coordinating with the private sector on restoration and recovery of CIKR. Activities to restore and facilitate the recovery of CIKR are primarily the responsibilities of the private sector, who owns the majority of these components. The restoration and repair of these facilities is integral to the recovery of the community, and therefore almost always require the assistance of the federal and state governments. The NRF guides the emergency management stakeholders in working with the owners and operators of these facilities to ensure that critical services return (which include, e.g., water, power, natural gas and petroleum, emergency communications, and health care).

Coordinating mitigation grant programs to help communities reduces the potential impacts of future disasters. The NRF addresses the most important concept behind recovery, which is to ensure that new disaster information is applied such that preexisting hazard vulnerabilities are effectively reduced.

At a certain point in the recovery operation, it will be determined that operations no longer require the services of a full JFO and that office will be closed. At this point, ongoing activities are led by the individual agencies that hold recovery responsibilities under the NRF. Federal partners then work directly with their regional or headquarter offices to administer and monitor recovery programs, support, and technical services.

Each of the primary and support agencies of ESF #14 has distinct programs aimed at facilitating recovery, based on their individual agency-specific expertise. The following subsections describe each agency's recovery function.

Coordination of Disaster Recovery

The practical work of implementing the recovery process occurs at the JFO. Two organizational structures, or branches, divide the recovery assistance functions. These branches assess state and local recovery needs at the outset of the disaster and relevant time frames for program delivery. The human services branch coordinates assistance programs to help individuals, families, and businesses meet basic needs and return to self-sufficiency. It is responsible for the donations management function. The infrastructure support branch coordinates assistance programs to aid state and local governments and eligible private nonprofit organizations to repair or replace damaged public facilities. The two branches assist in identifying appropriate agency assistance programs to meet applicant needs, synchronizing assistance delivery and encouraging incorporation of mitigation measures where possible. In addition to the work of the DRCs, applicant briefings are conducted for local government officials and certain private nonprofit organizations to inform them of available recovery assistance and how to apply.

Federal disaster assistance available under a major disaster falls into three general categories: individual assistance, public assistance, and hazard mitigation assistance. Individual assistance is aid to individuals, families, and business owners. Public assistance is aid to public and certain private nonprofit entities for emergency services and the repair or replacement of disaster-damaged public facilities. Hazard mitigation assistance is funding available for measures designed to reduce future losses to public and private property. A detailed description of the first two types of assistance follows.

FEMA'S Individual Assistance Recovery Programs

Individual assistance programs are oriented to individuals, families, and small businesses, and the programs include the Individuals and Households Program (IHP), SBA loans, disaster unemployment assistance (DUA), legal services, special tax considerations, and crisis counseling. The disaster victim must first register for assistance and establish eligibility before receiving this assistance. These programs are described next.

Individuals and Households Program

The Individuals and Households Program (IHP) is a program coordinated jointly by FEMA and the affected states. When a major disaster is declared, the IHP provides both money and services to people in the declared areas whose property has been damaged or destroyed and whose losses are not covered by insurance. To receive assistance under this program, disaster victims must register for assistance and first have their eligibility established.

IHP has two separate programs that address the needs of individuals and households. The housing assistance program works to ensure that people whose homes are damaged by a disaster have a safe place to live while it is repaired or replaced. The ONA program provides financial assistance to individuals and households who have disaster-related expenses or serious needs, but who do not qualify for Small Business Administration (SBA) loans (see next subsection). These two programs are designed to provide funds for expenses that are not covered by insurance. They are available only to U.S. citizen homeowners and renters, noncitizen nationals, or qualified aliens. The following is a list of the types of assistance available through this program and what each provides:

> *Temporary housing*: Funding that covers the cost of renting an alternate house or apartment when a victim's residence is uninhabitable due to disaster damage.
>
> *Repair*: Funding that covers the cost of repair to damage that was caused by the disaster, but which was not covered by insurance. These repairs must be geared toward making the home "safe and sanitary" to qualify.
>
> *Replacement*: Funding to cover the cost of replacing a home destroyed by a disaster.
>
> *Permanent housing construction*: Funding for the construction of a new home. This type of assistance occurs only in very unusual situations, in remote locations where no other type of housing is possible.
>
> *Other needs assistance (ONA)*: Funding for necessary and serious needs caused by the disaster. This includes medical, dental, funeral, personal property, transportation, moving and storage, and other expenses that FEMA approves. To receive ONA, the victim may first need to apply for an SBA loan.

Small Business Administration Disaster Loans

Following federally declared disasters, the U.S. Small Business Administration (SBA) normally provides federally subsidized loans to repair or replace homes, personal property, or businesses that sustained damages not covered by insurance. For many individuals, the SBA disaster loan program is the primary form of disaster assistance. The SBA can provide three types of disaster loans to qualified homeowners and businesses:

- Home disaster loans to homeowners and renters to repair or replace disaster-related damage to home or personal property

- Business physical disaster loans to business owners to repair or replace disaster-damaged property, including inventory and supplies
- Economic injury disaster loans, which provide capital to small businesses and to small agricultural cooperatives to assist them through the disaster recovery period

Disaster Unemployment Assistance

The Disaster Unemployment Assistance (DUA) program provides unemployment benefits and re-employment services to individuals who have lost their jobs as a result of the disaster. Benefits begin with the date the job was lost, and can be continued for up to 26 weeks after the presidential declaration date. The DUA program is available to people who are not covered by other unemployment insurance programs or who cannot qualify for other unemployment compensation.

Legal Services

Following a disaster, the Young Lawyers Division of the American Bar Association may be contracted by FEMA to provide free legal assistance to disaster victims. These services are provided to low-income individuals who, prior to or because of the disaster, are unable to afford adequate legal services to meet their postdisaster-related needs. Legal advice under this program is limited to cases that will not result in any attorney or other fees. The assistance that participating lawyers provide typically includes the following:

- Assistance with insurance claims (life, medical, property, etc.)
- Counseling on landlord/tenant problems
- Assisting in consumer protection matters, remedies, and procedures
- Replacement of wills and other important legal documents destroyed in a major disaster

Special Tax Considerations

Taxpayers who have sustained a casualty loss from a declared disaster may deduct that loss on the federal income tax return for the year in which the casualty actually occurred, or elect to deduct the loss on the tax return for the preceding tax year. To qualify, victims' losses must be greater than 10% of the adjusted gross income for the tax year by at least $100. Additionally, the Internal Revenue Service (IRS) can expedite refunds due to taxpayers in a federally declared disaster area. This service is available to any taxpayer in a federally declared disaster area.

Crisis Counseling

The Crisis Counseling Assistance and Training Program (CCP) is designed to provide supplemental funding to states for short-term crisis counseling services. Two separate portions of the CCP can be funded: immediate services and regular services. A state may request either or both types of funding. The immediate services program is intended to enable the state or local agency to respond to the immediate mental health needs with screening, diagnostic, and counseling techniques, as well as outreach services such as public information and community networking. The regular services program is designed to provide up to 9 months of crisis counseling, community outreach, and consultation and education services to people affected by the disaster. To be eligible for crisis counseling services funded by this program, the person must be a resident of the designated area or must have been located in the area at the time the disaster occurred. The person must also have a mental health problem that was caused or aggravated by the disaster or its aftermath, or he or she must benefit from services provided by the program.

Public Assistance Programs

Public assistance, oriented to public entities, is designed to facilitate the repair, restoration, reconstruction, or replacement of public facilities or infrastructure damaged or destroyed by a federally declared disaster. Eligible applicants include state governments, local governments, and any other political subdivision of a state, Native American tribes, and Alaska Native villages. Certain private nonprofit (PNP) organizations may also receive assistance, including educational, utility, irrigation, emergency, medical, rehabilitation, and temporary or permanent custodial care facilities, and other PNP facilities that provide essential services of a governmental nature to the general public.

As soon as is possible and practical following a disaster declaration, the state, assisted by FEMA, briefs state, local, and PNP officials to inform them of the assistance available and how to apply for it (Figure 9–8). To receive this assistance, a Request for Public Assistance must be filed with the state within 30 days of the time the area is designated as eligible. Following the briefing, a "Kickoff Meeting" is conducted where damages are discussed, needs assessed, and a plan of action put in place. A team made up of federal, state, and local representatives initiates the project, including documenting the eligible facilities, the eligible work, and the eligible cost for fixing the damages to every public or PNP facility identified by state or local representatives. The team prepares a project worksheet (PW) for each project. Projects are grouped into the following categories:

- *Category A*: Debris removal
- *Category B*: Emergency protective measures

FIGURE 9–8 Birmingham, AL, June 17, 2011 — FEMA Associate Administrator William Carwile (center) listens to a report during a general staff meeting at the Joint Field Office, along with Alabama State Coordinating Officer Jeff Byard (left) and Federal Coordinating Officer Mike Byrne. The meetings help coordinate all of the state and federal resources to continue the recovery process. (Source: FEMA photo/Tim Burkitt)

- *Category C*: Road systems and bridges
- *Category D*: Water control facilities
- *Category E*: Public buildings and contents
- *Category F*: Public utilities
- *Category G*: Parks, recreational, and other

FEMA reviews and approves the PWs and obligates the federal share of the costs (75% or more) to the state. The state then disburses funds to local applicants.

Other Federal Agency Disaster Recovery Funding

Other federal agencies have programs that contribute to social and economic recovery. Most of these additional programs are triggered by a presidential declaration of a major disaster or emergency under the Stafford Act. However, the Secretary of the Department of Agriculture and the administrator of the SBA have specific authority relevant to their constituencies to declare a disaster and provide disaster recovery assistance. All of the agencies are part of the structure of the NRF.

Conclusion

The motives behind the establishment of the DHS are almost as numerous as the number of agencies it involves, and include politics, power, public relations, or a real need to improve the federal response and recovery systems because of the new spectrum of threats made apparent by the September 11 attacks. For whatever reason or combination of reasons, a system that had demonstrated its operational capabilities in both natural disasters and terrorism events in Oklahoma City, New York, and the Pentagon became subject to significant and ongoing change. As a result of the integration of different agencies and the need for new procedural systems to operate together, the NRP was developed with the NIMS. NIMS and the NRF (that has since replaced the NRP) together serve as references and guidelines to determine how the nation's first responders and agencies involved in response operate.

The effort to include citizens and the private sector as active partners is commendable. Programs developed under the CCCs provide the opportunity to build strong communities. However, they have been poorly supported by the political leadership and are underfunded. Further collaboration with the business sector will allow for enhanced preparedness and protection of the critical infrastructure and provide a better understanding of its vulnerabilities and how to respond if it is attacked.

As a final point, it is essential to bear in mind that the massive integration of many agencies into one has its drawbacks: independence is compromised and the overall redundancy of the system decreases. The NRF and NIMS define how different agencies operate together but it should not jeopardize or change the agencies' own integrity and mission. Although redundancy is an attribute that all organizations try to get rid of, it is also what often saves the day during a crisis situation. "Too efficient" systems with minimal backup, no duplication of function, and low flexibility/adaptability have been shown to be more vulnerable to unexpected situations, to fail in a worse manner, and to be less agile when responding to and dealing with an emergency. Thus, an excessive integration to reduce redundancy can cause the involved agencies to depend on each other rather than empower each other — and this might lead the way for a catastrophic chain reaction of failure to occur in certain conditions.

Key Terms

Demobilization: The orderly, safe, and efficient return of a resource or resources to their original location and status.

Disaster Declaration: The process by which the chief executive official of a jurisdiction (e.g., the mayor, governor, or president) identifies a situation as being beyond the capacity of that particular jurisdiction to be responsed. Under established statutory authorities at the state and federal levels, disaster declaration frees up various resources in support of the affected governments.

Emergency Declaration: Any occasion or instance for which, in the determination of the president, federal assistance is needed to supplement state and local efforts and capabilities to save lives and to protect property and public health and safety, or to lessen or avert the threat of a catastrophe in any part of the United States. An emergency declaration is more limited in scope and without the long-term federal recovery programs of a major disaster declaration. Generally, federal assistance and funding are provided to meet a specific emergency need or to help prevent a major disaster from occurring.

Emergency Support Function (ESF): Used by the federal government and many state governments as the primary mechanism at the operational level to organize and provide assistance. ESFs align categories of resources and provide strategic objectives for their use. ESFs exist within the NRF, and in most state and local emergency operations plans. ESFs utilize standardized resource management concepts such as typing, inventorying, and tracking to facilitate the dispatch, deployment, and recovery of resources before, during, and after an incident.

Federal Response Plan: A plan guiding the overall delivery of federal assistance in Stafford Act (presidentially declared) disasters that was replaced by the National Response Plan in 2004.

Incident Command System (ICS): A system by which emergency incidents of all sizes are managed, developed by the federal, state, and local wildland fire agencies during the 1970s. ICS is structured to facilitate activities in five major functional areas: command, operations, planning, logistics, and finance/administration. In some circumstances, intelligence and investigations may be added as a sixth functional area.

Individual Assistance: Individual assistance programs are oriented to individuals, families, and small businesses, and the programs include the Individuals and Households Program, Small Business Administration loans, disaster unemployment assistance, legal services, special tax considerations, and crisis counseling. The disaster victim must first register for assistance and establish eligibility before receiving this assistance.

Joint Field Office: The JFO coordinates federal incident support to the state, allowing the integration of diverse federal resources. Within the JFO, there is one key operational group and two key officials, including the Unified Coordination Group and the State Coordinating Officer.

Joint Information Center (JIC): A JIC may be established in emergency situations in order to coordinate the release of emergency information and other public affairs functions. The JIC serves as a focal point for coordinated and timely release of incident-related information to the public and the media. Information about where to receive assistance is communicated directly to victims and their families in an accessible format and in appropriate languages.

Long-Term Recovery: This is the period that involves the restoration of lives and livelihoods beyond the emergency phase of the disaster, once lifelines and critical societal components have been restored or replaced. This phase falls squarely within the direction of Emergency Support

Function #14, "Long-Term Community Recovery," and often continues for several months or years after the disaster has ended.

Multiagency Coordination System (MACS): A system designed to help coordinate activities that occur above the field level, and to prioritize demands for critical or competing resources. Examples of multiagency coordination include a state or county emergency operations center, a state intelligence fusion center, the National Operations Center, the FEMA National Response Coordination Center, the Department of Justice/FBI Strategic Information and Operations Center, the FBI Joint Operations Center, and the National Counterterrorism Center.

National Incident Management System (NIMS): A system that provides a proactive approach guiding government agencies at all levels, the private sector, and nongovernmental organizations to work seamlessly to prepare for, prevent, respond to, recover from, and mitigate the effects of incidents, regardless of cause, size, location, or complexity, in order to reduce the loss of life or property and harm to the environment.

National Response Framework (NRF): A document released in 2008 to replace the National Response Plan that guides how the nation conducts all-hazards response. The framework documents the key response principles, roles, and structures that organize national response. It describes how communities, states, the federal government, and private-sector and nongovernmental partners apply these principles for national response. It also describes special circumstances where the federal government must exercise a larger role, including incidents where federal interests are involved and catastrophic incidents where a state would require significant support. It was designed to allow all response stakeholders to provide a unified national response.

National Response Plan: A plan released in 2004 to replace the Federal Response Plan that guided the response actions of local, state, and federal resources to major "incidents of national significance." This plan was replaced in 2008 by the NRF.

NRF Cooperating Agency: Cooperating agencies have specific expertise and capabilities that allow them to assist the coordinating agency in executing incident-related tasks or processes. When the procedures within a support annex are needed to support elements of an incident, the coordinating agency will notify cooperating agencies of the circumstances.

NRF Coordinating Agency: Coordinating agencies are responsible for implementing the processes detailed in NRF annexes. These federal agencies support DHS incident management efforts by providing the leadership, expertise, and authorities to implement critical and specific aspects of the response. When the functions of a particular support annex are required, the agency serving as the coordinator must carry out various responsibilities as stipulated in the NRF.

Posse Comitatus Act: A law passed in 1878 that restricts the use of the armed forces to perform domestic law enforcement.

Presidential Major Disaster Declaration: Any natural catastrophe (including any hurricane, tornado, storm, high water, wind-driven water, tidal wave, tsunami, earthquake, volcanic eruption, landslide, mudslide, snowstorm, or drought), or, regardless of cause, any fire, flood, or explosion, in any part of the United States that in the determination of the president causes damage of sufficient severity and magnitude to warrant major disaster assistance under the Stafford Act to supplement the efforts and available resources of states, local governments, and disaster relief organizations in alleviating the damage, loss, hardship, or suffering caused thereby.

Public Assistance: Public assistance, oriented to public entities, is designed to facilitate the repair, restoration, reconstruction, or replacement of public facilities or infrastructure damaged or destroyed by a federally declared disaster. Eligible applicants include state governments, local governments and any other political subdivision of a state, Native American tribes, and Alaska Native villages. Certain private nonprofit (PNP) organizations may also receive assistance, including educational, utility, irrigation, emergency, medical, rehabilitation, and temporary or permanent custodial care facilities, and other PNP facilities that provide essential services of a governmental nature to the general public.

Short-Term Recovery: This is the period when recovery actions that begin immediately upon occurrence of the disaster, which overlap with response actions, are taken. This phase includes actions such as providing essential public health and safety services, restoring interrupted utility and other essential services, reestablishing transportation routes, and providing food and shelter for those displaced by the incident. Although called *short term*, some short-term recovery activities may last for weeks. Short-term recovery actions are addressed in several functional areas of the NRF.

State Coordinating Officer (SCO): The SCO plays a critical role in managing the state response and recovery operations following presidential disaster declarations. The governor of the affected state appoints the SCO, and lines of authority flow from the governor to the SCO, following the state's policies and laws. For events in which a declaration has not yet occurred but is expected (such as with an approaching hurricane), the Secretary of Homeland Security or the FEMA administrator may predesignate one or more federal officials to coordinate with the SCO to determine resources and actions that will likely be required, and begin deployment of assets.

Strategic National Stockpile: CDC's Strategic National Stockpile (SNS) consists of strategically placed repositories of medicine and medical supplies that can be called on to protect the public in the event of a public health emergency severe enough to deplete local supplies. Once federal and local authorities agree that the SNS is needed, medicines will be delivered to any state in the United States within 12 hours. Each state has plans to receive and distribute SNS medicine and medical supplies to local communities as quickly as possible.

Unified Command: A system that allows for more efficient multijurisdictional or multiagency management of emergency events by enabling agencies with different legal, geographic, and functional responsibilities to coordinate, plan, and interact with each other in an effective manner. Unified command allows all agencies with jurisdictional authority or functional responsibility for the incident to jointly provide management direction to an incident through a common set of incident objectives and strategies and a single incident action plan. Under unified command, each participating agency maintains its authority, responsibility, and accountability.

Unified Coordination Group: The Unified Coordination Group is comprised of senior officials from the states and key federal departments and agencies, and is established at the JFO. Using unified command principles, this group provides national support to achieve shared emergency response and recovery objectives.

Urban Search and Rescue: Urban search and rescue (US&R) involves the location, rescue (extrication), and initial medical stabilization of victims trapped in confined spaces. Although structural collapse is the most common origin of trapped victims, transportation accidents, mines, and collapsed trenches may also cause such to occur. US&R is considered a "multihazard" discipline, as it may be needed for a variety of emergencies or disasters, including earthquakes, hurricanes, typhoons, storms and tornadoes, floods, dam failures, technological accidents, terrorist activities, and hazardous materials releases.

Zoonotic: A disease that can be spread between animals and people.

Review Questions

1. In your opinion, what are the most important differences between the NRF, the NRP, and the FRP?
2. Do you feel that the creation of the Department of Homeland Security has improved emergency response in the United States? Why or why not?
3. If you were an appointed local emergency manager, would you be satisfied with the actions of the federal government in terms of preparedness for large-scale emergency events? What would be the greatest benefits and problems for you under this new structure (the NRF) from a response perspective? Answer the same question from a regional emergency manager officer and a FEMA high-level officer point of view.
4. What was the basis of the decision to create the National Incident Management System (NIMS)? Why wasn't the ICS used instead? What benefits are gained by having an NRF that is based on the NIMS?
5. The establishment of the Department of Homeland Security, and the many subsequent changes to the national emergency management framework, are seen by many local emergency managers as inhibiting their efforts to establish an effective all-hazards emergency response capacity. What are your opinions on this stance? Explain your answer.

References

American Corporate Council Association (ACCA), 2002. 107th Congress Homeland Security Legislation. http://www.acc.com/infopaks/homeland/legislativechart.pdf.

Bea, Keath, W. Krouse, D. Morgan, W. Morrissey, and C. Redhead. 2003. Emergency Preparedness and Response Directorate of the Department of Homeland Security. Congressional Research Service. http://www.fas.org/sgp/crs/RS21367.pdf.

Bullock & Haddow, LLC, 2003. Personal interviews with the Chief of Staff and Deputy Chief of Staff of the Federal Emergency Management Agency, unpublished.

Department of Homeland Security, 2007. FY 2007 Homeland Security Grant Program. http://www.dhs.gov/xlibrary/assets/grants_st-local_fy07.pdf.

Environmental Protection Agency, 2008. "National Oil and Hazardous Substances Pollution Contingency Plan." http://www.epa.gov/OEM/content/lawsregs/ncpover.htm.

Federal Bureau of Investigation, 2001. Domestic Terrorism Concept of Operations Plan. http://www.fbi.gov/publications/conplan/conplan.pdf.

Federal Emergency Management Agency, 1992. Federal Response Plan. http://www.library.findlaw.com/1992/Apr/1/127810.html.

Federal Emergency Management Agency, 2001. Federal Radiological Emergency Response Plan. http://www.fas.org/nuke/guide/usa/doctrine/national/frerp.htm.

Federal Emergency Management Agency, 2004. National Response Plan. http://www.dhs.gov/xlibrary/assets/NRPbaseplan.pdf.

Federal Emergency Management Agency, 2008. National Response Framework. http://www.fema.gov/emergency/nrf/.

Federal Emergency Management Agency. 2008. Number of Declarations per Calendar Year Since 1998. Washington, DC. http://www.fema.gov/government/grant/pa/stat1.shtm.

Washington Post. 2005. War plans drafted to counter terror attacks in U.S. The Washington Post, August 8, p. A1. http://www.washingtonpost.com/wp-dyn/content/article/2005/08/07/AR2005080700843_pf.html.

10

Mitigation, Prevention, and Preparedness

What You Will Learn

- The definitions of mitigation, preparedness, and prevention
- Overview of mitigation and preparedness programs
- Where terrorism fits in the classical life cycle of emergency management
- Preparedness for chemical, biological, and radiological incidents
- Community issues in preparedness
- Private-sector involvement in mitigation and preparedness

Introduction

Mitigation and preparedness constitute one-half of the classic emergency management cycle, with response and recovery completing the sequence (Figure 10–1). Mitigation and preparedness generally occur before a disaster ever occurs, although postdisaster mitigation and preparedness, conducted in recognition that similar events are likely in the future, make these two activities somewhat general to the entire emergency management cycle. This is in contrast to response and recovery, which by definition are only possible in the aftermath of a disastrous event.

Mitigation refers to a sustained action taken to reduce or eliminate risk to people and property from hazards and their effects. Mitigation activities address either or both of the two components of risk, which are probability (likelihood) and consequence. By mitigating either of these components, the risk becomes much less of a threat to the affected population. In the case of natural disasters, the ability of humans to limit the probability of a hazard is highly dependent on the hazard type, with some hazards such as hurricanes or tornadoes impossible to prevent, while avalanches, floods, and wildfires are examples of hazards for which limiting the rate of occurrence is possible.

In general, however, mitigation efforts for natural hazards tend to focus on improved consequence management. In terms of man-made disasters, however, there is a much greater range of opportunities to minimize both the probability and the consequences of potential incidents, and both are applied with equal intensity. Mitigation in terms of terrorism, which is a much more complicated process, is discussed later in this chapter.

Preparedness can be defined as a state of readiness to respond to a disaster, crisis, or any other type of emergency situation. In general, preparedness activities can be characterized as the human component

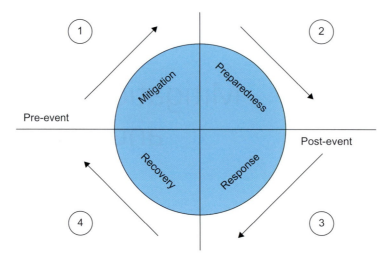

FIGURE 10–1 The four classical phases of disaster management.

of predisaster hazard management. Training and public education are the most common preparedness activities, and, when properly applied, they have great potential to help people survive disasters. Although preparedness activities do little to prevent a disaster from occurring, they are very effective at ensuring that people know what to do once the disaster has happened.

The concepts of mitigation and preparedness have been altered since September 11, 2001, when terrorism became viewed as the primary threat facing America. As such, terms like *terrorism prevention* and *terrorism preparedness* have become more popular. One must question, in light of these new terms, whether there is any real difference between the traditional definitions of *preparedness* and *mitigation* and what is being conducted in light of the new terrorism hazard.

In January 2008, the National Response Plan (NRP) was replaced by the National Response Framework (NRF), and as such much of the emergency management terminology and functions have changed accordingly. The following section describes several of these changes as they relate to mitigation, prevention, and preparedness.

First, the document's title has been changed appropriately to reflect its true nature — namely, that it provides guidelines, rules of engagement, and an organizational framework for all stakeholders of a disaster response involving the federal government rather than offering specific steps of action as is typical in an EOP.

Second, the NRF does not attempt to redefine the phases of emergency management as occurred in the NRP. In the NRP, prevention was introduced as a distinct phase in the incident management cycle, and in many (but not all) references, as a replacement for mitigation. The NRF makes no direct reference to the emergency management cycle, and refers more sensibly to the terms *prevention* and *mitigation*. *Mitigation* is used comfortably and consistently as part of the all-hazards approach, thereby providing clarity throughout the document. The choice not to push prevention as a distinct emergency management phase is consistent with former Department of Homeland Security (DHS) Secretary Michael Chertoff's vision to establish DHS as managing all hazards rather than having a distinct focus on terrorism. The term *prevention* is most closely associated with terrorism, and therefore finds little applicability in any generalized emergency management approach.

The third major difference relates to the adjustments made to general terms that better accommodate the involvement and partnership of nonfederal stakeholders. These entities are better defined in terms of their role with regard to the emergency support functions (ESFs). The final difference is that the framework commits the federal government to the development of specific emergency response plans based on the 15 incident scenarios identified by the Homeland Security Council. Because incident scenario planning tends to create a rigid response functionality, it is difficult to agree with the approach taken. In such an approach, flexibility is sacrificed and problems may arise when real incidents do not fit the expected parameters. Additionally, this should be seen as a departure from the all-hazards approach as so many of the scores of known hazards are omitted or disregarded, though it is true that these 15 scenarios may be useful as an exercise tool. (For more complete information regarding the NRF and the changes it brings, see DHS, 2011a; Public Broadcasting System, 2006.)

Whether we call it prevention or mitigation, proactive incident management is crucial for minimizing the loss of human life, injuries, financial losses, property damage, and interruption of business activities. Specific methods of prevention and mitigation change from hazard to hazard, and incident to incident, but the goals are the same.

Using the all-hazards approach, whether you are mitigating for earthquakes or floods or preparing for a potential terrorist threat, the classic mitigation planning process is an effective guide for the overall process. The traditional mitigation planning process, still conducted by the Federal Emergency Management Agency (FEMA) today under its DHS umbrella, consists of four stages: (1) identifying and organizing resources; (2) conducting a risk or threat assessment and estimating losses; (3) identifying mitigation measures that will reduce the effects of the hazards and creating a strategy to deal with the mitigation measures in priority order; and (4) implementing the measures, evaluating the results, and keeping the plan up-to-date. This chapter expands on these concepts.

Mitigation and preparedness are vital for sustainable emergency management because strategies geared strictly toward post disaster response tend to be costlier than those accounting for predisaster opportunities. However, it can be difficult to convince decision makers to invest in mitigation and preparedness activities.

The next section focuses on mitigation, prevention, and preparedness activities in an effort to identify ongoing programs, as well as new developments as they fit into each subject.

Mitigation Plans, Actions, and Programs

Mitigation activities include many different methods and strategies that have the common goal of reducing the risk associated with potential hazards. To provide a deeper understanding of mitigation, it is important to first understand the nature of natural, man-made, and terrorism risk.

There are many different definitions of *risk*, each of which may be appropriate within specific circumstances. Kaplan 1997, an acclaimed risk management expert, argues that rather than providing a full definition of *risk*, one must ask three major questions in considering a specific hazard: (1) What can happen? (2) How likely is it? (3) What are the consequences? This indirect definition provides a much more flexible starting point with which to begin our discussion of risk and how to mitigate it. It also sheds additional light on the complexity of treating risks, which are clearly dynamic in nature. How we consider those risks — and rank them according to our concern — is a factor of the combined answers of those three questions. For instance, although traffic accidents occur on a daily basis, their consequences tend to be relatively minor. Very large meteor strikes, on the other hand, are very rare, but when they do occur, their consequences are globally catastrophic. Each hazard must be considered for its individual characteristics, and it is up to the individual, community, or society that is making the analysis to determine what level of effort will be made to address each according to these individual risk components.

The uncertainty component of risk, contained within the probability of disastrous event occurrence, places the greatest burden on those who are treating a full portfolio of risks that must be compared in relation to each other. Uncertainty forces us to ask ourselves questions that are often difficult and based more on expert judgment than on concrete evidence, such as, "What is the probability that a 7.0-magnitude earthquake will happen in San Francisco Bay within the next 10 years?" or "What is the probability that terrorists will attack and damage a nuclear power plant in the United States?" The probability component of risk is important because it is an equally weighted parameter that helps us to quantify and prioritize mitigation actions when dealing with multiple risks. The determination of probabilities for events is often a difficult and complicated process. Although several quantitative methods and tools are available that can be used to determine probabilities, these often tend to be too complex for communities to use. Qualitative methods have been developed to ease this problem, which in turn allows for much easier comparison of risk by communities that attempt treating their risks. The sidebar titled, "Qualitative Representation of Likelihood" illustrates but one example of a system of estimation used to establish qualitative risk likelihood rankings.

Qualitative Representation of Likelihood

This particular qualitative representation system uses words to describe the chance of an event occurring. Each word or phrase has a designated range of possibilities attached to it. For instance, events could be described as follows:

- Certain: 99% chance of occurring in a given year (one or more occurrences per year)
- Likely: 50%–99% chance of occurring in a given year (one occurrence every 1 to 2 years)
- Possible: 5%–49% chance of occurring in a given year (one occurrence every 2 to 20 years)
- Unlikely: 2%–5% chance of occurring in a given year (one occurrence every 20 to 50 years)
- Rare: 1%–2% chance of occurring in a given year (one occurrence every 50 to 100 years)
- Extremely rare: 1% chance of occurring in a given year (one occurrence every 100 or more years)

Note that this is just one of a limitless range of qualitative terms and values assigned that can be used to describe the likelihood component of risk. As long as all hazards are compared using the same range of qualitative values, the actual determination of likelihood ranges attached to each term does not necessarily matter.

The second component of risk, hazard consequence, is a detailed examination of the total unwanted impact of the disaster to the community, government, or the interested stakeholders. Consequence is often given an assigned monetary value in order to facilitate comparison with other hazards, but there are many intangible consequences that are very difficult to quantify in such absolute terms but which have to be considered as well if a comprehensive risk analysis is expected (Table 10–1). Interestingly, the consequences of disasters also have a probabilistic nature. In practice, it is quite hard to assign a single monetary value to the expected damage; probability distributions are used to model the most likely damage estimates. For this reason, qualitative applications of consequence estimation have also been developed. An example is presented in the sidebar "Qualitative Representation of Consequence."

Table 10–1 Tangible and Intangible Consequences of Disasters

Consequences	Measure	Tangible Losses	Intangible Losses
Deaths	Number of people	Loss of economically active individuals	Social and psychological effects on remaining community
Injuries	Number and injury severity	Medical treatment needs, temporary loss of economic activity by productive individuals	Social and psychological pain and recovery
Physical damage	Inventory of damaged elements by number and damage level	Replacement and repair cost	Cultural losses
Emergency operations	Volume of manpower, person-days employed, equipment, and resources expended to relief mobilization cost, investment in preparedness capability	Stress and overwork in relief participants	
Disruption to economy	Number of working days lost, volume of production lost	Value of lost production opportunities, and in competitiveness and reputation	
Social disruption	Number of displaced persons, homeless	Temporary housing, relief, economic production	Psychological, social contacts, cohesion, community morale
Environmental impact	Scale and severity	Cleanup costs, repair costs	Consequences of poorer environment, health risks, risk of future disaster

Source: United Nations Development Programme, *Vulnerability and Risk Assessment*, 2nd ed., Cambridge: Cambridge Architectural Research Limited, 1994.

Qualitative Representation of Consequence

As was true with the qualitative representation of likelihood, words or phrases that have associated meanings can be used to describe the effects of a past disaster or the anticipated effects of a future one. These measurements can be assigned to deaths, injuries, or costs (often, the qualitative measurement of fatalities and injuries is combined). The following is one example of a qualitative measurement system for injuries and deaths:

- Insignificant: No injuries or fatalities
- Minor: Small number of injuries but no fatalities; first-aid treatment required
- Moderate: Medical treatment needed but no fatalities; some hospitalization
- Major: Extensive injuries, significant hospitalization; fatalities
- Catastrophic: Large number of fatalities and severe injuries; extended and large numbers requiring hospitalization

Table 10–2 Example of a Qualitative Risk-Level Analysis Matrix

Likelihood	Consequences				
	Insignificant	Minor	Moderate	Major	Catastrophic
Almost certain	High	High	Extreme	Extreme	Extreme
Likely	Moderate	High	High	Extreme	Extreme
Possible	Low	Moderate	High	Extreme	Extreme
Unlikely	Low	Low	Moderate	High	Extreme
Rare	Low	Low	Moderate	High	High

Source: Emergency Management Australia, "Emergency Risk Management: Application's Guide," Australian Emergency Manual Series, 2000.

Once both of these factors (probability and consequence) have been determined, it is possible to compare risks against each other, primarily for the purposes of treating the risks through intervention measures. Normally, only limited funds exist for this purpose and, as such, not all risks can be treated. Risk comparison allows for a prioritization of risk, which can help those performing mitigation and preparedness ensure that they are spending their limited funds most wisely. Table 10–2 provides one example of a risk matrix that can be used to compare risks to each other.

Having provided a basic description of the components of risk, it is appropriate to move on to the mitigation of risk. In applying mitigation, risk managers try to minimize probability or consequence or both. In practice, however, it is not always easy, or even possible, to address both. And because each risk is unique, there are different strategies that must be identified, assessed, and applied for successful risk intervention. For example, assume one seeks to minimize the risk of an earthquake. How can one minimize the probability of its happening? In terms of modern science, unfortunately, there is no known way of doing so, and this is true for many natural hazards despite humankind's best efforts. However, one can still mitigate the risk of an earthquake by minimizing its consequences. For the earthquake risk, several known and proven strategies are available to minimize such consequences, such as adopting and enforcing earthquake-resistant building codes, educating the public about earthquakes, and developing robust earthquake response plans.

In dealing with the newly expanded terrorism risk, the mitigation strategy would likely take on a much different approach. In this case, the opportunity to minimize the likelihood of the event's occurrence is very possible, and has been done countless times with great success. Through actionable intelligence collection on terrorist activity, and by infiltration of its social and communication networks, it is possible to stop terrorists before they proceed with their plots. Therefore, theoretically, the probability component of terrorism risk can be reduced through mitigation (or "prevention"). Of course, minimizing this likelihood component is a very complex task, requiring governments to allocate significant resources to build and manage necessary systems, establish international partnerships, and build networks to identify and detain terrorists.

The consequence component of terrorism risk can also be mitigated. However, unlike most natural disasters that have a limited range of possible consequences, the options available to terrorists are limited only by their imagination. Terrorists have limitless targets, including facilities, infrastructures, and organizations, so many different strategies must be employed to minimize the impacts of terrorist attacks to each of these potential targets. DHS has developed a manual titled *Reference Manual to Mitigate Potential Terrorist Attacks against Buildings* (the sidebar "FEMA 426"). This manual discusses the importance of minimizing the impacts of potential terrorist attacks against buildings. Buildings, however, are but one target. Presumably, it may be impossible to mitigate all possible consequences only because to do so would surely exhaust even the richest nation's financial resources. It would seem, then, that the best measures would seek multiple-use solutions, such as building a robust mass-casualty public health system that would not only serve to mitigate the impact of terrorism on humans but also mitigate the consequences of other natural and technological hazards that also may affect the population.

The threat of terrorism is not new. Throughout history there have been terrorist organizations and terrorist attacks in all parts of the world, including North America, Europe, and Australia; however, the September 11 attacks resulted in such severe consequences that, not unexpectedly, terrorism became the primary issue on the U.S. government's agenda.

Mitigating the terrorism risk is important in order to minimize potential damage that may result from what is known to be a very real threat, but it is vital to remember that combating terrorism is a complex and long-term task, one that requires both patience and sacrifice. Therefore, all stakeholders — including the government, the public, the private sector, the media, and academia — need to appreciate the benefit of applying mitigation on an all-hazards approach such that all known risks are treated, not only terrorism. Clearly, as has been shown in the years following the September 11 attacks, there are much more likely hazards — hurricanes and floods being the greatest — that have much greater potential to cause harm in terms of both likelihood and consequence. Hurricanes Katrina and Rita and the 2011 tornadoes that struck Joplin, MO, and Tuscaloosa, AL, are just some of many recent examples.

DHS continues to provide funding for predisaster and postdisaster mitigation projects through FEMA and its other relevant directorates. Details of those initiatives are provided in the next sections.

Federal Insurance and Mitigation Administration (FIMA)

The Federal Insurance and Mitigation Administration (FIMA) is responsible for a vast majority of the U.S. government's hazard mitigation activities, including the National Flood Insurance Program (NFIP). FIMA performs several organizational activities that serve to promote protection, prevention, and partnerships at the federal, state, local, and individual levels. The overall mission of FIMA is to protect lives and prevent the loss of property from natural and other hazards. FIMA employs the all-hazards approach through a comprehensive risk-based emergency management program. (See sidebar "What FIMA does and Mitigation Value to Society.")

What FIMA Does and Mitigation Value to Society

What FIMA Does

FIMA manages the National Flood Insurance Program (NFIP) and a range of programs designed to reduce future losses to homes, businesses, schools, public buildings, and critical facilities from floods, earthquakes, tornadoes, and other natural disasters.

Mitigation focuses on breaking the cycle of disaster damage, reconstruction, and repeated damage. Mitigation efforts provide value to the American people by creating safer communities and reducing loss of life and property. Mitigation includes such activities as:

- Complying with or exceeding NFIP floodplain management regulations.
- Enforcing stringent building codes, flood-proofing requirements, seismic design standards, and wind-bracing requirements for new construction or repairing existing buildings.

- Adopting zoning ordinances that steer development away from areas subject to flooding, storm surge, or coastal erosion.
- Retrofitting public buildings to withstand hurricane-strength winds or ground shaking.
- Acquiring damaged homes or businesses in flood-prone areas, relocating the structures, and returning the property to open space, wetlands, or recreational uses.
- Building community shelters and tornado-safe rooms to help protect people in their homes, public buildings, and schools in hurricane- and tornado-prone areas.

Mitigation's Value to Society

1. Mitigation creates safer communities by reducing losses of life and property.
2. Mitigation enables individuals and communities to recover more rapidly from disasters.
3. Mitigation lessens the financial impact of disasters on individuals, the Treasury, and state, local, and tribal communities.

Source: FEMA, 2011, Federal Insurance and Mitigation Administration (FIMA), http://www.fema.gov/about/divisions/mitigation.shtm.

FIMA administers the nationwide risk-reduction programs authorized by the U.S. Congress and is composed of the following divisions:

The Risk Analysis Division applies engineering and planning practices in conjunction with advanced technology tools to identify hazards, assess vulnerabilities, and develop strategies to manage the risks associated with natural hazards. The division runs the following FEMA mitigation programs:

- Flood Map Modernization
- National Dam Safety Program
- Mitigation Planning

The Risk Reduction Division works to reduce risk to life and property through the use of land use controls, building practices, and other tools. These activities address risk in both the existing built environment and future development, and they occur in both pre- and postdisaster environments. The division is in charge of the following programs:

- National Earthquake Hazards Reduction Program (NEHRP)
- Hazard Mitigation Grant Program (HMGP)
- Flood Mitigation Assistance Program (FMA)
- Pre-Disaster Mitigation Program (PDM)
- Severe Repetitive Loss Program (SRL)
- Repetitive Flood Claims Program (RFC)

- Building Science
- Community Rating System (CRS)

The *Risk Insurance Division* helps reduce flood losses by providing affordable flood insurance for property owners and by encouraging communities to adopt and enforce floodplain management regulations that mitigate the effects of flooding on new and improved structures. The Division's prime responsibility is to run the NFIP, through which affordable flood insurance is provided to communities vulnerable to flood hazards, and impacts of floods are minimized through enforcement of floodplain management for new and altered buildings and structures (FEMA, 2011a). FEMA mitigation programs and their funding levels are described in subsequent sections.

Flood Map Modernization

Flood Map Modernization is a multiyear program to improve existing flood maps in the United States and to create new maps based on new technology and standards for those localities that require flood maps for which no previous maps exist. The need for flood map modernization arises because of the dynamic nature of flood hazards that change with geography. Changing information management standards, improvements in information delivery methods such as the Internet, and advances in technologies such as GIS (geographical information systems) are other drivers behind flood map modernization.

The resulting maps and data better serve the needs of all parties that use those maps. FEMA Risk Analysis Division takes the lead in this program and acts as the main integrator of data, creator of geographic maps, and the clearinghouse for the dissemination of all flood map products. Community planners, public policymakers, local officials, developers, builders, insurance companies, and individual property owners can all benefit from those map products made available by the program.

National Dam Safety Program

National Dam Safety Program is an initiative of the FEMA Risk Analysis Directorate. The program was created by the Water Resources and Development Act of 1996 and has since been reauthorized twice with new legislation introduced in 2002 and 2006.

The primary goal of the program is to provide funding for states to be used in dam safety-related activities. In that scope, states use program funds to provide dam safety training, increase the frequency of dam safety inspections, create and test emergency response plans, and promote dam safety awareness through videos and other educative material. Between FY 1998 and FY 2004, the program provided approximately $22 million to states. Other components of the program include dam safety research and dam safety training.

Mitigation Planning Program

The Mitigation Planning Program administered by FEMA's Risk Analysis Division creates multihazard mitigation planning manuals, how-to guidelines, and best-practice documents. Since the program has an all-hazards mitigation scope, it works closely with several partners in different areas of interest and expertise. Some of the program partners include the American Planning Association, Association of State Floodplain Managers, Institute for Business and Home Safety, and National Institute for Building Sciences.

The program also works closely with the (postdisaster) HMGP and the PDM administered by FEMA's Risk Reduction Division (FEMA, 2011d).

National Earthquake Hazards Reduction Program

The NEHRP was established by the Earthquake Hazards Reduction Act of 1977 to "reduce the risks of life and property from future earthquakes in the United States." In 1980, the act was amended to include the National Institutes of Standards and Technology (NIST, then the National Bureau of Standards) and to designate the newly created FEMA as the lead agency. FEMA coordinated NEHRP until 2003, when legislation transferred FEMA's management role in the program to NIST. In this capacity, FEMA planned and managed the federal response to earthquakes, funded state and local preparedness exercises, and supported seismic design and construction techniques for new buildings and retrofit guidelines for existing buildings.

As part of this program, the U.S. Geological Survey (USGS) conducts and supports earth science investigations into the origins of earthquakes, predicts earthquake effects, characterizes earthquake hazards, and disseminates earth science information. Additionally, the National Science Foundation (NSF) provides funding to earthquake engineering research, basic earth science research, and earthquake-related social science.

In addition to its lead management role for the program, NIST conducts and supports engineering studies to improve seismic provisions of building codes, standards, and practices for buildings and lifelines (FEMA, "NEHRP," 2007).

FEMA's Mitigation Grant Programs

FEMA currently has five mitigation grant programs: the Hazards Mitigation Grant Program, Pre-Disaster Mitigation Grant Program, Flood Mitigation Assistance Grant Program, Severe Repetitive Loss Grant Program (SRL), and Repetitive Flood Claims Grant Program (RFC), all of which are administered by the Risk Reduction Division of the Mitigation Directorate.

Hazards Mitigation Grant Program

Authorized under Section 404 of the Stafford Act, the Hazard Mitigation Grant Program (HMGP) provides grants to states and local governments to implement long-term hazard-mitigation measures after a major disaster declaration. The purpose of the program is to reduce the loss of life and property due to natural disasters and to enable mitigation measures to be implemented during the immediate recovery from a disaster declaration. HMGP funding is only available in states following a presidential disaster declaration. Eligible applicants follow:

- State and local governments
- Indian tribes or other tribal organizations
- Certain private nonprofit organizations

Individual homeowners and businesses may not apply directly to the program; however, a community may apply on their behalf. HMGP funds may be used to fund projects that will reduce or eliminate the losses from future disasters. Projects must provide a long-term solution to a problem — for example, elevation of a home to reduce the risk of flood damages as opposed to buying sandbags and pumps to fight the flood. In addition, a project's potential savings must be more than the cost of implementing the project. Funds may be used to protect either public or private property or to purchase property that has been subjected to, or is in danger of, repetitive damage.

The HMGP is directly funded by FEMA's Disaster Relief Fund. The amount of HMGP funds that will be made available depends on the combined funding made available from the Disaster Relief Fund for the Public Assistance Program and the Individual Assistance Program. The Public Assistance Program makes funds available to communities in repairing or replacing roads, bridges, and other public infrastructure after a disaster occurs. The Individual Assistance Program provides grants for individuals and families in the aftermath of disasters.

According to FEMA's "Hazard Mitigation Assistance Unified Guidance: June 1, 2010," "HMGP funding is allocated using a "sliding scale" formula based on a percentage of the estimated total federal assistance under the Stafford Act, excluding administrative costs for each presidential major disaster declaration. Applicants with a FEMA-approved State or Tribal Standard Mitigation Plan may receive

- Up to 15% of the first $2 billion of the estimated aggregate amount of disaster assistance;
- Up to 10% for the next portion of the estimated aggregate amount more than $2 billion and up to $10 billion; and
- 7.5% for the next portion of the estimated aggregate amount more than $10 billion and up to $35.333 billion.

In the aftermath of the severe 2004 hurricane season, which included Hurricanes Frances, Jeanne, Ivan, and Charley, FEMA provided a record $359 million in mitigation funding to the State of Florida through the HMGP. As of November 26, 2007, Hurricane Katrina- and Rita-related HMGP grants exceeded $1.47 billion (FEMA, 2011c, 2011j, 2011k).

Pre-Disaster Mitigation Program

The Pre-Disaster Mitigation (PDM) Program was authorized by Section 203 of the Robert T. Stafford Disaster Assistance and Emergency Relief Act (as amended by Section 102 of the Disaster Mitigation Act of 2000). Funding for the program is provided through the National Pre-Disaster Mitigation Fund to assist state and local governments (including Indian tribal governments) in implementing cost-effective hazard mitigation activities that complement a comprehensive mitigation program. Recipients of this grant must be participating in the NFIP if they have been identified as being at special risk from flood hazards (i.e., have a "Special Flood Hazard Area"), and must have a mitigation plan in effect. The PDM was funded in FY 2006, FY 2007, and FY 2008 at $49.5 million, $100 million, $114 million, respectively. FY 2009 funding was $90 million, FY 2010 was $100 million, and FY 2011 was $100 million, respectively. The president's FY 2012 budget request included $84.9 million for the program (DHS, 2011a; DHS, 2012; FEMA, 2011f).

Flood Mitigation Assistance Program

The Flood Mitigation Assistance (FMA) Program provides funding to assist states and communities in implementing measures to reduce or eliminate the long-term risk of flood damage to buildings, manufactured homes, and other structures insurable under the NFIP. Three types of grants are available under FMA: planning, project, and technical assistance grants. FMA planning grants are available to states and communities to prepare flood mitigation plans. NFIP-participating communities with approved flood mitigation plans can apply for FMA project grants. FMA project grants are available to states and NFIP-participating communities to implement measures to reduce flood losses. Ten percent of the project grant is made available to states as a technical assistance grant. These funds may be used by the state to help administer the program.

Severe Repetitive Loss Program

The Severe Repetitive Loss Program (SLP) is a proactive mitigation initiative of the NFIP to reduce or eliminate flood-related damages and insurance claims for the approximately 83,000 residential properties that qualify as structures with severe repetitive flood damage potential. Structures with severe repetitive flood loss potential are defined as structures that meet the following criteria:

- Have four or more NFIP claim payments over $5,000 each, given that at least two such claims have occurred within 10 years of each other, and the total amount paid to the policy holder exceeds $20,000; or
- Have two or more separate claims payments where the total amount paid for the building portion of such claims exceeded the value of the property, given that two such claims have occurred within 10 years of each other.

The SLP has been in effect since the Flood Insurance Reform Act of 2004. This program reduces the cost of NFIP claims made by owners of highly vulnerable structures by funding mitigation projects that strengthen those structures against flood damage. Among qualifying projects are flood proofing (historical properties only), relocation, elevation, acquisition, mitigation reconstruction (demolition rebuild), and minor physical localized flood control projects. The program is funded at $40 million per fiscal year from 2005 to 2009 (FEMA, 2008d, 2008g).

Repetitive Flood Claims Program

Another program introduced by the Flood Insurance Reform Act of 2004 is the RFC. The program is conceptually similar to the SLP, but the criterion to qualify for the program is more relaxed. Any state or community that had at least one claim to the NFIP can apply for RFC funding to finance projects to reduce the vulnerability of properties against floods. RFC funds can only be spent to improve structures that are located within a state or community that is ineligible for the FMA due to cost share or capacity to manage the activities.

Other FEMA Mitigation Directorate Programs

National Flood Insurance Program

Congress established the National Flood Insurance Program (NFIP) with the passage of the National Flood Insurance Act of 1968. The NFIP is a federal program enabling property owners in participating communities to purchase insurance as a protection against flood losses in exchange for state and community floodplain management regulations that reduce future flood damages. Flood insurance is designed to provide an alternative to disaster assistance to reduce the escalating costs of repairing damage to buildings and their contents caused by floods. Flood damage is reduced by nearly $1 billion a year through communities implementing sound floodplain management requirements and property owners' purchasing of flood insurance. Additionally, buildings constructed in compliance with NFIP building standards suffer approximately 80% less damage annually than those not built in compliance. And, every $3 paid in flood insurance claims reduces $1 in disaster assistance payments (FEMA, 2005).

The importance of flood insurance was again proven following Hurricanes Katrina, Rita, and Wilma in 2005, when the NFIP paid more than $16 billion in claims (Figure 10–2). As more communities meet floodplain management eligibility requirements and participate in the program, they will continue to minimize flood risk, while enjoying greater financial protection from inevitable flood damages. As these benefits become more and more apparent to homeowners with each disaster that occurs, participation in the NFIP should continue to increase over time. Figure 10–3 provides an overview of the growth in the number of flood insurance policies issued by the NFIP. NFIP funding increased from $2.5 billion to $2.8 billion from FY 2006 to FY 2008. The president's FY 2009 budget request included $3.16 billion

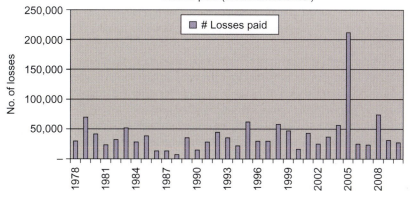

FIGURE 10–2 Losses paid by National Flood Insurance by year. (Source: FEMA, 2011, "Number of Losses Paid by Calendar Year," http://www.fema.gov/business/nfip/statistics/cy2010_lossespaid.shtm)

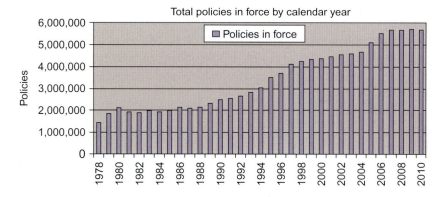

FIGURE 10–3 Growth in national flood insurance policies since 1978. (Source: FEMA, 2011, "Total Policies in Force by Calendar Year" from this site — http://www.fema.gov/business/nfip/statistics/cy2010_totpif.shtm)

in mandatory and discretionary funding for the program (NFIP, 2008; Insurance Information Institute, 2008; FEMA, 2011g; DHS, 2008).

Prevention Actions and Programs

Prevention refers to actions taken to avoid an incident or to intervene in an effort to stop an incident from occurring in order to protect lives and property. The draft National Incident Management System of August 2007 defines prevention as follows:

> *Actions to avoid an incident or to intervene to stop an incident from occurring. Prevention involves actions to protect lives and property. It involves applying intelligence and other information to a range of activities that may include such countermeasures as deterrence operations; heightened inspections; improved surveillance and security operations; investigations to determine the full nature and source of the threat; public health and agricultural surveillance and*

testing processes; immunizations, isolation, or quarantine; and, as appropriate, specific law enforcement operations aimed at deterring, preempting, interdicting, or disrupting illegal activity and apprehending potential perpetrators and bringing them to justice. (FEMA, 2007a, p. 156)

According to DHS, the NRP (now called the National Response Framework) may be implemented for threats or potential incidents of national significance to prevent or intervene in order to lessen the impact of an incident. Prevention activities may include heightened inspections; improved surveillance and security operations; public health and agricultural surveillance and testing; immunizations, isolation, or quarantine; and, as appropriate, specific law enforcement operations aimed at deterring, preempting, interdicting, or disrupting illegal activity and apprehending potential perpetrators and bringing them to justice (FEMA, 2005).

As the prevention activities described by DHS imply, most of these activities are related to the prevention of terrorist incidents. Prevention actions related to terrorism threats and incidents include law enforcement activities and protective activities. All federal law enforcement activities are coordinated by the attorney general, generally acting through the FBI. During an incident, initial prevention efforts include, but are not limited to, the following actions:

- Collecting, analyze, and apply intelligence and other information.
- Conducting investigations to determine the full nature and source of the threat.
- Implementing countermeasures such as surveillance and counterintelligence.
- Conducting security operations, including vulnerability assessments, site security, and infrastructure protection.
- Conducting tactical operations to prevent, interdict, preempt, or disrupt illegal activity.
- Conducting attribution investigations, including an assessment of the potential for future-related incidents.
- Conducting activities to prevent terrorists, terrorist weapons, and associated materials from entering or moving within the United States.

As defined within the NRF, any activity that attempts to prevent terrorist attacks can be considered a prevention measure. Several specific DHS prevention programs are discussed in greater detail in Chapter 5.

Several of the recommendations made by the 9/11 Commission, discussed in Chapter 2, also include prevention components. The following examples are provided:

Prevention of proliferation of weapons of mass destruction and their acquisition by terrorist groups: The 9/11 Commission underlines that about two dozen terrorist groups including al-Qaeda have attempted to acquire or develop chemical, biological, radiological, and nuclear weapons. Most of those weapons can be developed relatively inexpensively if the necessary knowledge is available to terrorists. The possible consequences of an attack involving those weapons are very likely to be devastating. Therefore, preventing the proliferation of such weapons or materials that are necessary in their development is a critical task that needs to be performed. The commission recommends that the United States has to work with the international community to get this done. The commission recommends that the United States should sustain its support for the Cooperative Threat Reduction Program, which aims to secure the weapons and highly dangerous materials still scattered in Russia and other countries of the Soviet Union.

Prevention of financial strength and flexibility of terrorist organizations: The United States and its allies made an effort to paralyze the financial networks of terrorists in the recent aftermath of 9/11. This effort aimed to reduce or eliminate the ability of terrorist groups to support their operations and maintain their existence. The experience showed that tracking and blocking of money that is potentially connected to terrorist groups is a very difficult job that demands not only international cooperation but also the convenience of national laws of international partners. Therefore, other innovative ways of reducing the financial strength and flexibility of terrorist organizations are necessary.

Prevention of terrorist travel: With the advancements in and increased frequency of international travel, terrorist groups were able to gain the mobility to conduct attacks in different parts of the world. This gives an opportunity to governments to identify the terrorist as they enter the transportation system or the country through its border checkpoints. This is a critical task that may prevent some terrorist attacks or at least the penetration of terrorists from one country to another one. But the fact that terrorists also use local resources and people in their activities makes the challenge even tougher.

Prevention of terrorist access to critical infrastructures and key assets: The 9/11 Commission recommends that the improvements being made to protect U.S. borders such as use of terrorist lists, biometric screening, biometric passports, and other threat-related information be shared with and implemented at access points to critical infrastructures and key assets. Such assets may include nuclear power plants, dams, and other infrastructures of national significance and consequences (9/11 Commission, 2004).

Preparedness Actions and Programs

Preparedness within the field of emergency management can best be defined as a state of readiness to respond to a disaster, crisis, or any other type of emergency situation. It includes those activities, programs, and systems that exist before an emergency that are used to support and enhance response to an emergency or disaster.

Preparedness is important to the overall emergency management cycle because it provides for the readiness and testing of all actions and plans before actual application occurs in response to a real incident or disaster.

Examples of preparedness for natural hazards are organizing evacuation drills from buildings in case of fires or other threats, providing first-response training to employees so that they can assist each other and their neighbors in small emergencies (Figure 10–4), and preparing a family disaster plan that covers topics such as the designation of a location where family members will meet if they get separated during an event and what personal papers (e.g., prescriptions and insurance records) they might need in the aftermath of an event. More specific examples include the logistical planning for tugboats operating around oil refineries such that they become responsible for responding to fire emergencies in the refinery, or providing training and relocating necessary hazardous materials (HAZMAT) teams to areas where the risk of radiological emergencies is higher, such as nuclear power plants.

In the aftermath of September 11, terrorism preparedness has become a more pressing issue. The risk of terrorists gaining access to and using weapons of mass destruction (WMDs), such as biological, chemical, and radiological agents, forced the U.S. government to establish an adequate response capability, capacity, and expertise to protect American citizens against a potential attack and respond to it in case these weapons are used. Citizens, who are the most likely targets of these attacks, must be adequately prepared if any response effort is to be successful. DHS has been given the responsibility for this task, although several other federal government agencies, including the Centers for Disease Control and

FIGURE 10–4 Mays Landing, NJ, April 17, 2010 — Community Relations Specialists Paul Williams and Joseph Bonaccorse (right) team up with Community Emergency Response Team Nancy E. Neglia (left) and Dwight L. Neglia to inform residents of the flood-affected area of the FEMA registration process. FEMA Community Relations specialists are going door to door to inform residents about the assistance available. (Source: Photo by Michael Medina-Latorre/FEMA)

Prevention (CDC) and the Department of Education, for example, provide guidance on a full range of terrorism preparedness activities.

Preparedness Against Biological and Chemical Attacks and Accidents

Preparedness against biological and chemical attacks and accidents poses a distinct challenge due to the unique consequences that they inflict and the relatively limited experience of emergency management professionals in dealing with them. This unique challenge is being addressed by many local, state, federal, private, and nonprofit agencies throughout the United States. In fact, the majority of preparedness funding under the Department of Homeland Security targets these WMD hazards.

Specific Challenges for Biological/Chemical Terrorism Incident Management

Deliberate biological or chemical incidents will present critical challenges to both the intended targets and those in charge of managing the incident that results. These agents, as with all WMDs, present public health threats that are not typically seen in either day-to-day or even major incidents of natural or accidental man-made nature. As such, the methods by which citizens and response officials can prepare for these attacks have only just begun to emerge in the past few years. Chemical incidents do occur with regularity, but it is very rare for them to deliberately target a human population.

Both chemical and biological agents, when used as weapons, have a significant potential to overwhelm the capabilities of the public health infrastructure. There have been several attempts to design a comprehensive framework to prepare for and manage mass-casualty medical incidents. The specific response challenges that those defining new preparedness methods must take into account are listed here:

- The existence of a chemical or biological attack may be hard to verify, due to delayed consequences or symptoms.
- The incident may involve multiple jurisdictions, which may make it much more difficult to organize a coordinated response.
- It may be time consuming to identify and isolate the type and source of the chemical or biological agent present on site.
- The incident may have a pinpoint target where a specific crowd is targeted, or may be designed to impact a larger geographic area and even larger crowds, both of which will likely create large crowds of morbidities if not mortalities.
- If large numbers of the public are impacted by the incident, the demand for health care may quickly exceed local, or even regional, medical resources.
- The identification of the involved chemical(s) or biological agent(s) may consume the capacity of local medical laboratories making it mandatory to integrate use of neighboring laboratories.
- Resources of the medical system may be consumed by not only the victims but also by those who perceive themselves as possible victims who may not be real victims.
- The emergency management officials may have to make extremely difficult public policy decisions very quickly, where lives may have to be sacrificed to save other lives.
- It may be necessary to quarantine the impacted region to insulate the nonimpacted geographies from potential contamination.
- The medical units may have to triage arriving victims if the incoming demand dramatically exceeds the capacity of available resources.
- To decontaminate the impacted geographies and those who were contaminated by the release, necessary decontamination systems, equipment, and human resources may be necessary at multiple locations.
- The medical system may not only have to deal with the physical disease caused by the chemical or biological release but also with the mental impacts of the "mass paranoia" the incident may have triggered.

These are but a small subset of the potential challenges that must be met. Individual events will present individual response factors that may or may not be known beforehand. To address these issues, physical (equipment, tools, technology), financial, knowledge, and human resources are all necessary. More importantly, a comprehensive system to address these challenges is necessary, and the adequate utilization of such a system demands the provision of training and exercises to those who will be dependent on such a system in a time of crisis.

Comprehensive Medical and Health Incident Management System

The Medical and Health Incident Management System (MaHIM) designed by Joseph A. Barbera and Anthony G. Macintyre is one of the most recent and most comprehensive analytical tools designed to help communities develop their own medical mass-casualty incident management capacity. The system not only focuses on developing local capacities, but also proposes a framework that can be used to integrate interjurisdictional capacities, should the incident spread beyond local jurisdictional borders.

The goal of the framework is to define as a single system encompassing the medical and public health functions and processes required for adequate management of a mass-casualty incident. The system has been designed with an all-hazards approach where special consideration is given to bioterrorism.

The MaHIM system defines the goal of medical consequence management in a mass-casualty incident as follows: to maximally limit morbidity (injury or illness) and mortality (deaths) in the population exposed to a major hazard and to return the community to normalcy as soon as possible. The three primary medical objectives to attain this goal are as follows:

- *Reduce hazard exposure*: Avoid or minimize the hazard exposure to patients and the population after hazard "release."
- *Increase hazard resistance*: Maximize patient and population resistance to the hazard impact after exposure.
- *Promote/achieve healing from hazard effects*: Maximize the rate and degree of patient and population healing from the hazard impact.

To achieve these goals, the system utilizes principles of effective local and regional organization to provide a detailed description of necessary medical and health emergency operations, and the associated subfunctions and processes. The system underlines the importance of responsibility and authority. It defines the operational requirements for surge capacity, and provides detailed explanations about support functions critical to system's operation. Figure 10–5 details the MaHIM management process.

MaHIM provides a new vision for the health and emergency medical service communities, and gives them an actionable tool with which they can now structure their preparedness and management efforts in a more systematic fashion. The system describes in detail all functional areas that should be included in a comprehensive, mass-casualty health incident management system. The system is currently being implemented in Arlington County, Virginia, as part of a pilot project. The project includes restructuring

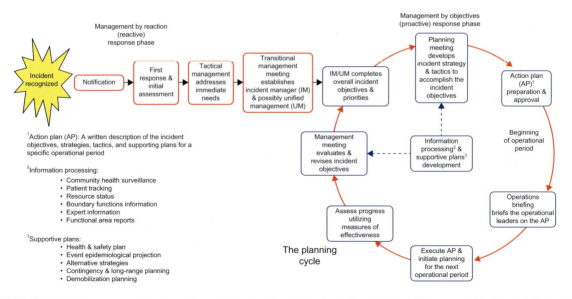

FIGURE 10–5 MaHIM management process. (Source: "Planning Cycle," U.S. Coast Guard Incident Management Handbook, U.S. Coast Guard COMDTPUB P3120, April 17, 2001)

the county's entire emergency medical system. A more detailed functional description of the system can be downloaded from the following website: http://www.gwu.edu/~icdrm/publications/MaHIM%20 Model%20Web%20Version%20FEB%2003.pdf (Barbera and Macintyre, 2002, 2003).

Nuclear and Radiological Preparedness

The Nuclear Regulatory Commission (NRC) is the primary federal government agency in charge of regulating the commercial radiological operations within the United States. The NRC's mission is to regulate the nation's civilian use of by-product, source, and special nuclear materials to ensure adequate protection of public health and safety, to promote the common defense and security, and to protect the environment.

A key component of the mission of the NRC is to ensure adequate preparedness measures are in place to protect the health and safety of the public. These actions are taken to avoid or reduce radiation dose exposure and are sometimes referred to as *protective measures*.

The overall objective of NRC's Emergency Preparedness (EP) program is to ensure that nuclear power plant operators are capable of implementing adequate measures to protect public health and safety in the event of a radiological emergency. As a condition of their license, operators of these nuclear power plants must develop and maintain EP plans that meet comprehensive NRC EP requirements. Increased confidence in public protection is obtained through the combined inspection of the requirements of emergency preparedness and the evaluation of their implementation.

The NRC assesses the capabilities of nuclear power plant operators to protect the public by requiring the performance of a full-scale exercise at least once every 2 years that includes the participation of government agencies. These exercises are performed in order to maintain the skills of the emergency responders and to identify and correct weaknesses. They are evaluated by NRC regional inspectors and FEMA regional evaluators. Between the times when these 2-year exercises are conducted, additional drills are conducted by the nuclear power plant operators that are evaluated by the resident inspectors (Nuclear Regulatory Commission, 2005).

Terrorism Preparedness and Mitigation: Community Issues

The terrorism threat knows no geographic, social, or economic boundaries. Every citizen and every community is potentially at risk. Although the DHS focuses on federal and state efforts to prepare for and combat terrorism, local communities are struggling to address the terrorism risk. The following sections explain several initiatives that have been launched to deal with community issues concerning the terrorist threat.

Corporation for National and Community Service

The mission of the Corporation for National and Community Service (CNCS), an independent federal agency under the White House, is to provide opportunities for Americans of all ages and backgrounds to engage in service that addresses the nation's educational, public safety, environmental, and other human needs to achieve direct and demonstrable results. In doing so, the corporation fosters civic responsibility, strengthens the ties that bind citizens together, and provides educational opportunities for those who make a substantial commitment to service.

CNCS is an important initiative for homeland security efforts at the local community level because it provides a significant portion of the total federal funding that goes to volunteer organizations and local communities that are trying to improve their homeland security capabilities.

Following the tragic events that occurred on September 11, 2001, state and local government officials have increased opportunities for citizens to become an integral part of protecting the homeland and supporting local first responders. Officials agree that the formula for ensuring a more secure and safer homeland consists of preparedness, training, and citizen involvement in supporting first responders. In January 2002, President George W. Bush launched the USA Freedom Corps to "capture the spirit of service that has emerged throughout our communities following the terrorist attacks."

Citizen Corps, a vital component of USA Freedom Corps, was created to help coordinate volunteer activities that can make communities safer, stronger, and better prepared to respond to emergencies. It provides opportunities for people to participate in a range of measures to make their families, their homes, and their communities safer from the threats of crime, terrorism, and disasters of all kinds.

Citizen Corps is coordinated nationally by FEMA. In this capacity, FEMA works closely with other federal entities, state and local governments, first responders and emergency managers, the volunteer community, and the White House Office of the USA Freedom Corps. One of the initiatives supported by Citizen Corps is the Community Emergency Response Teams (CERT). The program trains citizens to be better prepared to respond to emergency situations in their communities. When emergencies happen, CERT members can give critical support to first responders, provide immediate assistance to victims, and organize spontaneous volunteers at a disaster site. CERT members can also help with nonemergency projects that help improve the safety of the community.

The CERT course is taught in the community by a trained team of first responders who have completed a CERT Train-the-Trainer course conducted by their state training office for emergency management, or FEMA's Emergency Management Institute (EMI), located in Emmitsburg, Maryland. CERT training includes disaster preparedness, disaster fire suppression, basic disaster medical operations, and light search and rescue operations. As of 2008, there were more than 2,800 CERT programs active in many states, counties, and communities nationwide. For more information on CERT, see the CERT website at www.citizencorps.gov/programs/cert.shtm.

Another important Citizen Corps initiative is the Medical Reserve Corps (MRC) program, which coordinates the skills of practicing and retired physicians, nurses, and other health care professionals, as well as other citizens interested in health issues who are eager to volunteer to address their community's ongoing public health needs and to help their community during large-scale emergency situations.

Local community leaders develop their own MRC units and identify the duties of the MRC volunteers according to specific community needs. For example, MRC volunteers may deliver necessary public health services during a crisis, assist emergency response teams with patients, and provide care directly to those with less serious injuries and other health-related issues. More information on the MRC program can be found at http://www.medicalreservecorps.gov.

The Neighborhood Watch Program (NWP) and Volunteers in Police Service (VIPS) programs are other Citizen Corps homeland security–related programs.

A relatively new partner program of the Citizen Corps initiative is the Fire Corps program. Launched in 2004, Fire Corps is a partnership between the International Association of Fire Chiefs' Volunteer and Combination Officers Section (IAFC/VCOS), the International Association of Fire Fighters (IAFF), the National Volunteer Fire Council (NVFC), and the U.S. Fire Administration (USFA). Its mission is to help career, volunteer, and combination fire departments supplement existing personnel resources by recruiting citizen advocates. The purpose of the program is to help fire departments expand existing programs — or assist in developing new ones — that recruit citizens who donate their time and talents to support the fire service in nonoperational roles. Within the first 4 years of its existence, Fire Corps has expanded its organization to many states. Currently, the organization has a division advocate for all 7 divisions across the United States, and 52 state advocates that represent 28 states. More information about Fire Corps can be found at http://firecorps.org (Fire Corps, 2008).

The president's FY 2012 budget requested $9.8 million for the program (DHS, 2011b).

The American Red Cross

The American Red Cross (ARC) has always been one of the most important partners of the federal, state, and local governments in disaster preparedness and relief operations. Some of the daily community operations of the Red Cross chapters include senior services, caregivers' support, provision of hospital and nursing home volunteers, lifeline (an electronic personal emergency response service), transportation to medical/doctor's appointments and other essential trips, food pantry and hot lunch programs, homeless shelters and transitional housing services, school clubs and community service learning programs and projects, youth programs (violence and substance abuse prevention, peer education and mentoring, leadership development camps), food and rental assistance, language banks, and community information and referral.

From the first $10.3 million in federal grants provided to involve citizen volunteers in homeland security efforts in 2002, the ARC received $1,778,978, which was distributed by the national headquarters to many individual chapters. The recipient of the greatest portion of these funds was the Greater New York chapter, which received $500,000 of the funds for the recruitment, training, and mobilization of 5,000 new disaster volunteers equipped to respond to another terrorist attack on a local level. These volunteers work with Red Cross service delivery units in New York to train additional volunteers, exponentially increasing the city's force of disaster relief workers.

In 2002, another $371,978 was given to the ARC National Headquarters for a nationwide program aimed at increasing volunteers in communities most vulnerable to terrorist attacks. The grant supported a yearlong program with 30 Community Preparedness Corps (CPC) members working in 19 chapters. Corps members worked in chapters to ensure that all community members — totaling some 27 million — have a "family disaster response plan." They tailored plans for those with language barriers and disabilities and for children and the elderly. At the same time, CPC volunteers focused on minimizing intolerance across the country by teaching international humanitarian law and the principles of the International Red Cross Movement (humanity, independence, neutrality, impartiality, voluntary service, unity, and universality).

Corps members also recruited and trained an estimated 400 new volunteers and instructors who made the educational programs available to additional vulnerable communities. Ultimately, corps members working through Red Cross chapters will create a network of hundreds of skilled volunteers across the country.

Additional grants have since been awarded to Red Cross chapters nationwide. In California, funds have been dedicated to the implementation of homeland security measures in Los Angeles, San Francisco, and Sacramento. The Oregon Trail Chapter that was awarded a grant funding 400 new volunteers will perform 1,500 hours of service to disaster preparedness. On the East Coast, the Red Cross developed "Disaster Resistant Neighborhood" programs across eight wards of Washington, DC. Through the program these communities created disaster response plans. The southeast Pennsylvania chapter received a grant to create an alliance of more than 100 nonprofits in the Philadelphia area to form the Southeast Pennsylvania Voluntary Organization Active in Disaster (VOAD) to help citizens prevent, prepare for, and respond to disasters.

In 2003, the ARC participated in the TOPOFF 2 national training exercise. The Red Cross used this exercise to practice the screening of emergency shelter residents and supplies for radiation exposure, the logistical support when national stockpiles of medications were mobilized, and keeping the public informed as the national threat level reached the highest "red" alert. In the same year the Red Cross was actively involved with the development of the new NRP. The ARC was the only nongovernmental organization that was invited to the discussions.

Throughout 2004, the Red Cross taught 11 million Americans critical life-saving skills such as first aid, water safety, caregiving, CPR, and the use of automated external defibrillators (AEDs). In addition, the number of people attending presentations or demonstrations for Together We Prepare, community disaster education awareness, and the Masters of Disasters program climbed 6% to 3.9 million. Those programs aim to create safer families and communities.

Another 2004 initiative from the Red Cross involved expanding to diverse audiences with important preparedness and other information. To achieve this goal, the Red Cross expanded and detailed its Spanish-language website and first-aid and preparedness print materials. In cooperation with the CDC, the Red Cross initiated a multiyear project to develop and disseminate terrorism preparedness materials to the public.

In 2005, the year of several major hurricanes, some criticism emerged regarding the way the ARC handled its duties during those disasters. In the days leading to the landfall of Hurricane Katrina at the shores of Florida, the ARC was initially praised for its proactive approach in prestaging volunteers and mass care resources, but as the disaster unfolded and showed its destructive face in larger geographies, issues concerning the ARC response to the disaster became more apparent. At the center of the problem were issues between FEMA and the ARC regarding rules of engagement as partners under the new NRP. A Government Accountability Office (GAO) study that looked at the relationship of the two agencies during and after Katrina sheds light on some of the specific issues.

One major issue was the different interpretation of emergency support function 6 (ESF #6) responsibilities and process flow by FEMA and the ARC. The ARC and FEMA are the designated primary agencies for ESF #6 in charge of mass care, housing, and human services. The ARC is directly responsible for mass care. The NRP tasks an ESF #6 coordinator, a FEMA official with the oversight and coordination of all ESF #6 activities including mass care, which according to the ARC is not a perfect model since it designates the oversight of a core ARC competency to a non-ARC official. Therefore, during its response to Katrina, ARC in some instances bypassed the ESF #6 coordinator and tried to work with the FEMA Operations Section Chief. This resulted in tensions between the ARC and FEMA, and in many instances undermined a very much needed partnership between the two agencies.

Another issue that the ARC was criticized for was the frequently changing personnel at facilities that required ongoing working relationships with the staff of other agencies, primarily FEMA. Those short shifts also reduced the exposure of ARC representatives to the operational environment of the ESF #6. The primary explanation for this problem was the ARC's predisposition for involvement in disasters with much shorter life spans, and requiring shorter periods of continuous staffing — neither of which describe the needs of the Hurricane Katrina response where ESF #6 was active for more than 3 months. Also, since a significant portion of ARC personnel are volunteers, it is more difficult to engage those individuals in longer-term deployments than shorter ones.

In its response to GAO findings, the ARC underlined that it followed the guidance provided in the NRP as it worked with FEMA during Hurricane Katrina. Nevertheless, it is also mentioned that ARC and FEMA are in the process of developing policies and procedures to formalize their agreement on seemingly gray areas of responsibility and ESF #6 operations. Regarding the issues of frequent ARC personnel changes in ESF #6, ARC reports that it has improved the content of its ESF #6 training and hired 14 permanent employees to be trained in ESF #6 procedures and deployed at strategic locations in multiple states to coordinate with state emergency management agencies and officials (GAO, 2006; PBS, 2005; DHS, 2004).

Two other issues the ARC faced during its response to Hurricane Katrina were the fraudulent money transfers by some ARC subcontractors, and unacceptably long wait times on phone-based services.

ARC provides cash payments to disaster victims to help them get through the first few days of a disaster until other means of relief become available. During Hurricane Katrina, ARC established call centers manned by subcontractors to register and provide cash payments to hurricane victims using the money wiring services of a private contractor. The procedure did not have adequate checks and protection against fraudulent money transfers; therefore a group of employees working for the subcontractor staffing the call center found loopholes to transfer money to themselves and their relatives who were not victims of the hurricane. None of those workers were actual ARC employees or volunteers. ARC has also been criticized by people trying to reach the call centers in that wait times were extremely long, and in many instances, hours. Some experts explain those management problems are the result of the unique financial structure of the ARC, which heavily relies on donations; donors generally want their money spent strictly on direct assistance of hurricane victims rather than fixing administrative or managerial problems. This may minimize budgets to fix problems related to functions such as operations, finance, and accounting (Washington Post, 2005).

The Role of the Private Sector in Mitigation and Preparedness Activities

The events of September 11 brought to light the importance of private-sector involvement in crisis, emergency, and disaster management. Since that time, an ever-expanding list of private entities has begun focusing on their needs in this area. This section discusses the essentials of private-sector business continuity planning and disaster management. Most of the components discussed next have been learned as a result of experience with natural disasters or man-made accidents; however, the September 11 attacks have proved that those important components of classical crisis management are also important for terrorism risk management:

Business impact analysis (BIA): The management-level analysis by which an organization assesses the quantitative (financial) and qualitative (nonfinancial) impacts, effects, and loss that might result if the organization were to suffer a business-interrupting event. Performing BIA as a preparedness measure is important because findings from BIA are used to make decisions concerning business continuity management strategy.

Crisis communications planning: Decision making about how crisis communications will be performed during an emergency is important because communication is a critical success factor for effective crisis management. Preventing rumors about your corporation as well as telling your story before someone else does it for you is only possible via a predefined communication policy.

Information technology (IT) and systems infrastructure redundancy planning: There are different techniques and approaches regarding the enforcement of systems redundancy. Each company is unique, with its own IT and system needs and processes; therefore, customized approaches have to be employed to build more reliable systems infrastructure (e.g., backup databases, software, hardware, and network redundancy).

Geographic location and backup sites: The selection of the geographic location of headquarters and offices and the distribution of key executives in those buildings are strategically important decisions with regard to minimizing potential losses (both human and physical) during a disaster. The availability of backup sites that allow employees to continue operations in case of physical loss of or damage to a primary facility is a key success factor, but, unfortunately, is usually difficult to justify in terms of cost and benefit.

Transportation planning: The transportation infrastructure is one of the most sensitive infrastructures to emergency and disaster situations. Overloaded transportation infrastructure during crisis is usually a reason for microdisasters in the midst of bigger ones. Therefore, realistic transportation planning is important for a successful response.

Crisis leadership: Research and experience have shown that during crisis situations, people (e.g., employees, staff, and customers) need someone to tell them what is going on and explain what is being done about it, even if the information this person communicates is obsolete or redundant. Strong leadership also helps people to regain self-esteem and motivates them to commit to the efforts to overcome the crisis.

Insurance: It is important for companies to have a feasible but protective insurance policy. Realistic risk assessments and modeling are necessary to establish this economic feasibility.

Corporate Preparedness and Risk Management in the Sarbanes–Oxley Era

The Sarbanes–Oxley Act of 2002, written by Senator Paul Sarbanes (D-MD) and Representative Paul Oxley (R-OH), was created to protect investors by improving the accuracy and reliability of corporate disclosures. The act is in direct response to financial fraud discovered in the cases of both Enron and WorldCom. However, it was created to cover issues beyond fraud (establishing a public company accounting oversight board, auditor independence, corporate responsibility, and enhanced financial disclosure), and is now a driving force behind corporate business continuity planning. Although the phrase *business continuity planning* is not once mentioned in the language of the act, continuity professionals claim that Section 404 of the act implies that such measures must be taken for compliance. Section 404 of the act reads as follows:

SEC. 404. MANAGEMENT ASSESSMENT OF INTERNAL CONTROLS.

(a) RULES REQUIRED — The Commission shall prescribe rules requiring each annual report required by Section 13(a) or 15(d) of the Securities Exchange Act of 1934 (15 U.S.C. 78m or 78o(d)) to contain an internal control report, which shall

   (1) state the responsibility of management for establishing and maintaining an adequate internal control structure and procedures for financial reporting; and

   (2) contain an assessment, as of the end of the most recent fiscal year of the issuer, of the effectiveness of the internal control structure and procedures of the issuer for financial reporting.

(b) INTERNAL CONTROL EVALUATION AND REPORTING — With respect to the internal control assessment required by subsection (a), each registered public accounting firm that prepares or issues the audit report for the issuer shall attest to, and report on, the assessment made by the management of the issuer. An attestation made under this subsection shall be made in accordance with standards for attestation engagements issued or adopted by the Board. Any such attestation shall not be the subject of a separate engagement (Sarbanes–Oxley Act of 2002, http://thomas.loc .gov/cgi-bin/query/F?c107:6:./temp/~c107×5GHak:e143423).

Section 404 of the Sarbanes–Oxley Act requires companies to include an internal control report that states the responsibility of management for establishing and maintaining an adequate internal controls structure and procedures for financial reporting in their annual report. In addition, it requires management to ensure that the effectiveness of the internal control structure is assessed on an annual basis. The section also requires the external auditing entity to report on management's assessment of the effectiveness of the company's internal controls and procedures with respect to standards defined by the Public Company Accounting Oversight Board. Compliance with the act became effective in April 2005 for most companies.

Even though the section still focuses on financial record management and process control, in order to really ensure those things, it is almost a prerequisite for the company to ensure adequate protection and continuity of its entire core processes. This is where the "business continuity" aspect of the act becomes evident.

To protect the financial processes and records from misconduct or fraud, and to ensure data integrity and resilience, the first step is to identify the risks, threats, and vulnerabilities that may endanger those expectations defined by the act. This is possible through a comprehensive risk and vulnerability assessment followed by a BIA to identify the business consequences of possible adverse incidents. The BIA is usually considered as one of the main building blocks of business continuity planning, because its findings usually help the corporations identify and prioritize the risks it has to mitigate, and provide an understanding of recovery goals.

At present, it is too early to comment on whether there is full consensus between what the Sarbanes–Oxley Act demands from corporations and how the corporations interpret those expectations and what they are going to do about it. But it is true that business continuity concepts will adequately address some of the expectations of the act. Business continuity service providers seem to capitalize on this connection and enlarge the market for their services and products. The fact that the Sarbanes–Oxley Act places responsibility for compliance on top management makes it inevitable that these corporations will increase investments aimed at compliance. Business continuity is one of the answers.

Based on recent reports (2007), corporate spending on the Sarbanes–Oxley Act increased until 2005 and stabilized at about $6 billion a year. This includes all the money that corporations spend to comply with the requirements of the 2002 Act (Reuters, 2007b).

A recent business continuity planning-focused journal article has indicated that compliance may require more than basic business continuity planning. The article explained that the act will make senior management involvement in the planning process inevitable, and thus will require them to think about and find solutions beyond their organizations, while paying more attention to service-level agreements, continuity of vendors, and suppliers (Benvenuto, 2004; Berman, 2004; Williams, 2005).

Exercises to Foster Preparedness

The Homeland Security Council (HSC), in partnership with DHS, and state and local homeland security agencies, has developed 15 all-hazards planning scenarios for use in national, federal, state, and local homeland security preparedness activities. These scenarios are designed to be the foundational structure for the development of national preparedness standards from which homeland security capabilities can be measured (Figure 10–6).

Conclusion

Mitigation, prevention, and preparedness programs are vital to the safety and security of the nation. Since the onset of civilization, people have worked to limit their vulnerability to hazards once they recognized that those hazards existed. Since the attacks of September 11, the focus of mitigation has shifted primarily to mitigation, prevention, and preparedness for terrorist attacks, but the real threat has proven to be the traditional natural and man-made hazards that existed both before and after the attacks began. It is the responsibility of government, which rests most clearly on the Department of Homeland Security, to protect the nation from the consequences of disastrous events. For that reason, it is vital that the all-hazards approach to mitigation, prevention, and preparedness be maintained.

FIGURE 10–6 Anniston, AL, January 21, 2011 — Health-care workers rush to decontaminate a simulated victim during an exercise at the Center for Domestic Preparedness, located in Anniston, Alabama. These students were attending the Hospital Emergency Response Training (HERT) for mass-casualty incidents course that places emergency response providers in a realistic mass-casualty training scenario. For more information on the CDP's more than 50 specialized programs and courses, please visit their website at: http://cdp.dhs.gov.

Key Terms

All-Hazards Planning: The disaster planning and preparedness philosophy that advocates for holistic preparedness and flexible disaster planning to ensure the response can be improvised to deal with the many unknowns of any disaster situation. In one sense, it is the opposite of "Scenario Planning."

Avian Influenza: An infection typically seen in birds, although in rare cases human transmission has been observed. Among four strains of the virus known to be infectious for humans, H5N1 is the most dangerous one. Avian influenza is also called "bird flu" in daily use.

Bird Flu: Please refer to Avian Influenza.

Business Continuity Planning (BCP): The process of identification and remediation of commercial and organizational impacts of disasters through planning and strategy. Business continuity planning typically involves strategizing for the continuity and protection of the human resource, critical business processes, information systems, infrastructure, and organizational reputation.

Business Impact Analysis (BIA): The management-level analysis by which an organization assesses the quantitative (financial) and qualitative (nonfinancial) impacts, effects, and loss that might result if the organization were to suffer a business-interrupting event. Performing BIA as a preparedness measure is important because findings from BIA are used to make decisions concerning business continuity management strategy.

Community Emergency Response Team (CERT): A community initiative of Citizen Corps to create disaster-resistant communities by training and disaster awareness. CERTs are composed of volunteers trained in basic disaster and medical response. As of 2008, there are more than 2,800 CERT programs all over the United States.

Crisis Management: A proactive management effort to avoid crisis, and the creation of strategy that minimizes adverse impacts of crisis to the organization when it could not be prevented. Effective crisis management requires a solid understanding of the organization, its strategy, liabilities, stakeholders, and legal framework combined with advanced communication, leadership, and decision-making skills to lead the organization through the crisis with minimizing potential loss.

Crisis: A critical turning point with impact to the future state of a given system. Although mostly signaling a deteriorating status of the system, if managed correctly, a crisis can be potentially beneficial. Example: Increased customer confidence to a company that has managed to survive a major crisis in the industry provides competitive advantage.

Disaster Recovery Planning (DRP): The planning effort that primarily deals with the continuity and timely recovery of physical and logical components of information systems infrastructure and applications. The first goal in DRP is to ensure a redundant infrastructure that provides for continuity of information technology (IT) systems that support critical business processes. The second goal is to develop a prioritized recovery strategy for systems and applications based on their criticalities for the organization in case of an inevitable system failure or a catastrophic incident.

Epidemic: An infection that affects the public in a larger proportion than day-to-day diseases and infections to the degree that resources of national medical care systems are exhausted or significantly constrained. Epidemics also typically have impacts on the social and economic infrastructures.

Emergency Support Function (ESF): A specific area of expertise deemed critical for a successful disaster operation as identified by the federal disaster response framework. The Federal Response Plan (12 ESFs), the National Response Plan (15 ESFs), and the new National Response Framework (15 ESFs) each identify the various ESFs as appendices. The ESFs in the National Response Framework follow: ESF #1 — Transportation, ESF #2 — Communications, ESF #3 — Public Works and Engineering, ESF #4 — Firefighting, ESF #5 — Emergency Management, ESF #6 — Mass Care, Housing, and Human Services, ESF #7 — Resource Support, ESF #8 — Public Health and Medical Services, ESF #9 — Search and Rescue, ESF #10 — Oil and Hazardous Materials Response, ESF #11 — Agriculture and Natural Resources, ESF #12 — Energy, ESF #13 — Public Safety and Security, ESF #14 — Long-Term Community Recovery, and ESF #15 — External Affairs.

Federal Response Plan (FRP): A signed agreement among 27 federal departments and agencies, including the American Red Cross, that provided a mechanism for coordinating the delivery of federal assistance and resources to augment efforts of state and local governments overwhelmed by a major disaster or emergency; replaced by the National Response Plan.

Hazard: A potential source of danger or unsafe environment.

Influenza: A contagious infection of the respiratory tract. Common symptoms include fever, muscular pain, general tiredness, and chills. Symptoms are typically felt stronger than those caused by the common cold.

Man-Made Disaster: Sometimes also called *technological disaster*. Man-made disasters have two common elements: (1) They are not primarily induced by a naturally occurring process. (2) In most instances, the cause of the disaster is human error or failure of systems designed by humans. Examples of man-made disasters include oil spills, radiological incidents, chemical releases, and transportation disasters.

Mitigation: A sustained effort taken to reduce or eliminate risk to people and property from hazards and their effects.

Natural Disaster: A disaster that is primarily induced by the destructive power of nature. Examples of natural disasters include hurricane, earthquake, tsunami, and snowstorm.

National Planning Scenarios (NPS): Fifteen disaster scenarios, each corresponding to one particular natural, technological, or terrorist hazard threats, which together or individually allow for a standard against which plans, capabilities, and policies may be exercised and otherwise tested or measured.

National Response Framework (NRF): Presents the guiding principles that enable all response partners to prepare for and provide a unified national response to disasters and emergencies—from the smallest incident to the largest emergency catastrophe; defines key principles, roles, and structures that organizes the way the nation responds; replaced the National Response Plan.

National Response Plan (NRP): A national-level plan which replaced the Federal Response Plan and which was created in keeping with the national Incident Management System model to align federal coordination structures, capabilities, and resources into a unified, all-discipline, and all-hazards approach to domestic incident management.

Pandemic: An epidemic that impacts a large region or has global impacts.

Postdisaster Mitigation: Mitigation activities typically performed in the aftermath of a disaster either to provide a safer environment for the ongoing response or recovery effort or to mitigate potential impacts of the next disaster based on immediate lessons learned from a current one.

Predisaster Mitigation: Mitigation activities engaged prior to the occurrence of the disaster to minimize its impact when it occurs.

Preparedness: A state of readiness to respond to a disaster, crisis, or any other type of emergency situation.

Prevention: Actions taken to avoid an incident or to intervene in an effort to stop an incident from occurring for the purpose of protecting lives and property.

Risk: According to Stan Kaplan, risk is comprised of three components: scenario, probability of scenario, and consequence of scenario.

Tabletop Exercise: A mock disaster game in which participants playing different roles such as decision maker, incident commander, or first responder typically gather around a table and discuss/decide their responses to the incident scenario presented by a moderator. The goal of a tabletop exercise is to simulate a disaster situation for the purposes of exposing the participant to the stressful decision-making conditions of a disaster. Tabletop exercises typically conclude with a debrief session where various parties discuss their respective roles, goals established, priorities, and challenges faced regarding the scenario played.

Terrorism: There are more than 100 definitions of terrorism in the literature. The United Nations defines terrorism as "an anxiety-inspiring method of repeated violent action, employed by (semi-) clandestine individual, group or state actors, for idiosyncratic, criminal or political reasons, whereby — in contrast to assassination — the direct targets of violence are not the main targets."

TOPOFF (abbreviation for "top officials"): TOPOFF is a congressionally mandated annual disaster preparedness and response exercise designed to improve the incident management/decision-making capability of the nation's top officials at every level of the government during an incident of national significance.

Review Questions

1. What are the initiatives that help local communities to mitigate/prepare against potential terrorist attacks? Why is community preparedness an important component of homeland security?

2. What mitigation/preparedness role does the private sector have in terms of homeland security? Do you believe that the private sector learned lessons from the 9/11 terrorist attacks?

3. Try to define terrorism mitigation using the common definition of mitigation in terms of the all-hazards approach. (Hint: Define risk as a combination of probability and consequence, and list all potential activities that can reduce both components of the potential terrorist event.)

4. What is the importance of international consensus and cooperation for terrorism mitigation/preparedness?

5. Take a quick look at the FEMA document, FEMA 426, Reference Manual to Mitigate Potential Terrorist Attacks against Buildings (available at www.fema.gov). What are the two most important factors to minimize damage caused by car bombs to buildings?

References

American Red Cross, 2003. Largest terrorism response drill in U.S. history begins, May 12. http://www.redcross.org/news/ds/terrorism/030512TOPOFF.html.

American Red Cross, 2008. Frequently asked questions. http://www.redcross.org/faq/0,1096,0_383_,00.html.

American Society of Civil Engineers, 2007. Dam Safety Act signed by president. https://www.aawre.org/pressroom/news/grwk/event_release.cfm?uid53912.

Association of State Dam Safety Officials, 2005. What is the National Dam Safety & Security Program and why should it continue? http://www.damsafety.org/media/Documents/Legislative%20Handouts/NDSPA%20Handout.pdf.

Barbera, J.A., Macintyre, A.G., 2002. Medical and Health Incident Management (MaHIM) System: A Comprehensive Functional System Description for Mass Casualty Medical and Health Incident Management. Institute for Crisis, Disaster, and Risk Management, The George Washington University. Washington, DC.

Barbera, J.A., Macintyre, A.G., 2003. *MaHIM*. Presentation at the ICDRM/SAIC Monthly Emergency Management Forum. George Washington University. Washington, DC, 2003.

Benvenuto, N., 2004. The relationship between business continuity and Sarbanes-Oxley. Protiviti KnowledgeLeader. http://www.protiviti.com/downloads/PRO/pro-us/articles/FeatureArticle_20040312.html.

Berman, A., 2004. Business continuity in a Sarbanes-Oxley world. Disaster Recovery Journal, Spring. http://www.drj.com/articles/spr04/1702-01.html.

Citizen Corps, 2003a. Citizen Corps councils. http://www.citizencorps.gov/councils/.

Citizen Corps, 2003b. Community emergency response team. http://www.citizencorps.gov/programs/cert.shtm.

Citizen Corps, 2003c. Medical reserve corps. http://www.citizencorps.gov/programs/medical.shtm.

CNN, 2008. Katrina timeline. http://www.cnn.com/SPECIALS/2005/katrina/interactive/timeline.katrina.large/frameset.exclude.html.

Cone, E., Gallagher, S., 2001. Cantor Fitzgerald — forty seven hours. www.baselinemag.com/print_article/0,3668,a517022,00.asp.

Congressional Research Service, 2007a. Aging infrastructure: Dam safety. www.fas.org/sgp/crs/homesec/RL33108.pdf.

Congressional Research Service, 2007b. FY2008 appropriations for state and local homeland security. http://www.fas.org/sgp/crs/homesec/RS22596.pdf.

Coppola, D.P., 2003a. A Report on the First Annual Conference on the Community and Homeland Security. Washington, DC: Haddow and Bullock, LLC (March).

Coppola, D.P., 2003b. Annotated Organizational Chart for the Department of Homeland Security. Bullock & Haddow, LLC, Washington, DC.

Corporation for National Community Service, 2005. Congressional budget justification for FY 2006. http://www.nationalservice.gov/pdf/2006_budget_justification.pdf.

Corporation for National Community Service, 2006. National service responds: The power of hope and help after Katrina. http://www.nationalservice.gov/pdf/katrina_report.pdf.

Corporation for National Community Service, 2007a. The power of help and hope after Katrina by the numbers: Volunteers in the Gulf. http://www.nationalservice.gov/pdf/katrina_volunteers_respond.pdf.

Corporation for National Community Service, 2007b. A resource guide for the strategic initiatives. http://www.nationalservice.org/pdf/07_0913_resourceguide_strategicplan.pdf.

Department of Homeland Security, 2003. Family Preparedness Guide. Washington, DC.

Department of Homeland Security, 2004. National Response Plan Appendix ESF #6." Washington, DC. http://www.au.af.mil/au/awc/awcgate/nrp/esf06.pdf.

Department of Homeland Security, 2007a. Budget in brief 2008. http://www.dhs.gov/xlibrary/assets/budget_bib-fy2008.pdf.

Department of Homeland Security, 2007b. Overview: FY 2007 homeland security grant program. http://www.dhs.gov/xlibrary/assets/grants-2007-program-overview-010507.pdf.

Department of Homeland Security, 2007c. The National Response Framework. http://www.fema.gov/pdf/emergency/nrf/nrf-base.pdf.

Department of Homeland Security, 2007d. What's new in the NRF. http://www.in.gov/dhs/files/whatsnew.pdf.

Department of Homeland Security, 2008. Budget in brief 2009. http://www.dhs.gov/xlibrary/assets/budget_bib-fy2009.pdf.

Department of Homeland Security, 2011a. The National Response Framework. http://www.fema.gov/emergency/nrf/index.htm.

Department of Homeland Security, 2011b. Overview: FY 2011 Homeland Security Grant Program. http://www.fema.gov/pdf/government/grant/2011/fy11_hsgp_factsheet.pdf.

Emergency Management Australia, 2000. Emergency Risk Management: Applications Guide. Emergency Management Australia, Sydney.

European Commission, 2008. Threats to health — avian influenza. http://ec.europa.eu/health/ph_threats/com/Influenza/ai_human_en.htm.

Federal Emergency Management Agency, 2001. Multi-hazard mitigation planning. http://www.fema.gov/plan/mitplanning/index.shtm.

Federal Emergency Management Agency, 2003. Federal Emergency Management Agency 426: Reference Manual to Mitigate Potential Terrorist Attacks against Buildings. http://www.fema.gov/plan/prevent/rms/rmsp426.

Federal Emergency Management Agency, 2005. National Flood Insurance Program.

Federal Emergency Management Agency, 2007a. Draft National Incident Management System. http://www.fema.gov/emergency/nims/.

Federal Emergency Management Agency, 2007b. Plan ahead for an earthquake. http://www.fema.gov/plan/prevent/earthquake/index.shtm.

Federal Emergency Management Agency, 2007c. About the National Dam Safety Program. http://www.fema.gov/plan/prevent/damfailure/ndsp.shtm.

Federal Emergency Management Agency, 2008a. FY 2007 Flood Mitigation Assistance (FMA) Program. http://www.fema.gov/government/grant/fma/fma2007.shtm.

Federal Emergency Management Agency, 2008b. FY 2007 repetitive flood claims grant recipients. http://www.fema.gov/government/grant/rfc/rfc_fy07_recipients.shtm.

Federal Emergency Management Agency, 2008c. FY 2008 Flood Mitigation Assistance (FMA) Program. http://www .fema.gov/government/grant/fma/fma2008.shtm.

Federal Emergency Management Agency, 2008d. Guidance for severe repetitive loss properties. www.fema.gov/pdf/ nfip/manual200610/20srl.pdf.

Federal Emergency Management Agency, 2008e. Repetitive Flood Claims (RFC) Program (Fiscal Year 2007). http://www .fema.gov/government/grant/rfc/rfc_fy2007.shtm.

Federal Emergency Management Agency, 2008f. Repetitive Flood Claims (RFC) Program (Program Overview). http:// www.fema.gov/government/grant/rfc/index.shtm.

Federal Emergency Management Agency, 2008g. Severe Repetitive Loss Program. http://www.fema.gov/ government/grant/srl.

Federal Emergency Management Agency, 2010. Hazard Mitigation Assistance Unified Guidance, June 1. http:// www.fema.gov/library/viewRecord.do?id=4225.

Federal Emergency Management Agency, 2011a. Federal Insurance and Mitigation Administration (FIMA). http:// www.fema.gov/about/divisions/mitigation.shtm.

Federal Emergency Management Agency, 2011b. About the National Dam Safety Program. http://www.fema.gov/ plan/prevent/damfailure/ndsp.shtm.

Federal Emergency Management Agency, 2011c. Hazard Mitigation Grant Program. http://www.fema.gov/ government/grant/hmgp/index.shtm.

Federal Emergency Management Agency, 2011d. Hazard Mitigation Planning. http://www.fema.gov/plan/ mitplanning/index.shtm#2.

Federal Emergency Management Agency, 2011e. Overview of Flood Map Modernization. http://www.fema.gov/plan/ prevent/fhm/mm_main.shtm.

Federal Emergency Management Agency, 2011f. Pre-Disaster Mitigation Grant Program. http:// www.fema.gov/ government/grant/pdm/index.shtm.

Federal Emergency Management Agency, 2011g. National Flood Insurance Program. http://www.fema.gov/plan/ prevent/floodplain/index.shtm.

Federal Emergency Management Agency, 2011h. Severe Repetitive Loss Program. http://www.fema.gov/ government/grant/srl/index.shtm.

Federal Emergency Management Agency, 2011i. Welcome to flood hazard mapping. http://www.fema.gov/plan/ prevent/fhm/index.shtm.

Federal Emergency Management Agency, 2011j. Frequently Asked Questions Mitigation Grant Programs. http://www. fema.gov/government/grant/hmgp/

Federal Emergency Management Agency, 2011k. Louisiana Post-Katrina Recovery. http://www.fema.gov/hazard/ hurricane/2005katrina/6year/iafm.shtm.

Fire Corps, 2008. Fire Corps National Advisory Committee Meets. http://firecorps.org/page/630/show_item/172/News .htm.

Frase-Blunt M., 2003. Operation Topoff 2. http://www .aamc.org/newsroom/reporter/august03/bioterrorism.htm.

Government Accountability Office, 2000. Federal Emergency Management Agency Disaster Relief Fund. www.gao.gov/cgi-bin/getrpt?GAO/RCED-00-182.

Government Accountability Office, 2006. Hurricanes Katrina and Rita: Coordination between Federal Emergency Management Agency and the Red Cross Should Be Improved for the 2006 Hurricane Season. http://www.gao .gov/new.items/d06712.pdf.

Infoplease.com., 2008. Hurricane Katrina Timeline. http:// www.infoplease.com/spot/hurricanekatrinatimeline.html.

Insurance Information Institute, 2008. National Flood Insurance Program. http://www.iii.org/media/facts/ statsbyissue/flood/.

Kaplan, S., 1997. The words of risk analysis. Risk Analysis 17 (4), 408–409.

Kayyem, N.J., Chang, E.P., 2002. Beyond Business Continuity: The Role of the Private Sector in Preparedness Planning. Belfer Center for Science and International Affairs, John F. Kennedy School of Government, Harvard University, Cambridge, MA.

Kulling, P., 1998. The Terrorist Attack with Sarin in Tokyo. Socialstyresen, Stockholm.

National Commission on Terrorist Attacks upon the United States (9/11 Commission), 2004. What to Do? A Global Strategy. Chapter 12. Washington, DC.

National Earthquake Hazard Reduction Program, 2007. NEHRP 2007 Annual Report. http://www.nehrp.gov/pdf/2007NEHRPAnnualReport.pdf.

National Earthquake Hazard Reduction Program, 2008. NEHRP 2009 Program Budget. http://www.nehrp.gov/pdf/ppt_budget_fy09.pdf.

National Flood Insurance Program, 2008. Flood statistics. http://www.floodsmart.gov/floodsmart/pages/statistics.jsp.

Nuclear Regulatory Commission, 2005. Emergency preparedness and response. http://www.nrc.gov/about-nrc/emerg-preparedness/faq.html.

Public Broadcasting Service, 2005. American Red Cross troubles, December 14. http://www.pbs.org/newshour/bb/health/july-dec05/redcross_12-14.html.

Public Broadcasting Service, 2006. Fixing FEMA online news hour with Secretary M. Chertoff, February 13. http://www.pbs.org/newshour/bb/fedagencies/jan-june06/fema_2-13.html.

Public Safety Canada, 2008. Is your family prepared? http://www.emergencypreparednessweek.ca.

Reuters, 2007a. WHO confirms human-to-human bird-flu case, December 27. http://www.reuters.com/article/scienceNews/idUSL2732429220071227.

Reuters, 2007b. Sarbanes-Oxley spending seen at $6 billion in 2007, February 22. http://www.reuters.com/article/fundsFundsNews/idUSN2217546720070222.

Smith, J.D., 2002. Business Continuity Management: Good Practice Guidelines. Business Continuity Institute, United Kingdom.

ThinkProgress.org., 2008. Katrina Timeline. http://thinkprogress.org/katrina-timeline.

U.S. Department of Health and Human Services, 2007. Pandemic preparedness planning for US businesses with overseas operations. http://www.pandemicflu.gov/plan/workplaceplanning/businessesoverseaspdf.pdf.

U.S. Department of Health and Human Services, 2008. General information on pandemic and avian flu. http://www.pandemicflu.gov/general/index.html.

United Nations Development Programme, 1994. Vulnerability and Risk Assessment, 2nd ed. Cambridge Architectural Research Limited, Cambridge.

Washington Post, 2005. Fraud alleged at Red Cross call centers, December 27. http://www.washingtonpost.com/wp-dyn/content/article/2005/12/26/AR2005122600654.html.

White House, 2005. National strategy for pandemic influenza. http://www.whitehouse.gov/homeland/nspi.pdf.

WikiBirdFlu.org., 2007. Relationship between bird flu and SARS. http://www.wikibirdflu.org/page/Relationship1between1Bird1Flu1and1SARS?t5anon.

Williams, B., 2005. Sarbanes-Oxley: Another driver for business continuity management. http://www.disaster-resource.com/articles/03p_029.shtml.

World Health Organization, 2003. SARS. http://www.wpro.who.int/health_topics/sars/.

World Health Organization, 2005. WHO checklist for influenza pandemic preparedness planning. http://www.who.int/entity/csr/resources/publications/influenza/FluCheck6web.pdf.

World Health Organization, 2008. Cumulative number of confirmed human cases of avian influenza A/(H5N1) reported to WHO. http://www.who.int/csr/disease/avian_influenza/country/cases_table_2008_01_11/en/index.html.

Yale Center for Public Health Preparedness, 2006. Preparedness glossary. http://publichealth.yale.edu/ycphp/Glossary.html.

11

Communications

What You Will Learn

- How risk communication efforts inform the public about what hazard risks they face and what they can do to prepare for or mitigate them
- How the federal government performs risk communication through the Ready.gov website and other efforts
- What role the news media has in informing the public about hazard risks
- How the federal government warns the public of terrorist risk through the National Terrorism Alert System (NTAS)
- The mission and assumptions that serve as the basis of crisis communications
- The growing role of social media and first informers in crisis communications
- How to build an effective disaster communications strategy

Introduction

Communicating messages to the general public is a critical yet underdeveloped aspect of effective emergency management. Such messages fall under three basic categories: risk communication, warning, and crisis communication. Risk communication involves alerting and educating the public to the risks they face and how they can best prepare for and mitigate these risks in order to reduce the impacts of future disaster events. Warning involves delivering notice of an actual impending threat with sufficient time to allow recipient individuals and communities to take shelter, evacuate, or take other mitigative action in advance of a disaster event. Crisis communication involves the provision of timely, useful, and accurate information to the public during the response and recovery phases of a disaster event.

Preparedness programs have been an active part of emergency management in this country for decades, and public education programs conducted by the Federal Emergency Management Agency (FEMA), the American Red Cross, the Salvation Army, local fire departments, and other public- and private-sector agencies have disseminated millions of brochures and checklists describing the risks of future disaster events and the steps that individuals and communities can take to reduce and prepare for them. In recent years, these programs have embraced new technologies to disseminate this information, including video and, most significantly, the Internet.

The design and implementation of warning systems has similarly advanced in the past decades. From the Civil Defense sirens to the Emergency Broadcast Network to weather radios, warning systems alerting the public to sudden or impending disaster events have become more sophisticated and widely used. Broadcasting timely information that allows individuals to make appropriate shelter and evacuation decisions is at the core of the warning systems designed for natural hazards such as tornadoes and tsunamis. Watch and warning notices for floods and hurricanes provide individuals and community leaders with valuable information on the path and potential destructiveness of severe storms that could result in flooding events. The public media — television, radio, and most recently the Internet — are the mechanisms most often used by emergency officials to issue watch and warning notices.

The importance of communicating with the public during the response and recovery phases of a natural or technological disaster event has only recently been fully embraced by emergency officials. Too often in the past, little value was placed on communicating with the public during and after a disaster event, and emergency officials had little training and interest in this area. This changed in the 1990s as FEMA, under the direction of James Lee Witt, made a commitment and marshaled the resources to develop and implement an aggressive public affairs program designed to deliver timely and accurate messages to the public in a time of crisis. The messages focused on what measures government and private-sector officials were taking to help a community in responding to and recovering from a disaster event and the methods by which individuals and communities could apply for and receive federal, state, and local disaster relief. FEMA established a working partnership with the media to deliver these messages through press conferences, individual interviews, satellite feeds, radio actualities, and the Internet. One of their greatest accomplishments in this regard was the publication of *Recovery Times*, a newspaper supplement developed and maintained by FEMA to be distributed by local newspaper outlets in disaster-affected areas. Over time, this public affairs model created by FEMA has gained wider acceptance by state and local emergency officials.

The threat of terrorism has altered the playing field for emergency managers by introducing new hazards that are not fully understood, creating an altered risk perception among members of the public (who are concerned about terrorism victimization), and presenting new response and recovery (mostly cleanup) procedures and practices, new information uncertainties, new restrictions on the release of information to the public, and new demands for public information.

Risk Communication

The federal government, through the Department of Homeland Security (DHS), has initiated several programs to achieve a goal of community and individual resilience to the effects of terrorism and other disasters. One of the primary methods employed to achieve such preparedness is public education.

Public education has long been recognized as an effective method for decreasing the damaging potential of hazards and risks, and the media are often central in such projects (Mullis, 1998). Furthermore, the role of the media in previous risk-related public education endeavors dealing with natural and technological hazards and public health issues has been well documented. From teaching citizens to build tornado-resistant safe rooms to minimizing tsunami drowning and preventing teen pregnancy, public and private agencies have partnered with, cooperated with, or utilized the various players collectively referred to as the *mass media* to achieve the goal of reducing public risk.

■ ■ Critical Thinking ■

Why are the news media considered such an important asset to emergency preparedness public education efforts? Are other sources more effective? Why or why not? Give examples to support your answer.

Emergency Management and Risk Communication in the United States

On November 25, 2002, President Bush signed into law the Homeland Security Act of 2002, investing in the new DHS the mission of protecting the United States from further terrorist attacks, reducing the nation's vulnerability to terrorism, and minimizing the damage from potential terrorist attacks and natural disasters. DHS began working to organize the federal response to the consequences of disasters but concentrated its efforts on preparedness and response capabilities to combat terrorism (as is evident by changes in federal funding trends). DHS officials were still operating under the same constraints of the previous administration in terms of what they could do to increase preparedness at the community level. DHS repeatedly acknowledged that, even in the event that a terrorist attack be declared a national disaster, local communities would need to be prepared to be self-sufficient for a minimum of 48 hours. However, public demand for more federal action and information required DHS to address these public education needs.

The Ready.gov campaign is DHS's primary effort to increase individual citizen preparedness at the community level. It is essentially a website, designed by the Ad Council, that offers citizens, businesses, and children with explicit directions detailing what they can do to prepare themselves and their families for all hazards, including terrorism. Initially, other efforts at informing the public, which are equal components in the larger public education effort, included the five-color–coded Homeland Security Alert System (HSAS) and more specific public announcements and alerts, such as the well-known "duct tape and plastic" incident (in which DHS Director Tom Ridge made a general appeal to people in the United States to buy those particular items to protect themselves from the effects of a possible WMD terrorist attack). In April 2011, DHS announced the implementation of the National Terrorism Advisory System (NTAS) that took the place of the HSAS.

Personal preparedness for disasters, as described by the Ready.gov website, includes three major components. They are "get a kit" (one that contains materials to ensure potable water, food, clean air, first aid, and special needs items), "make a plan" (in which individuals or families determine actions to be taken in the event of specific disasters), and "be informed" (generally by obtaining information about hazards and their associated personal mitigation and preparedness measures). To measure the effectiveness of a citizen's degree of terrorism–hazard preparedness, these three components must be used as performance measures. For the specific case of terrorism, "vigilance" (or actively looking for and reporting suspicious behavior that could be linked to terrorism) is included as a performance measure for personal terrorism preparedness (DHS, 2003).

Since late 2004, DHS has added two components to its Ready.gov site to expand on the specific groups that may benefit from the preparedness information they provide. The first group is the business community. The website instructs business owners and administrators on how to (1) plan to stay in business, (2) talk to your people, and (3) protect your investment. The second group is children.

Essential Components of Effective Risk Communication

Numerous components of effective risk communication have been identified as vital to the success of an effective campaign. Morgan and his colleagues (2002) conclude that effective risk communication requires authoritative and trustworthy sources. They add that if the acting communicators are perceived by the public as having a vested personal interest in the result of such preparedness, they may be skeptical about the communicators' intentions. Mileti (1999) contends that several characteristics must be considered in creating the messages, including the amount of material, speed of presentation, number of arguments, repetition, style, clarity, ordering, forcefulness, specificity, consistency, accuracy, and extremity of the position advocated. These characteristics are adjusted depending on whether the communicators intend to attract attention or enhance the acceptance of their message. Singer and Endreny (1993) claim that in order for a message to be considered comprehensive, it should contain an annual mortality associated with the hazard (if known), the "spatial extent" of the hazard, the time frame associated with the hazard, and the alternatives for mitigating the hazard.

Communicators must also ensure that their messages are understood by those whom they are trying to reach, which undoubtedly changes from community to community depending on the demographic makeup of each. Mileti (1999) writes, "Most hazard-awareness and education programs have assumed a homogeneous 'public,' and have done little to tailor information materials to different groups." He adds that hazard-awareness programs are more effective if they rely on multiple sources transmitting multiple messages through multiple outlets and that radio and television are best at maintaining hazard awareness, whereas printed materials tend to provide more specific instructions on what should be done.

These are obviously high standards when considering the strict time, length, and content guidelines within which journalists must work. Highlighting the difficulty of both creating and analyzing such endeavors and the need for such a study as this, Morgan and his colleagues (2002) write, "As practiced today, risk communication is often very earnest but also surprisingly ad hoc. Typically, one can find neither a clear analysis of what needs to be communicated nor solid evidence that messages have achieved their impact. Nor can one find tested procedures for ensuring the credibility of information."

Existing Government Public Awareness Campaigns

Ready.gov, with its partners in the public, private, and volunteer sectors, is the government's official risk communication website, providing information to three primary groups (Figure 11–1): Americans

FIGURE 11–1 Department of Homeland Security Ready.gov website.

(adult citizens), businesses, and children. Ready America, the original focus of the website, instructs the American public to perform three preparedness activities, namely:

Get a Kit
Make a Plan (Figure 11–2)
Be Informed

This site also provides more specific emergency preparedness information for three special populations:

Older Americans
People with disabilities
Pet owners

Ready Business was the second component developed in the DHS public education effort. Ready Business focuses on business continuity and crisis management concepts to help businesses prepare for and respond to disasters. Through this online instructional guide, businesses are instructed to take action in three primary subject areas.

Plan to Stay in Business: This includes the following actions:

Be informed (knowing what kinds of emergencies might affect the company)
Continuity planning (how to carefully assess how the company functions, both internally and
     externally)
Emergency planning (how to protect employees)
Emergency supplies (survival basics, including fresh water, food, clean air, and warmth)
Deciding to stay or go (basics for sheltering in place or evacuating)
Fire safety (fire is the most common source of business disasters)
Medical emergencies (information about first aid and CPR)
Influenza pandemic (basic information about how to get more information on pandemic planning)

Talk to Your People: This includes general advice on informing and educating employees in emergency management basics and response principles:

Involve coworkers (including all staff in the emergency planning process)
Practice the plan (planning and conducting emergency drills and exercises)
Promoting preparedness (encouraging employees to follow the Ready America advice)
Crisis communications plan (company planning on how to stay in contact with employees and
     customers in a disaster situation)
Employee health (addressing the special health needs of employees that arise in disasters)

Protect Your Investment: This instructs businesses in ways to ensure the safety of physical assets, including:

Insurance coverage
Planning for utility disruption
Securing facilities, buildings, and plants
Securing equipment
Protecting heating, ventilation, and air-conditioning systems
Ensuring cybersecurity

Family Emergency Plan

Make sure your family has a plan in case of an emergency. Before an emergency happens, sit down together and decide how you will get in contact with each other, where you will go and what you will do in an emergency. Keep a copy of this plan in your emergency supply kit or another safe place where you can access it in the event of a disaster.

Out-of-Town Contact Name: _____   Telephone Number: _____

Email: _____

Neighborhood Meeting Place: _____   Telephone Number: _____

Regional Meeting Place: _____   Telephone Number: _____

Evacuation Location: _____   Telephone Number: _____

Fill out the following information for each family member and keep it up to date.

Name:	Social Security Number:
Date of Birth:	Important Medical Information:
Name:	Social Security Number:
Date of Birth:	Important Medical Information:
Name:	Social Security Number:
Date of Birth:	Important Medical Information:
Name:	Social Security Number:
Date of Birth:	Important Medical Information:
Name:	Social Security Number:
Date of Birth:	Important Medical Information:
Name:	Social Security Number:
Date of Birth:	Important Medical Information:

Write down where your family spends the most time: work, school and other places you frequent. Schools, daycare providers, workplaces and apartment buildings should all have site-specific emergency plans that you and your family need to know about.

Work Location One
Address:
Phone Number:
Evacuation Location:

Work Location Two
Address:
Phone Number:
Evacuation Location:

Work Location Three
Address:
Phone Number:
Evacuation Location:

Other place you frequent
Address:
Phone Number:
Evacuation Location:

School Location One
Address:
Phone Number:
Evacuation Location:

School Location Two
Address:
Phone Number:
Evacuation Location:

School Location Three
Address:
Phone Number:
Evacuation Location:

Other place you frequent
Address:
Phone Number:
Evacuation Location:

Important Information	Name	Telephone Number	Policy Number
Doctor(s):			
Other:			
Pharmacist:			
Medical Insurance:			
Homeowners/Rental Insurance:			
Veterinarian/Kennel (for pets):			

FIGURE 11–2 Ready America Family Plan cover page. (Source: Department of Homeland Security, "Ready America," 2008, http://www.ready.gov/america/_downloads/familyemergencyplan.pdf)

The third and final component of the Ready.gov website is Ready Kids. This web page is designed to help parents and teachers educate children in grades 4 and 5 about emergency preparedness, emergency response, and how to help their family to prepare for disasters. The site contains simple and illustrated step-by-step instructions about the kinds of things families can do to be better prepared, and the role that

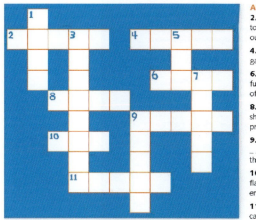

DEAR FAMILY,

Family Reproducible Worksheet

To prepare for emergencies, families can collect items that might be useful and put them in an emergency supply kit. Go to www.ready.gov and click on *Ready Kids* to find out how your family can prepare for unexpected situations. Then complete this crossword puzzle to give you an idea of what kinds of things should be part of your family's emergency supply kit.

CLUES

ACROSS:

2. _ _ _ _ _ light: A handy tool to have if the lights go out!

4. Every person needs one gallon of this per day!

6. This comfortable piece of furniture should not be part of a family's supply kit.

8. Furry family members that should be part of your preparedness plan.

9. Some people have a _ _ _ _ _ between meals if they are hungry.

10. You might find water, a flashlight, or a whistle in an emergency supply _ _ _.

11. Fun items that families can play together.

DOWN:

1. Families can create a communication _ _ _ _ so that they know where to meet and who to call during an emergency.

3. _ _ _ _ _ _ _ _ bag: Great for napping or keeping warm.

5. Every family member should carry a contact list with at least _ _ _ different phone numbers that will allow you to keep in touch during an emergency.

7. It's important to get the _ _ _ _ _ about different kinds of emergencies, so that you know what to expect.

9. Keep an extra pair of these in your supply kit to keep your feet dry!

FIGURE 11–3 Crossword puzzle from the Ready.gov Ready Kids website. (Source: Ready.gov, 2008)

children can play in this effort (Figure 11–3). The website was developed in consultation with several established children- and emergency-focused organizations, including:

American Psychological Association
American Red Cross
National Association of Elementary School Principals
National Association of School Psychologists
National Center for Child Traumatic Stress
National PTA
U.S. Department of Education
U.S. Department of Health and Human Services

■■ Critical Thinking ■

Do you believe that the Ready.gov website offers useful information to the public? If so, do you believe that average Americans will access this information and use it to their benefit? Why or why not? Can you think of a more effective way to communicate risk to the general public?

Warning

On April 20, 2011, DHS Secretary Janet Napolitano announced the implementation of the NTAS. The NTAS took the place of the much-maligned color-coded Homeland Security Advisory System (HSAS) (Figure 11–4) that had been in place since 2002.

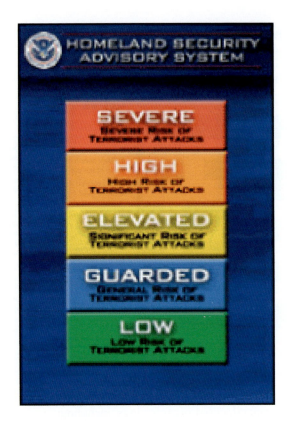

FIGURE 11–4 Homeland Security Advisory System (2002–2011).

Since its inception, concerns had been raised about the level of information provided through the HSAS. These concerns were shared by both the general public and members of the first-responder community (e.g., police, fire, and emergency medical technicians), as well as local officials responsible for ensuring public safety. The Partnership for Public Warning (PPW) was formed in January 2002 as a partnership among the private sector, academia, and government entities at the local, state, and federal levels for the purpose of better coordinating disaster warning programs. PPW is a nonprofit entity with its stated mission to "promote and enhance efficient, effective, and integrated dissemination of public warnings and related information so as to save lives, reduce disaster losses and speed recovery" (PPW, 2008). In May 2003, PPW published "A National Strategy for Integrated Public Warning Policy and Capability," which examined the current status of public warning systems, practices, and issues across the United States. The report stated, "Working together in partnership, the stakeholders should assess current warning capability, carry out appropriate research and develop the following:

- A common terminology for natural and man-made disasters
- A standard message protocol
- National metrics and standards

- National backbone systems for securely collecting and disseminating warnings from all official sources
- Pilot projects to test concepts and approaches
- Training and event-simulation programs
- A national multimedia education and outreach program (Partnership for Public Warning, 2003)

In her announcement concerning the NTAS, Secretary Napolitano stated, "The terrorist threat facing our country has evolved significantly over the past ten years, and in today's environment — more than ever — we know that the best security strategy is one that counts on the American public as a key partner in securing our country." DHS released the document entitled "A Public Guide to the NTAS" as part of its effort to announce its establishment (DHS, 2011). Additional information concerning the NTAS released by DHS in April 2011 is presented in the sidebar "National Terrorism Advisory System (NTAS)."

■ ■ ■ ───

National Terrorism Advisory System (NTAS)

Under NTAS, DHS will coordinate with other federal entities to issue detailed alerts to the public when the federal government receives information about a credible terrorist threat. NTAS alerts provide a concise summary of the potential threat including geographic region, mode of transportation, or critical infrastructure potentially affected by the threat, actions being taken to ensure public safety, as well as recommended steps that individuals, communities, businesses, and governments can take to help prevent, mitigate, or respond to a threat. NTAS Alerts will include a clear statement on the nature of the threat, which will be defined in one of two ways:

- "Elevated Threat": Warns of a credible terrorist threat against the United States
- "Imminent Threat": Warns of a credible, specific, and impending terrorist threat against the United States

Depending on the nature of the threat, alerts may be sent to law enforcement, distributed to affected areas of the private sector, or issued more broadly to the public through both official and social media channels — including a designated DHS webpage (www.dhs.gov/alerts), Facebook, and Twitter @NTASAlerts. NTAS alerts and posters will also be displayed in places such as transit hubs, airports, and government buildings.

NTAS threat alerts will be issued for a specific time period and will automatically expire. Alerts may be extended if new information becomes available or as a specific threat evolves.

─────────────────────────────

Source: DHS, 2011, http://www.dhs.gov/ynews/releases/pr_1303296515462.shtm.

── ■ ■ ■

As part of the announcement of the NTAS, DHS released the following information presented in the sidebars "A Public Guide to the NTAS" and "Frequently Asked Questions of the NTAS." A sample NTAS alert is presented in Figure 11–5.

National Terrorism Advisory System

Alert

www.dhs.gov/alerts

DATE & TIME ISSUED: XXXX

SUMMARY

The Secretary of Homeland Security informs the public and relevant government and private sector partners about a potential or actual threat with this alert, indicating whether there is an "imminent" or "elevated" threat.

DURATION

An individual threat alert is issued for a specific time period and then automatically expires. It may be extended if new information becomes available or the threat evolves.

DETAILS

• This section provides more detail about the threat and what the public and sectors need to know.

• It may include specific information, if available, about the nature and credibility of the threat, including the critical infrastructure sector(s) or location(s) that may be affected.

• It includes as much information as can be released publicly about actions being taken or planned by authorities to ensure public safety, such as increased protective actions and what the public may expect to see.

AFFECTED AREAS

▪ This section includes visual depictions (such as maps or other graphics) showing the affected location(s), sector(s), or other illustrative detail about the threat itself.

HOW YOU CAN HELP

• This section provides information on ways the public can help authorities (e.g. camera phone pictures taken at the site of an explosion), and reinforces the importance of reporting suspicious activity.

• It may ask the public or certain sectors to be alert for a particular item, situation, person, activity or developing trend.

STAY PREPARED

• This section emphasizes the importance of the public planning and preparing for emergencies before they happen, including specific steps individuals, families and businesses can take to ready themselves and their communities.

• It provides additional preparedness information that may be relevant based on this threat.

STAY INFORMED

• This section notifies the public about where to get more information.

• It encourages citizens to stay informed about updates from local public safety and community leaders.

• It includes a link to the DHS NTAS website http://www.dhs.gov/alerts and http://twitter.com/NTASAlerts

If You See Something, Say Something™. Report suspicious activity to local law enforcement or call 911.

The National Terrorism Advisory System provides Americans with alert information on homeland security threats. It is distributed by the Department of Homeland Security. More information is available at: **www.dhs.gov/alerts.** To receive mobile updates: **www.twitter.com/NTASAlerts**
If You See Something Say Something™ used with permission of the NY Metropolitan Transportation Authority.

FIGURE 11–5 A sample NTAS alert. Source: DHS, 2011, http://www.dhs.gov/xlibrary/assets/ntas/ntas-sample-alert.pdf

A Public Guide to the NTAS

The National Terrorism Advisory System

The National Terrorism Advisory System, or NTAS, replaces the color-coded Homeland Security Advisory System (HSAS). This new system will more effectively communicate information about terrorist threats by providing timely, detailed information to the public, government agencies, first responders, airports and other transportation hubs, and the private sector.

It recognizes that Americans all share responsibility for the nation's security, and should always be aware of the heightened risk of terrorist attack in the United States and what they should do.

NTAS Alerts

After reviewing the available information, the Secretary of Homeland Security will decide, in coordination with other Federal entities, whether an NTAS Alert should be issued.

NTAS Alerts will only be issued when credible information is available.

These alerts will include a clear statement that there is an imminent threat or elevated threat. Using available information, the alerts will provide a concise summary of the potential threat, information about actions being taken to ensure public safety, and recommended steps that individuals, communities, businesses, and governments can take to help prevent, mitigate, or respond to the threat.

The NTAS Alerts will be based on the nature of the threat: in some cases, alerts will be sent directly to law enforcement or affected areas of the private sector, while in others, alerts will be issued more broadly to the American people through both official and media channels.

NTAS Alerts contain a sunset provision indicating a specific date when the alert expires — there will not be a constant NTAS Alert or blanket warning that there is an overarching threat. If threat information changes for an alert, the Secretary of Homeland Security may announce an updated NTAS Alert. All changes, including the announcement that cancels an NTAS Alert, will be distributed the same way as the original alert.

The NTAS Alert — How can you help?

Each alert provides information to the public about the threat, including, if available, the geographic region, mode of transportation, or critical infrastructure potentially affected by the threat; protective actions being taken by authorities; and steps that individuals and communities can take to protect themselves and their families, and help prevent, mitigate or respond to the threat.

Citizens should report suspicious activity to their local law enforcement authorities. The "If You See Something, Say Something™" campaign across the United States encourages all citizens to be vigilant for indicators of potential terrorist activity, and to follow NTAS Alerts for information about threats in specific places or for individuals exhibiting certain types of suspicious activity. Visit www.dhs.gov/ifyouseesomethingsaysomething to learn more about the campaign.

Alert Announcements

NTAS Alerts will be issued through state, local, and tribal partners, the news media, and directly to the public via the following channels:

- Via the official DHS NTAS webpage — http://www.dhs.gov/alerts
- Via email signup at — http://www.dhs.gov/alerts

- Via social media
    - Facebook — http://www.facebook.com/NTASAlerts
    - Twitter — http://twitter.com/#!/NTASAlerts
- Via data feeds, web widgets, and graphics — http://www.dhs.gov/alerts. The public can also expect to see alerts in places, both public and private, such as transit hubs, airports and government buildings.

Source: DHS, 2011, "NTAS Guide: National Terrorism Advisory System Public Guide," http://www.dhs.gov/xlibrary/assets/ntas/ntas-public-guide.pdf

Crisis Communications

Communications has become an increasingly critical function in emergency management. The dissemination of timely and accurate information to the general public, elected and community officials, and the media plays a major role in the effective management of disaster response and recovery activities. Communicating preparedness, prevention, and mitigation information promotes actions that reduce the risk of future disasters. Communicating policies, goals, and priorities to staff, partners, and participants enhances support and promotes a more efficient disaster management operation.

Communications failures by government responders in Hurricane Katrina were noted in a report prepared by the U.S. House of Representatives that stated, "The lack of a government public communications strategy and media hype of violence exacerbated public concerns and further delayed relief." The House report also asked "why coordination and information sharing between local, state and federal governments was so dismal ... Why situational awareness was so foggy, for so long ... Why unsubstantiated rumors and uncritically repeated press reports — at times fueled by top officials — were able to delay, disrupt, and diminish the response." (Select Bipartisan Committee to Investigate the Preparation for and Response to Hurricane Katrina, 2006)

The purpose of this section is:

- To define the mission of an effective disaster communications strategy
- To examine communicating in the era of homeland security
- To examine the various forms of media that emergency managers have historically relied on and the new forms of media that are changing how disaster news and information is shared with the public
- To detail the seven elements that we believe will comprise an effective crisis communications capability in the future

Mission

The mission of an effective disaster communications strategy is to provide timely and accurate information to the public in all four phases of emergency management:

- *Mitigation*: To promote implementation of strategies, technologies, and actions that will reduce the loss of lives and property in future disasters

- *Preparedness*: To communicate preparedness messages that encourage and educate the public in anticipation of disaster events
- *Response*: To provide to the public notification, warning, evacuation, and situation reports on an ongoing disaster
- *Recovery*: To provide individuals and communities affected by a disaster with information on how to register for and receive disaster relief

The foundation of an effective communications strategy is built on five critical assumptions (see the sidebar entitled "Five Critical Assumptions for a Successful Communications Strategy"):

- Customer Focus
- Leadership Commitment
- Inclusion of Communications in Planning and Operations
- Good Information
- Media Partnership

Five Critical Assumptions for a Successful Communications Strategy

1. Customer Focus — Understand what information your customers and your partners need and build communications mechanisms that deliver this information in a timely and accurate fashion.
2. Leadership Commitment — The leader of the emergency/homeland security operations must be committed to effective communications and must participate fully in the communications process.
3. Inclusion of Communications in Planning and Operations — Communications specialists must be involved in all emergency/homeland security planning and operations to ensure that communicating timely and accurate information is considered when action decisions are being considered.
4. Timely and Accurate Information — Effective communications is based on the timely collection, analysis and dissemination of information from the impacted area in accordance with basic principles of effective communications such as transparency and truthfulness.
5. Media Partnership — The media (i.e., television, radio, Internet, newspapers, etc.) are the most effective means for communicating timely and accurate information to the public. A partnership with the media involves understanding the needs of the media and including trained staff who work directly with the media to get information to the public. And now that citizen journalists and new media technologies (cell phones, laptops, digital cameras) have become more vital and accepted sources of information and imaging from the front lines of a disaster, methods for incorporating these data and information must also be implemented.

Customer Focus

An essential element of any effective emergency management/homeland security system is a focus on customers and customer service. This philosophy should guide communications with the public and with all partners in emergency management. A customer service approach includes placing the needs and interests of individuals and communities first, being responsive and informative, and managing expectations.

The customers for emergency management/homeland security are diverse. They include internal customers, such as staff, other federal agencies, states, and other disaster partners. External customers include the general public, elected officials at all levels of government, community and business leaders, and the media. Each of these customers has specific information needs, and a good communications strategy considers and reflects their requirements.

Leadership Commitment

Good communications starts with a commitment by the leadership of the emergency management organization to sharing and disseminating information both internally and externally. One of the lessons learned from Hurricane Katrina is, "We need public officials to lead. Communicating confidence to citizens and delivering on promises are both critical in crises" (Kettl, 2005).

The leader of any disaster response and recovery effort must openly endorse and promote open lines of communications among the organization's staff, partners, and publics in order to effectively communicate (Figure 11–6). The leader must model this behavior in order to clearly illustrate that communications is a valued function of the organization.

Inclusion of Communications in Planning and Operations

The most important part of leadership's commitment to communications is inclusion of communications in all planning and operations. This means that a communications specialist is included in the senior management team of any emergency management/homeland security organization and operation. It means

FIGURE 11–6 Milwaukee, WI, June 18, 2008 — Michael Morgan, Secretary of the Wisconsin Department of Administration, and Dolf Diemont, Federal Coordinating Officer for Disaster 1768, speak at the opening of a Disaster Recovery Center in Milwaukee. FEMA public affairs personnel work closely with the state in a disaster situation. (Source: Photo by Ed Edahl/FEMA)

that communications issues are considered in the decision-making processes and that a communications element is included in all organizational activities, plans, and operations.

In the past, communicating with external customers, and in many cases internal customers, was not valued or considered critical to a successful emergency management/homeland security operation. Technology has changed that equation. In today's world of 24-hour television and radio news and the Internet, the demand for information is never-ending, especially in an emergency response situation. Emergency managers must be able to communicate critical information in a timely manner to their staff, partners, the public, and the media.

To do so, the information needs of the various customers and how best to communicate with these customers must be considered at the same time that planning and operational decisions are being made. For example, a decision process on how to remove debris from a disaster area must include discussion of how to communicate information on the debris removal operation to community officials, the public, and the media.

Again the response to Hurricane Katrina clearly illustrates the downside of failing to include consideration of communications issues in conducting a response operation. The Lessons Learned report prepared by White House Homeland Security Advisor Francis Townsend noted, "The lack of communications and situational awareness had a debilitating effect on the Federal response. The Department of Homeland Security should develop an integrated public communications plan to better inform, guide, and reassure the American public before, during, and after a catastrophe. The Department of Homeland Security should enable this plan with operational capabilities to deploy coordinated public affairs teams during a crisis" (Townsend 2006).

Situational Awareness

Situational awareness is key to an effective disaster response. Knowing the number of people killed and injured, the level of damage at the disaster site, the condition of homes and community infrastructure, and current response efforts provides decision makers with the situational awareness needed to identify need and appropriately apply available resources. The collection, analysis, and dissemination of information from the disaster site are the basis for an effective communications operation in a disaster response.

This is also true during the disaster recovery phase especially early in the recovery phase when the demand for information from the public, and therefore the media, is at its highest. Developing effective communications strategies to promote community preparedness and/or mitigation programs requires detailed information about the nature of the risk that impacts the community and how the planned preparedness programs will help individuals and communities to be ready for the next disaster and the mitigation programs will reduce the impacts of future disasters.

FEMA's National Incident Management System (NIMS) includes a section on Public Information in its Incident Command System (ICS) component. One of the three top command staff reporting to the Incident Commander in ICS is the Public Information Officer (see Figure 11–7).

FEMA's NIMS document states, "Public Information consists of the processes, procedures, and systems to communicate timely, accurate, and accessible information on the incident's cause, size, and current situation to the public, responders, and additional stakeholders (both directly affected and indirectly affected). Public information must be coordinated and integrated across jurisdictions and across agencies/organizations; among Federal, State, tribal, and local governments; and with the private sector and NGOs. Well developed public information, education strategies, and communications plans help to ensure that lifesaving measures, evacuation routes, threat and alert systems, and other public safety information is coordinated and communicated to numerous audiences in a timely, consistent manner. Public Information includes processes, procedures, and organizational structures required to gather, verify, coordinate, and disseminate information" (FEMA, 2007) (Figure 11–7).

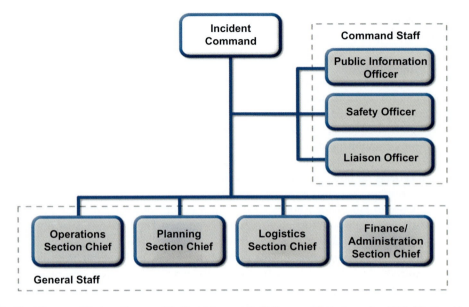

FIGURE 11–7 Incident Command System: Command Staff and General Staff. (Source: FEMA, December 2008, "National Incident Management System, http://www.fema.gov/pdf/emergency/nims/NIMS_core.pdf)

Media Partnership

The media plays a primary role in communicating with the public. No government emergency management/homeland security organization could ever hope to develop a communications network comparable to those networks already established and maintained by television, radio, newspapers, and online news outlets across the country. To effectively provide timely disaster information to the public, emergency managers must establish a partnership with their local media outlets.

The goal of a media partnership is to provide accurate and timely information to the public in both disaster and nondisaster situations. The partnership requires a commitment by both the emergency manager and the media to work together, and it requires a level of trust between both parties.

Traditionally, the relationship between emergency managers and the media has been strained. There is often a conflict between the need of the emergency manager to respond quickly and the need of the media to obtain information on the response so it can report it just as quickly. This conflict sometimes results in inaccurate reporting and tension between the emergency manager and the media. The loser in this conflict is always the public, which relies on the media for its information.

It is important for emergency/homeland security managers to understand the needs of the media and the value they bring to facilitating response operations. An effective media partnership provides the emergency/homeland security manager with a communications network to reach the public with vital information and provides the media with access to the disaster site, access to emergency/homeland security managers and their staff, and access to critical information for the public that informs and ensures the accuracy of their reporting.

Communications Infrastructure

FEMA built a substantial communications infrastructure to support its communications objectives. Resources were devoted to hiring and training staff with experience in working with the media and community and providing these employees with the tools they needed to be successful. FEMA built and maintained a television studio with satellite capabilities and an audio studio with radio broadcast capabilities. The agency also established an interactive website where radio actualities and print information could be posted instantaneously. FEMA hired still and video photographers who were dispatched to the field, filing their photos electronically each night. These photos were then made available to media outlets around the country via the Internet.

Local emergency managers developed similar capabilities on a smaller scale in communities around the country. A research project conducted by graduate students at George Washington University found that many jurisdictions in the Washington, D.C., metro area have built varying degrees of communications infrastructure such as communications plans, web and fax communication capabilities, and trained staff who served them well during recent natural and man-made events.

Terrorism Application

As noted earlier, Mayor Giuliani was an effective communicator in the aftermath of the World Trade Center attacks. He quickly assumed the role of principal government spokesperson, providing information, solace, and comfort to victims and their families, fellow New Yorkers, the nation, and the world through a series of planned and unplanned media events and interviews over the course of the days and months after September 11. Giuliani has been praised for his candor, his sensitivity, and his availability during these efforts. He has set a standard by which public officials will be judged in future tragedies.

In Washington, D.C., a different communications scenario surfaced in the days and weeks after the first anthrax-contaminated letter was discovered in the office of the then U.S. Senate Majority Leader Tom Daschle in October 2001. A series of public officials and scientists issued often-conflicting information to the public as both the officials and the public struggled to understand the nature and the reach of the anthrax threat. The failure to communicate accurate and timely information reduced public confidence in the government response and increased the confusion and misinformation surrounding the events.

What factors made Mayor Giuliani's efforts successful and caused the situation in Washington to worsen? What type of information and infrastructure support did Giuliani have that may or may not have been available to the public officials in Washington? Was the commitment to inform the public different in New York City than it was in Washington, D.C.?

A study of the anthrax attacks, funded by the Century Foundation, concluded that "the timely flow of information from experts to the public via the mass media will be the nation's best protection against panic and potential disaster" (Thomas, 2003). To reach this goal, the media and public officials will need to change the way they work together and possibly establish new protocols for determining the methods by which sensitive information is collected and disseminated to the public. These issues must ultimately be balanced against the public's right to know. As the study found, the public is often smarter and better informed than both the media and public officials believe (Thomas, 2003).

A report entitled "What Should We Know? Whom Do We Tell? Leveraging Communications and Information to Counter Terrorism and Its Consequences" found that the dissemination of information before a terrorist incident is as critical, if not more so, as delivering timely and accurate information during and after a crisis (Chemical and Biological Arms Control Institute, 2002). Preincident planning and coordination and public education and awareness campaigns are critical elements in establishing clear lines of communications among responding agencies, significantly improving the opportunities to collect accurate information and make it available to the public through the mass media. Again, changes in current practices and relationships among responders and with the media must occur to meet the information needs before, during, and after future terrorist attacks (Chemical and Biological Arms Control Institute, 2002).

Communicating in the Era of Homeland Security

Communicating with the public is an area that needs to be improved if the nation is going to have a truly effective homeland security system. From its inception, the DHS has shown little interest in communicating with the public, and when it has the results have not always been positive — the "duct tape and plastic" fiasco and past reports of former DHS Secretary Ridge questioning terror alert warnings serve as classic examples. DHS communications have improved during the Obama Administration, but DHS and its state and local partners still need to address three factors in order to further improve their communications with the American people.

First, there must be a commitment from the leadership, not only at DHS and its state and local partners, but also at all levels of government including the executive level to communicate timely and accurate information to the public. This is especially important in the response and recovery phases to a terrorist incident.

In a disaster scenario, the conventional wisdom that states information is power, and that hoarding information helps to retain such power, is almost categorically reversed. Withholding information during disaster events generally has an overall negative impact on the well-being of the public, and on the impression the public forms about involved authorities. In practice, sharing of information is what generates authority and power, when that information is useful and relates to the hazard at hand. A good example of this fact are the actions of former New York City Mayor Rudy Giuliani after the September 11 attacks. Giuliani went to great lengths to get accurate and timely information to the public in a time of crisis, and his efforts both inspired the public and greatly enhanced the effectiveness of the response and recovery efforts he guided.

Historically, DHS leadership and the political leadership have been reluctant to make this commitment to share information with the public. This is something that must change if they expect the American people to fully comprehend the homeland security threat and to become actively engaged in homeland security efforts. Few citizens have any idea of what actual terrorism risks they face, and fewer can actually relate those risks in any comparable fashion to the risks they face every day.

Second, homeland security officials at all levels must resolve the conflict between sharing information with the public in advance and in the aftermath of a terrorist incident that has value for intelligence or criminal prosecution purposes. This is directly linked to the commitment issue discussed in the previous paragraphs and has been repeatedly cited by homeland security officials as reasons for not sharing more specific information with the public.

Also at issue is the question of when to release relevant information to the public without compromising intelligence sources and/or ongoing criminal investigations. This is an issue that rarely if ever confronts emergency management officials dealing with natural and unintentional man-made disasters. Therefore, there is little precedent or experience for current homeland security officials to work with in crafting a communications strategy that balances the competing need for the public to have timely and accurate information with the need to protect intelligence sources and ongoing criminal investigations. To date, the needs of the intelligence and justice communities have clearly been judged to outweigh those of the public — but at a cost.

Withholding information leaves the public vulnerable and suspicious of the government. Lucy Dalglish, executive director of the Reporters Committee for the Freedom of the Press, said her task, and the task of journalists, was to convince government officials that over the long run transparency can build trust and save lives: "The same information that a terrorist can use to do great damage can possibly give families information about which escape route to use to get away from a nuclear power plant. I think we're going to find that if we have a flu pandemic, the information that can be used to terrorize and scare people can also be used to save their lives. I think what we have to do is work very hard at convincing people that access to information is ultimately going to be our friend" (May, 2006).

The recent implementation by the Obama Administration of the national Terrorism Advisory System that replaced the much-maligned Homeland Security Advisory System (HSAS) is a critical first step in reestablishing trust with the public for the warning system. From this starting point, additional communications mechanisms can be developed to ensure that the public gets timely and accurate information both in advance of any terrorist incident and during the response and recovery phases in the aftermath of the next terrorist attack.

Third, more effort must be invested by federal departments and agencies to better understand the principal terrorist threats that our nation faces (i.e., biological, chemical, radiological, nuclear, and explosives), and to develop communications strategies that educate and inform the public about these threats with more useful information. The 2001 Washington, D.C., anthrax incident is a perfect example of uninformed or misinformed public officials sharing what is often conflicting and, in too many instances, wrong information with the public.

The nation's public officials must be better informed about these principal risks and be ready and capable of explaining complicated information to the public. As the anthrax incident made clear, this is not a luxury, but a necessity if the response to similar incidents in the future is to be successful.

Decades of research and a new generation of technologies now inform emergency managers as they provide information about hurricanes, tornadoes, earthquakes, and hazardous materials incidents to the public. A similar research effort must be undertaken for these five new terrorist risks and communications strategies that will ensure that homeland security officials at all levels are capable of clearly explaining to the public the hazards posed by these threats.

These communications strategies must consider how to communicate to the public when incomplete information is all that is available to homeland security officials. In the vast majority of cases, this partiality of information is probable. A public health crisis will not wait for all the data to be collected and analyzed, nor will the public. Homeland security officials must develop strategies for informing the public effectively, as the crisis develops, by forming effective messages that are able to explain to the public how what is being said is the most accurate information available based on the information that, likewise, is available — despite its incomplete nature. Clearly, this is not an easy task, but it is not impossible. The public will increasingly expect such communications efforts, so the sooner such a system is in place, the better the next incident will be managed.

Disaster Communications in a Changing Media World

The media is constantly changing and emergency/homeland security managers must keep up with these changes to have an effective communications operation. Historically, traditional media such as radio, television, and newspapers delivered emergency messages to the public.

The radio has become over time an integral part of communicating warning messages to the public before the next tornado or hurricane strikes. In turn, radio has often been the sole source of information in the immediate aftermath of a massive disaster that cuts off electricity to the disaster area for days at a time because of the availability of transistor and crank radios that do not require electricity.

Television has become a big part of disasters in the past 50 years. The pictures and stories that are generated by disaster events are a natural fit for television. It was the size of the satellite photo of Hurricane Floyd on television coupled with evacuation warnings from local, state, and federal officials transmitted by television that prompted 3 million residents in Florida, Georgia, and South Carolina to

FIGURE 11–8 Nashville, TN, May 5, 2010 — Nashville resident and disaster survivor Amy Frogge uses social media to display pictures that document the flood and damage to her home in Davidson County. FEMA is responding to the severe storms and flooding that damaged or destroyed thousands of homes in May 2010 across Tennessee. (Source: Photo by David Fine/FEMA)

evacuate their homes as the storm threatened the Eastern Seaboard. It is also television that graphically communicated the sorry events that occurred in New Orleans after Hurricane Katrina.

Over time, television has changed considerably. The three national networks and usually three to four local stations in any given community have given way to hundreds of channels available nationwide along with 24/7 news channels and the Weather Channel, and they are available across the country.

The rise of the Internet as a source for disaster and emergency-related information and news has been spectacular. A survey conducted in April 2008 by the Canadian Centre for Emergency Preparedness (CCEP) found that the Internet has passed newspapers on the list of emergency information sources used by the Canadian public. Television and radio are ranked 1 and 2 on this list, but it may not be long before the Internet grabs even more of the public's attention especially as older and low- to moderate-income individuals and families gain access to the Internet.

The media continues to change with the advent of "first informers," ordinary citizens armed with a cell phone who can take pictures and/or video at the disaster site and add commentary and post their submissions on the Internet or provide them to CNN or MSNBC or other outlets (Figure 11–8). Some of the first photos and commentaries coming out of the Asian tsunami disaster in 2004 were filed by these "first informers" who were one there when the tsunami struck and survived to provide information and images of the damage and destruction.

The Evolution of New Media Use in Disasters

The magnitude and frequency of natural disasters are increasing. According to the Center for Research on the Epidemiology of Disasters, there were four times as many weather-related disasters in the last 20 years than in the previous 75 years. With this new "Age of Extreme Weather," has come the evolution and maturation of new media tools and technologies, a dramatic rise in the number of citizen journalists, and an almost annual increase in their contribution to the flow of new information during disasters.

Even though the 1990s was a time of transformation in communications technology with the emergence of the World Wide Web, 24/7 cable television, and an array of digital tools — from affordable and widely available wireless mobile devices and high-resolution satellite maps — new media was not a factor in natural disaster coverage or recovery until 2001.

In the aftermath of the September 11, 2001, terrorist attacks, citizen-shot videos of the attacks on the Twin Towers dominated news coverage and Americans turned to the Internet for information. But the sharp spike in traffic froze and crashed websites. In many ways, 9/11 was the last disaster covered under the old model of crisis communications: Newspapers printed "Extra" editions, people turned to television for news and "the familiar anchors of the broadcast networks — Tom Brokaw, Peter Jennings, and Dan Rather — took on their avuncular roles of the past for a nation looking for comfort and reassurance" (May, 2006).

Every disaster since 9/11 has involved more citizen journalists and expanded the use and utility of the new media tools and technologies. In 2003, during China's SARS epidemic, people used text messaging to exchange information the government tried to suppress (Hattotuwa, 2007). Three major disasters within nine months — the Asian tsunami (2004), the London transit bombings (2005), and Hurricane Katrina (2005) — marked the coming of age of participatory media.

The December 26, 2004, Asian tsunami has been defined as "the turning point — a before-and-after moment for citizen journalism." Blogs, websites, and message boards provided news and aid — and in real time. One blog, "waveofdestruction.org" logged 682,366 unique visitors in four days (Cooper, 2007). Wikipedia — a group-created website that is editable by any user — became the site for basic information, particularly for hotlines that allowed people to search for missing loved ones and find housing, medical, and other assistance.

Minutes after four bombs rocked London's transportation system, a definitive webpage "July 7, 2005 London Bombings" was started with five sentences on Wikipedia. The page "received more than a thousand edits in its first four hours of existence as additional news came in." Users added links to traditional news sources, and information was posted about what public transportation was shut down, listing contacts to help track a missing person and offering directions to commuters trying to get home. "What was conceived as an open encyclopedia in 2001 [became] a general purpose tool for gathering and distributing information quickly ..." (Shirky, 2008).

In September 2005, Hurricane Katrina, a category 3 hurricane, tore through New Orleans, Louisiana, Mobile, Alabama, and Gulfport, Mississippi. Over 1,500 people were killed and tens of thousands left homeless. Blogs became the primary information-providing tool used by both traditional media and citizen journalists. Staff reporters for New Orleans' daily newspaper, the *Times-Picayune*, created a blog that for a time became the front page of their news operation. It enabled members of the community isolated by flood waters and debris to show and tell each other what they were seeing (Gillmor, 2006).

Message boards provided critical information about shelter locations, family tracing, and missing persons. Internet expert Barbara Palser counted 60 separate online bulletin boards that were created to locate missing people within 2 weeks of the storm. "These sites included major portals such as Yahoo and Craigslist, an array of newspaper and television sites, websites hosted by government and relief organizations, and individual technologists, including a group of programmers who enlisted about 2,000 volunteers to create a database called the Katrina PeopleFinder Project." PeopleFinder was established "to create a consolidated database of missing people built outside the traditional, centralized institutions (i.e., FEMA, Red Cross)" (May, 2006). Google Earth and Google Map that provide and use online satellite imagery were used to illustrate damage assessments — particularly to the Gulf Coast and barrier islands (Laituri, 2005).

After the Java earthquake in 2006, mobile phones became mobile news services. Internews, an international media support group, worked with 180 Indonesian journalists to set up a text messaging service that helped local radio stations to report on the recovery (Hattotuwa, 2007).

In October 2007, wildfires in Southern California resulted in the loss of nearly 2,200 homes and over $1 billion in damages and marked a major step forward in the integration of mainstream media and citizen journalists. "Local media has been highlighting user-submitted photos and videos, and embedding new technology in their prime coverage. San Diego's public television station, KPBS, used Twitter to give its audience updates when its website went down, and the Twitter updates now have a prominent place on their home page" (Glaser, 2007).

San Diego TV station News 8 responded to the crisis by taking down its entire regular website and replacing it with a rolling news blog, linking to YouTube videos of its key reports, plus Google Maps showing the location of the fire (Stabe, 2007). Also on the site were links to practical information that viewers needed, including how to contact insurance companies, how to volunteer or donate to the relief efforts, evacuation information, and shelter locations. "It's an exemplary case study in how a local news operation can respond to a major rolling disaster story by using all the reporting tools available on the Internet" (Catone, 2007).

The Google Map (Internet GIS) tool was used to develop maps of shelter locations and fire updates (Wagner, 2007).

Social media experts were able to track cell phone calls on the island of Haiti after the 2010 earthquake in order to track the spread of cholera. Thousands of Twitter messages from individuals in or near the site of the 2010 Japanese earthquake and tsunami provided the first messages, pictures, and videos of the massive destruction caused by these twin events. Individuals, voluntary groups, and government agencies used various social media sites to communicate recovery and reconstruction messages in Joplin, Missouri, in the aftermath of the 2011 tornadoes.

Clearly, a symbiotic relationship is emerging between citizen journalists and the mainstream news media. With every new major disaster, the mainstream media's use of Internet-facilitated reporting increases. Government, however, has been slow to appreciate the power or potential of the new media tools and Internet culture.

New Media: New World

When disasters happened in the past, we learned about them after the fact. No more. New technologies — laptops, cell phones, text messaging systems, digital cameras, the Internet — have changed the way news is gathered and distributed. These technologies have also profoundly altered the flow of information, undermining the traditional gatekeepers and replacing the centralized, top-down model used by the government and professional media with a more dynamic flow of information that empowered citizens and created ad hoc distributive information networks.

According to Gillmor, the days of news as a "lecture" — when traditional media told the audience what was news — are done. Now news is more of a conversation and the lines have blurred between producers and consumers: "The communications network itself will be a medium for everyone's voice, not just the few who can buy multimillion-dollar printing presses, launch satellites, or win the government's permission to squat on the public's airwaves... (Gillmor, 2006).

The once passive audience has become an active participant in the creation and dissemination of news, and the flow of information is no longer controlled by journalists and government agencies. The increasing participation and power of ordinary citizens in emergency communications are starting to have more observable consequences. The Aspen Institute report, *First Informers in the Disaster Zone: The Lessons of Katrina,* noted in its conclusion, "... there was a difference in how the online environment changed the media mix and altered the flow of information during and after the disaster .... At times the traditional flow of information from government to media to public reversed course .... As one pair of new media experts put it, Katrina 'revealed extraordinary changes taking place within a society increasingly connected by digital networks, a society at the cusp of a new era in human history in which individuals possess an unprecedented capacity to access, share, create and apply information'" (May, 2006).

One participant in the Aspen Institutes assessment of lessons learned from Katrina was Jon Donley, the editor of NOLA.com — the *New Orleans Times-Picayune*'s online companion and the primary source of news when the daily could not print in the weeks following the hurricane. He explained that the new media had fostered a two-way flow of information, in contrast to the old paradigm in which information flows down from government and media to a passive audience. "I would really encourage everybody to think about this new media age that we're in, where the audience isn't playing that game anymore. We have had a revolution" (May, 2006).

In addition to forcing the traditional media to reconsider and redefine its role in disaster communications, the new participatory media enhanced the amount of information and number of sources and added to the problems endemic in disaster — the need to sort truth from rumor and the tension between media demanding transparency and accessibility and government officials changed with managing information during a disaster.

The information available to citizens at times of crises is often inadequate, incorrect, or dated. According to Gillmor and Hattotuwa, "Studies show that the problem lies not with the technologies (or lack thereof) but with the culture of information sharing. The access, dissemination and archiving of information is often controlled by government's agencies, institutions who have a parochial interest in controlling its flow — what gets out where, to whom, how and when" (Gillmor, 2007).

"If we waited for the government to release information during a disaster, it would be days before the public would know anything," complained to one participant in the Aspen Katrina assessment. Chet Lunner, acting director of state and local government coordination in DHS and a former national reporter for the Gannett News Service, spoke from the government's perspective in the Aspen session. He disagreed with a comment from CNN's David Borhman that the government instinct in a crisis was to hide. "They are not hiding. They are sort of defensive, in a crouch … because [they] don't trust the media" (May, 2006).

The challenge now for traditional news sources and cautious governmental hierarchies is to plan for and maximize the use of an increased and accelerated flow of information, to seize the opportunity to share information and build community that online media creates.

In recent years, FEMA and DHS have embraced all forms of new media and begun to engage the public in new forms of communications. In November 2009, FEMA stated why it was becoming involved in social media, "FEMA has been engaging in Web 2.0 tools and on social media sites nationwide as part of its mission to prepare the nation for disasters." FEMA's goals with social media are to provide timely and accurate information related to disaster preparedness response and recovery, provide the public with another avenue for insight into the agency's operations, and engage in what has already become a critical medium in today's world of communications. FEMA's social media ventures function as supplemental outreach, and as appropriate channels for unofficial input (FEMA, 2011). FEMA's and DHS's Internet and social media presence has grown considerably since 2009 (see the sidebar "Social Media at the Department of Homeland Security").

Social Media at the Department of Homeland Security

The Department of Homeland Security is using "Web 2.0," social media technologies and Web sites to provide information in more places and more ways. The following is a list of tools and sites that DHS (including its component agencies) uses to provide up-to-date information "straight from the source".

Web 2.0 and Communications on Department Sites

Online Subscription Services

- RSS and Atom feeds at the Department of Homeland Security: http://www.dhs.gov/xutil/feeds.shtm
- E-mail updates from the Department of Homeland Security: http://www.dhs.gov/xutil/gc_1193765609028.shtm

Media Galleries

- Department and component links to multimedia: http://www.dhs.gov/ynews/gallery/

Blogs

- The Blog @ Homeland Security, Department of Homeland Security: http://www.dhs.gov/journal/theblog/
- TSA Blog, Transportation Security Administration: http://www.tsa.gov/blog/
- Coast Guard Compass, U.S. Coast Guard: http://coastguard.dodlive.mil/
- Chief's Corner, U.S. Fire Administration: http://www.usfa.dhs.gov/about/chiefs-corner/
- FEMA Blog, FEMA: http://blog.fema.gov/
- The Beacon, U.S. Citizenship and Immigration Services: http://blog.uscis.gov/
- The U.S. Coast Guard maintains additional blogs that are not on Department sites, which can be found at: http://www.dhs.gov/xabout/gc_1245941465213.shtm#1

Mobile Web Sites

- FEMA: http://m.fema.gov/
- TSA: http://www.tsa.gov/mobile
- ICE: http://m.ice.gov/

Podcasts

- U.S. Coast Guard: http://www.uscg.mil/top/podcast.asp

Widgets

- Federal Hurricane Response Widget, Department of Homeland Security: http://www.dhs.gov/files/programs/gc_1220128923561.shtm
- Emergency Preparedness and Response Widgets, FEMA: http://www.fema.gov/help/widgets/
- Wait Time Calculator, Transportation Security Administration: http://www.tsa.gov/travelers/waittime.shtm
- Most Wanted, Latest News, Detainee Locator, ICE: http://www.ice.gov/news/widgets/

Web 2.0 and Communications on Non-Government Sites
Blogspot

- Coast Guard All Hands, U.S. Coast Guard: http://coastguardallhands.blogspot.com/

Facebook

- Department of Homeland Security: http://www.facebook.com/homelandsecurity
- U.S. Department of Homeland Security Blue Campaign: http://www.facebook.com/home.php#!/bluecampaign
- FEMA: http://www.facebook.com/fema
- ICE: http://www.facebook.com/homelandsecurity#!/wwwICEgov
- U.S. Coast Guard: http://www.facebook.com/uscoastguard

Flickr

- U.S. Coast Guard, U.S. Coast Guard: http://www.flickr.com/photos/coast_guard/

iTunes

- Transportation Security Administration: itms:\--itunes.apple.com-WebObjects-MZStore.woa-wa-viewPodcast?id = 310038315

Ning

- Our Border, Department of Homeland Security: http://ourborder.ning.com/

Twitter

- DHSJournal, Department of Homeland Security: http://twitter.com/DHSJournal
- National Terrorism Advisory System (NTAS), Department of Homeland Security: http://twitter.com/#!/NTASAlerts
- Citizen Corps, FEMA: http://twitter.com/citizen_corps
- FEMA: http://twitter.com/fema
- Craig Fugate, FEMA: http://twitter.com/craigatfema
- FEMA Region 1: http://twitter.com/femaregion1
- FEMA Region 2: http://twitter.com/femaregion2
- FEMA Region 3: http://twitter.com/femaregion3
- FEMA Region 4: http://twitter.com/femaregion4
- FEMA Region 5: http://twitter.com/femaregion5
- FEMA Region 6: http://twitter.com/femaregion6
- FEMA Region 7: http://twitter.com/femaregion7
- FEMA Region 8: http://twitter.com/femaregion8
- FEMA Region 9: http://twitter.com/femaregion9
- FEMA Region 10: http://twitter.com/femaregion10
- FEMA LRO: http://twitter.com/femalro
- Ready.Gov: http://twitter.com/ReadydotGov
- Science and Technology Directorate: http://twitter.com/dhsscitech
- Transportation Security Administration: http://twitter.com/TSABlogTeam
- U.S. Citizenship and Immigration Services: http://twitter.com/uscis
- U.S. Coast Guard: http://twitter.com/uscoastguard
- CG Compass; U.S. Coast Guard: http://twitter.com/cgcompass
- iCommandant, U.S. Coast Guard: http://twitter.com/iCommandantUSCG
- U.S. Customs and Border Protection: http://www.twitter.com/customsborder
- U.S. Fire Administration, FEMA: http://www.twitter.com/usfire/
- U.S. Immigration and Customs Enforcement: http://www.twitter.com/wwwicegov

YouTube

- U.S. Department of Homeland Security: http://www.youtube.com/ushomelandsecurity
- FEMA: http://www.youtube.com/user/fema
- Transportation Security Administration: http://www.youtube.com/user/TSAHQpublicaffairs
- U.S. Coast Guard: http://www.youtube.com/uscgimagery
- U.S. Customs and Border Protection: http://www.youtube.com/customsborderprotect
- U.S. Immigration and Customs Enforcement: http://www.youtube.com/wwwicegov

The Department is not currently using Myspace*, Picasa*, Vimeo*, or virtual worlds like Second Life*. If you find any sites that seem like they are from the Department and are not listed above, they are not used by the Department. Refer to this list for future updates. You can sign up for email updates, too.

For more information about social media within government see webcontent.gov.

*Links to non-federal organizations are provided solely as a service to our users. These links do not constitute an endorsement of these organizations or their programs by the Department of Homeland Security or the federal government, and none should be inferred. The Department of Homeland Security is not responsible for the content of the individual organization's Web pages found on these sites.

The Department of Homeland Security's policies on privacy and intellectual property can be found at the *Notices* page.

Source: DHS, 2011. "Social Media at the Department of Homeland Security," http://www.dhs.gov/xabout/ gc_1238684422624.shtm

Building an Effective Disaster Communications Capability in a Changing Media World

The world of emergency management/homeland security is changing rapidly. The onslaught of major catastrophic disasters around the world, the projected impact of global climate change, and the continuing threat of terrorism have forced the emergency management/homeland security community to reexamine all of its processes, including communications. Managing information before, during, and after a disaster or terrorist attack has changed significantly in recent years and emergency/homeland security operations at all levels — local, state, and national — must recognize and acknowledge this change and adapt accordingly.

As we have noted earlier in this chapter, the biggest change in disaster communications has come with the emergence of the "first informers" — citizen journalists — and their use of new, widely available online and digital technologies to gather and share information and images. No organization working in the emergency management/homeland security field — government, nongovernmental groups, voluntary agency, private sector — can ignore the role these "first informers" and their information networks will play in future disasters.

In the future, emergency management/homeland security organizations must establish partnerships with both the traditional media outlets and the new media in order to meet their primary communications mission of providing the public with timely and accurate information before, during, and after a disaster.

The purpose of this section is to detail the seven elements that we believe will comprise an effective disaster communications capability in the future. These seven elements include:

- A Communication Plan
- Information Coming In
- Information Going Out
- Messengers
- Staffing
- Training and Exercises
- Monitor, Update, and Adapt

A Communication Plan

Disaster communication plans can take several forms. Planning for communicating in disaster response focuses on collecting, analyzing, and disseminating timely and accurate information to the public.

A disaster response communication plan will include protocols for collecting information from a variety of sources including citizen journalist, analyzing these data in order to identify resource needs and to match available resources to these needs, and then disseminating information concerning current conditions and actions to the public through both traditional and new media outlets. The plan will identify trusted messengers who will deliver disaster response information to the public. The plan will identify how disaster communications will be delivered to special needs and non-English-speaking populations.

The disaster response communications plan will include a roster of local, state, and national media outlets, reporters, and first informers. This roster will be contacted to solicit information and to disseminate information back out to the public. Finally, the plan should include protocols for monitoring the media, identifying new sources of information collection or dissemination, and evaluating the effectiveness of the disaster communications. This information would be used to update the plan.

The communications plan must place a premium on delivering this information to the targeted audiences and must identify the appropriate communications mechanisms to communicate these messages. Information collection from the field from a wide variety of sources must be a priority in the communications plan for the recovery phase. Community relations staff, community leaders, and first informers are good sources of information on the progress of recovery activities and can provide valuable perspective of the mood of the individuals and communities impacted by the disaster. These sources are also effective in identifying communities, groups, and individuals who have been passed over by recovery programs. It is in the recovery phase that consensus is sought since crucial long-term decisions have to be made at the state and community levels.

Information Coming In

Information is the basis of effective disaster communications. In disaster response, receiving and processing regular information concerning conditions at a disaster site and what is being done by agencies responding to the disaster allows disaster communicators to provide timely and accurate information to the public. In collecting this information, no potential source should be ignored and all possible sources should be encouraged to forward relevant information. To be successful in this task, you should identify all potential sources of information and develop working relationships with these various sources *before* the next disaster strikes. You must also be prepared to identify and partner with new sources of information as they come on the scene in the aftermath of a disaster.

Potential disaster information sources include:

- Government damage assessment teams: Government disaster agencies at every level have staff responsible for assessing damages in the aftermath of a disaster. For a major disaster, a damage assessment team may include representatives from local, state, and federal response agencies. The information collected will include deaths, injuries, damage to homes, infrastructure, and the environment, and other critical data.
- First responders: These are among the first on the scene at any disaster, equipped with the necessary communications devices and trained to be observant.
- Voluntary agencies: These groups often have members or volunteers located in the disaster areas trained in damage assessment who can make first and ongoing assessments. For example, the Red Cross has extensive experience in reporting damage to homes and numbers of people evacuated and in shelters.
- Community leaders: Trusted leaders who have their own neighborhood network or work with community-based organizations with networks into the community can be a valuable source of on-the-ground information.

- First informers: Individuals in the disaster site with the wherewithal to collect information and images and to communicate that information and images by cell phone, handheld device, or laptop.
- New media: Blogs (weblogs), Google Earth, Google Map, Wikis (Wikipedia), SMS (text messaging postings — Twitter), Flickr, Picasa (photo survey sites), YouTube (video sharing sites).
- Online news sites: Aggregate of community news, information, and opinion.
- Traditional media: Television, radio, and newspaper reporters, editors, and news producers can be good sources of information especially if they have deployed news crews to the disaster area before or just after a disaster strikes.

Having identified the potential information sources in your area, you must reach out to these sources to develop a working partnership and to put in place whatever protocols and technologies are needed to accept information from these sources. Government response agencies and voluntary agencies practicing NIMS and ICS will know what information to collect. You must reach out to the nongovernmental, nontraditional information sources before the next disaster to let them know what information you need and how to communicate that information to you.

Ideas for developing these working partnerships with nongovernmental, nontraditional information sources include:

- Building neighborhood communications networks: Partner with community-based organizations, churches, and neighborhood associations to build neighborhood communications networks. Local residents can be trained in information collection, maybe as part of Community Emergency Response Team (CERT) training, and local community leaders can be entrusted to collect this information and forward it to emergency officials. These networks could also be used to send messages from emergency officials to neighborhood residents through trusted community leaders.
- Creating and distributing a disaster information protocol for first informers: List what information you will be seeking over the course of a disaster response and get this list out to the public. Make sure they know where to e-mail or post the information and images they collect.
- Establishing a point of contact within your organization for information sources: Designate staff that will work with information sources during a disaster and are accessible.
- Creating an electronic portal for information from the field: Wikis and weblogs (blogs) can accept and aggregate comments from users, set up a Twitter website that can be updated via text messages, and create a homepage on YouTube and Flickr.
- Including first informers and traditional and new media outlets in disaster response training and exercises: Incorporate these information sources into your disaster exercises to identify issues and gaps and to update plans accordingly. Media are not always included in exercises nor are first informers, but by including these groups in your exercises you make the exercise more authentic and you create an opportunity to identify difficult issues prior to facing them in the next disasters and you can make appropriate adjustments. It is also a chance to get to know each other.
- Meeting with traditional and new media types on a regular basis: Another way to create personal relationships with these critical partners in any disaster response.
- Including information sources in your after-action debrief: Their perspectives and experiences can be used to update plans and operations.

Many of these information sources can be identified as part of a hazard mitigation and preparedness campaign. Working relationships can be developed during these nondisaster periods that will facilitate information collection and flow in disaster response.

Information Going Out

If information coming in is the basis for disaster communication, then information going out is the goal. Timely and accurate information can save lives in disaster response and in hazard mitigation and preparedness programs. In getting information to the public, you must use all available communications mechanisms including:

- Traditional media: Television, radio, newspapers, and the Internet
- New media: Post new information on community websites, blogs, wikis, and bulletin boards; share timely photos and video online; and tell traditional media that online outlets are being updated routinely
- Neighborhood communications networks: Trusted community leaders who go door to door

Historically, emergency officials have disseminated disaster information to the traditional media by means of press conferences, briefings, tours of the disaster site, one-on-one interviews with disaster officials, press releases, situation reports, and postings on the Internet. Radio actualities, photographs, and videotape have also been provided to traditional media. In major disasters, emergency management agencies have used satellite uplinks and video and audio press conferences to reach traditional media outlets across large sections of the country.

Disseminating information through new media outlets is something new for emergency officials and will require patience and understanding of how these new media functions with their audiences. Most of this work can occur during nondisaster periods. This is the time to learn more about Wikipedia, Twitter, blogs, Flickr, Facebook, YouTube, and social networking sites, and to discover how you as an emergency manager can best use these new media to deliver preparedness and hazard mitigation messages as well as communicate with their target audiences in the disaster response and recovery phases.

Prior to the next disaster, you might consider:

- Starting a blog: Get your message out there about the risks your community faces: how to take action to reduce those risks and protect your family, home, and business; how to prepare for the next disaster; when to evacuate and how; what will happen when your organization responds; and how members of your community can become first informers.
- Creating a bulletin board: This could serve as a link to community leaders involved in hazard mitigation and preparedness programs in the neighborhoods and could be accessed by all community members before, during, and after a disaster.
- Establishing accounts and actively engaging in Twitter, Facebook, YouTube, and other active social media sites: This presents opportunities to engage in an ongoing dialogue with the public and has proved to be an effective means for communicating emergency messages and receiving real-time emergency information.
- Getting on Wikipedia: Load preparedness and hazard mitigation information and links for more information on the site. Understand that this site will grow with information added by readers.
- Starting a YouTube site: That features "How To" videos on how to disaster-proof your home, office, and business. Post videos that explain how to survive the next disaster (how much water and food to have on hand; where to go for information).
- Creating a Google Map: This is of the locations of designated shelters and evacuation routes.

When the next disaster strikes, consider:

- Regular updates on your blog: This allows you a direct link to members of your community. Include time in your schedule to get interactive and answer questions and inquiries.
- Regular updates on your bulletin board: Again another opportunity to talk directly to members of the community, to get interactive.
- Review and update Wikipedia: Place your information in the Wikipedia file on the disaster and keep it regularly updated. Update disaster aid and shelter information and links to missing persons sites and correct inaccurate information and confront rumors.
- Post on Twitter, Facebook, and other social media sites: Emergency messages and information from you to the public and collect information from reliable individual sources.
- Post on YouTube: Videos from informational briefings, from affected neighborhoods, and appeals for help.
- Update Google Map: To show locations of open shelters, hospitals.
- Display on Google Earth: Locations of affected areas.

Maintain and regularly update all of these sites during the recovery phase.

Messengers

The person who delivers the messages plays a critical role in disaster communications. The messenger(s) puts a human face on disaster response and this person(s) is critical to building confidence in the public that people will be helped and their community will recover. Public Information Officers (PIOs) regularly deliver information and messages to the media and the public. However, the primary face of the disaster response should be an elected or appointed official (i.e., mayor, governor, county administrator, city manager) or the director of the emergency management agency, or both. These individuals bring a measure of authority to their role as messenger and in the case of the emergency management director, someone who is in charge of response and recovery operations.

The public wants to hear from an authority figure and the media wants to know that the person they are talking to is the one making the decisions. Elected officials who served as successful messengers in recent disasters include California Governor Arnold Schwarzenegger during the 2007 southern California wildfires, New York City Mayor Rudy Giuliani during the September 11 attacks, Florida Governor Jeb Bush during the four hurricanes that struck Florida in 2004, and Oklahoma Governor Frank Keating during the 1995 Oklahoma City bombing. Successful emergency managers as messengers include former FEMA Director James Lee Witt and California Office of Emergency Services Director Dick Andrews in the 1994 Northridge Earthquake and Craig Fugate with the Florida Division of Emergency Management during recent hurricanes, tornadoes, and wildfires in Florida. Former FEMA Director Witt and Former President Clinton worked very well together in delivering messages concerning federal relief programs in numerous disasters in the 1990s.

Prior to the next disaster or terrorist attack, each emergency management/homeland security agency should determine whether an elected or appointed official will serve as the primary messenger alone or in tandem with the emergency agency director. It is best to work out in advance what types of information will be delivered by which messenger. Protocols for briefing books and situational updates should be developed. A determination should be made as to who will lead press briefings and news conferences, who will be available to the media for one-on-one interviews, and who will be involved in communicating with the new media outlets. Again, all of these activities can be shared by the elected/appointed official and the emergency agency director.

Emergency management/homeland security agencies should also designate appropriate senior managers who will be made available to both the traditional and new media to provide specific information on their activities and perspective. This is helpful in even the smallest disaster when persons with expertise in specific facets of the response can be very helpful in delivering disaster response information and messages.

Staffing

Not many emergency management/homeland security agencies have a single communications specialist much less a communications staff. Federal agencies such as FEMA, DHS, HHS, and others involved in disaster have extensive communications staff. Most state emergency management/homeland security operations have at least a communications director. The depth of staff support for communications varies widely. Emergency management/homeland security agencies in major cities in the United States often have communications directors and in some case extensive communications staff. Small- to mid-sized cities and communities are unlikely to have a communications director or staff.

The time has come for all organizations involved in emergency management/homeland security to establish an ongoing communications staff capability. For agencies in small- to mid-sized communities, this may require enlisting help from the local government's communications staff. One way to do this is to provide funding for a percentage of this individual's time each month. In this way, communications activities required during nondisaster periods could be acquired on a consistent basis. This will also allow for the local government communications staff and director to be better informed of the emergency management/homeland security agency's activities and be better prepared to work with the emergency/homeland security agency director during disaster response and recovery.

For large cities and federal and voluntary agencies with existing communications staff, it is now a matter of reordering priorities to meet the demands of working with the new media. Staff will be required to establish and maintain working relationships with new media outlets and to interact with the various blogs, bulletin boards, social networking sites, and other new media outlets that serve their community. At minimum, there should be one designated staff person on the communications staff who is responsible for the day-to-day interaction with new media. Additional staff should be made available in a major disaster to work with these groups.

The new media designated staff would also work with new media outlets in promoting hazard mitigation and preparedness campaigns in the community and serve as the staff support for the establishment and maintenance of neighborhood communications networks working with trusted leaders in the community.

Training and Exercises

An effective disaster communications operation requires well-trained messengers and staff and should be a vital part of all disaster exercises. Elected/appointed officials, agency directors, and public information officers should all receive formal media training in order to become comfortable working with the media to communicate disaster messages to the public. Media training teaches how to communicate a message effectively, helps with learning techniques for fielding difficult questions, and provides the opportunity to practice delivery outside the crucible of a crisis. If possible, media training should be provided to senior staff who may appear in the media.

Staff training should come in several forms including:

- Media relations: Learn how to work with traditional and new media including meeting deadlines, responding to inquiries, scheduling interviews, understanding what types of information each media outlet requires, and how a news operation works

- New media: Learn what a blog is, how social networking works, and how to establish and maintain a neighborhood communications network
- Marketing: Learn how to pitch a story idea for a preparedness program or hazard mitigation project to all forms of media, how to develop supporting materials for preparedness and hazard mitigation campaigns, and how to evaluate the effectiveness of such efforts

Communications operations must always be included in future disaster exercises. It is highly recommended that these exercises include reporters from traditional media outlets, representatives from the new media including bloggers, and online news sites. Working with new media and online news sites should be included in the exercise such as updating and correcting a Wikipedia site and posting information on a community bulletin board. Community leaders involved in neighborhood communications networks should also be included in the exercise.

Monitor, Update, and Adapt

Staff should be assigned to regularly monitor all media outlets. Summaries of news stories in the traditional media should be compiled regularly. Staff should routinely monitor new media outlets and provide regular summaries of news on these sites. This activity is especially important during a disaster response. Through monitoring, the media staff is capable of identifying problems and issues early in the process and can shape communications strategies to address these issues before they become big problems. This is also an opportunity to identify trends in how information flows through the media to the public and to identify areas for improvement of message development and delivery. Regular monitoring will identify rumors and misinformation and speed corrections.

The information collected as part of monitoring activities can be used to update communications plans, strategies, and tactics. This data can be used to determine how to allocate staff resources and to update training and exercise programs. Emergency management agencies must be constantly on the lookout for emerging communications technologies and opportunities.

Conclusion

The experience of emergency managers with natural disasters provides at minimum a guide to the development of effective terrorism-related communications strategies. However, there is much work to be done to adapt existing risk, warning, and crisis communications models to the new hazards, the new partners, and the new dynamic between response and recovery and criminal activity associated with the new terrorist threat. One thing will remain constant: Communication with the public about the terrorist threat must receive the same attention and resources that are now going to new technologies, new training programs, and new organizations. It has never been more important that public officials talk to the public, and it has never been more difficult than it is now. If this problem is not addressed properly, it can only compound in the worst way the terrible consequences of any terrorist incident.

Key Terms

Comprehensive Emergency Management: An emergency management philosophy that seeks to reduce risk and prevent injuries, damages, and fatalities by treating hazards before, during, and after an event has occurred. There are generally four accepted functions performed in comprehensive emergency management: mitigation, preparedness, response, and recovery.

Crisis Communication: The provision of timely, useful, and accurate information to the public during the response and recovery phases of a disaster event.

Mass Media: Channels of communication for popular consumption, which could include books, magazines, advertisements, newspapers, newsletters, radio, television, the Internet, cinema, theater, and videos, among many others.

National Terrorism Advisory System: A robust terrorism advisory system that provides timely information to the public about credible terrorist threats and replaced the former color-coded Homeland Security Advisory System (HSAS).

News Media: A subcomponent of the mass media focused on presenting current news to the public.

Ready.gov: A government-sponsored website developed by the Advertising Council to educate the public, businesses, and children about hazard risks in the United States.

Risk Communication: Any communication intended to supply laypeople with the information they need to make informed, independent judgments about risks to health, safety, and the environment (Morgan et al., 2002).

Warning: The delivery of notice of an actual impending threat with sufficient time to allow recipient individuals and communities to take shelter, evacuate, or take other mitigative action in advance of a disaster event.

Review Questions

1. Identify and discuss the four critical assumptions underlying the crisis communications efforts of the Federal Emergency Management Agency (FEMA) in the 1990s.
2. Discuss the role of the mass media in risk and crisis communications.
3. Review the content and communication delivery mechanisms used in the Department of Homeland Security's Ready.gov campaign. Do you feel this is useful information that could effectively prepare the public for a disaster?
4. How would you reengineer the Homeland Security Advisory System (HSAS)? How many alert levels would you include, what colors and titles would you associate with each alert level, and what preparedness messages designed for individuals and communities would you associate with each alert level?

References

BBC News, 2008, Burmese blog the cyclone (May 8). http://www.news.bbc.co.uk/2/hi/asia-pacific/7387313.stm.

Bowman, S., Willis, C., 2003. We Media: How Audiences are Shaping the Future of News and Information. The Media Center at the American Press Institute.

Burma News, 2008. Burmese journals face restriction on cyclone coverage (May 13). http://www.myamarnews.blogspot.com/2008/05/burmese-journals-face-restrictions-on.html.

Catone, J., 2007. Online citizen journalism now undeniably mainstream, readwriteweb. (October 26). http://www.readwriteweb.com/archives/online_citizen_journalism_mainstream.php.

Cooper, G., 2007. Burma's bloggers show power of citizen journalism in a crises. Reuters Alert Net (October 3). http://www.alertnet.org/db/blogs/30708/2007/09/3-134022-1.htm.

DHS, 2011, NTAS guide: National terrorism advisory system public guide. http://www.dhs.gov/xlibrary/assets/ntas/ntas-public-guide.pdf.

DHS, 2011. Social media at the Department of Homeland Security. http://www.dhs.gov/xabout/gc_1238684422624.shtm.

FEMA, 2007. National Incident Management System: FEMA 501/Draft August 2007. FEMA, Washington, DC.

Ferrara, L., 2007. AP's "NowPublic" Initiative, Remarks at the Associated Press Managing Editors' Conference. Fast Forward to the Future (October 2). http://www.j-lab.org/apme07notesp5.shtml.

Gillmor, D., 2006. We the Media: Grassroots Journalism by the People, for the People. O'Reilly Media Inc.

Gillmor, D., Hattotuwa, S., 2007. Citizen journalism and humanitarian aid: boon or bust? ICT for Peacebuilding. http://ict4peace.wordpress.com/2007/07/30/citizen-journalism-and-humanitarian-aid-bane-or-boon/.

Glaser, M., 2007. California Wildfire Coverage by Local Media, Blogs, Twitter, Maps and More. MediaShift (October 25). http://www.pbs.org/mediashift/2007/10/the_listcalifornia_wildfire_co_1.html.

Global Voices Online, Myanmar cyclone 2008. http://www.globalvoicesonline.org/specialcoverage/myanmar-cyclone-2008/.

Hattotuwa, S., 2007. Who is afraid of citizen journalists? Communicating Disasters, TVA Asia Pacific and UNDP Regional Centre in Bangkok, 2007.

Kettl, D.F., September 2005. The Worst Is Yet to Come: Lessons from September 11 to Hurricane Katrina. Fels Institute of Government, University of Pennsylvania.

Laituri, M., Kodrich, K., 2008. On Line Disaster Response Community: People as Sensors of High Magnitude Disasters Using Internet GIS. Sensors, Colorado State University. http://www.mdpi.org/sensors/papers/s8053037.pdf.

May, A.L., 2006. First Informers in the Disaster Zone: The Lessons of Katrina. The Aspen Institute.

Rincon, J., 2008. Myanmar: Citizen videos in Cyclone Nargis aftermath. Reuters Global News Blog (May 16). http:// www.blogs.reuters.com/global/tag/burma/.

Select Bipartisan Committee to Investigate the Preparation for and Response to Hurricane Katrina, 2006. A failure of initiative: Final report of the special Bipartisan Committee to investigate the preparation for and response to Hurricane Katrina. Government Printing Office (February 15). http://www.gpoacess.gov/congress/index.hmtl.

Shirky, C., 2008. Here Comes Everybody: The Power of Organizing Without Organizations. The Penguin Press, New York, NY.

Stabe, M., 2007. California wildfires: A round up. OJB Online Journalism Blog (October 25). http:// www.onlinejournalismblog.com/2007/10/25/california-wildfires-a-roundup/.

Townsend, F.F., 2006. The Federal Response to Hurricane Katrina Lessons Learned. The White House, February 2006.

Wagner, M., 2007. Google Maps and Twitter are essential resources for California fires. Information Week (October 24). http://www.informationweek.com/blog/main/archives/2007/10/google_maps_and.html.

Washkuch, F., 2008. Relief groups turn to Twitter amid crises. PR Week (May 20). http://www.prweekus.com/Relief-groups-turn-to-Twitter-amid-crises/article/110368/.

YouTube, http://www.youtube.com/user/AfterNargisYgn.

12

Science and Technology

What You Will Learn

- How homeland security research and development funding is distributed among various federal government agencies
- What research and development efforts are performed by the Department of Homeland Security, and by what offices that work is done
- Where in the federal government structure research and development are performed in the areas of weapons of mass destruction and information and infrastructure
- The names and functions of the various government research facilities
- The source and function of maritime homeland security research
- Where homeland security research and development efforts are occurring outside the Department of Homeland Security

Introduction

The Department of Homeland Security (DHS) announced at the time of its establishment that it "is committed to using cutting-edge technologies and scientific talent" to create a safer country. In this vein, the Science and Technology Directorate (S&T) was formed, which still exists today despite the many iterations of DHS organizational change. The S&T Directorate was tasked under the original development plans with assuming the research needs of the new department, and for organizing the scientific, engineering, and technological resources of the country in order to adapt their use to the newly recognized needs under the counterterrorism drive created by the September 11, 2001, terrorist attacks. Universities, the private sector, and federal laboratories have all become important DHS partners in this endeavor.

Overview of Involved Agencies and Budgets

Although the DHS has the most prominent stake in homeland security–related research efforts, there are many other agencies that are involved in homeland security R&D efforts dispersed throughout the federal government. As DHS was gaining center-stage prominence in the homeland security effort and was emerging as a leading agency for these issues, many research and scientific programs were under way under the other agencies' management that preceded the Department's creation. The efforts of these organizations were almost immediately given new direction and resources to use in the fight against a more prominent

Table 12–1 Federal Homeland Security R&D Appropriations ($ in millions)

Agency	FY 2002	FY 2003	FY 2004	FY 2005	FY 2006	FY 2007	FY 2008	FY 2009	FY 2010	FY 2011
Agriculture	175	155	40	161	105	45	129	97	85	88
Commerce	20	16	23	73	62	59	68	76	135	177
DOD	259	212	267	1,079	1,270	1,175	1,278	1,505	2,376	2,115
Energy	50	48	47	67	68	68	71	81	89	90
DHS	266	737	1,028	1,240	1,300	1,005	996	1,033	887	1,054
EPA	95	70	52	33	40	41	53	74	66	42
HHS	177	1,653	1,724	1,795	1,827	1,829	1,815	2,106	1,871	1,929
NASA	73	73	88	89	93	97	94	109	20	6
NSF	229	271	321	326	329	329	357	358	370	395
DOT	106	7	3	2	3	1	2	1	0	0
All others	0	0	32	42	41	42	40	36	47	4
Total	1,451	3,243	3,626	4,893	5,138	4,691	4,902	5,475	5,946	5,900

Source: Office of Management and Budget, Budget of the U.S. Government FY 2008, 2008, http://www
.whitehouse.gov/omb/budget/fy2008/; American Association for the Advancement of Science (AAAS), 2011,
AAAS XXXVI: Research and Development FY2012, http://www.aaas.org/spp/rd/rdreport2012/.

terrorist hazard — a "shot in the arm," so to speak. Table 12–1 lists the agencies involved in the home-land security R&D field and their recent budgets.

Department of Homeland Security

Before the establishment of DHS, most R&D efforts dealing with issues relevant to homeland security were dispersed among a wide variety of agencies, and this situation remains. However, the clear trend since 2003 has been to make DHS a focus for such R&D, and as of 2008 over one-fifth of all R&D funding is managed by DHS (placing it second only after HHS). Inside DHS, the S&T Directorate has been established in order to coordinate and manage R&D efforts. For the first 3 years of the directorate's existence, R&D efforts were dispersed throughout the various directorates and independent agencies (e.g., the Coast Guard). However, as early as FY 2006, all R&D efforts were consolidated under S&T. A more detailed description of S&T and the research this directorate conducts follows.

DHS Science and Technology Directorate

The Science and Technology Directorate (S&T), led by an undersecretary of homeland security, is the primary R&D office within the Department of Homeland Security. Since November 12, 2009, S&T has been led by Dr. Tara O'Toole. In her testimony at two Congressional hearings held in March 2011, Dr. O'Toole outlined the current vision for S&T to achieve its mission to "strengthen America's security and resiliency by providing knowledge products and innovative technology solutions for the Homeland Security Enterprise."

The S&T Directorate current organizational chart is presented in Figure 12–1. The mission and organizations aligned with the four Lead Groups in the S&T organization are described in the following sidebar.

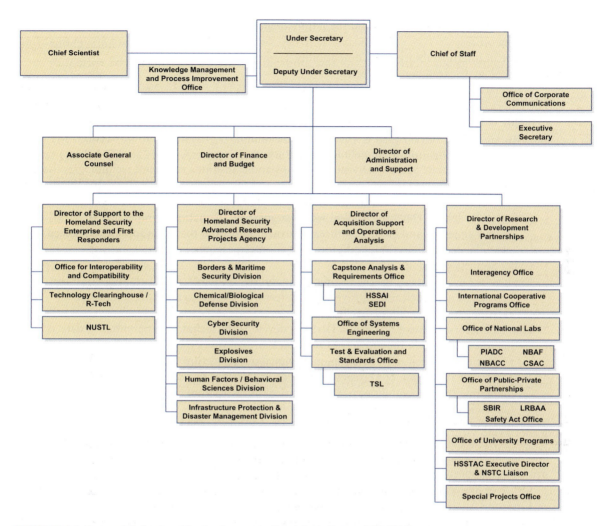

FIGURE 12–1 Science and Technology Directorate organizational chart. (Source: DHS, 2011)

DHS Science and Technology Directorate Lead Groups

- The Director of Support to the Homeland Security Enterprise and First Responders Group (FRG) identifies, validates, and facilitates the fulfillment of First Responder requirements through the use of existing and emerging technologies, knowledge products, and the acceleration of standards. This organization manages working groups, teams, and stakeholder outreach efforts to better understand the requirements of first responders. FRG manages the following offices:

Office of Interoperability and Compatibility

Technology Clearinghouse/R-Tech

National Urban Security Technology Laboratory (NUSTL)

- The Director of Homeland Security Advanced Research Projects Agency manages a portfolio of highly innovative programs that are transforming the future mission space for Homeland Security. HSARPA projects push scientific limits to address customer-identified needs. HSARPA manages the following technical divisions:

Borders & Maritime Security Division develops and transitions tools and technologies that improve the security of our nation's borders and waterways, without impeding the flow of commerce and travel.

Chemical/Biological Defense Division works to increase the nation's preparedness against chemical and biological threats through improved threat awareness, advanced surveillance and detection, and protective countermeasures.

Cyber Security Division

Explosives Division develops the technical capabilities to detect, interdict, and lessen the impacts of non-nuclear explosives used in terrorist attacks against mass transit, civil aviation, and critical infrastructure.

Human Factors/Behavioral Sciences Division develops the technical capabilities to detect, interdict, and lessen the impacts of non-nuclear explosives used in terrorist attacks against mass transit, civil aviation, and critical infrastructure.

Infrastructure Protection & Disaster Management Division focuses on identifying and mitigating the vulnerabilities of the 18 critical infrastructure and key assets that keep our society and economy functioning.

- The Director of Acquisition Support and Operations Analysis (ASOA) serves as a conduit for Department components seeking support on a range of technical and analytical requirements and document development throughout the acquisition life cycle. ASOA is made up of three primary components including:

Office of Systems Engineering (SYS)

Capstone Analysis & Requirements Office (CAR)

Test & Evaluation and Standards Office (TES)

- The Director of Research and Development Partnerships (RDP) conducts effective stakeholder outreach and engagement through close partnerships with eight Departments of science and technology groups. The RDP groups include:

Interagency Office

International Cooperative Programs Office

Office of National Laboratories

Plum Island Animal Disease Center (PIADC)

National Biodefense Analysis and Countermeasures Center (NBACC)

National Bio- and Agro-Defense Facility (NBAF)

Chemical Security Analysis Center (CSAC)

Office of Public–Private Partnerships

Small Business Innovative Research Office (SBIR)

Long Range Broad Agency Announcement Office (LRBAA)

SAFETY Act Office
Commercialization Office
Office of University Programs
Homeland Security Science and Technology Advisory Committee (HSSTAC)
Executive Director & National Science and Technology Council (NSTC) Liaison
Special Projects Office

Source: DHS, 2011, http://www.dhs.gov/xabout/structure/editorial_0530.shtm.

In her Congressional testimony before the House Committee on Appropriations, Subcommittee on Homeland Security on March 30, 2011, Dr. O'Toole stated that "S&T instituted an inclusive and comprehensive strategic planning process" that resulted in the development of five strategic goals for S&T. Dr. O'Toole also outlined planned S&T activities to "address all five mission areas described in the 2010 Quadrennial Homeland Security Review, and include both late-stage "applied" technology development efforts, and more fundamental research." The following sidebars "S&T Strategic Goals" and "Science and Technology Directorate Research, Development, and Innovation Activities" present Dr. O'Toole's detailed explanations of current S&T goals and activities.

S&T Strategic Goals

S&T Goal #1 — Rapidly develop and deliver knowledge, analyses, and innovative solutions that advance the mission of the Department.

- *Ongoing Review of the R&D Portfolio*
- *Becoming Best-in-Class at Technology Foraging, Outreach to Private Sector*

S&T Goal #2 — Leverage S&T's technical expertise to assist DHS Components' efforts to establish operational requirements, and to select and acquire needed technologies

- *Test and Evaluation*
- *Supporting Departmental Acquisition Requirements and Systems Engineering*

S&T Goal #3 — Strengthen the Homeland Security Enterprise and First Responders' capabilities to protect the homeland and respond to disasters

S&T Goal #4 — Conduct, catalyze, and survey scientific discoveries and inventions relevant to existing and emerging homeland security challenges

- *Supporting University Centers of Excellence*
- *Stewardship of Laboratory Infrastructure for Homeland Security*

S&T Goal #5 — Foster a culture of innovation and learning in S&T and across DHS that addresses mission needs with scientific, analytic, and technical rigor.

- *Build a Culture of Innovation and Learning*
  The full text of this document is available on the companion website.

Source: DHS, 2011, Under Secretary Tara O'Toole, Science and Technology Directorate, before the House Committee on Appropriations, Subcommittee on Homeland Security, S&T Fiscal Year 2012 Budget Request, http://www.dhs.gov/ynews/testimony/testimony_1301519363336.shtm.

S&T Budget

The amount of funding under the overall DHS budget dedicated to science and technology has steadily risen each year since the department's creation. This growth signifies the steadily increasing role that technology is taking on in modern emergency management, especially in the area of terrorism prevention and response. It is important to remember that these funds are only in addition to similar project funds being supplied by many other federal agencies, which together comprise a much larger homeland security–related R&D budget (see Table 12–2).

The S&T Directorate is responsible for setting the national agenda and giving direction and setting priorities for R&D efforts in other departments and agencies, regardless of the funding source. S&T is unique among federal R&D agencies in that it has responsibility for the entire cycle of science and technology (i.e., from product research to bringing the product to the market and deploying it).

The S&T Directorate established the Homeland Security Advanced Research Project Agency (HSARPA). This agency, based on the existing model of the Defense Advanced Research Project Agency (DARPA) in the Department of Defense (DOD), distributes resources within the directorate, awards money for the extramural grants, develops and tests potential technologies, and accelerates or prototypes development of technologies for deployment. The directorate has also created a Homeland Security Advisory Committee consisting of 20 members appointed by the undersecretary representing first responders, citizen groups, researchers, engineers, and businesses to provide science and technology advice to the undersecretary. DHS has also created a new federally funded R&D center (FFRDC), the Homeland Security Institute, to act as a think tank for risk analyses, simulations of threat scenarios, analyses of possible countermeasures, and strategic plans for counterterrorism technology development. Table 12–1 presents the homeland security R&D budget for those departments and agencies currently involved in homeland security R&D. Various successes identified by DHS are listed in the sidebar "Science and Technology Directorate Accomplishments."

Table 12–2 Department of Homeland Security R&D (S&T Directorate) Budget ($ in millions)

FY 2004	FY 2005	FY 2006	FY 2007	FY 2008	FY 2009	FY 2010	FY 2011	FY 2012
$912,751	$1,115,450	$1,467,075	$846,916	$830,118	$932,587	$1,006,471	$1,006,471	$1,176,432 (requested)

Science and Technology Directorate Accomplishments in FY 2010

- SAFETY Act
- Borders/Maritime Standards Program
- Explosives Standards
- System Assessment and Validation for Emergency Responders (SAVER) Program
- International Programs
- Container Security Device (CSD)
- Hybrid Composite Container
- Scholars and Fellows
- Laboratory Construction
- National Biodefense Analysis and Countermeasures Center (NBACC)
- Internet Measurements Techniques Project (formerly Internet Route Monitoring)
- Process Control Systems (PCS) Security Project
- Real-Time Data Processing and Visualization Project
- Compliance Assessment Project (CAP)
- Converged Interoperable Communications
- Air Cargo Project
- Automated Threat Recognition (ATR)
- Risk Prediction Project
- Validation of SPOT (Screening Passenger by Observation)
- Decision Support Tools Project
- Facility Restoration Demonstration Project
- Chemical Security Analysis Center (CSAC) Project
- Contractor-to-Federal Employee Conversions (DHS, 2011, FY 2012 Budget in Brief)

See the companion website for the full text of this document.

Critical Thinking

In your opinion, is federal funding better spent on all-hazards first-responder preparedness, or on R&D efforts to find new emergency management solutions for terrorist hazards? Based on the FY 2012 funding levels for both of these activities (listed throughout this chapter), would the American public be better served by transferring funding from R&D to first-responder preparedness, or vice versa? Explain your answer.

R&D Efforts Focused on Weapons of Mass Destruction

The DHS website states, "The S&T Directorate will tap into scientific and technological capabilities to provide the means to detect and deter attacks using weapons of mass destruction. S&T will guide and organize research efforts to meet emerging and predicted needs and will work closely with universities, the private sector, and national and Federal laboratories." This effort can be subdivided into two fields: chemical and biological, and radiological and nuclear. In both fields, the Directorate's aim is to carry research to develop sensors to detect such weapons from production to employment. The different organizations within the federal sector that will support and serve the R&D efforts of S&T are detailed in the following section.

Chemical, Biological, Radiological and Nuclear Defense Information and Analysis Center

The Chemical, Biological, Radiological and Nuclear Defense Information Analysis Center (CBRNIAC), formerly known as the CBIAC, is a full-service DOD Information Analysis Center (IAC). The CBRNIAC is the authoritative resource for DOD Chemical, Biological, Radiological and Nuclear (CBRN) Defense and Homeland Security scientific and technical (S&T) information.

The CBRNIAC generates, acquires, processes, analyzes, and disseminates CBRN Defense Science and Technology Information (STI) in support of the Combatant Commanders, warfighters, the Reserve Components, the CBRN Defense Research, Development, and Acquisition community, and other federal, state, and local government agencies. The CBRNIAC assists these agencies in implementing high-priority research and development (R&D) initiatives by:

- Identifying and acquiring relevant data and information from all available sources and in all media
- Processing data and acquisitions into suitable storage and retrieval systems
- Identifying, developing, and applying available analytical tools and techniques for the interpretation and application of stored data and acquisitions
- Disseminating focused information, datasets, and technical analyses to managers, planners, scientists, engineers, and military field personnel for the performance of mission-related tasks
- Anticipating requirements for CBRN Defense STI
- Identifying and reaching out to emerging CBRN Defense organizations (Department of Defense, 2011, https://www.cbrniac.apgea.army.mil/About/Pages/default.aspx).

Defense Threat Reduction Agency

The Defense Threat Reduction Agency (DTRA, www.dtra.mil) safeguards national interests from weapons of mass destruction (WMDs) (chemical, biological, radiological, nuclear, and high explosives) by controlling and reducing the threat and providing quality tools and services for the war fighter. DTRA performs four essential functions to reach its mission: combat support, technology development, threat control, and threat reduction. Moreover, the agency's work covers a broad spectrum of activities:

- Shaping the international environment to prevent the spread of WMDs
- Responding to requirements to deter the use and reduce the impact of such weapons
- Preparing for the future as WMD threats emerge and evolve

  The activities concerning homeland security are as follows:

- DTRA draws on the disparate chemical and biological weapons defense expertise within the DOD to increase response capabilities.
- The Advanced Systems and Concepts Office (ASCO) stimulates, identifies, and executes high-impact seed projects to encourage new thinking, address technology gaps, and improve the operational capabilities of DTRA.

Department of State

The Department of State (www.state.gov) contributes to the counterterror effort related to WMDs through diplomatic and intelligence gathering efforts. The Department of State provides information and assessments of potential chemical and biological weapons sources throughout the world and analyzes what different countries and groups are doing to increase, decrease, or support WMD development and stockpiling.

Centers for Disease Control and Prevention

The Centers for Disease Control and Prevention (CDC, www.cdc.gov) is recognized as the lead federal agency for protecting the health and safety of people by providing credible information to enhance health decisions and promoting health through strong partnerships. CDC serves as the national focus for developing and applying disease prevention and control, environmental health, and health promotion and education activities designed to improve the health of the people of the United States, with the mission to promote health and quality of life by preventing and controlling disease, injury, and disability. CDC provides information about the effects and treatment for exposure to chem-bio weapons and has valuable expertise in its 12 centers, institutes, and offices. The most prominent and relevant of the 12 follow:

- The National Center for Chronic Disease Prevention and Health Promotion prevents premature death and disability from chronic diseases and promotes healthy personal behaviors.
- The National Center for Health Statistics provides statistical information that will guide actions and policies to improve the health of the American people.
- The National Center for HIV, STD, and TB Prevention provides national leadership in preventing and controlling human immunodeficiency virus infection, sexually transmitted diseases, and tuberculosis.
- The National Center for Infectious Diseases prevents illness, disability, and death caused by infectious diseases in the United States and around the world.
- The National Immunization Program prevents disease, disability, and death from vaccine-preventable diseases in children and adults.
- The Epidemiology Program Office strengthens the public health system by coordinating public health surveillance; providing support in scientific communications, statistics, and epidemiology; and training in surveillance, epidemiology, and prevention effectiveness.
- The Public Health Practice Program Office strengthens community practice of public health by creating an effective workforce, building information networks, conducting practice research, and ensuring laboratory quality.

Lawrence Livermore National Laboratory

The Lawrence Livermore National Laboratory (LLNL, www.llnl.gov) provides information about nuclear and radiological weapons. Its activities are explained more broadly in the R&D section.

U.S. Nuclear Regulatory Commission

The U.S. Nuclear Regulatory Commission (NRC, www.nrc.gov) is an independent agency established to regulate civilian use of nuclear materials. The NRC's mission is to regulate the nation's civilian use of by-product, source, and special nuclear materials to ensure adequate protection of public health and safety, to promote the common defense and security, and to protect the environment. The NRC's regulatory mission covers three main areas:

- *Reactors*: Commercial reactors for generating electric power and nonpower reactors used for research, testing, and training
- *Materials*: Uses of nuclear materials in medical, industrial, and academic settings and facilities that produce nuclear fuel
- *Waste*: Transportation, storage, and disposal of nuclear materials and waste, and decommissioning of nuclear facilities from service

The NRC carries out its mission by conducting several activities, but most of them are not directly related to the homeland security purpose. The commission performs them as part of its mission to regulate the normal use of radiological material, but many of its capabilities and resources can be used during a radiological or nuclear incident. The major contribution fields are commission direction setting and policymaking, radiation protection, establishment of a regulatory program, nuclear security and safeguards information on how to promote the common defense and security, public affairs, congressional affairs, state and tribal programs, and international programs.

Efforts Aimed at Information and Infrastructure

DHS has been given the primary responsibility for detecting and deterring attacks on the national information systems and critical infrastructures, and the S&T Directorate is developing a national R&D enterprise to support this mission. The three main issues concerning information and infrastructure are as follows: Internet security, telecommunication, and the security systems. The directorate coordinates and integrates several organizations to accomplish its mission, as discussed in the next sections.

SANS Institute

The SANS (Systems Administration, Audit, Network, Security) Institute (www.sans.org) is active in the fields of information security research, certification, and education, and provides a platform for professionals to share lessons learned, conduct research, and teach the information security community. Besides the various training programs and resources aimed at informing its members and the community, the centers described below are part of SANS.

- *Internet Storm Center*: This center was created to detect rising Internet threats. It uses advanced data correlation and visualization techniques to analyze data from a large number of firewalls and intrusion detection systems in over 60 countries.
- *Center for Internet Security (CIS) and SCORE*: CIS formalizes the best practice recommendations once consensus between the SANS Institute and SCORE is reached and the practices are validated. The latter become minimum standard benchmarks for general use by the industry. Both organizations rely on and have very broad contact with the field experts.

CERT Coordination Center

The CERT Coordination Center (CERT/CC, www.cert.org) is located at the Software Engineering Institute (SEI), an FFRDC at Carnegie Mellon University in Pittsburgh, PA. SEI was charged by DARPA in

1988 to set up a center to coordinate communication among experts during security emergencies and to help prevent future incidents.

The CERT/CC is part of the larger SEI Networked Systems Survivability Program, whose primary goals are to ensure that appropriate technology and systems management practices are used to resist attacks on networked systems and to limit damage and ensure continuity of critical services in spite of successful attacks, accidents, or failures. The center's research areas are summarized below.

- *Vulnerability analysis and incident handling*: Analyze the state of Internet security and convey that information to the system administrators, network managers, and others in the Internet community.
- *Survivable enterprise management*: Help organizations protect and defend themselves. To this end, risk assessments that help enterprises identify and characterize critical information assets and then identify risks to those assets have been developed, and the enterprise can use the results of the assessment to develop or refine their overall strategy for securing their networked systems.
- *Education and training*: The center offers training courses to educate technical staff and managers of computer security-incident response teams as well as system administrators and other technical personnel within organizations to improve the security and survivability of each system.
- *Survivable network technology*: The center focuses on the technical basis for identifying and preventing security flaws and for preserving essential services if a system is penetrated and compromised. The center does research for new approaches to secure systems and analysis of how susceptible systems are to sophisticated attacks and find ways to improve the design of systems.

National Communications System

Through the National Communications System (NCS, www.ncs.gov), DHS supports the telecommunications critical infrastructure and R&D of tools and technology to prevent disruption or compromise of these services. The NCS was established in 1963 as a "single unified communications system to serve the president, DOD, diplomatic and intelligence activities and civilian leaders." The NCS mandate included linking, improving, and extending the communications facilities and components of various federal agencies, focusing on interconnectivity and survivability. The NCS's national security and emergency preparedness (NS/EP) capabilities were broadened in 1984 when it began coordinating and planning NS/EP telecommunications to support crises and disasters.

With the U.S. Information Agency being absorbed into the U.S. State Department in October 2000, the NCS membership currently stands at 24 members. The NCS also participates in joint industry–government planning through its work with the President's National Security Telecommunications Advisory Committee (NSTAC), with the NSC's National Coordinating Center (NCC) for Telecommunications, and the NCC's subordinate Information Sharing and Analysis Center (NCC-ISAC).

The NCS comprises numerous programs and committees that represent the majority of the national efforts in the field of communication for national emergencies and crises. The President's National Security Telecommunications Advisory Committee (NSTAC) and the Office of the Manager NCS (OMNCS) have been given the tasks of providing access control, priority treatment, user authentication, and other survivability features supporting NS/EP telecommunications to the Advanced Intelligent Network (AIN).

The OMNCS staff resources are organized into four branches: Technology and Programs, Critical Infrastructure Protection (CIP) with the NCC, Plans and Resources, and Customer Service.

The OMNCS is responsible for:

- Providing the expertise for the planning, implementing, administering, and maintenance of approved NS/EP communications programs and NCS baseline activities

- Conducting technical studies, analyses, and assessments pertaining to the effectiveness of NS/EP communications programs and the effects of these programs on the Nation's critical infrastructures
- Consulting with the Committee of Principals (COP), the NCS Council of Representatives (COR), and the President's National Security Telecommunications Advisory Committee (NSTAC) on issues pertaining to NS/EP telecommunications
- Participating on federal councils and boards, such as the Government Sector Coordinating Council and the National Infrastructure Advisory Council (NIAC), that develop telecommunications policies, standards, national initiatives, and performing research on emerging technologies
- Monitoring international emergency telecommunications planning activities and offering assistance to international emergency planning groups
- Developing, planning, and implementing NCS strategic goals and objectives
- Assisting individual NCS member organizations in developing efficient cost-effective solutions to complex communication/information requirements and resolutions to organizational communication/information issues (DHS, 2011, www.ncs.gov)

The OMNCS has established an AIN Program to address the emerging technology and an associated AIN Program Office to plan, coordinate, and oversee the effort. Two very important examples of initiatives follow:

- The Alerting and Coordination Network (ACN) provides a stable emergency voice communications network connecting telecommunications service providers' Emergency Operations Centers (EOCs) and Network Operations Centers (NOCs) to support NS/EP telecommunications network restoration coordination, transmission of telecommunications requirements and priorities, and incident reporting when the Public Switched Telephone Network (PSTN) is inoperable, stressed, or congested. The ACN is operational 24 hours a day, 7 days a week, to support the NCC during normal and emergency operations.
- The Emergency Notification Service (ENS) is a full-time service established to notify critical government personnel during emergencies using multiple communication channels, including telephone, short message service (SMS), pager, and e-mail. Within minutes of receiving an activation order from an authorized representative of an organization, an automated process makes multiple attempts to reach intended recipients until they confirm delivery or until a predetermined number of attempts have been made. After 30 minutes, a report detailing confirmation of delivery is returned to the originator of the notification. Messages can be recorded in advance or when the notification is initiated and can be sent as a general notification or a sensitive notification.

To initiate, coordinate, restore, and reconstitute NS/EP telecommunications services or facilities, the NCS continues to develop new capabilities and reevaluate or upgrade older ones.

Laboratories and Research Facilities

The R&D function is the most important aspect of the S&T Directorate. It relies on several existing agency programs to accomplish this task, including DOD, Department of Energy (DOE), and U.S. Department of Agriculture (USDA) programs, among others. A significant portion of the funding attached to these programs comes from DOD's National Bioweapons Defense Analysis Center, responsible for nearly the entire biological countermeasures portfolio.

S&T's Office for National Laboratories coordinates DHS interactions with DOE national laboratories with expertise in homeland security. The office has the authority to establish a semi-independent DHS headquarters laboratory within existing federal laboratories, national laboratories, or FFRDC to supply scientific and technical knowledge to DHS and has done so with at least five national laboratories. In addition to Livermore, DHS has established four other laboratories-within-laboratories at the Los Alamos, Sandia, Pacific Northwest, and Oak Ridge National Laboratories. DHS will also establish one or more university-based centers for homeland security.

The national and federal laboratory system possesses significant expertise in the area of WMDs in addition to massive computing power. These laboratories include the following:

- *DOE National Nuclear Security Administration Laboratories*: Lawrence Livermore Laboratory, Los Alamos National Laboratory, and Sandia National Laboratory
- *DOE Office of Science Laboratories*: Argonne National Laboratory, Brookhaven National Laboratory (BNL), Oak Ridge National Laboratory, Pacific Northwest National Laboratory, and other DOE laboratories
- *Department of Homeland Security Laboratories*: Environmental Measurements Laboratory (EML) and Plum Island Animal Disease Center
- *Department of Health and Human Services Laboratories*: HHS operates several laboratories focused on wide-ranging health and disease prevention issues
- *U.S. Customs Laboratory and Scientific Services*: The U.S. Customs Laboratory and Scientific Services perform testing to determine the origin of agricultural and manufactured products.

This section starts with an overview of the facilities cited above and relevant programs and then discusses other R&D activities, such as the university-based center approach, and partnerships between DHS and other agencies.

Lawrence Livermore National Laboratory

The Homeland Security Organization at Lawrence Livermore National Laboratory (LLNL, www.llnl.gov) provides comprehensive solutions integrating threat, vulnerability, and trade-off analyses, advanced technologies, field-demonstrated prototypes, and operational capabilities to assist federal, state, local, and private entities in defending against catastrophic terrorism. The center is also dedicated to pursuing partnerships with universities and the private sector to fulfill its mission.

Los Alamos National Laboratory

Los Alamos National Laboratory (LANL, www.lanl.gov) is a DOE laboratory, managed by the University of California, and is one of the largest multidisciplinary institutions in the world. The Center for Homeland Security (CHS) was established in September 2002 to engage the laboratory's broad capabilities in the areas of counterterrorism and homeland security. It provides a single point of contact for all external organizations.

The organization's emphasis is on the key areas of nuclear and radiological science and technology, critical infrastructure protection, and chemical and biological science and technology. Current LANL projects with a key role in homeland security include the following:

- BASIS (the Biological Aerosol Sentry and Information System), a biological early warning system that was tested and installed at the 2002 Salt Lake City Winter Olympics.

- A novel nuclear detector, the Palm CZT Spectrometer, is also in development and deployment, providing real-time gamma and neutron detection and isotope identification in a handheld device.
- LANL has also been active in the anthrax bacterial DNA analysis and the computerized feature identification tool known as GENIE, for Genetic Image Exploitation.

Sandia National Laboratory

The Sandia National Laboratory (www.sandia.gov) has been active since 1949 in the development of science-based technologies that support national security. Through science and technology, people, infrastructure, and partnerships, Sandia's mission is to meet national needs in following six key areas:

- Nuclear weapons
- Nonproliferation
- Defense systems and assessments
- Homeland security
- Science, technology, and engineering
- Energy and infrastructure assurance

Argonne National Laboratory

Argonne National Laboratory (www.anl.gov) is one of the DOE's largest research centers. It is also the nation's first national laboratory, chartered in 1946. Argonne's research falls into four broad categories:

- *Basic science*: This program seeks solutions to a wide variety of scientific challenges. This includes experimental and theoretical work in materials science, physics, chemistry, biology, high-energy physics, and mathematics and computer science, including high-performance computing.
- *National security*: This program has increased in significance in recent years. This program uses Argonne capabilities developed over previous years for other purposes that help counter the terrorist threat. These capabilities include expertise in the nuclear fuel cycle, biology, chemistry, and systems analysis and modeling. This research is helping develop highly sensitive instruments and technologies to detect chemical, biological, and radioactive threats and identify their sources. Other research is helping to detect and deter possible weapons proliferation or actual attacks.
- *Energy resources*: This program helps to insure that a reliable supply of efficient and clean energy exists in the future. The laboratory's scientists and engineers are working to develop advanced batteries and fuel cells, as well as advanced electric power generation and storage systems.
- *Environmental management*: This program includes work on managing and solving environmental problems and promoting environmental stewardship. Research includes alternative energy systems, environmental risk and economic impact assessments, hazardous waste site analysis and remediation planning, treatment to prepare spent nuclear fuel for disposal, and new technologies for decontaminating and decommissioning aging nuclear reactors.

Industrial technology development is an important activity in moving benefits of Argonne's publicly funded research to industry to help strengthen the nation's technology base.

Brookhaven National Laboratory

Established in 1947 on Long Island, New York, Brookhaven National Laboratory (BNL, www.bnl.gov) is a multiprogram national laboratory operated by Brookhaven Science Associates for the DOE. BNL's role for the DOE is to produce excellent science and advanced technology with the cooperation, support, and appropriate involvement of our scientific and local communities. The fundamental elements of BNL's role in support of the four DOE strategic missions follow:

- To conceive, design, construct, and operate complex, leading edge, user-oriented facilities in response to the needs of the DOE and the international community of users
- To carry out basic and applied research in long-term, high-risk programs at the frontier of science
- To develop advanced technologies that address national needs and to transfer them to other organizations and to the commercial sector
- To disseminate technical knowledge, educate new generations of scientists and engineers, maintain technical capabilities in the nation's workforce, and encourage scientific awareness in the general public

  Major programs that are managed at the laboratory include the following:

- Nuclear and high-energy physics
- Physics and chemistry of materials
- Environmental and energy research
- Nonproliferation
- Neurosciences and medical imaging
- Structural biology

Oak Ridge National Laboratory

The Oak Ridge National Laboratory (ORNL, www.ornl.gov) is a multiprogramming science and technology laboratory managed for the DOE by UT-Battelle, LLC. Scientists and engineers at ORNL conduct basic and applied R&D to create scientific knowledge and technological solutions that strengthen the nation's leadership in key areas of science; increase the availability of clean, abundant energy; restore and protect the environment; and contribute to national security. In their national security mission, ORNL provides federal, state, and local government agencies and departments with technology and expertise to support their national and homeland security needs. This technology and expertise are also shared with the private sector.

Pacific Northwest National Laboratory

The Pacific Northwest National Laboratory (PNNL, www.pnl.gov) is a DOE laboratory that delivers breakthrough science and technology to meet selected environmental, energy, health, and national security objectives; strengthen the economy; and support the education of future scientists and engineers.

PNNL's mission in national security supports the U.S. government's objectives against the proliferation of nuclear, chemical, and biological WMDs and associated delivery systems. About one-third of PNNL's $600 million annual R&D budget reflects work in national security programs for the Departments of Energy, Defense, and most other federal agencies. The focus is on issues that concern the

Air Force, Army, Defense Advanced Research Projects Agency, Defense Threat Reduction Agency, Navy, and nuclear nonproliferation.

Scientists and engineers at PNNL are finding ways to diagnose the life of the Army's Abrams tank, developing technologies that verify compliance with the Comprehensive Nuclear Test Ban Treaty, helping North Korea secure spent nuclear fuel in proper storage canisters, and training border enforcement officials from the United States and foreign countries.

Other Department of Energy Laboratories and Objectives

The DOE (www.energy.gov) also has other affiliated organizations in addition to the ones cited above that focus on various homeland security issues. The topics addressed in these facilities include:

- *Cybersecurity protection*: These programs are aimed at protecting the information and systems that the DOE depends on, which only increases in scope as it grows in dependence on newer technologies.
- *Managing operations security*: This program seeks to manage security operations for DOE facilities in the national capital area and to develop policies designed to protect national security and other critical assets entrusted to DOE.
- *Preventing the spread of WMDs*: DOE plays an integral part in nuclear nonproliferation, countering terrorism, and responding to incidents involving WMDs. The department does this by providing technology, analysis, and expertise developed through this program.

Environmental Measurements Laboratory

The Environmental Measurements Laboratory (EML, www.eml.st.dhs.gov), a government-owned, government-operated laboratory, is directly part of the S&T Directorate. The laboratory advances and applies the science and technology required for preventing, protecting against, and responding to radiological and nuclear events in the service of homeland and national security.

EML's current programs focus on issues associated with environmental radiation and radioactivity. Specifically, EML provides DHS with environmental radiation and radioactivity measurements in the laboratory or field, technology development and evaluation, personnel training, instrument calibration, performance testing, data management, and data quality assurance.

Plum Island Animal Disease Center

The Plum Island Animal Disease Center (PIADC, www.ars.usda.gov/plum/) became part of DHS on June 1, 2003. Although the center remains an important national asset in which scientists conduct basic and applied research and diagnostic activities to protect the health of livestock on farms across the nation from foreign disease agents, it was also tasked with a new mission to help DHS to protect the country from terrorist threats, including those directed against agriculture.

The USDA is responsible for research and diagnosis to protect the nation's animal industries and exports from catastrophic economic losses caused by foreign animal disease (FAD) agents accidentally or deliberately introduced into the United States. While continuing its mission, it works closely with DHS personnel to fight agroterrorism.

On September 11, 2005, the Department of Homeland Security announced that the Plum Island Animal Disease Center would be replaced by a new federal facility, the National Bio- and Agro-Defense Facility (NBAF). The NBAF will research high-consequence biological threats involving zoonotic (i.e., transmitted from animals to humans) and FADs. It will allow basic research; diagnostic development, testing, and validation; advanced countermeasure development; and training for high-consequence live-stock diseases. The new facility is being designed to:

- Integrate those aspects of public and animal health research that have been determined to be central to national security
- Assess and research evolving bioterrorism threats over the next five decades
- Enable the Departments of Homeland Security and Agriculture (USDA) to fulfill their related homeland defense research, development, testing, and evaluation (RDT&E) responsibilities

Department of Health and Human Services Laboratories

The Department of Health and Human Services (www.hhs.gov) operates several laboratories focused on various health and disease prevention issues. The laboratories have extensive programs, and more details can be found later in this chapter.

U.S. Customs Laboratory and Scientific Services

DHS Customs and Border Protection Laboratories and Scientific Services (LSS) (www.cbp.gov/xp/cgov/import/operations_support/labs_scientific_svcs/) coordinates technical and scientific support with all CBP trade and border protection activities. The mission of the program is to provide rapid, quality scientific, forensic, and WMDs services to the CBP officials and other counterparts. One of the principal responsibilities of the CBP science officers is to manage the Customs Gauger/Laboratory Accreditation program. The program calls for the accreditation of commercial gaugers and laboratories so that their measurements and analytical results can be used by customs for entry and admissibility purposes. The staff edits and publishes the Customs Laboratory Bulletin, which, as a customs-scientific journal, is circulated internationally and provides a useful forum for technical exchange on subjects of general customs interest. U.S. Customs and Border Protection maintains the following laboratory facilities:

- *Springfield (VA) Laboratory*: The Springfield Laboratory is a centralized facility that provides scientific support to CBP headquarters and the laboratories listed below. This facility provides analytical services to CBP legal and regulatory functions and to CBP offices that require scientific support, and develops new analytical methods and evaluates new instrumentation.
- *New York (NY) Laboratory*: The New York CBP services the greater New York City area including the New York Seaport, JFK Airport, the Port of Newark, and Perth Amboy. The laboratory provides scientific, forensic, and WMD services to CBP customers, including radiation detection, chemical WMD detection and identification, participation in the LSS national WMD strike team, and membership in the Food Emergency Response Network (FERN).
- *Chicago (IL) Laboratory*: The Chicago Laboratory services all of the New England states, Illinois, Iowa, Nebraska, Wisconsin, Michigan, Kansas, Missouri, Indiana, part of Minnesota, and New York except the New York City Metro area. This facility provides technical advice and analytical services to CBP officers, U.S. Immigration and Customs Enforcement (ICE) agents, border patrol officers, and other entities on a wide range of issues. These services assist CBP officers in collecting revenue based on import duties and enforcing the law. The services provided to ICE agents and border patrol officers pertain primarily to law enforcement and forensics-related issues.
- *Savannah (GA) Laboratory*: The Savannah Customs Laboratory serves ports from Philadelphia, PA, to Key West, FL. The facility conducts chemical and physical testing of all types of commodities, narcotics, and other controlled substances. The Savannah Laboratory operates two state-of-the art, custom-built mobile laboratories to meet the on-site testing needs of southeastern U.S. ports used for the detection of materials for WMD.

- *Southwest Regional Science Center (Houston, TX)*: The Southwest Regional Science Center provides technical and scientific services to all of the ports of entry and Border Patrol sectors in the following eight states: Alabama, Tennessee, Mississippi, Louisiana, Arkansas, Oklahoma, Texas, and New Mexico. This geographic area contains 80% of the border between the United States and Mexico. This facility provides technical and scientific services to manage, secure, and control the nation's border and to prevent terrorists and terrorist weapons from entering the United States. Services provided include forensic crime scene investigation, WMD interdiction, and trade enforcement.

- *Los Angeles (CA) Laboratory*: The Los Angeles Laboratory services all of southern California, and southern Nevada, including Las Vegas, Arizona, and the California–Mexico border in these areas. The staff of chemists, textile analysts, and physical scientists is trained to assist in meeting the CBP mission in areas of trade, forensics, and WMDs. Among the laboratory's functions are forensic support such as evidence collection and analysis of trace, controlled substances and pharmaceuticals; technical support for chemical, biological, explosives, and radiation WMD issues; and latent print processing at the crime scene or in the laboratory.

- *San Francisco (CA) Laboratory*: The laboratory serves the northern two-thirds of California, as well as the states of Oregon, Washington, North Dakota, South Dakota, Minnesota, Alaska, Hawaii, Colorado, Utah, Nevada, Montana, and Idaho. Major ports located in this service area include San Francisco, Portland, Seattle, Blaine, Anchorage, Honolulu, and Denver. This facility provides technical advice, forensic, and other scientific services to the CBP officials and other agencies on a wide range of imported and exported commodities.

- *San Juan (PR) Laboratory*: The San Juan Laboratory serves the ports of Puerto Rico and the U.S. Virgin Islands. This facility conducts chemical and physical testing of a wide variety of importations and forensic samples. Most of the facility's specialization has been in the area of controlled substances and other forensic samples. The San Juan Laboratory provides vital technical support and training to local and foreign law enforcement officials in areas such as WMD, radioactive material detection, crime scene management, and narcotics field test kits.

Academic Research Institutions

Universities, their research centers, institutes, and qualified staff represent a very important portion of the scientific research in the United States. These facilities account for an estimated one-third of the total federal budget available for R&D activities. The S&T Directorate has already started to show its recognition of the importance of these institutions in the overall homeland security R&D effort through both awarding them R&D grants and funding Homeland Security Centers of Excellence on their campuses.

Homeland Security Centers of Excellence

The S&T Directorate, through its Office of University Programs, is furthering the homeland security mission by engaging the academic community to create learning and research environments in areas critical to homeland security. Through the Homeland Security Centers of Excellence program, DHS has invested in university-based partnerships to develop centers of multidisciplinary research where important fields of inquiry can be analyzed and best practices developed, debated, and shared. The department's Homeland Security Centers of Excellence (HS-Centers) bring together the nation's best experts and focus its most talented researchers on a variety of threats that include agricultural, chemical, biological, nuclear/radiological, explosive, and cyberterrorism as well as the behavioral aspects of terrorism. The current HS-Centers are listed in the "Homeland Security Centers of Excellence" sidebar. In FY 2012, $29.9 million in funding will be available for university programs.

Homeland Security Centers of Excellence

There are currently 12 Centers of Excellence across the country.

The Center for Risk and Economic Analysis of Terrorism Events (CREATE), led by the University of Southern California, develops advanced tools to evaluate the risks, costs, and consequences of terrorism.

The Center for Advancing Microbial Risk Assessment (CAMRA), led by Michigan State University and Drexel University established jointly with the U.S. Environmental Protection Agency, fills critical gaps in risk assessments for mitigating microbial hazards.

The Center of Excellence for Zoonotic and Animal Disease Defense (ZADD), led by Texas A&M University and Kansas State University, protects the nation's agricultural and public health sectors against high-consequence foreign animal and emerging and zoonotic disease threats.

The National Center for Food Protection and Defense (NCFPD), led by the University of Minnesota, defends the safety and security of the food system by conducting research to protect vulnerabilities in the nation's food supply chain.

The National Consortium for the Study of Terrorism and Responses to Terrorism (START), led by the University of Maryland, informs decisions on how to disrupt terrorists and terrorist groups through empirically grounded findings on the human element of the terrorist threat.

The National Center for the Study of Preparedness and Catastrophic Event Response (PACER), led by Johns Hopkins University, optimizes our nation's preparedness in the event of a high-consequence natural or man-made disaster.

The Center of Excellence for Awareness & Location of Explosives-Related Threats (ALERT), led by Northeastern University and the University of Rhode Island, will develop new means and methods to protect the nation from explosives-related threats.

The National Center for Border Security and Immigration (NCBSI), led by the University of Arizona in Tucson (research co-lead) and the University of Texas at El Paso (education co-lead), are developing technologies, tools, and advanced methods to balance immigration and commerce with effective border security.

The Center for Maritime, Island and Remotes and Extreme Environment Security (MIREES), led by the University of Hawaii and Stevens Institute of Technology, focuses on developing robust research and education programs addressing maritime domain awareness to safeguard populations and properties in geographical areas that present significant security challenges.

The Coastal Hazards Center of Excellence (CHC), led by the University of North Carolina at Chapel Hill and Jackson State University in Jackson, Miss., performs research and develops education programs to enhance the nation's ability to safeguard populations, properties, and economies from catastrophic natural disaster.

The National Transportation Security Center of Excellence (NTSCOE) was established in accordance with HR1, Implementing the Recommendations of the 9/11 Commission Act of 2007, in August 2007. The NTSCOE will develop new technologies, tools, and advanced methods to defend, protect, and increase the resilience of the nation's multimodal transportation. It comprises seven institutions:

- Connecticut Transportation Institute at the University of Connecticut
- Tougaloo College
- Texas Southern University

- National Transit Institute at Rutgers — the State University of New Jersey
- Homeland Security Management Institute at Long Island University
- Mack Blackwell National Rural Transportation Study Center at the University of Arkansas
- Mineta Transportation Institute at San José State University

The Center of Excellence in Command, Control and Interoperability (C2I), led by Purdue University (visualization sciences co-lead) and Rutgers University (data sciences co-lead), will create the scientific basis and enduring technologies needed to analyze massive amounts of information to detect security threats.

Source: DHS, 2011, http://www.dhs.gov/files/programs/editorial_0498.shtm.

Maritime Research

The scope of the S&T Directorate encompasses the pursuit of a full range of research into the use, preservation, and exploitation of the national waterways and oceans. The U.S. Coast Guard Research and Development Center is in charge of conducting research to support defense of this resource and of the homeland.

U.S. Coast Guard

The Research and Development (R&D) Center is the Coast Guard's (www.uscg.mil) sole facility performing research, development, test, and evaluation (RDT&E) in support of the Coast Guard's major missions of maritime mobility, maritime safety, maritime security, national defense, and protection of natural resources. The center has as its mission "to be the Coast Guard's pathfinder, anticipating and meeting future technological challenges, while partnering with others to shepherd the best ideas into implementable solutions."

The Coast Guard RDT&E program produces two types of products: the development of hardware, procedures, and systems that directly contribute to increasing the quality and productivity of the operations and the expansion of knowledge related to technical support of operating and regulatory programs.

R&D Efforts External to the Department of Homeland Security

The majority of homeland security R&D funding is provided to federal agencies other than the DHS.

Department of Health and Human Services

National Institutes of Health

The National Institutes of Health's (NIH, www.nih.gov) most relevant effort in homeland security R&D is in bioterrorism-related research. It has conducted work in the field for much longer than the existence of the DHS, but it emerged as a high-priority R&D agency after the 2001 anthrax mail situation. Budget allocations, which tend to be a reliable predictor of federal priorities, have clearly indicated that this dedication to bioterrorism detection and countermeasures remains. In the FY 2012 budget, NIH saw a minor increase in homeland security research funding of 3.1% from the previous year, up to $1.929 billion.

NIH is clearly the leader within the federal government for homeland security R&D efforts for its biodefense research portfolio. The biodefense priorities of NIAID include, in addition to biodefense research, the development of medical countermeasures against radiological and nuclear threats, and medical countermeasures against chemical threats.

Centers for Disease Control and Prevention
The Centers for Disease Control and Prevention (CDC, www.cdc.gov) is another component of HHS that traditionally performed WMD terrorism R&D. However, with the opening of the Biodefense Advanced Research and Development Agency, CDC homeland security R&D funds have diminished. In fact, the majority of CDC terrorism activities, which are not R&D in nature, include the management of the Strategic National Stockpile (SNS) and funding for state and local responders to upgrade their abilities to prepare for and manage WMD events.

Biodefense Advanced Research and Development Agency
As part of its expanding effort to fund anthrax research and other R&D related to defenses against terrorist threats, the Office of the Secretary of Health and Human Services funded biodefense R&D in the Biodefense Advanced Research and Development Authority (BARDA, www.hhs.gov/aspr/barda/index.html). BARDA funds advanced R&D of new biodefense countermeasures as part of an HHS-wide effort to secure an adequate supply of such countermeasures for the SNS.

Department of Defense

The Department of Defense (DOD) has had a fluctuating budget for homeland security R&D since 2001. In FY 2012, DOD R&D funding decreased by 11%, to a total allocation of $2,115 billion. The vast majority of DOD R&D funding is provided through the Defense Advanced Research Projects Agency (DARPA), which works mainly on applications that serve the needs of the military (e.g., biological warfare defense and the Chemical and Biological Defense Program). The outcome of this research, however, often has applications that can be applied by civilian first responders despite the military origin of the projects that generated them. The DOD Chemical and Biological Defense Program (CBDP) is another research-oriented agency that performs homeland security research activities.

Department of Agriculture

Even more so than DOD, the USDA has witnessed widely fluctuating R&D budgets since the September 11 terrorist attacks. Actual fiscal year funding amounts have varied from less than $50 million to over $170 million. Since 9/11, USDA has invested a considerable amount of research effort toward developing security mechanisms to protect dangerous pathogens, which could be used as terror weapons and are located in many laboratories dispersed throughout the United States. Increases in funding in FY 2006 and 2007 were dedicated to renovating facilities that performed animal research and diagnosis at the National Centers for Animal Health in Ames, Iowa. These efforts are aimed at protecting the U.S. food supply from acts of sabotage and terrorism — both of which could have potentially devastating effects on the U.S. economy. The FY 2012 funding for USDA homeland security R&D efforts is $88 million, an increase of almost 4% over the previous year.

Environmental Protection Agency

The Environmental Protection Agency (EPA) has seen steady but small federal allocations of Homeland Security R&D funding since September 11. Since that year EPA research related to homeland security has been focused primarily on drinking water security research (which would involve EPA efforts to develop better surveillance and laboratory networks for drinking water supplies to counter potential terrorist threats) and decontamination research (to develop better technologies and methods for decontaminating terrorist attack sites). EPA also conducts threat and consequence assessments and tests potential biodefense and other decontamination technologies. Much of this work is conducted at EPA's National Homeland Security Research Center (NHSRC) in Cincinnati. NHSRC develops expertise and products that are used to prevent, prepare for, and recover from public health and environmental emergencies arising from terrorist threats and incidents. Research and development efforts focus on the following five primary areas:

- *Threat and consequence assessment*: Investigates human exposure to chemical, biological, and radiological contaminants to define dangerous levels of these contaminants and establish protective cleanup goals.
- *Decontamination and consequence management*: Focuses on decontamination of buildings and outdoor environments, as well as the safe disposal of contaminated materials.
- *Water infrastructure protection*: Protects the nation's drinking water sources and distribution systems and ensures the safety of wastewater collection, treatment, and disposal procedures.
- *Response capability enhancement*: Works directly with emergency responders and local governments to provide tools and information needed to make informed decisions in the event of an attack.
- *Technology testing and evaluation*: Evaluates technologies that show potential for use in homeland security applications. These evaluations are used by water utility operators, building owners, emergency responders, and others to make informed decisions when purchasing security technology.

National Institute of Standards and Technology

The Department of Commerce (DOC) is home to the National Institute of Standards and Technology (NIST), which funds R&D in cryptography and computer security and which provides scientific and technical support to DHS in these areas.

National Science Foundation

The National Science Foundation (NSF) funds research to combat bioterrorism in the areas of infectious diseases and microbial genome sequencing. These programs increased to $395 million in FY 2012.

Conclusion

Homeland security represents an entirely new spectrum of issues of R&D and technology and an opportunity to revitalize old issues under the homeland security umbrella. Establishing DHS and the S&T Directorate brought a new, major player into the federally supported R&D efforts. There was much discussion and disgruntlement within the research community concerning the lack of involvement of the NSF in the development of the homeland security R&D agenda. In fact, several people questioned the need for the S&T as opposed to just increasing the NSF's or NIST's portfolios.

With a spectrum of activity varying from research to development to deployment, and a span of subjects from bioterrorism to personal protective equipment, from communication tools to nonproliferation, and from detection devices to mass production of vaccines, the S&T Directorate has been given a monumental task. The directorate not only coordinates the R&D facilities of many organizations but also has the authority to set priorities in others. The university-based HS-Centers provide a level of funding

FIGURE 12–2 New York City, NY, September 29, 2001 — Lobby of hotel near the World Trade Center site. (Source: Photo by Andrea Booher/FEMA News Photo)

that has not been available for some time and provide one of the best funded opportunities for specific R&D to benefit emergency management.

Although the context of change leaves little room for conclusions, the extraordinary budget given to the S&T Directorate either in existing programs or in new ones will provide the emergency-management and first-responder communities new capabilities never before imagined. It is to be hoped that these technological "toys" do not give a false sense of confidence and overshadow the real requirements of building an improved capacity to mitigate, prepare for, respond to, and recover from the risks of terrorism (Figure 12–2).

The changes that can be implied with the establishment of the university-based centers should be watched closely. These centers comprise the most concrete platform for the partnership, or "integration," of academia, the private sector, and the federal government in support of homeland security. The establishment and progress of these centers must be followed carefully in order to discover the answer to two fundamental questions:

- How ready are these sectors to work together? That is, can the most basic goal of survival and safety of the homeland be a motivation strong enough to overcome the sectors' administrative and functional differences?
- Will real integration occur? The R&D field may be the place that shows whether integration at the large scale as proposed by the DHS is really possible or not. This field is probably the most appropriate one because research, development, and deployment are very close functions. But this task may be more difficult than it seems because it involves many different organizations, whose cooperation, successes, or failures can put the success of the entire organization at risk.

Key Terms

BioWatch: A program aimed at detecting the release of pathogens into the air, thereby providing warning to the government and public health community of a potential bioterror event. This is performed through the use of aerosol samplers mounted on preexisting EPA air-quality monitoring stations that collect air, passing it through filters. These filters are manually collected at regular, reportedly 24-hours, intervals and are analyzed for potential biological weapon pathogens using polymerase chain reaction (PCR) techniques. Although filters from the BioWatch program were initially shipped to and tested at a federal laboratory in California, state and local public health laboratories now perform the analyses.

MANPADS: A man-portable air defense system is a missile firing device, used to destroy aircraft, that is easily carried or transported by a person.

SAFECOM: A communications program of the DHS Office for Interoperability and Compatibility that, with its federal partners, provides research, development, testing and evaluation, guidance, tools, and templates on communications-related issues to local, tribal, state, and federal emergency response agencies.

Review Questions

1. Identify the four lead groups of research in the DHS Science and Technology Directorate and explain what each does to contribute to counterterrorism efforts.
2. Define in your own words why HSARPA was established, and explain its scope and objectives.
3. What are the Homeland Security Centers of Excellence, and what are the research and development goals of each?
4. What government laboratories are working to develop WMD countermeasures? What specific areas of research is each focused on?
5. What government laboratories are working to protect critical information and infrastructure from terrorist attack? What specific areas of research is each focused on?

References

American Association for the Advancement of Science (AAAS), 2011. AAAS XXXVI: Research and Development FY2012. http://www.aaas.org/spp/rd/rdreport2012/.

DHS, 2011, Under Secretary Tara O'Toole, Science and Technology Directorate, before the House Committee on Appropriations. Subcommittee on Homeland Security. S&T Fiscal Year 2012 Budget Request. http://www.dhs.gov/ynews/testimony/testimony_1301519363336.shtm.

Department of Homeland Security, 2003. Medical treatment of radiological casualties. http://www.appc1.va.gov/emshg/docs/Radiologic_Medical_Countermeasures_051403.pdf.

National Emergency Management Association, 2003. National Response Plan. www.nemaweb.org/docs/national_response_plan.pdf.

Office of Homeland Security, 2002. National strategy for homeland security. http://www.whitehouse.gov/homeland/book.

Telecommunications Service Priority, 2003. Welcome to the TSP website, National Coordination Center for Tele-communications (NCC), December 4. http://www.tsp.ncs.gov/.

13

The Future of Homeland Security

Introduction

This chapter is provided to identify and briefly explain several of the most pressing issues confronting the role of emergency management and disaster assistance programs in homeland security, both in general and specific to the Department of Homeland Security (DHS). Just as the Federal Emergency Management Agency (FEMA) has been the federal government leader in the national emergency management system since its 1979 inception, DHS has assumed a similar leadership role in the creation and management of a national system to ensure the security of the nation.

Even now, 10 years after the September 11 attacks, a measure of how effectively DHS can perform in this leadership position and exactly what role emergency management and disaster assistance functions will ultimately play within DHS and the national homeland security system have not been adequately developed. The massive failure of the federal government's response to Hurricane Katrina in August 2005 and the ongoing failure of the recovery efforts nearly 6 years later indicate very clearly that this single critical issue is yet to be resolved.

We believe that FEMA's history offers two important lessons for DHS as it progresses in its difficult mission. First, it is critical for DHS to take all the necessary steps to ensure that the nation's emergency management and disaster assistance capabilities, especially those at the federal government level, are not marginalized. Additionally, these emergency management agencies must be given the tools that enable them to effectively manage the new terrorist threat with which they are confronted. Second, terrorism, in all of its forms, must not become the singular risk driving DHS policy. In the absence of an all-hazards approach coupled with the growing risk caused by global climate change, the scene will surely be set for a repeat of the Hurricane Katrina fiasco.

The FEMA History Lesson

Prior to 1979, federal emergency management and disaster preparedness, response, and recovery programs and capabilities were scattered among numerous federal government agencies, including the White House. There was little, if any, coordination among these disparate parts. Communicating with the federal government during a disaster had become such a problem that the National Governor's Association petitioned then president Jimmy Carter to consolidate all federal programs into a single agency.

On April 1, 1979, President Carter signed the executive order that established the Federal Emergency Management Agency, moving federal disaster programs, agencies, and offices from across the federal government into a single executive branch agency. The director of FEMA was charged with integrating these diverse programs into one cohesive operation capable of delivering federal resources and assistance through a new concept called the *integrated emergency management system*. This system was centered on an all-hazards approach.

With the election of President Ronald Reagan in 1980, the focus of FEMA's policies and programs shifted dramatically from an all-hazards approach to a single focus on nuclear attack planning through its Office of National Preparedness. At the same time, agency leadership and personnel struggled to integrate its many diverse programs. This focuses on a single low-probability/high-impact event and the inability of the agency's many parts to function effectively as one led to the disastrous responses to Hurricane Hugo, the Loma Prieta earthquake, and Hurricane Andrew. There were numerous calls for the abolition of FEMA, including from several members of Congress.

President Bill Clinton, elected in 1992, appointed the first FEMA director who was an experienced emergency manager. Under James Lee Witt's leadership, FEMA once again adopted an all-hazards approach, became a customer-focused organization that worked closely with its state and local emergency management partners, and effectively responded to an unprecedented series of major disasters across the country. These included not only major natural disasters but also terrorist events such as the first World Trade Center bombing and the Oklahoma City bombing.

By the time of the election of President George W. Bush in 2000, FEMA had gained the trust of the public, the media, its partners, and elected officials in all levels of government. FEMA functioned as a single agency as envisioned when it was created in 1979 and possessed one of the most favorable brand names in government.

The emphasis on the national security functions of FEMA was highlighted when new FEMA Director Joe Allbaugh was reinstated to the Office of National Preparedness and all indications were that FEMA would once again focus on national security issues.

This process was accelerated after the September 11, 2001, terrorist attacks. FEMA became part of the new DHS, and the all-hazards approach, while acknowledged in speeches, was replaced by a single focus on terrorism. More importantly, the director of FEMA no longer reported directly to the president and was replaced in the president's cabinet by the DHS secretary. In the first major reorganization of DHS that began in July 2005, the FEMA of the 1990s was disassembled and its parts spread throughout the department.

In August 2005, Hurricane Katrina stuck the Gulf Coast and history repeated itself. DHS/FEMA was unable to provide the support needed by state and local officials for adequate response and hundreds of Americans died as a result. DHS/FEMA continues to fail to this day in the recovery phase as well. As this chapter is written in July 2011, FEMA's reputation has finally begun to improve following its response to the tornadoes in Tuscaloosa, AL, and Joplin, MO, in 2011, but for most of the public FEMA's reputation remains as sullied as it was in August 1992 after the botched response to Hurricane Andrew.

Despite DHS's current organizational restructuring, serious questions remain concerning FEMA's and the federal government's capabilities in responding to a catastrophic disaster, whether it be a hurricane, earthquake, flood, or another terrorist attack. The nation's emergency management system remains broken. How it will be repaired and returned to its former capability remains to be seen.

Lessons for Homeland Security from the FEMA Experience

The writer George Santayana once famously said, "Those who ignore history are doomed to repeat it." There are two critical lessons to be learned from the FEMA experience that provide some perspective on how the DHS may function in the future.

First and foremost, it will take time for DHS to become a functioning organization. DHS was cobbled together in much the same way that FEMA was bringing together an estimated 178,000 federal workers from 22 agencies and programs in a very short time period. It took FEMA nearly 15 years and several reorganizations to effectively coordinate and deliver the full resources of the federal government to support state and local governments in responding to major disasters. DHS is less than 10 years old and has already undertaken three major reorganizations. If FEMA's experience is any kind of indicator, it will be at least another 5 years before DHS will achieve full functionality.

Second, the single focus on a low-probability/high-impact event (i.e., a major terrorist attack similar to September 11) will undermine DHS's capabilities in responding to high-probability/low-impact events. In terms of natural and traditional man-made disasters (hurricanes, earthquakes, hazardous materials incidents, etc.), these programs' capabilities have been marginalized. The 2005 hurricanes in Florida and the resulting congressional and media investigations of fraud and incompetence that characterized the federal response and the miserable performance in Hurricane Katrina are clear evidence of the negative impact this single focus can have in an all-hazards world.

DHS's primary mission is to prevent a terrorist attack on American soil. The emergency management and disaster assistance functions centered in FEMA contribute little to this mission. However, should another terrorist event occur in the future, as everyone concedes that it will, these emergency management and disaster assistance functions will be critical in preparing our people, reducing the impact, and mounting an effective response and recovery that gets Americans back on their feet quickly. Marginalizing these capabilities as it pursues its primary mission is a mistake that FEMA made in the past and one that DHS cannot afford to repeat now and in the future.

The Future of Emergency Management in Homeland Security

Rebuilding the nation's emergency management system, especially the role of the federal government in this system, does not conflict with the primary mission of DHS. In fact, it is a critical element in the overall homeland security strategy. However, we feel several steps must be taken to rebuild and enhance the nation's emergency management system and to return the federal government to a leadership role in this area.

Reestablish FEMA as an Executive Branch Agency

Moving FEMA out of DHS and consolidating its traditional mitigation, preparedness, response, and recovery programs will ensure that the all-hazards approach will be reinstated and that FEMA and its state and local partners will once again focus on dealing with all manners of disaster events including terrorist attacks. Emergency management professionals will once again be in charge of preparing the public, reducing future impacts through hazard mitigation, and managing the resources of the federal government in support of state and local governments in responding to major disasters and fostering a speedy and effective recovery from these events.

The post-Katrina reorganization of DHS and FEMA has returned the preparedness, mitigation, response, and recovery programs to FEMA. But this reorganization did not provide the FEMA administrator direct access to the president of the United States. Only the president can vest the authority in the FEMA administrator that is needed for a successful federal response.

Reestablishing FEMA outside of DHS will not conflict with DHS's primary mission to prevent terrorist attacks on American soil and will enhance those critical elements in the homeland security system that will be called upon when the next event occurs.

Re-create the Federal Response Plan

The Federal Response Plan (FRP) successfully guided the federal government's response to over 350 presidentially declared disasters from Hurricane Andrew through the September 11 attacks. The FRP was an agreement signed by department and agency heads from 32 federal departments and agencies and the American Red Cross.

The FRP had three critical elements:

1. The president designated and empowered the director of FEMA to direct the actions of the 32 signatories to the plan.
2. Each signatory to the plan agreed to make specific resources available during a major disaster event.
3. Each signatory to the plan would be reimbursed for any resources expended at the direction and authorization of FEMA.

The bottom line is that when the president declared a major disaster event, the FRP ensured that the full resources of the federal government would be brought to bear in support of state and local government and directed by FEMA. No single agency was expected to carry the full federal responsibility and everyone knew that the director of FEMA was in charge.

The FRP was replaced first by the National Response Plan in 2004 and most recently by the National Response Framework in 2008.

The National Response Framework is just what its title indicates, a framework for how the nation as a whole will prepare for and respond to a major disaster. It is not a plan for managing the federal response to a major disaster and, similar to the National Response Plan, fails to designate what agency will direct the federal response.

A major step in rebuilding the nation's emergency management system and rebuilding the trust of the state and local emergency managers and the public must be re-creating the FRP with FEMA returned to the role of directing the plan. The FRP is a proven method for delivering federal resources in support of state and local efforts in a timely and cost-efficient manner.

Encourage Community-Based Homeland Security

Since September 11, 2001, the federal government has taken the lead in homeland security and the vast majority of policy and program initiatives have focused on federal capabilities and responsibilities. With the exception of the Citizen Corps program and Web-based awareness campaigns such as Ready.gov, very little has been done to effectively involve the American public in homeland security activities.

The "Redefining Readiness" study conducted by the New York Academy of Medicine identified numerous problems with the assumptions of homeland security planners in developing smallpox and dirty bomb plans without input from the public. Involving the public in developing community-based homeland security plans is critical to the successful implementation of these plans.

This study and others have discovered that a large segment of the public is ready and willing to participate in these planning efforts and to be part of a community-based effort to deal with the new homeland security threats. Mechanisms for involving the public in this process are needed.

The bottom line is that the general public must be involved in the development and implementation of community homeland security plans, and DHS and its partners in state and local government should invest more resources in developing the planning processes needed to involve the public in the nation's homeland security system.

Improve Communications

Communicating with the public is another area that needs to be improved if the nation is going to have a truly effective homeland security system. To date, DHS has shown little interest in communicating with the public, and when it has, the results have not always been positive — the "duct tape and plastic" fiasco serves as a classic example. FEMA's failed communications in Hurricane Katrina is another. DHS and its state and local partners need to address three factors to improve its communications with the American people.

First, there must be a commitment from the leadership, not only at DHS and its state and local partners, but at all levels of government, including the executive level, to communicate timely and accurate information to the public. This is especially important in the response and recovery phases to a terrorist incident.

In a disaster scenario, the conventional wisdom that states information is power and hoarding information helps to retain such power is almost categorically reversed. Withholding information during disaster events generally has an overall negative effect on the well-being of the public and on the impression the public forms about involved authorities. In practice, sharing of information is what generates authority and power, when that information is useful and relates to the hazard at hand. To date, DHS leadership and the political leadership have been reluctant to make this commitment to share information with the public. This is something that must change if they expect the American people to fully comprehend the homeland security threat and to become actively engaged in homeland security efforts. Few citizens have an idea of what actual terrorism risks they face, and fewer can actually relate those risks in any comparable fashion to the risks they face every day without notice.

Second, homeland security officials at all levels must resolve the conflict between sharing information with the public in advance and in the aftermath of a terrorist incident that has value for intelligence or criminal prosecution purposes. This is directly linked to the commitment issue discussed in the previous paragraphs and has been repeatedly cited by homeland security officials as reasons for not sharing more specific information with the public.

This is a very difficult issue that DHS has tried to ignore in the past. The continued frustration among the public and state and local officials with the Homeland Security Advisory System (HSAS) was just one sign that this issue would not solve itself or just go away.

Also an issue is the question of when to release relevant information to the public without compromising intelligence sources and/or ongoing criminal investigations. This is an issue that rarely, if ever, confronts emergency management officials dealing with natural and unintentional man-made disasters. Therefore, there is little precedent or experience for current homeland security officials to work within crafting a communications strategy that balances the competing need for the public to have timely and accurate information with the need to protect intelligence sources and ongoing criminal investigations. To date, the needs of the intelligence and justice communities have clearly been judged to outweigh those of the public.

The implementation of the National Terrorism Alert System (NTAS) that replaced the much maligned HSAS will hopefully be a critical first step in reestablishing trust with the public for a terrorism warning system. From this starting point, if the commitment is there among the homeland security leadership, additional communications mechanisms can be developed to ensure that the public gets timely and accurate information both in advance of any terrorist incident and during the response and recovery phases in the aftermath of the next terrorist attack.

Third, more efforts must be invested by federal departments and agencies to better understand the principal terrorist threats that our nation faces (i.e., biological, chemical, radiological, nuclear, and explosives) and to develop communications strategies that educate and inform the public about these threats with more useful information. The 2001 Washington, DC, anthrax incident is a perfect example of uninformed or misinformed public officials sharing what is often conflicting and, in too many instances, wrong information with the public.

The nation's public officials must become better informed about these principal risks and be ready and capable of explaining complicated information to the public. As the anthrax incident made clear, this is not a luxury, but a necessity if the response to similar incidents in the future is to be successful.

Decades of research and a new generation of technologies now inform emergency managers as they provide information about hurricanes, tornadoes, earthquakes, and hazardous materials incidents to the public. A similar research effort must be undertaken for these five new terrorist risks and communications strategies that will ensure that homeland security officials at all levels are capable of clearly explaining to the public the hazards posed by these threats.

These communications strategies must consider how to communicate to the public when incomplete information is all that is available to homeland security officials. In the vast majority of cases, this partiality of information is probable. A public health crisis will not wait for all the data to be collected and analyzed, nor will the public. Homeland security officials must develop strategies for informing the public effectively, as the crisis develops, by forming effective messages that are able to explain to the public how what is being said is the most accurate information available based on the information that, likewise, is available — despite its incomplete nature. Clearly, this is not an easy task, but it is not impossible. The public will increasingly expect such communications efforts, so the sooner such a system is in place, the better the next incident will be managed.

Partner with the Business Sector

The DHS and numerous business groups, such as the Business Roundtable, U.S. Chamber of Commerce, ASIS International, acknowledge that an effective partnership between the government and business groups must be maintained as part of the nation's homeland security efforts. This is only logical considering that the nation's economic security depends in part on the success of the nation's national security policies. A number of steps have been taken in the recent years to enhance this partnership, but there remains more work to be done in aligning the full strengths of the public and private sector in the homeland security mission space.

President Barack Obama stressed the convergence of economic and national security policies in the May 2010 release of his National Security Strategy. The Quadrennial Homeland Security Review also noted this relationship by including the private sector as part of the defined group of stakeholders referred to as the "homeland security enterprise." During the pandemic of 2009, DHS, HHS, and DOC were lauded by businesses for holding numerous joint conference calls with industries of every size, providing access to the latest scientific data, coordinated messaging, and protective actions leaders could take to protect their employees. A number of private-sector elements within DHS are focused on improving the effectiveness of government coordination with the private sector as well as creating the opportunity for business to partner with government. But this is a two-way street and government cannot do so much; industry too must be prepared to share essential information and collaborate.

The DHS Private Sector Office created a private-sector resources catalog[1] to centralize all the services offered to the private sector in the homeland security space from across the department. A Loaned Executive Program was created to allow experts from industry to serve in limited appointments within DHS to share their specific expertise. Recommendations for improving information sharing have been developed with industry leaders including the National Infrastructure Advisory Council and the Critical Infrastructure Partnership Advisory Council. The Office of Infrastructure's Protective Security Advisors (PSAs) work closely with owners and operators of critical infrastructure as well as the DHS Office of

---

[1] For details on numerous DHS programs involving the private sector see http://www.dhs.gov/privatesector.

Intelligence & Analysis and state and local personnel at the fusion centers to constantly address the dynamic risk environment. The PSAs are consistently referenced by business and state and local government leaders as vital to their all-hazards response and risk management activities.

However, in the nearly 10 years since the attacks of September 11, 2001, more focus and commitment can be directed in ensuring the private sector is a ready and prepared partner for the next crisis. There has been some progress and cooperation, but there is no overall strategy in place to incorporate the business sector into the government's emergency management planning for homeland security.

Numerous issues must be resolved before such a strategy can be designed and implemented. A significant issue that must be addressed is how the government will protect and use confidential information that it is asking or requiring the business community to provide. The business community, which has vast institutional knowledge about this privacy issue as well as countless other issues that have been presented in the homeland security approach, must be included in the planning process not only for terrorism response planning. According to FEMA, over 3,000 private-sector entities participated in the 2011 National Level Exercise simulating an earthquake along the New Madrid Seismic Zone. When combined with a more holistic strategy for private-sector capability alignment across the homeland security mission areas, these many initial actions could have significant longer term impact.

One possible avenue for establishing and nurturing an effective partnership with the business sector is to start at the community level. Issues such as what the government will do with confidential information are likely to be less critical at the community level, allowing for lessons to be learned in progressive steps.

As another voice in what the future direction of homeland security, Bridger McGaw suggests the following four opportunities offer future homeland security leaders the ability to improve the effectiveness of homeland security policies and programs:

Opportunity #1: Evolve Emergency Management for the Cyber-Age
The interdependencies between critical infrastructure and cyberspace only continue to increase, requiring more attention from public and private sector leaders.

Public and private sector decision makers should integrate cybersecurity measures into business continuity plans and incident response and recovery plans, and clearly lay out how their respective organizations will work together to respond to events during a cyber incident.

Opportunity #2: Support Information Sharing and Intelligence Fusion Centers
The 9/11 Commission made it clear that removing barriers to information sharing would improve counterterrorism actions by government agencies. Leaders in the national security community must make this effort a long-lasting reality. Success of the information-sharing effort cannot be under-valued.

Opportunity #3: Integrate Journalists as "First Amendment Responders"
Effective emergency response always cites the use of the "traditional" and "new" media for providing the public with assurance and direction in a crisis. Journalists can no longer play a reactive role in homeland security and need to be embraced as true partners in the homeland security enterprise in advance of the next crisis.

Opportunity #4: Invest in the Next Generation of Homeland Security Professionals
Ensuring the quality and effectiveness of the future homeland security workforce should be a national priority. Trained and knowledgeable experts are in high demand across the spectrum of critical

homeland security capabilities in both the public and private sectors. Defining the capabilities and knowledge that future homeland security professionals should possess must be undertaken while the subject matter and department are still evolving.

These four opportunities offer a place to focus attention where real progress can be achieved with long-lasting positive impact towards enhancing the resiliency of our nation.

Bridger McGaw is a graduate of Harvard College and the John F. Kennedy School of Government and was a homeland security policy and strategic communications consultant. He has held several positions as policy adviser, public affairs officer, and press secretary to senior leaders in the Department of Defense, White House, Capitol Hill, and state and local governments. McGaw served on the Century Foundation's 2006 Task Force on homeland security. The ideas and opinions of the writer are his own.

Conclusion

We believe that the FEMA experience from 1979 to the present may be a harbinger of the Department of Homeland Security's fate as it struggles in the coming decade to establish an integrated and effective national homeland security system. At a minimum, FEMA's experiences should serve as a cautionary tale for homeland security officials at the federal, state, and local levels of government.

The Hurricane Katrina experience should also serve as a warning to DHS that a coordinated federal response is critical during a major catastrophic event and that marginalizing the strong national emergency management system built on a partnership of federal, state, and local emergency operations in the 1990s was a terrible mistake.

One final note on the FEMA experience: At the core of FEMA's success in the 1990s was its focus on the needs of its customers, the American people. FEMA policies and programs from that period were driven by the needs of disaster victims and by the needs of community residents who wanted to reduce the terrible impacts of future events. Since its inception in 2002, the DHS and its partners in the federal government have been focused almost exclusively on their own needs. Policies and programs have been designed and implemented that meet the needs of these governmental departments and agencies and that were not informed by the needs of the public, their supposed customers.

If the officials at DHS that work in homeland security at the state and local levels change one thing in the future, it is critical that they shift their focus from themselves to the public, and that they plan and implement policies and programs with the full involvement of the public and their partners. It worked very well for FEMA, so there is no reason why it should not do the same for DHS.

References

Criss, K., 2005. E-mail message to George Haddow, July 14.

Peckenpaugh, J., 2004. Regional Homeland Security Offices Will Be Small. GovExec.Com, March 24. http://www.govexec.com/story_page.cfm?articleid528072&printerfriendlyVers51&.

For details on numerous DHS programs involving the private sector see www.dhs.gov/privatesector

Index